W9-AYS-366

Hip Hop Desis

Refiguring American Music

A series edited by Ronald Radano and Josh Kun

Charles McGovern, contributing editor

Nitasha Tamar Sharma

Hip Hop Desis

South Asian Americans, Blackness,

and a Global Race Consciousness

Duke University Press
Durham and London 2010

© 2010 Duke University Press
All rights reserved
Printed in the United States of
America on acid-free paper ∞
Designed by C. H. Westmoreland
Typeset in Quadraat by
Tseng Information Systems, Inc.
Library of Congress Cataloging-in-
Publication Data appear on the last
printed page of this book.

Duke University Press gratefully acknowledges the support of the Northwestern University Research Grants
Committee, which provided funds
toward the production of this book.

frontispiece: Deejay Bella spins
at a 4th of July event. Photograph
courtesy of Deejay Bella.

This book is dedicated with eternal love
to my parents, Miriam and Jagdish Sharma,

to Makaya McCraven with love
for his unending support and brilliance,

to the South Asian American hip hop artists
who make much more than music,

and to Ronald Takaki, who made generations
of activist scholars

Contents

Preface

The lives of South Asians in America, or *desis*—a term meaning "of the land" from the Hindi/Urdu word *desh*, or country—are both historically constituted and circumscribed by global processes and the limitations of what is possible today. Yet some members of this community, such as South Asian American hip hop artists, take active roles in their surroundings by disrupting seemingly fixed ideologies in order to generate new possibilities. In chapter 1 of this volume, "Alternative Ethnics," I explore the artists' ambivalent relationships to ethnicity and the influence of South Asian parents and peers from recollections of their childhood and college experiences. While nearly half of the artists grew up in middle-class, mostly White neighborhoods (as most desis do) where they have contended with racism from a young age, the other half came from racially and class-diverse neighborhoods in which they grew up alongside Blacks and participated in creating hip hop culture. Thus, class alone does not explain who becomes a hip hop artist; however, where the artists grew up had broad implications for their interactions with Blacks and their experiences with racism. I illustrate the critique by these artists of expectations of ethnic authenticity expressed within American South Asian communities as hegemonic notions of desiness—that is, as conservative responses to displacement, racism, and a desire to fit high up in American society. Their production of "ethnic hip hop" illustrates a process of sampling.

These individuals turn toward alternatives by rejecting not only desi norms but those of the dominant White society as well. Neither an insular ethnic identity nor assimilation with aspirations toward Whiteness is an option. After all, the racism they experience from Whites is doubled by South Asians' own racism toward Blacks. This tension conflicts with their emerging politics that attempt to understand and overcome racist practices. Thus, in chapter 2 I illustrate how South Asian hip hop artists "branch out" (Flores quoted in Lipsitz 2004) or turn toward communities and expressions that speak to their sense of difference, injustice, and artistic expression, as do some Latinos—another Brown population. George Lipsitz samples Juan Flores's concept to explain that "the polylateral points of connection afforded by 'branching out' enable Puerto Rican New Yorkers opportunities to remain 'ethnic' without being either 'always ethnic' or 'only ethnic,' to create new identities without having to surrender the historical consciousness and situated knowledges specific to their group" (33). In this volume I reveal that desis who become producers of hip hop enter Black social and hip hop worlds in their childhoods rather than later as a rebellious phase of adolescence. I explore how desi artists develop their understanding of race and conceive of relations between South Asians and Blacks through their relationships with Blacks. They express these worldviews through "racialized hip hop."

In chapter 3, "Flipping the Gender Script," I discuss how desi artists negotiate gender and sexual expectations within both hip hop and South Asian America. Female artists in particular must come to grips with hip hop's misogyny, which they engage by crafting pro-womanist work spaces. My ethnography contests theories that assert the appeal of stereotypical racialized masculinities for non-Black men by exploring other possible interpretations for the role of hip hop in the crafting of desi gender and sexual identities, both straight and queer. Desi women in hip hop, in fact, engage with tropes of Black masculinity, including players and pimps, to express themselves in the business of music. I explore these dynamics by tracing the moves by desis within the hip hop industry and in their intraethnic and interracial romances.

Following my discussion of ethnicity, race, gender, and sexuality, I illustrate in chapter 4 the appeal of hip hop to these artists by highlighting the counterhegemonic message of early rap music, the sonic pleasure they derived from it, and the voice it gave them to represent their identities. Hip hop offers them the vocabulary, ideology, and methodology for crafting their own resistant and racialized worldviews that speak to questions of alienation and belonging, equality and inequality. In "The Appeal of Hip Hop, Ownership, and the Politics of Location" I discuss how Black Nationalism and race pride teaches these artists how to develop a racialized identity. However, it does not speak to their sense of ethnicity or their transnational ties. Thus, I analyze how they transform Black Power into Brown Pride in response to racism and their attempts to belong to the nation not as model minorities, eternal foreigners, or deracialized "honorary Whites." They face the racial politics of authenticity, an essentialist test seemingly impossible to pass for people who are not of African descent. Chapter 4 illustrates how these artists conceive of Blackness in hip hop. The way they conceptualize themselves as legitimate Brown creators of Black popular culture offers an ethnographic account of cross-racial alliances.

In chapter 5, "Sampling South Asians," I expand my attention more broadly on dual flows of power and appropriation. I show how South Asian American youth and mainstream hip hop culture since 2001 reveal examples of "appropriation as othering" (by which one appropriates in order to reaffirm the distance between racial groups) and "appropriation as identification" (through which borrowing practices signal a bridging across differences). The heightened racialization and profiling of Brown people in the millennium directly impacts the themes in the artists' music as well as their visibility. Analyzing the borrowing practices between members of two groups who do not share a clear hierarchical relationship expands the literature on appropriation that tends to focus on exchanges between Blacks and Whites. The descriptions in this book are complemented with the artists' online videos and Web sites. Where appropriate I provide Web site information, and I highly recommend this multimedia approach to best illustrate the comportment of the artists and their music.

I conclude this volume by reflecting on the use by artists of lessons learned from hip hop that extend beyond the realm of music in their social justice activism. Their extramusical political commitments, which take them beyond national and racial borders, reveal their global race consciousness in action.

Acknowledgments

For someone whose memory resembles Swiss cheese (it is full of holes), remembering everyone who has helped make this book a reality over the past decade is a daunting yet gratifying exercise. I apologize in advance to those I have forgotten to mention; your influence is nonetheless reflected in these pages. My biggest thanks and praises go to each and every artist I met over the course of conducting fieldwork and who agreed to take part in this project at a time when many academics were unclear about who or what "hip hop" or "desis" referred to. Many of these desi hip hop artists have become dear friends and have shaped this project well into the editing phases, particularly Bella, Chirag, Kiran, Sammy, Nimo, Swapnil, Vivek, D'Lo, Roger, Asad, Fahad, and Joseph. Your words, vision, and actions have inspired me for years and I hope that inspiration and consciousness is reflected in this work. I also wish to thank K B, D'Lo, Chee Malabar, and Sammy for granting permission to use their words in the epigraphs. I could not have completed this project without the enormous guidance, support, and comedic relief of my dear friends, colleagues, and interlopers, including my dissertation writing group at the University of California, Berkeley: Aaron Bobrow Strain, Rebecca Dolhinow, and Susan Shepler; my tireless dear friends and intellectual interlocutors: Carleen Basler, Jinah Kim, Kristi and the quints, Heather Lee, Anastasia Panagakos, Dana Petersen, Elizabeth Schainbaum, Cathy Schlund-Vials, Zulema Valdez, and Andrew Yinger; and Laura Helper-Ferris, who helped me get back on track. While I do not envy your task of having read (numerous!) versions of my text, I cannot thank the following people enough for their thoughtful, fair, and solid advice: Richard Iton, Martha Biondi, Sherman Bryant, George Lipsitz, John Marquez, Oliver Wang, John Jackson, Gayatri Gopinath, Dwight McBride, Vijay Prashad, and the anonymous and fabulous reviewers enlisted by Duke University Press. If I had a voice, I would sing aloud unending praises of Courtney Berger at Duke University Press for her strong guiding hand, patience, and kindly delivered praise; would every author be so lucky to work with her! Supportive mentors, inspirational leaders, and patient colleagues include Evelyn Nakano Glenn, Mary Hancock, Darlene Clark Hine, Mattison Mines, Triloki Pandey, Gary Okihiro, Victoria Robinson, Ved Vatuk, and Ji-Yeon Yuh. The time and resources necessary for the research, writing, and editing of this book were made possible by generous grants and fellowships from the following institutions: University of California, Santa Barbara; University of California, Berkeley; Institute for the Study of Social Change; Social Science Research Council; Amherst College, particularly my colleagues in American studies; and Northwestern University, with a special shout out to all the faculty and staff in Asian American studies and African American studies, especially to Greg Jue, Marjorie McDonald, and Suzette Denose. I am thankful to Peter Holderness for the author photo and to the Asian American studies program at Northwestern University for providing funding for the index, professionally prepared by Diana Witt. I hope this book reflects the immensely supportive role and social justice ideals of my dearest mentor and professor, Ronald Takaki. And none of this has any meaning were it not for my family who engaged me with their perspectives, encouraged me over the years, read my work (or, wisely, didn't!), and trusted my voice: a big mahalo to Arun Sharma, Agnes Zsigmondi, and Kinga McCraven.

Introduction

Claiming Space, Making Race

We . . . classify everyone on this earth who is not White as members of the Black Nation. Japanese are members of the Black Nation. Mexicans are members of the Black Nation. Chinese are members of the Black Nation. All of your Indians and Africans are of the Black Nation. We are the majority, not the minority.
—Malcolm X speaking at the American Embassy, 1961

I didn't ever take the Black experience as my own per se but I did identify with it . . . The immigrant and, really, any racial or nationalistic discourse in this country, is framed first and foremost by the Black experience in this country. You don't have to identify with it in order to understand it, but you need to know that the discussion begins there. I guess it made me realize that a lot of immigrants who solely identified with the White experience were incorrect and needed to understand that.
—Jonny, Indian hip hop journalist

I arranged to interview Vivek, a Harvard alumnus and recent Yale Law School graduate, at the Ninth Circuit Court of Appeals in downtown San Francisco. I was meeting him at his office, where he was interning for "one of the most leftist judges." Despite our formal surroundings and heightened security precautions—a Black security guard buzzed me in and Vivek had to escort me to his stately office—the slim, vivacious Indian was dressed casually.

A skull cap covered his closely shorn hair and he wore a silver hoop in each ear. Complaining about his *chappals* (Indian sandals) cutting into his feet, he removed them once we got to his office. Peeling off clothing like layers of identity, he also shed his green *kurta* (a flowing Indian top), under which he had on an old green Adidas T-shirt and jeans. Vivek, an Indian American rapper, is one of hip hop's *desis*, a term commonly used, especially among the second generation, to refer to South Asians in America.

Vivek was characteristically expressive during our interview. His voice often reached a crescendo when he was excited. In a hurry to get things out he rarely finished sentences but rather left them with implied endings before skipping on to new ideas. But when he spoke slowly and softly, reverently even, I paid special attention, as that was when he relayed a most intriguing confession: Vivek told me, cautiously, that he was Black. To forestall any confusion, he clarified that he considered himself to be part of a "wider Black consciousness."

I translate Vivek's conception, a worldview shared by all of the artists in this study, as a *global race consciousness*. This phrase highlights the knowledge of how power-holding groups have created conceptions of group difference that exploit others for self-gain rather than an unexamined reification of "race." This reorientation refers to race as a matter of critical understanding—of ways of thinking about and being in the world rather than a reference to an individual's biology or phenotype. Thus, this notion refers not to racial categories (e.g., "Black," "Asian," etc.) but rather to understanding how and why Western Europeans created such categories, which non-Whites have since come to adopt. Central to this understanding—or consciousness—is the comprehension of how various racisms impact interminority relations and maintain the material and ideological supremacy of Whites. These are historical processes that have shaped global racial formations; they impact, for instance, the relationships between "Asian" and "Black" diasporas across national borders. Yet the development of such a worldview is politically enabling as these artists put this awareness of power to work on behalf of their own anti-racist and social justice agendas.

Vivek's identification as Black and his acknowledgment of racism is atypical in light of the tendency of South Asians to sidestep racial matters, particularly our minority status in the United States, while praising our cultural strengths and economic successes. In contrast is his consideration of the commonalities of South Asians and Blacks linked by historical and global processes rooted in colonialism that have differentially racialized and displaced these groups. The alternative visions of hip hop desis emerge from and contest hegemonic discourses common within mainstream American, South Asian, and hip hop communities that assume "sameness" (i.e., shared ancestry) unites, while "differences" (i.e., race) divide. How and why do Vivek and the other artists come up with this conception when so many South Asians in the United States view Blacks as their antithesis—as a group that lacks strong cultures, is dangerous, and has questionable moral and intellectual abilities? And what accounts for the political ideologies of hip hop desis with cross-racial identifications who insist that South Asians and Blacks share interests? This book unfolds to reveal the artists' responses to these questions and illustrates their expression of a global race consciousness through political acts of music making and everyday activism.

This project explains how and why some young South Asians negotiate their racial invisibility in the United States by developing newly racialized identities that express a political consciousness of interminority solidarity. The artists in this study craft new ways of being desi, or alternative desiness, by drawing upon the concept of Blackness, the most visible and salient example of a racial identity in the United States. And these desis express their perspectives in the most popular and generationally relevant expression of Blackness at this time—hip hop. Desis borrow and expand upon Blackness by elaborating upon its possibilities as an empowering rather than denigrated identity, not limited to people of African descent. They identify not only as "diasporic ethnics" linked to global communities as charted out in the literature on South Asian Americans but also as "American minorities." The identifications of hip hop desis are multiscalar; they traverse and often transcend the boundaries of time, nation, and racial categorization, thereby overriding the limits of "identity." These artists develop self-conceptions that allow them to belong to a community strictly drawn along notions of sameness (ethnicity, religion, class) while expressing a racialized consciousness that emphasizes commonality formed in the negotiation of difference among people of color. A global race consciousness emerges from and illustrates the artists' negotiations and identifications as non-Whites in America, as non-Blacks within hip hop worlds, and as South Asians with a diasporic sensibility. What motivates these youth, whom the census categorizes racially as Asians, to embrace a racial identity modeled on Blackness? I reveal how desi hip hoppers express their identifications with Blacks by infusing traditionally United States–bound and Black-centered themes in hip hop with a diasporic sensibility and a global lens. As cultural brokers and as independent music producers, desis who create conscious hip hop music alter the contours of desiness, Blackness, hip hop, and even Americanness. I analyze their creation of new cultural formations as a process that infuses "culture" with "politics" and vice versa.

My work in this ethnography focuses on hip hop artists who are 1.5-generation and second-generation South Asians in America.[1] The members of this group include twenty-four male and female, gay and straight, upper-middle-class and lower-middle-class Indian, Pakistani, Sri Lankan, Nepali, Bengali, and Indo-Fijian hip hop rappers, DJs, music producers, record label owners, and journalists who are mostly rooted in the Bay Area of northern California where the bulk of this ethnography takes place. Three central questions frame my study. First, why do some members of an upwardly mobile, middle-class immigrant community identify with Blacks, a group that many Americans perceive to be "disadvantaged"? Second, how do South Asians use hip hop to create and express racialized second-generation identities? And, finally, how do the artists forge political alliances between South Asians and Blacks through Black popular culture? The artistic and political interminority collaborations of desis are critical responses to the increasing social, economic, political, and ideological gaps between Blacks and Asians in the United States that have the potential to erupt in intergroup conflict, as occurred in Los Angeles in 1992 (Gooding-Williams 1993; Kim 1999). Hip hop's desis disrupt popular and divisive discourses about model (Asian) and not-so-model (Black) minorities by connecting themselves to Black histories, thereby forming an important critique of the "possessive investment in Whiteness" (Lipsitz 1998b) that persists through portrayals of racial groups as incommensurably different.

This book illustrates twenty-first-century multiracial politics for equality and justice expressed through Black popular culture. The lives, lyrics, and worldviews of desi performers reveal a two-pronged approach to "race" that I engage throughout the book. First, they must contend with commonly accepted notions of "race" in the United States. They grapple with the significance of living in racially marked bodies reflected in categories like "Asian" or "Black" created by those in power and that affect their life chances and daily experiences. European and American colonialists and imperialists constructed White normativity by conceptualizing Asians and Blacks as deviant groups on each side of the spectrum with regard to matters of intelligence, physical ability, and so forth. Second, desi artists create new and empowering meanings of "race" that capture the interplay of identification and distancing by pushing beyond existing national boundaries and racial categories. A global race consciousness affirms but breaks beyond the real impacts of socially constructed notions of race in the United States through broad-scale identifications. I chart how a sense of alienation and belonging of hip hop desis motivates their education on historical and global links with other subjugated communities across time and space. Their thoughts and actions reconfigure our common assumptions of "sameness" and "difference." The bond of desis with members of a group they have been defined as in opposition to reconceptualizes "race" rooted not in shared biology and identity but in a shared ideology and consciousness of how power operates through racism. These desis excavate the past in order to come to a conception of power attuned to the overlapping causes of group inequality, including the colonials' enslavement of Africans and their indenture of Indians and Chinese. These performers not only learn about alternative narratives of Black and South Asian displacements and migrations, but their collaborative practices also reflect historical precedents of South Asian and Black alliances in places like the West Indies and England. This past inspires desi artists to harness the power of agency and knowledge in their cultural-political work as hip hop artists to resist current forms of oppression and to articulate new grounds for future collaborations. This ethnography illustrates a model of racial politics unhinged from the body and rooted in a sense of connection across meaningful differences that cultivate multiracial alliances for justice.

Who Are Hip Hop's Desis?

While the number of hip hop–producing South Asians is small, there are more than is realized by most in the music industry. This is the case even with the popular Black DJs and radio personalities in the Bay Area who worked with some of the artists in this project. Desis in hip hop are also virtually invisible to the general population of South Asians in the United States, who share the surprise and skepticism of some Blacks. Having started rhyming and mixing records in their preteens, most of the artists are now in their third decade of producing Black popular culture. So what accounts for their invisibility?

Americans are largely unaware of desi hip hoppers partly because they do not form a community in a traditional or imagined sense (Anderson 1983). They do not always identify as a group or live within a geographically circumscribed area, and when I started this project few artists even knew of co-ethnics in hip hop. Several factors have led to a greater awareness of these artists, particularly in desi circles, including their growing numbers in hip hop, their artistic productivity, new networking technologies, and their lengthy musical careers. Nonetheless, a search for a cyber community devoted to "desi hip hop" is likely only to reveal the Web sites of scholars like myself, newspaper and magazine articles that refer to these artists as a group, and individual artists who self-promote. These performers, often the only desi in their local hip hop communities, are scattered in cities across the United States and produce their music independently. I put them in touch with one another over the past decade and mention their names, albums, and Web sites in my interviews and lectures. South Asian art festivals have also begun to introduce them to one another and to desi audiences. Contact among the artists has led to some collaboration; often, however, they distinguish among themselves based on the kinds of hip hop they produce, their target audiences, and their philosophies toward hip hop.

There is no genre of "desi hip hop." Their sounds and roles in hip hop culture are too diverse. In 2008 I cohosted "Hiphopistan: South Asians in Hip Hop," a multiday series of concerts and panels in Chicago that featured some of the artists in this book.[2] I wanted to showcase the variety of productions by South Asians and to create

HipHopistan
South Asians in Hip Hop
April 17-19, 2008
Chicago, IL

Thursday, April 17: Performance & Afterparty at McCormick Place Hyatt Regency
Friday, April 18: Discussion & Performance at University of Chicago Lab School
Saturday, April 19: Workshops at Northwestern University

Full Schedule & Ticketing Information online at... http://hiphopistan.uchicago.edu

The Hiphopistan weekend events took place in Chicago in 2008 and featured eight South Asian American hip hop artists. Hiphopistan poster courtesy of Samip Mallick.

a "community" among artists and academics who shared artistic and political challenges and concerns. While the artists may have felt isolated in their childhoods as one-of-a-kind desis, they have now met others who share their passions and predicaments, if not their tastes in musical production and performance. These forums are validating because they reveal not only the presence of a growing number of South Asian artists but also the range and maturity of their art. Few entities reflect this emergent social formation; in addition to Hiphopistan, the artists have been celebrated in the documentary *Brown Like Dat: South Asians and Hip Hop* (dir. Raeshem Nihjon 2005) and some contributed to an edited volume by artists and academics, *Desi Rap: Hip-Hop and South Asian America* (Nair and Balaji 2008). The present volume is the first ethnography of South Asian American hip hop artists, and as such it analyzes the intersection of South Asians, Blacks, and hip hop music and details how hip hop desis emerge from and contribute to racial politics at the turn of the twenty-first century.

Despite the artists' dispersal and heterogeneous styles, there are factors that unify them. Though they move often and live on the East, West, and "Third" (the Midwest and the South) coasts as well as overseas, most of the artists have deep connections to the San Francisco-Oakland Bay Area of northern California. The particular racial demographics and dynamics of the Bay Area, and its political and hip hop histories, leave its imprint upon most of these artists, whether they grew up in the region or migrated there in adulthood. The liberal politics and possibilities of California—a demographic microcosm of the nation's future—resonate in the form and content of this music and in the artists' global race consciousness. They share an understanding of the world emerging from and reflecting their dedication to a form of popular culture that is rife with racial and gender tensions, authenticity tests, and meager payoffs when it comes to finances or fame. Before I move on to the major concepts and context of this book, I will introduce some of hip hop's desis, whom I refer to as "artists," "desi artists," or "performers."

"Hip hop's been my first culture," says Rawj, an MC in the multi-racial hip hop group Feenom Circle based in the Bay Area.[3] Rawj is a Punjabi American whose Punjabi Indian immigrant parents settled in Richmond, California, one of the birthplaces of hip hop. Rawj grew up alongside Black and Filipino peers in the 1970s and

Chee Malabar on a video shoot in New York.
Photograph courtesy of Richard Louissaint.

1980s with hip hop, and he later attended community college and graduated from the University of California system in the 1990s. KB, a South Indian American rapper also from Richmond who attended the same predominantly Black high school as Rawj, was managing a number of local rap acts by the time he was seventeen. After graduating from the University of California, KB, along with three other desi men, Sammy, Swap, and Nimo, formed Karmacy, which is possibly the best-known Indian hip hop act among American desi audiences. Chee Malabar was a new arrival in the 1980s, an eleven-year-old immigrant to San Francisco from Baroda, South India, who learned English by rapping with Black school friends he mistook for Africans. He later formed Himalayan Project with his Chinese American rapping partner, Rainman, and completed his fifth album, a solo project produced by Zeeb titled *Oblique Brown*.

Hip hop saved D'Lo, a male-identified gay Sri Lankan who, all the while feeling like a boy trapped in a girl's body, grew up in a mostly White Southern California neighborhood contending with racism and homophobia.[4] D'Lo is one of the few desi female MCs. Around the same time, Deejay Bella, whose Gujarati parents moved to Southern California and then to Las Vegas, was becoming "ob-

Claiming Space, Making Race 9

sessed" with music.[5] She spent all of her time and money buying records and learning how to spin and mix them. Jonny, a fellow Gujarati living in northern California, embarked on a career in hip hop journalism after graduating from the same California university that Rawj attended. Jonny moved to New York City and began writing for hip hop magazines and working for MTV. In Staten Island, New York, three young Pakistani Muslim cousins, Asad, Fahad, and Ali, who were about a decade younger than the other artists, were coming of age and, inspired by the rap group Public Enemy, transformed into MC Humanity, MC AbstractVision, and DJ Ali. In Danbury, Connecticut, Vivek—the North Indian American whose voice opens this book—was growing up with Black friends listening to rap music. Soon he began writing lyrics on topics relevant to his life as a budding social justice worker. The artists' divergent styles and identities, however, lead them to identify with one another as South Asian *hip hop artists* rather than as *South Asian* hip hop artists.

Ethnic Hip Hop and Racialized Hip Hop

Desi hip hoppers represent a broader spectrum of Asian and Pacific Island American youth, including Filipinos, Chinese, Cambodians, and Samoans, who define themselves through Black popular culture. They highlight the underanalyzed impacts of American Blacks and their cultures upon the "new second generation," or the United States–born children of post-1965 immigrants from Asia, Latin America, and the Caribbean (Rumbaut 1994). Hip hop studies scholars have similarly underexamined the participation and impacts of Asian Americans and hip hop, thereby reinforcing the invisibility of Asian Americans in U.S. racial discourse. In this volume I illustrate cross-racial interactions beyond a one-way flow of South Asians into Black cultural realms; desis engage and impact the very meanings of Blackness and the expressions of Black popular culture. "Cross-fertilization" is how Vivek describes the kinds of racial, religious, and cultural interactions that he facilitates: "One of the things that I have enjoyed in my life is that I stand at some kind of strange position, having like massive [numbers of] Black people at the house dancing *dandia raas*![6] That was dope! You know, that was beautiful. The year before I brought like fifteen kids . . . ten Black people, three or four White people, and three or four Indian people from New Haven to a Navratri [the Hindu festival of Nine Nights] with like five hundred people! You know, we were in there, I dressed people up in *salwar kameez* [traditional Indian clothing], you know? And they were lovin' it!" These actions dialogically impact desis who produce hip hop and the lives of those around them.

In my work in this book I analyze how the artists contend with multiple and often competing expectations within their ethnic and hip hop communities. Are they confused ethnics who turn their backs on their ancestries? Are they drawn to the rebellious and tough images of Blackness in mainstream rap music? The artists develop strategies that bridge the distinct identities of ethnicity and race. For instance, Vivek, the son of immigrants from the Kutch Desert region of Gujarat, incorporates his knowledge and sense of ethnic identity with his awareness of Black histories and concerns. As the MC recalls, "When I did present a Kwanzaa principle last year—I had the one that was collective work—I told a Birbal [a close advisor to Akbar the Great] story as I presented it. And so [this is] one of the things that I enjoy being able to do . . . ! Or when I dance with that West African group: my solo moves, some of them are from bhangra! When I dance solo some of them are break dancing, which fits into West African [dance], too, which is from when I was little. I grew up dancing street-type shit." These forms of intertextual citation, or *sampling*, illustrate the everyday lives of these artists. Some of them produce what I term "ethnic hip hop," in which they incorporate South Asian languages, instruments, and immigrant themes. It is through ethnic hip hop (the topic of chapter 1) that desi artists such as KB, Swap, Nimo, and Sammy and their group, Karmacy, operate as cultural brokers who translate between generations of American South Asians. This kind of desi hip hop contests hegemonic desiness, or the expectations that ethnic gatekeepers place upon co-ethnics, thereby restricting what qualifies as "authentic" ethnicity to proscribed beliefs and behaviors. In the subgenre of ethnic hip hop, desi artists express alternative desiness; they also convey a diasporic sensibility to their Black peers and to multiracial audiences who may be more familiar with hip hop music centered on United States themes.

These desis' diasporic sense of ethnicity, or their global connection to other South Asians based on shared ancestry, immigration, and cultural practices, is mediated by their relationship to co-ethnics and to Blacks rather than primarily to Whites—the focus of most scholars on Asian American ethnicity. Desi hip hop artists develop simultaneous and multiple scales of identification not captured in the scholarship that views immigrants strictly through the lens of ethnicity. These performers forge a sense of *ethnic* belonging to fellow Indians or Pakistanis, for example, by recasting the meanings of ethnicity; they also create *panethnic* "South Asian" or "desi"—rather than Asian American—communities as a result of the processes of racialization that South Asians in the United States undergo (and did even prior to 9/11); and they express *racial* identifications as minorities in solidarity with Blacks, a uniquely racialized and oppressed group. In chapter 2 I illustrate how the artists uncover historical, political, and sonic connections between South Asians and Blacks that frame their identifications with Blacks. While most Americans across racial categories are unaware of historical and contemporary connections between Asians and Blacks (such as the relationship between Martin Luther King Jr., Malcolm X, and Mahatma Gandhi, for example), why did the artists unearth these ties? Those bent on professing these hidden histories create "racialized hip hop."

Racialized hip hop is sonically and thematically familiar to American hip hop audiences with its lyrics that address inequalities and injustices against minorities. Bay Area artists such as Chee Malabar of Himalayan Project and Rawj of Feenom Circle produce this kind of music and in so doing become cultural brokers across the constructed divides of "Black" and "South Asian" by taking up themes considered irrelevant to many Asian Americans. While listeners often say that the creators of these songs "sound Black," desi hip hoppers do not adopt wholesale a Black identity. South Asians use hip hop to identify *with* Blacks rather than *as* Black.

The lives and musical productions of these performers illustrate the process of sampling—a patching together and rejecting of various influences. The artists craft alternative desiness, for instance, by applying race-conscious paradigms of hip hop to their studies of South Asian histories. Other scholars have applied the concept of sampling, taken from music production, to describe how individuals "cut 'n' mix" identities (Hebdige 1987) by weaving together existing signs and symbols into novel ethnic expressions (Maira 2002). I use sampling as a metaphor for music, identity, and community formation that is anti-essentialist and dialogic or that is never created in a vacuum but always in dialogue with multiple influences. The way these artists stitch together their identities represents a broader phenomenon among young Americans. Yet how and what the artists sample in their expressions of ethnicity, race, gender, and sexuality and how these processes denaturalize seemingly stable categories of belonging is unique. Throughout this book I examine the role of appropriation and sampling—foundational practices of hip hop culture—in the way artists craft their identities, create art, and impact those around them.

The participants in this study expand monochromatic ethnographic and popular portraits of South Asians as middle-class suburban Hindu professionals and their college-attending youth (Jensen 1988; Lessinger 1995; Maira 2002; Purkayastha 2005). The political ideologies, educational trajectories, and interracial ties of these artists also challenge sociological predictions about the children of immigrants (Portes 1996; Portes and Rumbaut 2001). In particular, I take issue with segmented assimilation (Portes and Zhou 1993; Rumbaut 1994; Zhou and Bankston 1998), a theory that posits that only a negative connection can emerge from the impacts of American Blacks upon second-generation youth.[7] American Blacks are not the devalued or demonized underclass that exposes immigrant youth to "the adversarial subculture" of hip hop and lead them to the path of "downward assimilation" (Portes and Zhou 1993: 83; see Neckerman et al. 1999 for a rebuttal). My examination of desis in hip hop suggests new approaches to relations between native-born and immigrant minorities by focusing on collaborative and mutually constitutive exchanges.

Hi, My Name Is . . . :
South Asian Americans, Hip Hop, and Second-Generation Desis

When I began fieldwork for this project in the late 1990s I had been an avid fan of hip hop for less than a decade. Hip hop took its time crossing the Pacific to the oceanic outpost of Honolulu, Hawai'i, where my brother and I were born in the 1970s. Our parents were two transplants—professors who decided that Hawai'i would be the most hospitable place to raise *hapa*, or mixed race, children. (Our father is from a village in Uttar Pradesh, India, and our mother is the Brooklyn-born daughter of Jewish immigrants from Minsk, Russia). It was my brother's 1985 vinyl of "The Show" and "La Di Da Di (We Like to Party)" by Doug E. Fresh and the Get Fresh Crew that first turned me on to this new music, which was produced thousands of miles away in my mother's home state of New York.[8] In Hawai'i I had limited exposure to hip hop and the people who made it because there were so few Blacks other than those who were stationed on the military bases throughout the islands. Further, because we didn't have cable television I did not see the hip hop videos on Yo! MTV Raps. Indeed, it wasn't until the early 1990s when I moved to the mainland to attend college in northern California that I was finally introduced to my Black peers and the golden era of hip hop.

It was then that I also met other American-born South Asians along with the Black and White racial illogic of the continental United States. We were the second-generation children of professionals who had immigrated in large numbers to the United States as part of the second wave of Indian migration. The Immigration Act of 1965 opened quotas for skilled professionals, thereby leading to the entry of millions of immigrants from Asia, Latin America, and the Caribbean.[9] Indians were among those who found work in science, technology, medicine, and higher education and raised their children, including the artists in this study, during the 1970s and 1980s. These younger 1.5-generation and second-generation South Asians faced their parents' conceptions of national and religious divisions while beginning to craft their own diasporic pan-ethnic identities. By the 1990s, when we were in college, Indians in the United States had become the highest income earners and most educated of all groups, surpassing other Asians and Whites and inheriting the label "model minority," which formerly applied to East Asians.

The cultural thesis of the model minority myth plays a central role in the hegemonic desiness that hip hoppers contest. This myth is an ahistorical form of cultural racism that explains the economic and educational success of Asians in America, including South Asians, as a result of "Asian traits" of strong family and cultural values. Mainstream Americans hail Asians for enculturating their children with respect for elders and authority figures and for advocating education as the pathway to the American dream. Scholars have detailed the dangers of this ideology (Chang 1995; Palumbo-Liu

1999; Prashad 2000, 2001), but several points frame how Americans view Asians and, therefore, circumscribe how Asians and Blacks interact. The model minority myth denies everyday and institutional forms of racism against Asians, portrays them as apolitical non-agitators, and ignores the plight of less fortunate Asians, including first- and third-wave South Asian immigrants.[10] Therefore, this popular explanation hides the heterogeneity of past and present communities of South Asians in the United States. To support the view that everyone—even minorities—can make it in this meritoc-racy, the contemporary face of "Indians in America" is represented by second-wave immigrant Hindu Indian professionals who have become ethnic gatekeepers who define "proper desiness." Second-generation desis must negotiate these expectations; some choose to challenge them.

The artists in this study take up hip hop not only to challenge the model minority myth and issues concerning less fortunate South Asians but also to resist South Asian anti-Black racism. The preva-lence of cultural explanations for group difference since the 1960s and this myth's complementary facade has led many South Asians attempting to claim a higher status to adopt this framework (Raja-gopal 1995; Prashad 2000). The strength of "culture" and "family" are common ways that South Asians understand their "success" and speak about the "failures" of others, including Blacks. This ideological wedge between Asians and Blacks was, in fact, one of the reasons why the mainstream American media created the model minority myth; Whites deployed Asian Americans as "proof" of this nation's level playing field and of the end of racism. Such cul-turalist explanations became entrenched during the 1990s when multiculturalism celebrated South Asians' status as evidence that minorities could achieve the American dream *and* maintain their cultural distinctiveness.

Wealthy South Asians, in turn, use these concepts to explain to their children that success results from their allegiance to both the "benevolence" of their adopted nation and ethnic values of hard work, discipline, and filial piety rather than from structural, eco-nomic, and historical factors. Thus, even as growing numbers of working-class third-wave South Asian immigrants altered the rosy depiction of Indian professionals during the 1980s and 1990s, cul-turalist explanations for success dovetailed with the model minority myth in the minds of many second-generation youth. But this ideology rests uneasily with others, including those who turn to hip hop to articulate their concerns about South Asians who deny the struggles of minorities within *and outside* South Asian America.

The presence of desis in hip hop and particularly their cross-racial identifications with Blacks is surprising given this opposing conception of South Asians and Blacks and the material gaps (income, residential patterns, education) between them. Black and Brown worlds often do not mix, even among college students. Hip hop music and styles are overwhelmingly popular among desi youth (Maira 2002) despite the conspicuous absence of Black people. While the impacts of Blackness are often only implied in desi cultural worlds, Blacks continue to represent the most visible example of a minority identity for South Asians of all generations. Given the relative invisibility of Asians in America, however, Blacks are often less aware of or concerned about Asian Americans until policies, like affirmative action, explicitly frame Asians and Blacks as competitors.

In the 1990s, second-generation desis went on to college and came of age during the reign of multiculturalism (Prashad 2000), racial conflicts (e.g., the 1992 Los Angeles uprising), and the Silicon Valley hi-tech boom (Shankar 2008). Desi artists saw local hip hop acts rise to national fame while South Asians' increasing wealth and numeric presence led to the greater visibility of "Indians." As the official discourse on difference that impacted structural and funding decisions in universities, multiculturalism impacted desis' college education and identity exploration just as counterhegemonic narratives delivered in rhyme were filling the airwaves. The confluence of these economic policies and political and racial discourses directly affected the way that desi youth understood themselves.

Hip hop became the culture of their times for the second generation at large, just when media monopolies linked with transnational corporations to turn hip hop superstars into global commodities.[11] Many desi youths tended to embrace Black popular culture in ways similar to that of suburban White youths—that is, as avid consumers who could afford the commodities that mainstream rappers were increasingly rapping about and who consumed Blackness, itself, as if it were a commodity. And, encouraged by their parents, they maintained a physical distance from actual Black people. As the 1990s progressed, desis in California colleges were among the first to see—if not feel—the effects of anti-affirmative action policies and a heightened rhetoric of colorblindness. Some favored these policies, agreeing with the former University of California Regent and anti-affirmative action leader Ward Connerly that race-based policies "hurt" Asian Americans. Even on the relatively diverse and multicultural California university campuses prior to the banning of affirmative action in the 1990s I met desis who had never personally known even one Black person.

Hip hop desis, in contrast, speak directly to South Asian anti-Black racism and the mutual lack of South Asian and Black interaction. Their music explores alternatives to the cultural determinism of the model minority myth and offers ethnic alternatives that explore the potential of race-based identifications. The prominence of hip hop among all youth in the 1990s did not mean that young people across color lines came to know each other any better. It did, however, grant an opening to those invested in exploring inter-minority commonalities.

Claiming Space:
A Multiracial Look Back at Asian Americans in Hip Hop

Hip hop began in the early 1970s when minorities, particularly Blacks in urban areas, lost jobs as a result of deindustrialization. President Reagan's political and economic policies in the 1980s compounded the situation by removing the security of social services from the newly jobless and restricting children's opportunities for education and play. Black and Puerto Rican youth in the South Bronx responded to these strictures creatively by making use of the technology available to them. They hooked up speakers to stadium lights at local parks, played records on one and even two turntables to mix them back and forth to produce a continuous party track, chanted on microphones in rhyme, danced with fancy footwork reminiscent of Brazil's capoeira, and reclaimed the increasingly restricted and policed public spaces by tagging their pseudonyms on walls and subways with spray paint. This new culture, hip hop, started out as a localized expression of youthful exuberance and creativity but soon turned to urgent messages.[12] Sweeping to the West Coast, where Black and Brown men also earned pink slips from their jobs, gangsta rap emerged as the new angry face of Black America in the late 1980s, the time when desi artists were in high school. By the 1990s, when these second-generation members began to attend college, hip hop exploded commercially. Increasingly attractive to suburban White youth, other non-Blacks, and corporate marketers, hip hop's iconic rebellious male image was captured by N.W.A. (Niggaz with Attitude) from Compton, California.

Hip hop also emerged from parts of northern California, and the history and character of the Bay Area explains why some desi children, who were born just as hip hop itself was born in the 1970s, felt that they could be a part of a new kind of Black popular culture. Bay Area hip hop was particularly multiracial from its inception, from the Filipino DJ crews in Daly City to biracial rappers in Oakland, from Korean b-boys and b-girls to Mexican graffiti artists (see Wang 2005, 2006; Tiongson 2006). Racial politics accompanied racial mixing among Bay Area musicians; rappers are only the latest to deploy Black music for political and coalitional purposes (see Rios 2004; Watkins 2005; Arnold 2006).[13]

The origins and ownership of hip hop is a topic that dominates debates among hip hop heads and scholars alike. Historians such as Jeff Chang (2005) who evoke the multiracial origins of hip hop are interpreted by some as wanting to "take hip hop away from Blacks." But revisiting hip hop history informs debates over whom and what is incorporated into hip hop today without displacing the centrality of Blacks. Indeed, hip hop (like identities and cultures) is a *product* and *process* of multidirectional appropriations. The multivocality of hip hop contests accounts of its appropriation as a unidirectional power relation whereby the dominant group "takes" from the dominated. To analyze this notion I illustrate bidirectional flows of appropriation between South Asian and Black producers of hip hop (e.g., Mercer 1995; Ziff and Rao 1997).

The history of hip hop has been considered elsewhere (Rose 1994; Light 1999; Fricke and Ahearn 2002; Jeff Chang 2005) but a few points are worth mentioning in order to frame my consideration of Blackness and hip hop. A host of multiracial actors have produced the form of Black popular culture called hip hop that incorporates influences across color and culture lines. This perspective pulls together both the undeniable Blackness of hip hop rooted in the experiences of those who largely created the culture (see Perry

2004) and the contributions of Puerto Ricans, Mexicans, Filipinos, Samoans and others over the past thirty years (Flores 2000; Rivera 2003; Chang 2005; Wang 2005; Tiongson 2006). Kool Herc, a 1.5-generation immigrant from Jamaica, introduced the break-beat DJ style from his homeland to the Bronx. The Jamaican art of toasting, or chanting on the microphone over a beat, also informed rapping, while some of the earliest DJs, graffiti artists, and b-boys of the Rock Steady Crew included Puerto Rican youth from New York (see Chang 2005). The famous Nuyorican b-boy Pop Master Fabel noted that while many see Brazilian capoeira in the dance elements of hip hop, it was actually Bruce Lee and the Shaw Brothers's martial arts movies in the 1970s and 1980s that inspired young b-boys and b-girls (see Ongiri 2002; Kato 2007).[14] Thus, desi artists take part in a multicultural production of Black popular culture. This book is not concerned with defining an originary moment of hip hop creation (see Rose 1994 for an excellent history); detailing the important players that led to the emergence of this globally significant expression is likewise outside the scope of this project. Instead, I analyze how racism impacts the lives of those desi youths who turn to hip hop as a mode for analyzing racism. Why do they choose this form of Black popular culture to express themselves? A brief sketch of Asian Americans in hip hop helps frame this discussion.

Numerous Asian American youths who grew up alongside Blacks in the 1970s and 1980s "live, breathe, and bleed this rap shit," as one Pakistani MC says. Filipino Americans have earned some of the highest accolades for their turntablism while some Chinese Americans, like the members of the Mountain Brothers and the Miami rapper Jin, use their rhymes to battle, express witticisms, and demand representation (Wang 2007). The artist MC PraCh, a Cambodian refugee living in Long Beach, California, raps about the killing fields from which he fled and expresses a transnational identity (Schlund-Vials 2008). Asian Americans have always been in hip hop yet their invisibility mirrors their status in America as demographically outnumbered and often unrecognizable within Black and White United States conceptions of race. Despite their relative invisibility in hip hop, however, one of their biggest draws is to hip hop's potential for self-representation.

Generally speaking, South, East, and Southeast Asian Americans in hip hop contend with shared predicaments—notably, the audiences' misinterpretations of their motives for embracing Black culture and being Asian in a predominantly Black art form. Oliver Wang, a scholar on Asian American hip hop, specializes on the history of California Filipino DJ crews in the 1980s. Although there are differences in the subgroups and methodologies that Wang and I use, some of our findings overlap. Wang periodizes Asian American hip hop into three waves. The first wave occurred in the early 1990s and includes groups that used hip hop as a "tool for political agitation," expressed racial and ethnic identities, and were not bent on turning rap into a viable career (2007: 43). The second wave, dated to the mid-1990s, took a deracialized approach to their non-Black status and did not focus on their ethnicity (47). The third wave, which came at the end of the 1990s, is best represented by Jin, perhaps the most famous "Asian rapper." This Chinese American MC, signed by Ruff Ryder Records following his publicized freestyle battle success on Black Entertainment Television (BET), attracted mainstream audiences with his single "Learn Chinese." According to Wang, Jin dealt a preemptive strike with his racial otherness by incorporating copious references to his racial (Asian) and ethnic (Chinese) identities.

Desi artists in this project employ all of these approaches to race and politics simultaneously. Their hip hop practices and the content of their music also changes over the course of their decades-long careers.[15] Wang illustrates how East Asian rappers produce hip hop "*for, by,* and *about* Asian Americans" (44). Among desi artists, however, I found a split. There are those who tend to produce "ethnic hip hop," which may qualify as music *for, by,* and *about* (South) Asian Americans. And there are those who create "racialized hip hop" that addresses broader political issues by artists who do not want to restrict their appeal to desi audiences but rather want to attract "the tastemakers," or real hip hop heads. While this distinction can be sonically ascertained quite obviously, it is not firm; desi artists often change their music's content, sound, and target audiences over time. Unlike other Asian Americans, South Asians must also contend with their racialization as "Muslim-looking peoples." How do reactions to 9/11 impact the outlook of these artists, who were cognizant of anti-Asian racism well before 9/11?

This book analyzes desis' performances of Black popular culture as acts of "self-racialization" that are autonomous and responsive to the ways Americans have conceptualized them (Wong 2004). Detailing how desis negotiate their multiple positions of belonging as they claim space within an art form that prioritizes the male, Black, and working-class body contributes to authenticity debates. Called "rotten coconuts" (Sharma 2001) and "bruised bananas," common and scholarly accounts depict most Asian crossovers into Black culture as either a new form of "blackface" or an attempt to defeat emasculation by embodying Black male sexuality.[16] These compelling theories explain the general population of South Asian youth, whom I call "mainstream desis," but they do not apply to desis who chose to produce anti-racist hip hop and live in Black communities.

Observers most commonly apply theories about "why White kids love hip hop" (Kitwana 2005) to understand Asian Americans in hip hop, a problematic move given the non-White status of Asian Americans. The analysis by Amiri Baraka (LeRoi Jones) of White jazz artists' love of Black music emphasizes the conundrum of choice and race central to my discussion: "The white beboppers of the forties were as removed from the society as Negroes, but as a matter of choice. The important idea here is that the white musicians and other young Whites who associated themselves with this Negro music identified the Negro with this separation, this nonconformity, though, of course, the Negro himself had no choice" (Jones 1963: 188). Some desis, too, are drawn to Black cultural expressions precisely because they signify a break from mainstream society; however the motivations of second-generation youth negotiating their non-White, non-Black immigrant status—which, due to the racialization of non-Whites, they cannot fully choose—demands specific analysis (see Prashad 2001; Rana 2002; Chatterjee 2006; Nair and Balaji 2008). South Asians in America face racism. Unlike Whiteness, the relative "value" of a Brown identity, which has never overcome the stigma of "foreigner," has gone down in stock following 2001. Second, unlike the appeal of rebelliousness that Baraka says underlined Whites' love of jazz, South Asians do not become hip hop for purely rebellious reasons.

The costs of disavowal from their insular ethnic communities are too great for mere teenage rebellion by these performers. Sunaina Maira (2002) analyzes how Indian American youth use hip hop in remix subcultures to contend with their class, ethnic, sexual, gender, and racial anxieties. She reveals how some desi men renegotiate their racialized masculinity through hip hop culture. These New York youths are similar to the Bay Area mainstream college desis I observed during my fieldwork who consume hypersexualized images of Blackness at a distance from Black people. Second-generation desis, Maira explains, remix urban American notions of coolness with homeland nostalgia and ethnic authenticity. Desi hip hop artists contrast with these mainstream desis in their ideas about race and identity and in their approaches to hip hop culture. In fact, hip hop desis feel ambivalent about their own ethnic identities when confronted with hegemonic conceptions among desis that include a sense of ethnic exceptionalism, racial distance, insularity, and anti-Black racism. While a comfort to some, these factors actually make these artists open up to the influences of Black peers.

The presence of South Asians in hip hop affirms revisionist, multiracial histories of hip hop and highlights music's role in forging multiracial connections. Desis are drawn to hip hop's bond with Black people in ways that parallel Asian American jazz artists a generation older than them: "For them," writes the ethnomusicologist Deborah Wong, "the use of the category 'jazz' is both connecting and confining. The tie to African Americans is important to all of them, and jazz is the genre they have chosen to speak for and to that community . . . The Asian American political identification with jazz is thus as an African American music" (2004: 178). In contrast to dominant analyses of Asians, desi performers do not deracialize hip hop to make it "their own"; rather, they use Black music as Asian American jazz musicians do: to racialize themselves as minorities by drawing upon models of Blackness.

According to George Lipsitz (1994), particular cultural forms may resonate with members of various "aggrieved communities" in ways that enable them to form "families of resemblance." Similarly, some desis' political expressions take the form of and transform Black music through multiracial collaborations. While hip hop desis draw upon notions of Blackness to cultivate their own racial identities, they also identify as transnational ethnics (i.e., as Sri Lankan, Pakistani, etc.). Noting the problematics of some Black/Asian crossovers (Wang 2006), scholars are nonetheless optimistic. As Wong notes, "Still, the choice to move away from Whiteness is a racial performative that is anti-assimilationist and potentially bridge-building" (2004: 189). They engage in "lateral" and sometimes "reciprocal identification[s]," similar to those between some Black and White jazz musicians (232). But these are not sufficient explanations. In considering the case of desis in hip hop, I suggest several alternative theories for why, despite confronting the fraught and complicated racial, gender, and sexual politics of hip hop culture, these desis still choose to pursue musical careers. The concept of polyculturalism illustrates how the appropriation of Black popular culture by hip hop desis bears fruit through their multiracial production of new cultural formations.

Making Race:
Polycultural Sampling as Identity and Community Formation

American desis create identities, music, and communities through the use of sampling as they interact with new influences in novel contexts. Sampling, or the practice of cutting and remixing segments of preexisting forms to create a fresh product, is foundational to hip hop culture (Schloss 2004). The earliest DJs were technological innovators who, in light of scarce resources, produced tracks by mixing two records that played simultaneously. They reworked sound bytes—say a James Brown holler or part of a Malcolm X speech—filled with historical and shared references that produced a community of insiders. This sonic form of intertextual citation also exemplifies the "borrowing" of gender, sexual, and racial expressions. Desis, too, interweave multiple references upon their bodies and in their music to create inclusive communities of "resemblance."

Hip hop's defining practices make it especially open—or vulnerable—to productions by new groups of people. Non-Black influences became core elements of early hip hop and illustrate polyculturalism (Kelley 1999; Prashad 2001), the idea that people forge cultures by incorporating "outside" influences through interactions. In contrast to multiculturalism, polyculturalism asserts that no culture or group is a pure, bounded, and self-referential entity. "Culture," Prashad (2001) writes, "is a process (that may sometimes be seen as an object) with no identifiable origin. Therefore, no cultural actor can, in good faith, claim proprietary interest in what is claimed to be his or her authentic culture. 'All the culture to be had is culture in the making,' notes anthropologist Gerd Baumann. 'All cultural differences are acts of differentiation, and all cultural identities are acts of cultural identifications'" (66). The artists form desi identities and hip hop communities through polycultural, "cut 'n' mix" formations (Hebdige 1987). Sampling numerous influences in hip hop production contests the claims of sole authorship and the idea that cultures are static and self-contained.[17] Rather, individuals and collectives create identities through dialogic exchanges of polyculturalism as sampling.

Hip hop desis challenge an American expectation that culture and identity should align, and they elicit the suspicion of others who ask why an Indian would love hip hop. Polyculturalism, which contributes to debates about the ownership, purity, and membership of hip hop, offers one response. If people work across cultures to create new social formations, how can certain individuals "own" particular cultures or a shared set of values, ideas, practices, and their products? Polyculturalism emphasizes the multiple flows of appropriation that minimize essentialist interpretations of culture, a perspective equally applicable to hip hop and to diasporic South Asians' reconfigurations of ethnicity. Many Americans, however, feel that identity is rooted in biology and ancestry, around which communities should be organized. But, taken a step further, polyculturalism also suggests that individuals cannot claim to own particular identities, such as "Black" or "Asian," either.

This book illustrates the lives of a small segment of Asian America that chooses to engage in everyday meaningful contact with America's racial other. Rather than identifying strongly as ethnics (i.e., Indian) or assimilating into the dominant (White) American culture, desis drawn to hip hop create racial identities. They amplify the underanalyzed and implicit impacts of Blacks on the identity formation process of Asian and Latino youth. These artists are not engaged in "blackface"; they do not love hip hop's decontextualized and stereotyped images of racialized masculinity, hedonism, and rebellion. They come to identify hip hop as their culture because many of them grew up with it well before hip hop was mass produced.

As the children of recent immigrants, desi youth have few models of American-based identities within their own communities (see de Leon 2004). Ian Condry's findings that Black expressive forms resonate with some Japanese apply to desis in hip hop: "One paradox of hip-hop in Japan is that it was not supposed to mean anything to young Japanese, yet it does. They should not be hip-hop, yet they are" (2006: 207). The racially explicit and counterhegemonic messages of hip hop that analyze and challenge racism are taken up by these desis who apply them to their own experiences as distinctly racialized subjects. The demonization of Muslim-looking people following 9/11, which some of the artists have experienced firsthand in New York City, does not form (but certainly informs) the basis of their political ideologies, which developed earlier in their lives. From their life histories we learn that they represent a segment of Asian America that has always been concerned with the impact of racism on United States-born Asians even before they could properly articulate what race, racism, and racialization were.

The model minority myth and other cultural theories of difference obfuscate the fact that Whites have historically racialized Asians as the opposite of Blacks as part of the process of justifying White privilege. This understanding refers back to my first conception of race: desi artists must contend with Whites' racialization of South Asians. Americans have framed Asian immigrants as cultural rather than racialized populations, but desi hip hop artists push past such reductive depictions by embodying and performing ethnic, sexual, political, artistic, and racial identities. By theorizing the racial identity of non-White, non-Black immigrants we better understand their experiences and the choices of their United States–born children. Asians and Latinos, who often do not "fit" binary categories of race (Davis 1996), pose a "problem" to conceptions of identity only if we insist on a Black and White paradigm (Marable 1994; see also Pulido 2006; Kurashige 2008). Examining how members of these groups operate within and expand upon existing notions of race will allow scholars to revise these frameworks to better explain the dynamic and increasingly complex lives of Americans. Central to this reconceptualization of Asian Americans' racial status must be the recognition of the centrality of *racism* in second-generation lives; this includes the racism that youth face as well as the racism among co-ethnics against other minorities.

The range of identities available and desirable to South Asians in America centers not only on the fact of their non-Whiteness but also on their being *not Black*. Nonetheless, racism structures the lives of desis who are not "becoming White" despite those who argue otherwise (Yancey 2003; see also Bonilla Silva and Embrick 2006; cp. Tuan 1999).[18] The misconception of the honorary Whiteness of Asians is reinforced by South Asians' underreporting of racism and scholarly inattention to this phenomenon, particularly as it affects middle-class Asian Americans.[19]

Ethnicity, not race, has claimed the attention of most Asian American scholarship, and South Asians do not usually view themselves in racial terms. The ethnicity model emphasizes how immigrants retain culture and negotiate its loss. Within the context of multiculturalism, these theories also evade discussing power differentials and group inequality by discussing cultural identities and representation. Framing Asian American identity as strictly cultural does not illuminate the myriad factors that structure minorities' lives in the United States or that shape intergroup relations. Additionally, "culture" inadequately explains the differential standing of groups in American society and this ideology easily sidesteps the differential impacts of historical and institutional factors on the lives of Asians and Blacks, in this case.

By emphasizing the relational dynamics among Asians, Whites, and Blacks I wish to alleviate the overemphasis placed by scholars on exchanges between Asians and Whites to the neglect of those with Blacks. Racial triangulation analyzes Whites' racialization of Asians, including South Asians, as culturally foreign and unequal outsiders to the nation and Blacks as inferior subjects of the nation (Kim 1999). This theorization explains Americans' "relative valorization" of Asians compared to Blacks (Kim 2003) that frames the overall racial politics of South Asians in the United States who tend to accept this elevated position. But by complying with this racial ordering—by stamping the *girmit*, or contract (Prashad 2000: 104), of a supremacist system that disenfranchises all nondominant groups—they cosign their own relative devaluation.[20] By sidestepping "race," cultural notions of difference leave South Asian parents ill equipped to understand racism or explain race to their children. A relational conception of "race" may frame the problematic racial attitudes of many South Asians but it also constitutes the building blocks of desi hip hoppers' global race consciousness. This leads to my second conception of how some desis are "making race" in empowering ways, referring to their expansive communities and worldviews rather than to reified notions of identity, ethnicity, or authenticity.

Desi rappers and DJs understand how people create categories and infuse them with meaning. For instance, they agree that the heterogeneity of people of African descent denounces the singular notion of "Blackness" that implies a biological or genetic basis to a process that is actually socially and historically constructed (Hall 1983; Dyson 1993; Gilroy 1993a).[21] This knowledge propels these Brown performers to recuperate "desiness" and "Blackness" by engaging in meaning making. They strategically employ the seeming fixity of race through self-representations that push beyond imposed identities toward re-creation and empowerment (see Gilroy 2005). Thus the artists *make race* by rejecting and incorporating what is available to them and reaching out for those less-known samples, including aspects of South Asian and African diasporic formations in England and the Caribbean. In not being a biological concept tied to ancestry that is imputed upon individuals, "desi" becomes a racialized construct *selected* by some South Asians.

South Asians occupy a liminal position in American society: they stand between foreigner and citizen, between South Asian and American, between Black and White (van Gennep 1909; Turner 1969). Not even the racial designation "Asian American" properly describes their sense of self. Although historically South Asians fall into the larger narrative of Asians in America, their distinctions are important. Like Pacific Islanders and Filipinos, they fall outside mainstream conceptions of (East) Asians. Rather than being seen as "Orientals" or "Asians," Brown subcontinentals have been racialized as spiritual exotics and increasingly as Muslim fundamentalist Middle Easterners. Thus, I weave South Asians in and out of the story of Asian America.

This liminal status may be problematic for desis; after all, Michael Omi and Howard Winant (1994) explain that without a racial identity Americans would have almost no identity at all. However, desis in this project engage third spaces of possibility (Bhabha 1994) by engaging ambiguity *strategically* in order to endow categories ("desi," "South Asian") and ambiguous bodies with their own meanings. Indeed, I do not celebrate their social locations and choices as if they can ever overcome or transcend the circumscribing factors of race (see Morris 1995). Yet while their subjectivities emerge in response to United States racial binaries and discourses, the artists attempt to change some of the terms of engagement by critiquing racism and claiming explicitly racialized identities.

Their sliding, ambiguous positions offer potential spaces for Asian Americans to reframe Black and White racial poles by moving laterally across communities thought to be unlikely allies. What this work demonstrates is that these artists' racial liminality and their cross-fertilizations illustrate *différence* (Derrida 1982); or, according to Stuart Hall, a "'weave' of similarities and differences that refuse to separate into fixed binary oppositions" (2000: 216). Like liminality, desiness "arises in the gaps and aporias which constitute potential sites of resistance, intervention, translation" (216), and it offers the potential for rearticulation precisely due to its unfixed nature. South Asians can harness their racial instability and the ambiguity of desiness by endowing it with a new set of references, thereby shaping how others view them.

The artists in this ethnography harness ambiguity strategically to expand their options of being in the world beyond what is currently modeled for them by others. They broaden desiness to include political activism and conscious artistry. Some of them work alongside other young desi activists and artists who fight for the rights of marginalized South Asian populations, including the working class, undocumented immigrants, and gays and lesbians (Das Gupta 2006). Anti-racist youth who employ popular culture to speak truth to power embody Foucauldian notions of power as forms of resistance against hegemony, both of which are constituted through contestation and are therefore unstable. Desi artists find hip hop their preferred vehicle of expression as many aspects of this culture exemplify these same notions of resistance and empowerment.

The racial self-conceptions of desi artists illustrate the assertions among Mixed Race studies scholars against singular racial identities, or the idea that people must choose "only one" race. Instead, like people of mixed racial descent, the artists embrace "both/and" rather than "either/or" identifications. This reflects their tolerance for ambiguity, difference, and unresolved tensions, and they are more concerned with understanding rather than "overcoming" difference. Liminal individuals live in and through sameness and difference simultaneously expressed through their identification with multiple communities. As David Scott notes, "Against the old view of identity as self-presence, [Stuart Hall] urges that we think in terms of an open-ended process of *identification*. In this sense of it, identity is not a fixed and permanent entity existing continuously through time but an always unfinished *suturing* together of fragments" (2005: 14). In addition, desis forge identifications across constricting boundaries by "suturing together" samples to create multiracial communities rooted in shared interests. Hardly color-blind or idealistic, they engage upfront with racial ideologies that construct them as exotic others and fill the category of desiness with new meanings. We can understand the choices of desis in hip hop by contextualizing their predicaments within historical precedents of Afro-Asian relations.

Afro-Asian Precedents

I understood Vivek's hesitation to claim a Black identity during our interview. We had met recently and although he was familiar with my project, he didn't know my take on South Asian hip hoppers. After all, there have been historical examples of Asians claiming a non-White status not as a sign of coalition but for economic gain. In the 1980s the Association of Indians in America, whose members included business owners, petitioned to change their status from "White," as they were categorized for the 1970s census, to "Asian" (see Lessinger 1995). This was perhaps not so much a reflection of a politicized "Asian American" identity or a refutation of a "White" status; rather, for these particular individuals the motivation was to qualify for minority business loans. More recently, the High Court in South Africa allowed Chinese to be reclassified as "Black" so that they, too, could benefit from business and governmental policies for non-Whites. These changes have occurred at institutional levels and have garnered much attention, especially within the realm of popular culture. *Mississippi Masala* is Mira Nair's 1991 film about star-crossed lovers and relations between working-class Indian immigrants and Blacks in small-town Mississippi. In a telling scene a Gujarati Indian motel owner proclaims "United we stand, divided we fall!" to the Black owner of a carpet cleaning company (played by Denzel Washington). As the movie progresses, however, we realize this is only a strategic and momentary alliance that the Indian employed to avoid a lawsuit. These kinds of Indian identifications with Blacks for economic gains while they maintain geographical and economic separation are common (in East Africa, the West Indies, Europe, and the United States) and seem "insincere" (see Jackson 2005). Additionally, the aforementioned legal and institutional decisions have led some Blacks to feel mistrustful of Asians' identification with a minority position, which carries over to their skepticism toward South Asians in hip hop. For South Asians who pursue careers in hip hop, however, their claim to a minority status is not about economic profits (in fact, many of the artists decry the materialism of their ethnic communities, see Sharma 2007); rather, it is about political and artistic expression.

Researchers of Indians' attitudes about Blacks examine interracial tensions experienced by groups such as the Sidis of western India (see Jayasuria and Pankhurst 2003; Hawley 2008). Historians have also pointed to British colonial notions of race that may have encouraged Indians' anti-Black attitudes. Subcontinentals who worked in South Africa, Kenya, and Uganda (where Idi Amin expelled Indians) also found ways to remain separate from Black Africans through endogamous marriages and strong cultural identities (Lal, Reeves, and Rai 2007; Oonk 2007; Herzig 2008). Subcontinentals may have traveled with their ideas about otherness, including privileging themselves and fairness over Blacks and darkness, in their migration to the West Indies as indentured laborers and to England and the United States where such notions overlap with Western racial discourses.[22] And although African, Caribbean, and South Asian former British subjects came together as "Blacks" in England, as among the Southall Black Sisters, this unity began to fracture during the 1980s when other South Asians demanded particular representation and distinguished themselves from people of African descent.[23] Thus European colonial interests have crafted global and historical precedents of the conflicts between South Asians and Blacks. These tensions also arise in the United States because of the patterns of racialization and colonial displacement that locate these groups in sectors of the economy that induce competition and reify their differences.

Despite antagonisms that characterize interminority relations, the burgeoning scholarship in Afro-Asian studies uncovers historical precedents for Black and Asian alliances (Du Bois in Mullen and

Watson 2005). Vijay Prashad (2000) hails W. E. B. Du Bois's call for solidarity among Third World peoples across the globe and details a history of Indian and African collaboration among traders between Africa, over the Indian Ocean and into India and China, well before European "adventurers" added their own foul spices to the mix. In Walter Rodney's analysis of the Black Power movement in the Caribbean, he includes all non-White people in one definition of Black: "The black people of whom I speak, therefore, are non-whites—the hundreds of millions of people whose homelands are in Asia and Africa, with another few millions in the Americas" (1969: 16). He highlights the labor strikes held in concert by Black and Indian workers against exploitative conditions in the West Indies. Therefore, as Prashad writes, "The lack of connection between desi advancement on the backs of blacks and of the use of desis in a war against black Americans comes at the expense of a tradition of solidarity and fellowship that began at least a hundred years ago" (171).

The large-scale migration of Blacks and Asians to the United Kingdom since the 1950s makes Britain an important comparison for this study. The relationship between Blacks and Asians in the United States converges with and diverges from that in England; the nation-bound perspectives within American Ethnic Studies obfuscates these global and historical comparisons, thus leading to their underexamination. Many of the South Asians who came to England in the 1950s came, along with their African-descended compatriots, from the West Indies. They shared colonial pasts and a racist present in the "belly of the beast," which made economic advancement difficult. The migration histories and the overlapping racializations of people of African and South Asian descent in England are specific. They cannot be generalized into the United States context where a majority of South Asians arrived as professionals in the 1960s and 1970s and have rarely been categorized as Black, for either politically progressive or oppressive purposes. Additionally, the class differences between South Asians and Blacks in England are less extreme than they are in the United States due to each nation's differing labor demands, immigration patterns, and forms of racism.

In contrast to their shared immigration history in Britain, in popular United States discourse the citizen-foreigner dichotomy splits Blacks from Asians: despite immigration status or ethno-national identities, Americans often assume that all Blacks in the United States are African American; in contrast, irrespective of length of stay, citizenship status, or distance from Asia, Asians in America are assumed, like Latinos, to be recent immigrants. This divide between racialized Blacks and ethnicized Asians empha-sizes a link between slavery and an American minority status.[24] In speaking of the umbrella category "Black" in England, Stuart Hall explains that "one unintended effect was to privilege the Afro-Caribbean experience over that experienced by Asians" (2000: 224; see Modood 1994 for a critique of "Black"). In addition to charting the rise of the emergent Black British identity, postcolonial scholars criticize the hegemony of the Black authenticity of African Ameri-cans that neglects the experiences of others in the African diaspora (Gilroy 1993a). Their critique of racial essentialism and Hall's call to "the end of the innocent notion of the essential black subject" (1992: 32) highlights different ways of being "Black" in the world that should not be homogenized. Alternately, despite their differ-ences, in both the United States and England Blacks and Asians are linked by their racialization and experiences with racism. As Rehan Hyder writes, "For Britain's black and Asian minorities, the com-mon experiences of prejudice and racism have meant that a sense of cultural and ethnic identity has assumed a particularly important role in many aspects of everyday life" (2004: 17). Although less ana-lyzed, racism is also formative for South Asians on this side of the Atlantic.

In addition to their attention to multiple communities of color, some British race studies scholars offer theories applicable to the United States context (Gilroy 1993a; Brah 1996; Sharma, Hutnyk, and Sharma 1996; Hall 2000; Hesse 2000). They emphasize the dan-gers of essentialism and chart out possibilities for anti-essentialist multiracial solidarities. Although the case of England is particu-lar, the claims of these theorists who illustrate an inclusive com-parative race studies scholarship apply to the United States case—including, for example, that Blacks have ethnicities (Hall 2000); that South Asians and Blacks are both racialized minorities sub-ject to overlapping processes of historical and global exploitation, displacement, and racisms via coloniality (Hesse and Sayyid 2006); and that acknowledging these overlaps does not erase difference but allows minority groups to inhabit a stance of belonging-in-difference (Scott 2005: 2).

British South Asian musicians who incorporate rapping, such as M.I.A., Hard Kaur, and the band FunDaMental, along with American desi hip hoppers stand within this larger narrative of conflicting and cooperative relations, of overlapping and discrete histories.[25] At the same time, the choices by hip hop desis to defy ethnic expectations by committing their time, resources, and politics to art and to nondesi peers could only have emerged in this time and place and in this particular form. In this sense, they are "atypical desis," distinguished also from those of the mainstream second generation whose lives have been detailed in existing ethnographies.

Methods:
Comparative Racial Studies through Multisited Ethnography

I suggest a race-centered approach to Asian American studies and a comparative approach to the study of race. This methodology emphasizes the impact of race on immigrants and their youth and contributes to larger debates in ethnic studies. Histories impact the present, including how power and inequality are institutionally inscribed in contemporary societal structures such as in education, the job market, and the prison industrial system. Comparative approaches to race illustrate the specific and overlapping processes of racialization and highlight the dynamics of within-group and cross-group relations. The theories that emerge from comparative race projects interpret how a multitude of individuals live race in America. Therefore, this research furthers our understanding of race and racism and has the potential to illustrate models of interminority solidarities. In illustrating relations between immigrant and native-born minorities this project disrupts the Black and White binary and fills in the contours of contemporary interminority relations. It maps the emergent possibilities of coalitions and suggests models for their creation. Analyzing relations between two minority groups whose hierarchical relation to one another is under construction contributes to theories that explore the dialogic formation of individual and group identities.

In taking its cue from Asian American youth, Asian American

studies can move beyond the model minority myth, intergenerational conflict, internal Asian American community dynamics, and their relation only to Whites. A fuller picture of Asian America emerges when we expand our politics, recommit to the founding principles of Asian American studies that link the academy with community, and dedicate ourselves to knowledge production and cross-racial activism. This includes coming to grips with our commonalities without erasing important differences. If much of the literature on Asian Americans — the fastest-growing group in the United States — continues to focus on their ethnic and cultural identities and is still largely based on assimilation models of upward mobility, hip hop scholarship has been equally inward looking by focusing on issues of authenticity, corporate commodification, and the racial politics of Black popular culture. In pulling together Asian American studies and African American studies, this cultural studies ethnography details one basis of cross-racial social movements. Such a race-centered approach is also a defining feature of the music made by South Asian American hip hop artists.

Some of the most exciting work in South Asian American studies focuses on the lives of "atypical" desis, including those with "alternative" class, religious, and sexual identities (all of whom are represented in this project) (Gopinath 2005; Das Gupta 2006; Maira 2009). Depicting the various processes of racialization that affect Brown people, especially since 9/11, necessitates that we account for — and not just theorize — *actual* interracial relations. This project ethnographically illustrates the impacts of Black people and Black popular culture on the lives and worldviews of some South Asians.

Since 2000 South Asians in hip hop have shown me what a sampled cross-racial life looks like by supplementing my analyses of their lyrics and what they shared with me during taped conversations. Their lives reveal an integral and complex weaving together of passions, politics, practices, and ideologies that spill over the realm of music. Grounding theories within the realities of everyday lives is of paramount importance. Scholars are able to produce more accurate theories of appropriation and better understand relations between groups when they root their interpretations of how and why people appropriate by spending time with them, understanding their perspectives, and observing their relations with others. An ethnographic approach contests analyses that speak of borrowing practices as fixed and unidirectional. It also allows anthropologists to weigh people's words with their lifestyles.

This book stems from research spanning a decade, but it is particularly rooted in ethnographic research from 2000 to 2002 that includes intensive participant observation and recorded and informal interviews with over one hundred people, including the artists who are now mostly in their thirties. Although they are mostly male and straight, the artists include women and one who identifies as a boi (a term used within the LGBT community to, in this case, refer to a female-born person who does not fully or only identify as female or feminine). I also gained insight from nondesis, including African Americans, Africans, and Afro-Caribbean Islanders in hip hop and other music industries in the San Francisco Bay Area. Among other topics, we discussed hip hop, cultural ownership, and South Asian and Black relations.

In addition to countless conversations and get-togethers, I recorded forty-seven interviews that ranged from one to three hours, along with fifty-nine semistructured formal (written) and informal interviews. I corroborated the performers' past recollections with my own firsthand accounts of their cities and schools. Generally, I conducted tape recorded interviews in coffee shops, while the informal interviews and conversations occurred during the course of hanging out, driving, and at nightclubs and concerts. Although I spent a lot of time with the artists during the day (especially if I had arranged an interview), the majority of my fieldwork took place at night. Primary events and locations included concerts, hip hop and reggae nightclubs in the Bay Area, and house parties where some of the artists mixed records and freestyled. I also attended as many of the artists' live shows as possible; these were often in other states and in popular venues such as the House of Blues in Los Angeles and Manhattan's Knitting Factory. In addition, many of our conversations occurred over the twenty-two-month period by phone, through email, and in person as we drove to an event together or enjoyed a meal and drinks. Although my contact with the artists is more sporadic since the period of my fieldwork, I continue to speak and collaborate with some of them through the present.

I engaged other young and old South Asians who were not necessarily involved in hip hop but who had important perspectives on this topic. I met them at South Asian events; for instance at the Alliance of South Asians Taking Action (ASATA) meetings, the Indo-American Community Service Center (ICSC) in Santa Clara where I volunteered, at annual events (e.g., the India Day Festival held in Fremont), and on college campuses across the Bay Area.[26] In addition, I hosted parties and gatherings where different artists were able to meet one another and develop professional networks over time. While most of the ethnographic work took place in public places, I also spent hours talking with people in their homes and in mine as we browsed through our music collections and talked about music, politics, and relationships.

Conclusion

Overall, this book reveals how these artists take the tools provided from ethnic and racial communities—an immigrant sensibility, a sense of otherness, an articulation of racial pride, and a counter-hegemonic discourse—to craft expansive politics. By confronting ethnic and racial norms and articulating cross-racial links in rhyme, they change what being an American desi means. These performers also wish to alter the terms of understanding "difference" more generally: they present South Asians as unequal citizens in a White nation rather than honorific models, and they reframe South Asian and Black relations as mutually constitutive and created through lateral acts of cross-pollination.

Brown members of the hip hop generation claim space outside of ethnic parameters by engaging directly with their minority status, racism, and inequality. They contest the impossibility that Asians "would *choose* to move in the direction of color" (Wong 2004: 187). Their lives resound with the notes of cultural, social, and political cross-fertilizations between South Asians and Blacks. This book is an ode to the music and culture that became the poetics and politics of the desi hip hop artists and shaped my own craft and worldview. Hip hop plays a defining role in the development of new models of immigrant identity, one that privileges the cultivation of positive and progressive interracial relationships in an increasingly diverse world.

1.

Alternative Ethnics

Rotten Coconuts and Ethnic Hip Hop

In my freshman year of college I decided to go to the first Indus dance of the year. I hung out for a while and then went to my dorm room early. Two Indian guys (already two more Indian people than I had ever really known and hung out with) came to my dorm room after the dance.

They said, "Hey, everybody's talking about you. Yeah, they even have a nickname for you. They're calling you 'the rotten coconut.'"

I didn't get it. I said, "Rotten coconut? What does that mean?"

"They're saying that you're Brown on the outside, Black on the inside."

—KB, Indian American MC

Race, not ethnicity, is the explanatory and hermeneutic concept needed to describe the heterogeneous terrain of conflicting culture in the United States. Race, not ethnicity, articulates with class and gender to generate the effects of power in all its multiple protean forms. Ethnicity theory elides power relations, conjuring an illusory state of parity among bargaining agents. It serves chiefly to underwrite a functionalist mode of sanctioning a given social order. It tends to legitimize a pluralist but hierarchical status quo.

—E. San Juan Jr., *Racial Formation/Critical Transformations*

The South Indian American KB was born in the 1970s and grew up in the majority-Black city of Richmond, California, which is known for its own brand of hip hop and was once voted the "most dangerous city in the United States."[1] He began rapping at a young age and by the time he graduated from high school KB was managing the rapping careers of several of his Black friends. More attuned to the lives and tastes of these peers than to those of Indians, he contributed to the culture of their generation's namesake: hip hop. In the 1990s he attended college in Berkeley, and although its location is just a few miles south of Richmond it may have seemed a world away with its hippies, progressive politics, and racial mixing. In college KB continued with what he knew: he rhymed, expanded his mind, and wrote his BA thesis on the impact of popular media depictions of South Asians. At this time, KB met three other desi men and together they formed a hip hop group, Karmacy. The college environment contrasted with both his urban childhood and his later experience in the suburban private and mostly White high school he attended once his family could afford to send him there. At Berkeley he came across a community quite different from the one he claimed — he found desi youth culture just as it was beginning to form among the second-generation children of Indian professionals.

Having grown up without desi peers, KB decided to attend the first Indus dance in order to explore what this clique found so intriguing about socializing strictly among co-ethnics. His disillusionment with their insularity coupled with the "rotten coconut" incident related in the epigraph above was an experience encountered by other artists, and it heightened their ambivalence toward other young South Asians. The artists were also seeking a community but did not find it by retreating into a closely defined ethnic social group. Ethnicity was an ill-fitting cloak that neither protected them against negative experiences nor sufficiently expressed the totality of their beings.

The artists' interactions with co-ethnics reveal the benefits and limitations of both analyzing and building community in immigrant America around ethnicity. By ethnicity I refer to the sense of belonging that emerges from the combination of shared cultural practices and shared ancestry. My definition highlights the diasporic and transnational material and emotional ties among members of Indian, Sri Lankan, or Pakistani communities, for instance, and the fresh and prevalent impacts of immigration upon them. Of course, individuals experience ethnicity and race (the topic of the next chapter) simultaneously, and the dynamics internal to South Asian American ethnic communities, including hegemonic notions of desiness, develop through interracial relations. However, I pull the concepts of race and ethnicity apart for two reasons. First, I analyze the distinct impacts of desis and nondesis upon the artists, who generally socialize with members of these groups separately. Second, I theorize race and ethnicity differently, whereby ethnicity describes the pull and obligations toward a group defined by culture and ancestry while race refers both to imposed categories as well as to emergent identifications across existing categories. Race and ethnicity cannot be wholly disentangled and their impacts and definitions overlap at times; nonetheless, theirs is a tension that generates new theories to understand life. Analyzing these concepts in this way illustrates the separate and overlapping influences of co-ethnics and of Blacks upon desi artists who work within this nexus to rearticulate alternative forms of desiness by identifying with Blacks. A race-centered and critical approach to the limits of ethnicity yields theoretical clarity on the salience and incompleteness of analyzing Asian Americans as ethnics only.

Ethnicity is neither the only nor even the primary identity for all Asian American youth. And although many desis describe their peers as "White identified," Whiteness is not their only racial option.[2] This chapter addresses the shortcomings of theorists who assert that ethnicity is an internally cohesive identity and a positive reaction to immigrants' exclusion from mainstream America. South Asian American hip hop artists defy expectations of the new second generation by turning away from both an ethno-national identity (as "Sri Lankans," for instance) and from an assimilated mainstream White identity (Portes and Zhou 1993; Rumbaut 1994). Instead, I address why some second-generation immigrants choose to identify with Blacks (not all of whom represent "the underclass") when they do not have to. This phenomenon also begs a reconsideration of just how optional and flexible ethnicity is for South Asians (Leonard 1992; Kibria 2000), particularly when gatekeepers rigidify the "choices" of co-ethnics. Without recourse to Whiteness because of their racial otherness, they cannot voluntarily or symbolically choose whether, how, and when to "be ethnic" (Barth 1969; Glazer and Moynihan 1975; Gans 1996). Finally, ethnic identity is also not the only available reaction to racism, as predicted by reactive ethnicity.[3] We see this in the reformulations of desiness into panethnicity by these hip hoppers as they attempt to create expansive and inclusive communities.

Desi performers learn important lessons from their respective ethnic communities that cultivate diasporic sensibilities and membership in transnational communities with distinctive cultural practices that impact their music. Identifying strongly as "Indian" or "Nepali," they nonetheless feel constrained by their elders who define "real" or authentic ethnic expressions and norms. Part of the critical distance of hip hop desis stems from not fitting into such hegemonic conceptions; yet even those artists who *do* fit the parameters—who are North Indian, middle class, and upper caste—are sometimes critical of ethnic parochialism and chauvinism.

This chapter illuminates South Asian Americans' heterogeneity, hybridity, and multiplicity (Lowe 1996). Many studies reaffirm the dominant image of South Asians as Hindu Indians who have achieved upward mobility, maintain close family ties, and live the American dream. My work aligns with scholars who analyze the unequal heterogeneity within South Asian America—the maltreatment, disownment, and silencing of desis who are not heterosexual, Hindu, and middle class, for instance (Prashad 2000; Gopinath 2005; Das Gupta 2006). Dominant conceptions of proper desiness can push those who are marginalized and who disagree with such practices to disidentify with their ethnic communities. Hip hop desis are among a new generation of progressive youth who reconfigure themselves as members of groups outside the bounds of ethnicity.

Over the course of their childhood and college years, desi performers also reveal the kinds of progressive work that ethnicity, *reconfigured*, can take on to nourish alliances. Like other activist-oriented desi youths, these artists tussle with desi conservatism. Ethnographies have detailed how other Brown youths like those in this project "negotiate ethnicity" (Purkayastha 2005) as they contend with ethnic immersion, rejection, and reformulation. However, hip hoppers are unique desis for embracing Blackness and Black people and for their emphasis upon the role of Black popular culture in remixing ethnicity. Artists in this group create "ethnic hip hop" to articulate alternative iterations of desiness by working out contentious rather than essentialized or naturalized connections to ethnicity (Sharma 2008). Using their words, beats, and samples, they criticize parochial and conservative renditions of desiness that delimit "proper" ethnicity. Some create ethnic hip hop as their expression of ethnic allegiances and commitments to inclusiveness and commonality across differences. The artists take a role in shaping, through performance and lyrics, how desis present themselves to America, thereby impacting people's conceptions of South Asian Americans.

South Asian American rappers and DJs perform alternative identities that reject the assumed link between blood ties and belonging and look to history and power relations *within* ethnic communities. Desi youths who identify with Blacks reveal complex interactions that suggest nothing less than a reconfiguration of our notions about the role of ethnicity in the lives of Asian Americans. In fact, desi artists reveal how ethnicity also *enacts* racism upon others through conservative notions of authenticity that dovetail with mainstream racial politics. The conservative racial politics of hegemonic desiness becomes a motivating factor, in collusion with White racism and mainstream discourses that obfuscate its operations, to foster ambivalent feelings about ethnicity. This group reveals a willingness to trade the privileges of their ethnic and class status, indeed their very status of being non-Black. In turn, they embrace self-conceptions geared toward disenfranchised populations and open to social change. Ultimately, some individuals employ hip hop to express the alternative desiness that emerges from their critiques and embrace of particular aspects of South Asian cultures. This rearticulation opens up the very possibilities of community formation outside the bonds of ethnic identity, which I discuss in chapter 2.

Exceptional Desis?
Locating Hip Hoppers within South Asian America

The family biographies of South Asian hip hop artists in the United States are part of the overall story of the second wave of Asian immigrants who arrived following the Immigration Act of 1965. Desis who perform hip hop reflect the enormous ethnic, regional, linguistic, religious, caste, gender, sexual, and class diversity of South

Asians. Their parents, in partial response to their new status as "minorities," want their cultures to flourish within this adopted country in particularly crafted ways. First-generation ideas and family practices couple with class status and family structure to influence second-generation notions of ethnic authenticity that lead some desis to hip hop.

South Asians in America create a particular "hegemonic" form of ethnic identity, which Biju Mathew and Vijay Prashad (2000) call "Yankee Hindutva" due to the nexus of factors impacting their arrival. Global and historical forces (the British colonization of India and the Second World War) and economic and political policies (a postwar economic boom, the need for professionals in the United States, civil rights gains, and the opening up of immigration quotas in the 1960s) intersect with changing discourses of race that continue to justify White supremacy in the face of changing demographics. Skilled postcolonials arrived in 1960s civil rights America as the nation was reevaluating its approach to race from biological discourses to similarly problematic cultural understandings of difference. This shift led to the idea that these new immigrants were the "model minority," a culturalist ideology that "praised" Asians and disciplined Blacks with the corresponding theory of Black cultural pathology.

South Asian immigrants, eager to enculturate their youth, reinvented conservative elements of their cultures and explained group inequality in the United States through culturalist explanations. According to Vijay Prashad, "U.S. multiculturalism joins with desi conservatism to invoke certain aspects of desi culture as desi culture *tout courte*" (2000: 113). As the status of many professional Asians grew in the hourglass economy of the 1980s, so too did their distance from working-class communities, including third-wave South Asians and many Blacks and Latinos. South Asians generally adopted the idea that their success was due to strong cultural and family values and they encouraged their children with the notion that success was earned through hard work and persistence. This bootstraps theory coincided with governmental neoliberal economic policies that cut and privatized services (Dolhinow 2010). The professional status of some of the artists' families protected them from these changes, thereby enabling their parents to provide them with private schools and stable homes in predominantly White neighborhoods. But growing economic disparities hid the existence of those who did not fare as well. Those desi artists in less financially secure families, particularly those whose parents were separated, grew up in class-diverse minority neighborhoods and attended school systems with Black peers who were directly affected by changing economic conditions.

Hegemonic desiness emerged within this context among wealthier Indians who praised their financial and educational exceptionalism. The aims of these ethnic gatekeepers coincided with those of the American politicians and decision makers who advanced the idea that individuals are responsible for their own station in life. They used Asians to illustrate the end of institutional racism, and as long as these "models" supported the doctrine of progress, they would not pose a problem. Some Asian Americans, however, became troublemakers and crafted their own definitions of success.

Second-generation desis across all classes who were born in the 1970s and grew up in the Bay Area were particularly affected by the identity-based racial movements of the previous decade. The Black Panthers started in Oakland, California, and the Black Power movement influenced the Asian American, American Indian, and Chicano movements. The heightened race consciousness of Bay Area residents is in no small part due to the efforts of members of the Black Students Union and the pan-racial Third World Liberation Front who held the longest student strike in history at San Francisco State University, thereby creating the nation's first and second (at Berkeley) ethnic studies departments. Some of the artists attended these schools and were undeniably influenced by the logic and goals of these social movements well into the 1990s, despite the national sentiment that America had moved on. The pursuit of elite educations and economic advancement by South Asians and their closed ethnic circles make it difficult to ascertain the impact of these global and race-conscious politics upon desis. Indeed, as Glenn Omatsu (2000) describes, many desi youths illustrate the shift taken by Asian Americans from broad-based radical political and anti-war activism in the 1960s to a conservative and apolitical stance with the rise of second-generation professionals in the 1990s.[4] However, some individuals, like these desis, continue with the spirit of anti-racist and consciousness-raising movements, which infuse their music.

In this section I analyze the expectations, including ethnic insularity, cultural distinctiveness, and material success, within the artists' various South Asian communities that limited competing possibilities. The childhood experiences of artists from wealthier White neighborhoods and those from urban, racially mixed cities explain their ethnic ambivalence rooted in their critique of rigid expectations and conservatism. Hegemonic desiness opens them to other "families of resemblance" beyond the bounds of ethnicity (Lipsitz 1994).

Ethnic Insularity:
Middle-Class South Asians from Predominantly White Areas

Most of the desi artists' parents came from urban regions throughout South Asia; a smaller number came from Fiji, England, and the West Indies. Their fathers came to the United States as English-speaking doctors, engineers, and graduate students in science and medicine and their mothers worked as office managers, doctors' assistants, and homemakers.[5] Many of these families faced occupational downgrading in a gender- and race-segregated market. The shifts in family status from South Asia to the United States became a source of frustration for some artists, especially for those whose lives then became economically unstable. Nonetheless, despite the high cost of living in California and New York where most of the artists grew up, none of them came from poor families; rather, they represented a range of middle-class statuses. Nearly half of them were middle- and upper-middle-class members of nuclear families that lived in mostly White suburban-type neighborhoods in medium-sized cities like Fremont, California, home to hi-tech and other professionals.[6]

Along with "Indianness," wealthier South Asian families sought to maintain mainstream American markers of success: a suburban-type solid middle-class status, two-parent household, and access to White neighborhoods and schools. Members of the first generation drew strength from their cultural traditions, including filial piety, hard work, and the importance of secure futures and endogamous marriages. These expectations worked well with mainstream American ideas of how to integrate newcomers in ways that allow them their practices, given they cannot—or will not—be granted equal status.

The privileged class status that these artists shared with their White neighbors did not prevent them from routine encounters with racism. White high school classmates called one artist "dot," referring to the bindi that some South Asian women wear on their forehead; others were called "monkey" and "nigger" (and later "nigger-lover").[7] "They were so ignorant," stated one DJ, "they used to call me 'chink.'" Like other Asians (Chan 1991; Espiritu 1992, 1997), South Asians have been victim to multiple forms of racism: occupational downgrading, the glass ceiling, political invisibility, religious persecution, and hate crimes (including the Dotbusters, or individuals in New Jersey who violently targeted South Asians in the 1980s, and the fatal violence and unconstitutional detentions following 9/11). Despite such violence, South Asians tend to side-step racial matters and their victimization. When the MC D'Lo reported White harassment to his/her Sri Lankan father in the 1980s, he said, "Yeah, it happens and don't worry about it." His response was typical among South Asians who are often unfamiliar with how American racism works but who are nonetheless aware of it: "They tried not to make a big deal of it," said D'Lo.

A widespread response to racism faced by these postcolonial elites is ethnic insularity, a part of reactive ethnicity. South Asians have turned inward to foster communities and organizations along ethnic, regional, religious, and linguistic lines for solace from tensions at work. In the poem "From Silent Confusion to Blaring Healing" D'Lo muses: "Sometimes her fellow uprooted friends / tried to re-plant themselves in historical soil / soil common to their ancestors."[8] Similarly, Muslim artists report that their families participate in closed social circles based on religious sectionalism. "Pretty tribal" is how one Pakistani Shia MC from Staten Island describes his family. "Like many South Asian families we stuck to our niche community. . . . Most and maybe all of our social relations came out of the religious community. . . . We pretty much associate with ourselves."[9]

Rigid ethnic borders also help parents fulfill their central goal of raising children who will not only learn but embrace cultural and

South Asians in the United States continue to practice their religious
and cultural events. Author's photograph.

religious practices, gendered roles, and generational obligations
(Prashad 2000: 118). They pass down to their children beliefs akin
to the Protestant work ethic hand in hand with the importance of
family, community, and culture. Middle-class desis are subjected
to evaluation by co-ethnics through competition and gossip. "No
Shame," a poem in D'Lo's third collection, describes the predica-
ment of Sri Lankan kids under the eyes of such watchdogs:

> Have to politely ward off the gossip Aunties and
> dodge intrusively interrogating uncles. Have to
> tiptoe 'bout everything, have to look good, get the
> edumacation, go to med or law school.
> You know the boring background story.

Despite such monitoring, second-generation desi youth who grew
up during the 1980s — a decade in which Asian Americans faced increasing racial violence — employed similar insular strategies to
contend with racism (Maira 2002; Purkayastha 2005). Artists such
as D'Lo, Bella, and Jonny from middle-class suburban neighborhoods benefited from close-knit ethnic communities. Their families provided them with cultural practices, historical knowledge,

and a sense of belonging to a transnational community of real and fictive aunties and uncles that helped them find their footing in America (see Purkayastha 2005).

Many desis understand their cultural uniqueness in multicultural terms and they deny the relevance of race while racism shapes their daily lives. This is not the case for hip hop artists. Desis from White neighborhoods who created hip hop contest ethnic insularity and offer reflections rooted in an analysis of race and class rather than in culture. Jonny, a hip hop journalist from Fremont, California, sees that "a lot of Indians socialize together, still dislike other immigrant groups, and are quick not to embrace the Black experience in America as being similar to their own." He hypothesizes that, like his, other Indian families understand "race as a function of their own experiences as immigrants and as assimilants into the successful economic track of America (usually guided by the White experience)." His link between Indians' upward mobility (class) and their desire to align with Whites rather than Blacks (race) is an alternative to the culture-based analyses that underwrite the model minority myth.

Desis in hip hop criticize as parochialism the insularity of members of the first generation who "don't see the connection with anyone." First- and second-generation members of South Asian communities have reacted to life in America by cultivating strong internal ethnic bonds, but this move inward also signifies a troubling "strategy of disidentification" (Kibria 2000: 84) with Blacks and Latinos. The hip hoppers' ambivalence toward ethnicity partially stems from the reaction of elder immigrants who repress their experiences with racism while discriminating against other minorities. Thus, despite their access to a privileged identity, these artists do not find comfort in ancestry-based exclusivity.

Artists from wealthier families reveal some of the pressures faced by second-generation youth, including ethnic insularity, a focus on economic success, and a sense of exceptionalism. Despite the benefits of such a community, they sometimes question ethnicity because it requires them to sacrifice too many of their own interests and perspectives. Ethnicity is adopted by South Asians unevenly, even by those who *have access* to hegemonic desiness. What, then, do we learn about the "options" of those who grew up without strong ethnic networks in diverse and working-class neighborhoods?

The model minority image created by dominant Americans and embraced by many Asian immigrants characterizes the early family lives of the majority of desi youth generally, but it applies to the lives of only half of the artists. In contrast to their wealthier counterparts, most of the artists from lower-middle-class families lived in racially diverse neighborhoods in cities like Richmond, California, during the 1970s through 1990s when they went off to college. Recent scholars, dissatisfied with older conceptual models describing South Asians in America, focus on the particularities and politics of the second generation and disrupt the outmoded Black and White conception of race.[10] But the "social and economic positioning" of various South Asian populations have, like their counterparts in Britain, "become markedly more differentiated over time" (Hall 2000: 219). How do those from modest economic backgrounds re-create ethnicity? South Asian American studies often point to third-wave immigrants in the service sector as the face of working-class subcontinentals in the United States, yet not all second-wave professionals fared well. Class status does not determine whether or not a South Asian will produce Black popular culture and forge meaningful relationships with Blacks. However, it directly impacts the lives and options of Americans by affecting their residence, peers, engagement with institutions, and access to ethnic networks. Artists representing this group were particularly aware of what they termed their "atypical" experiences in contrast to mainstream desis.

Whereas their wealthier counterparts were primarily aware of their ethnic otherness, artists of this second set were less focused on White racism and noticed both class and race patterns. They took more time to describe their ambiguous class status, for instance. A Richmond-raised rapper considered his family "middle class" and described his as a "good home," despite living near people who were working class and "poor." "If you take my house and put it in a middle-class area, though," he clarified, "it would be working class." Coming from a "good home" referred often to material status in relation to neighborhood friends rather than nuclear family structure. The class status of these artists was often closer to that of their neighbors than to wealthy desis, who would not choose to live in these neighborhoods. Those who came from areas that lacked strong South Asian networks had restricted access to cultural capital, which in turn inhibited a strong sense of ethnic belonging. At the same time, it also offered these artists and their families some freedom from ethnic expectations.

While the families of wealthier artists tended to stay put, the upward mobility of this second set was more drastic. They moved to different neighborhoods and changed schools often. "Until college," the rapper KB explains, "I never went to any school for more than two years." In the 1980s Rawj and KB attended the same underfunded high school in Richmond, which the radio producer Asma (who also went there, but they did not know one another) estimates was about 65 percent Black and where hip hop culture was the norm. The two boys later transferred to separate private schools outside of Richmond. Rawj's family moved to a wealthy suburb that was "like Beverly Hills with Birkenstocks," after his mother remarried. "That was an experience," he exclaims: "I was fifteen, in high school, had never been around that many White people in my life and it was completely different!" The class and complexion of his new 'hood was accompanied with new acoustic tastes. "They didn't listen to hip hop!" he said incredulously of the students who were "on a whole different style: Pink Floyd, Nirvana, and shorts, raggedy clothes, and BMWs." "Somehow," says Rawj, who "felt like the Fresh Prince" after moving to the suburbs, "I got out of there without killing or strangling anybody!"[11]

Artists such as MCs Rawj and KB, radio producer Asma, rapping cousins Asad and Fahad from Staten Island, and the San Francisco MC Chee Malabar all experienced the complex economic and demographic patterns that make up racially diverse and lower-middle-class neighborhoods. But KB speaks for many of them when he says, "I just got so used to moving around and I got to experience a lot of different socio-economic backgrounds and cultures . . . I just had the feeling that some people were rich, some people were poor." These urban desis shared experiences that led to a critical consciousness that took both race *and* class differences into account at a young age.

The influence of ethnic gatekeepers who wish to cover up the "undesirable elements" among South Asians often extends beyond ethnic enclaves to impact these more isolated families. Cases of divorce and sexual transgressions among desi girls attract an especially watchful eye. "Many migrants," write Mathew and Prashad, "seek to re-invent their cultural environment to preserve themselves from the onslaught of what they see as an ahistorical and noncontradictory 'American culture'" (2000: 520). Ironically, many of the crafted requirements only serve to reinforce the ideas that many Americans have of "Indians" as unassimilable foreigners. Stuart Hall connects modern divisive discourses to the past. "One result," he writes, "is that the unresolved problems of social development have combined with the resurgent traces of older, still unrequited, ethnic and religious nationalisms, allowing the tensions in these societies to resurface in a multi-cultural form" (2000: 214). We see this surface in problematic gender and class politics as well as the religious divides that persist in the diaspora.

Families and communities use sanctions to regulate women's sexuality and marital practices as an aspect of ethnic identity, thus closely linking gender expectations with ethnicity (Mani 1993: 34). Asian immigrants often deem women to be the keepers of their culture, and thus ethnic identities hinge upon community-defined appropriate sexual and marital behaviors (Espiritu 2001; see also Rudrappa 2002). Divorce is rare among South Asians, some of whom consider it "Western" and "inferior" (Gupta 1999: 197, 194).[12] However, urban desi hip hoppers include a number of those whose parents had divorced or separated. Divorce led to a decline in household income that constrained where these artists could live, and split families were sometimes estranged from nearby South Asians who looked down upon their situations. These factors directly impacted the artists' relationship to co-ethnics. Rawj describes how "all of the families that we associated with, after she got divorced, they no longer associated with us, so that's another reason why I didn't grow up around Indians. And then as far as blood family that came here from India, there was a language barrier and there were conflicts with the parents, so we didn't really get too close, either." Desi communities give these single mothers difficulty over separation or divorce; their sanctions also trouble the artists' sense of belonging to a community whose norms coincide with conservative American "family values" discourses on heterosexuality and marriage (see Das Gupta 2006). For queer and transgender artists like D'Lo, the tests of ethnicity and sexuality can become overwhelming. For these reasons, having some breathing room away from ethnic ties can prove to be somewhat liberatory, albeit in limited ways, by encouraging other possible self-expressions.

Class also does not determine whether or not a particular youth will take a critical stance in relation to his or her ethnic community. Urban participants, written out of emerging definitions of proper desiness, did not fit the "typical" desi experience with regard to their class status, geographic distance from ethnic networks, less stable family structures, and their proximity to Black and Latino peers. While the ethnic ambivalence of wealthier artists stemmed from their critique of ethnic mores, urban artists faced the social sanctions that deemed them inauthentic before they were able to fully respond to what was expected of them.

Despite the cleavage in experiences between suburban and urban artists, each adapted to their context. Their ethnic ambivalence emerged for a variety of reasons, mostly tied to solidifying conceptions of what constituted proper desiness. Some found it impossible to fulfill religious, class, gender, and regional expectations while others were unwilling to do so. Suburban artists' experiences with racism reminded them of their racial difference, despite their shared class status with classmates and neighbors. Due to their racial liminality (van Gennep 1909; Turner 1967, 1969) as neither Black nor White and their shifting economic standing, urban artists understood the fluidity of categories and the ambiguity of their own race and class identities. Whether or not they were to embrace or retreat from claiming an ethnic identity would be sorted out in college and articulated through their music. Beforehand, though, the artists all had to contend with a shared set of ethnic expectations across class lines.

Sampling Ethnics: Shared Experiences among Desis in Hip Hop

Through an uneven process of ethnic engagement, dissociation, critique, and rearticulation, the artists began to "sample ethnicity" by rejecting aspects they found oppressive while taking and remixing those parts that resonated with them. The artists' relationship to ethnicity was framed by their experiences within their homes and at community functions and was reinforced by a sense of racial otherness at school. It took time for them to understand both what was expected of them and why through interactions with other South Asians. At times, they drew from the strengths that ethnic belonging and social capital offered them, learning from their elders the importance of stability, family responsibility, and education. But the set of values developing among American desis was tinged with the chauvinism, materialism, and exclusivity that accompanied community membership. Over time, many hip hop–oriented youths critiqued hegemonic desiness, sometimes using the same logic that they hoped to overcome. This process was engendered by a set of expectations about religion, marriage, economic mobility, and what constituted an "authentic desi," which elicited similar reactions among the artists.[13] The artists' dialogic engagement with ethnic formation ultimately encouraged their move toward Blacks and hip hop culture.

The religious hegemony of Indian Hindus, which can silence and disparage Sikhs and Muslims as well as Christians, can be an oppressive force in the lives of non-Hindu South Asians. Like other desi youth, the artists picked up religious practices within their families. Mothers were often responsible for exposing their children to religious practices such as taking them to the local *gurdwara* in El Sobrante or staging a *puja* (a religious ritual) at home for special events. At times the hip hop heads protested. Rawj says of his mother that "the way she tried to push the culture on me was through religion, and a little too much for me. So that's why I didn't learn it." Religion became an aspect of ethnic identity that other Americans at school disparaged (see Joshi 2006; see also Chen 2008). Non-Christian parents often enrolled their children in Catholic and Baptist schools, which they felt provided a better education than public schools. As D'Lo, a Hindu Tamil who attended school near Los Angeles, remembers: "In the books that we were reading, they would always bash on Hindus or other cultures in that these weren't followers of God, 'cause this was a Baptist school. And they were always targeting other Brown kids to convert them. So I converted. I was like, 'I love me some Jesus!' [Laughs] Jesus was my best fuckin' friend, you know?!" D'Lo's accommodation to religious hegemony, however comedic in retrospect, was not as easily applied to his/her phenotypic distinctiveness. Looks, in addition to being non-Christian in a largely Judeo-Christian nation, emphasized desi otherness and may account for the artists' reframing of religion in their lives. D'Lo was not dissuaded from religion or from identifying as a Sri Lankan Hindu, a topic that takes its place, front and center, in his/her performances. D'Lo, who writes, "Me-proud lover of God ~also~ as/in people," dedicates the written word first to God. In the poem "Legitimizing the Spirit Within" D'Lo proffers a poetic dialogue between him/herself, a believer in "God as people" and "God in people," and an atheist man s/he wishes to emulate "in case there isn't a God":

> I wanted to laugh like this and tell him
> That he himself is God!
> That he is the example of
> what every religious
> or spiritually based person
> wanted to be — aspired to be like

Contesting parents' lament that their youth are irreligious, the artists are less concerned than their elders about "purity" of form, and they craft unique religious practices that fit their circumstances.

Like D'Lo's play on his/her relationship to Jesus, other artists also shifted ethnic definitions of religiosity and, as they grew older, some of them remixed their practices with non-desi influences. The rapper Vivek and Deejay Bella (both Gujarati) have customized syncretic practices that fuse South Asian, Caribbean, and African-based traditions. Both strict vegetarians, Vivek identifies strongly with Jainism and Bella melds Sindhi Hindu religious practices with Rastafarianism. These "unlikely crossovers," which can be explained by historical precedents, hint at future cross-fertilizations that later come to characterize their lives. The British brought Indian "coolies" to replace African slave labor in Trinidad, Jamaica, and Guyana. Exchanges among these seemingly distinct populations led to the new fusions seen in contemporary Carnival celebrations despite concerns about cultural and religious "dilution" from racial mixing among members across these populations (see Khan 2004a, 2004b). In their youth, hip hop desis in the United States had trouble rearticulating religion and often upheld the same logic of fixed social expectations they later tried to work through.

The artists fell back on community descriptions of religion, ethnicity, and authenticity as essentialist and quantifiable entities: they implied that "cultural purity" and "real religious knowledge" "belonged" the most to those living in South Asia and that ethnicity was a quality subject to "dilution" through Americanization. Indian parents sometimes monitored the clothes and whereabouts of their children, "for fear they would 'lose' their Indianness," according to one Indian hip hop journalist. Many American desis sensed their parents' homeland nostalgia expressed through fossilized conceptions of ethnicity and often reproduced these dynamics of authenticity in their subcultures (see Maira 2002). MC Chee, a 1.5-generation Indian who lives in Los Angeles, located authenticity spatially within the boundaries of India and temporally in traditions of the past: "Being Indian is just like . . . that's where I come from I guess. I mean, I look around now—the way I'm dressed, the way I talk, the stuff I like—it has nothing to do with being Indian. You know? So how can I say I'm more proud to be Indian? If I was Indian, I would be living in India, you know, wearing a *dhoti* or a *lungi* [a wrap men wear] and I'd be praying or doing whatever that comes with being Indian." Thus, the artists borrowed cultural practices and essentialist conceptions from their ethnic communities. As they sorted through their meanings over time, however, the performers incorporated flexible practices into their notions of desiness (Ong 1998).

Dominant expectations also coalesce around the all-important issues of education (attending "the best" schools), income (wealthy), and stability (low-risk, high-income jobs). The artists dealt with these norms as they did with religion: they first found themselves subject to these requirements; they grappled with them; they found them to be too restrictive; and they took those aspects they found central to their self-conception while attempting to burst through rigid options to explore new ones. A member of the Indian American hip hop group Karmacy, KB, described how South Asians laud and berate particular careers, which constrains those who want to pursue other options: "If you're Indian, [and] every single person that you know is a doctor or a lawyer, what are you going to aspire to be? . . . Because if you're an Indian kid growing up in this country, no matter how much you don't want to believe it, there's a self-conscious mental block telling you that you can't be Michael Jordan." Parents urged their music-minded children to pursue lucrative and stable careers in business, medicine, and science. Parents who sacrifice for their children's futures understandably worry about the economic and personal health of their children, yet their hopes also morph into troublesome racial and class politics. Politicians and others have latched onto the upward mobility of Asians as the model of the proper way immigrants should insert themselves into the nation. Access to wealth has also made South Asians active consumers of property, including large McMansions and fancy cars, in an economy that, dependant upon them, praises these items as symbols of having "made it." Desi artists remix their competing ethnic-economic and music-passion obligations by getting trained in medicine and computers, for instance, while also producing hip hop music.

The notion that South Asian immigrants are often "significantly short on progressive politics" and are bent on class aspirations (Rajan and Sharma 2006: 14) disturbs desis bent on social justice. Some artists say that their parents' insularity and focus on money is tied to their "politically liberal, racially conservative" ideas, including those who are Democrats who may be in favor of state services for the poor but are against affirmative action. Many parents even discouraged their children's friendships with other minorities. Wealthy community leaders advance conservative ideas (Prashad 2000; Maira 2002; Das Gupta 2006), and even some Muslims, who tend not to gain equal representation within Indian organizations, share these ideas. A Muslim woman says of her otherwise Democrat and permissive parents that "definitely there's a capitalist side to their politics. And they are probably pretty classist, too." Like religion, therefore, success, defined in monetary and educational terms, is naturalized as an aspect tied to ethnicity — it *defines* one as an "Indian." Prevalent discourses within South Asian immigrant communities couple with American conceptions of meritocracy to infiltrate even the minds of those attempting to challenge these ideas. Without an alternative framework, artists also echoed the link between class and ethnicity. For example, one MC naturalizes this connection in his example of a friend: "As much as he's not Indian, in some ways he's completely Indian because he really feels he's superior toward other minorities. He's like, 'man, I *know* I got a good job. Shit, I'm Indian, I'm *supposed* to succeed. There's no way I should fail.'"

"New cosmopolitans" (Rajan and Sharma 2006) are members of a wealthy post-1965 group within the South Asian community that combines their access to privilege with a longing for their home-land. They epitomize the model minority in many ways and foster a "predominantly conservative, right-wing, and unabashedly capi-talist nexus" (14–15) that dovetailed with the rise of the New Right during the Reagan years. American South Asians, Prashad argues, "prefer to detach themselves from the minutiae of democracy and to attach themselves solely to the task of capital accumulation" (2000: 3).[14] Kasturi DasGupta suggests an alternative interpre-tation: "Arming their children with the best education, from the best colleges, with the best academic record is seen as imperative, if the conditions of 'color-prejudice' are to be mitigated" (1997: 61). DasGupta's connection between material success and racism is another example of South Asian Americans' "triple move" when it comes to race: denying the impacts of racism upon their com-munities, negotiating the effects of racism *upon them* by appealing to class mobility and security, while embracing (not stated in this example but present) explicit and implicit racist ideologies against *other* minorities for their class standing.

This single-minded focus on material success and high social status points to another cleavage within "the community": wealthy desis often ignore and deride struggling co-ethnics because, like divorced and queer South Asians, they mar South Asians' positive reputations (see Khandelwal 2002). This dangerous confluence of South Asian and American "values" has colored outsiders' views of South Asians as money-oriented and also partially accounts for rifts between wealthy immigrants from South Asia and more working-class Indians from Fiji and the Caribbean. Many second-generation youths heed their parents' advice regarding their choices of college, majors, and, ultimately, their jobs. However, desi artists, whose very careers signal a shifting path, attempt to address South Asians' embodiment of United States orientalist and model minority depic-tions of "passive" Asians "without a developed social conscious-ness" (Prashad 2000: 68).

Cultural capital is another component of constructions of Ameri-can desiness. While over time the artists often felt distant from other South Asians, mainstream desis also called into question their ethnic identity because, to those living "proper" desi lives, the artists lacked cultural capital. I asked a South Indian rapper who immigrated to the States when he was eleven whether or not he felt bad about this distance, even estrangement, from other desis. He responded, "No. I think I did more when I was [young] . . . When I needed them [when I first came to this country], they weren't there. You know what I mean? So now it's like, 'I don't need them.'" One's familiarity with cultural norms and knowledge, such as language fluency, knowing religious stories, being able to identify and cook regionally specific cuisine, knowledge about the subcontinent, and even looking identifiably South Asian are elements used by others to gauge one's "level" of ethnicity. These forms of cultural capital are also the ways that desi artists came to understand their "lack." It is difficult for those without strong ethnic networks to make up for the cultural knowledge that can be absorbed through sustained engagement with a cohesive community. All of the performers felt their lack of cultural capital in their adolescence and the majority had few to no deep relationships with non-family desis.[15] They called themselves "weird," "atypical," and "different" in comparison to mainstream South Asians and therefore needed to redefine desiness if they wanted to claim an ethnic identity.

Some of the artists chose to alienate themselves from hegemonic expectations while others were unable to claim these identities. Their ethnic choices pertaining to religion, education, class, politics, and cultural capital, therefore, were not uniform. They were surrounded by conceptions of success, belonging, and difference described in cultural terms but often rooted in primordial notions. Hegemonic desiness is therefore essentialist, tied to religion, nationality, and ancestry. These artists adopted similar ideas about ethnicity and religion as something one "had" or "didn't have," particularly in their childhoods. College, however, would introduce them to mainstream desi youth and an entirely new set of social interactions that changed the terms of the artists' relationships with co-ethnics and with ethnicity itself. It was there that they were able to develop anti-essentialist conceptions of desiness, which they articulated through ethnic hip hop.

College: Rejecting Desis

I got [to the University of California, Berkeley] at a time when most of the Indian population that was there was from White upper-class or upper-middle-class neighborhoods. And so I guess to them I spoke differently,

I walked differently, I talked differently, I dressed differently, and so they reacted to me that way. And it was a very big culture shock to me because, first, I had never hung out with Indians before and, second, I never realized the impact that my community had had on me.

—KB, rapper from Richmond, California

Desi artists, all of whom attended college in the 1990s, were part of the first generation to mark the presence of large numbers of South Asians in higher education. While the majority enrolled in the University of California system in Berkeley, Davis, and Los Angeles, a few attended state universities in San Francisco and Pennsylvania and some first took classes at a junior college before moving on to a university. There they confronted other mainstream desi students who grafted first-generation ideas onto their social worlds, thereby re-creating reified notions of ethnicity around which they formed their social cliques and politics. Identity-based cliques were common among desis and other minority students in college at a time when the mission statements of American universities averred "tolerance" and "diversity" while they banned affirmative action. These groups provide youth, including current college students, with a sense of security and identity in the same way that larger organizations do for the older generation. Finding a community in which to celebrate and share one's ethnic identity through cultural shows and organizations also draws these youths together (see Maira 2002: 120–32). Within these organizations, mainstream desis create age-appropriate norms through communities of "sameness" — members of dominant desi cliques share ancestries, languages, food, and their status as non-Whites. They also unofficially restrict inclusion by appraising the ethnic "fitness" of others. Parading social, class, ethnic, gender, and sexual norms as "desi pride" reflects "reverse assimilation," which is seen as a "necessary response to the bewildering conformism of college life in the United States" (Prashad 2000: 191). In this section, I analyze how desis in hip hop dealt with these inward-looking social formations.

Through tense and sometimes disappointing interactions with co-ethnics, the artists needed to figure out how to remain "desi" on their own terms. They, too, found ethnicity appealing, and they drew strength from Indians' relatively visible presence on campus. However, the organizations that students developed in order to give groups a space on campus sometimes ended up alienating co-ethnics who did not conform to ethnic ideals. South Asian hip hoppers realized that they were expected to pare down the extra-curricular commitments and extraethnic interests that formed the very basis of their identities. But in seeing how people socially constructed labels through contestation they helped develop the emerging and inclusive category "desi" to replace the label "Indian" by engaging in debates over the meanings of South Asianness. The presence, interests, and cultural adoptions by desis in hip hop de-naturalized ethnicity by unlinking ancestry from culture. They found that ethnicity was malleable; it could be contested as well as sampled.

College Cliques and Hegemonic Desiness

Although the college years can be an exciting time they were also disenchanting for some of the artists as familiar storylines crept onto a new stage. Racism was again played out, but this time within the intimacy of living conditions. A White student called an Indian DJ a "sand nigger." Jonny, a University of California, Davis, alumnus, explained that some guys in his dorm ("so white they were pink") nicknamed him "spot" in reference to the bindi. The California native says he "was bewildered that this was the college environment and, really, disappointed." Within the artists' first year at school, tensions abounded. In response, they thought to meet other South Asians for the first time.

The easiest way to find other desis is through student organizations, and on California campuses Indian groups such as Indus at the University of California, Berkeley, are among the largest. In these social and cultural groups, students bond over intergenerational conflicts, cultural practices, and the comfort of being surrounded by sameness within a context of difference. In addition to finding "all these people that look like [you]," students share the pressures and an identity as the children of immigrants who sacrificed so that they could attend college. The sheer numbers of South Asians on West Coast campuses during this period made them a zone for these youths to frame their identity *as* desis outside of a Black and White binary. Meena, a middle-class Indian American, describes the University of California, Berkeley, as "such a big place that you want to find people that are like you [and] have things in common with you." Gaining admittance into such a tightly woven clique can be seductive. The artists hoped that being around ethnic ambassadors—those who traveled to India, could speak the language, and were comfortable in their own skin—might increase their own knowledge. The artists' explorations not only turned out to be short-lived, however, but also they fueled their sense of rejection and negativity; later, these meetings proved useful for reconceptualizing ethnicity.

The college organizations of desi youth mirror immigrant organizations that aim to sustain culture in the context of assimilation. Both circulate cultural knowledge; however, they also replicate ethnic, class, religious, gender, and sexual divisions from the subcontinent. As Jonny says, "One of the most revealing things about college . . . was how splintered the ethnic factions could become. It was the first time I noticed White cliques and Black cliques and Chinese cliques and Indian cliques and lesbian cliques . . . The culture at college really causes you to become very self-aware of your race, [your] gender. There are a lot of identity politics involved, too, in what you study, who you socialize with, and everything." Although moving toward a more inclusive "South Asian" membership, Indian cultural organizations tend to represent Americanized and affluent North Indian Hindus. Among them, "being Indian" connotes the ethnic insularity, middle-class consumptive practices, and heterosexual norms advocated by the first generation (Prashad 2000: 122). Students considered active members to be culturally more "authentic" due to their cultural knowledge and because they socialized strictly with Indians. This in-group of mainstream desis establishes hegemonic desiness on campus, thereby impacting the decisions of desi hip hop artists.

Through their interactions with mainstream desis the artists, especially those from urban areas, felt especially "atypical." At first "it was kind of enriching," says Rawj, an MC who grew up with Black friends and who attended a junior college before transferring to University of California, Davis. "People sort of had the same experience I had; they're going through the same thing. But at the same time, it made me realize why I might be a bit different. And it was mostly because of my musical and my childhood experiences." The artists were distinguished by their performance of identity—their urban hip hop style, the way they walked, and the slang they incorporated into their speech, all of which were organic extensions of their past experiences. These visible and audible differences marked deeper cleavages that would later become painfully apparent.

Even those from middle-class suburbs felt disconnected. According to Radhika, who is Bengali and German, it was only upon interacting with the Indian Student Association, she says, "when I realized how culturally out of touch I was. I really felt like 'oh, none of them would really see me as an Indian because I don't know anything compared to them.'" She and Jonny were "freaked out" by their own lack of knowledge in their interactions with mainstream desis. They were also averse to socializing along ethnic lines due to internalized stereotypes that South Asians are "all science nerds and they're geeks and I didn't want to be like them." The idea of socializing along ethnic lines "repelled" Jonny, for whom the ethnic exclusivity of the Indian student club "just didn't seem right in a nonfamily context."

Desi students face a Catch-22 when confronting tight social cliques: students find it difficult to penetrate them, yet mainstream desis interpret those who choose not to participate in their groups as denying their cultural heritage, which consequently disqualifies them from membership. Rawj, a Punjabi American rapper, laughs, "It's like you need to be a member of The Mob in order to make friends! You have to be one of them." Because they chose not to participate, desi hip hop heads faced repercussions. As Jonny noted, "Occasionally I'd get the evil eye from a member or two [of the Indian student organization]: 'sellout eyes.'" Rawj considers that "maybe they *do* want to get to know people, but I don't know. I just found that it ends up being a status-oriented conversation." Still thinking about these issues today, albeit with a lighthearted tone, Rawj remembers how not funny it actually was: "It was terrible." Mainstream desis question the authenticity of nonconformists to mark those outside of their social realms and to monitor, in place of their parents, the sexuality of co-ethnics.

I asked Meena, a Berkeley student, to explain the tight social boundaries among campus desis; so rare are their interracial interactions, she says, that she has to "do a double take when I see someone that's not with an Indian person." Laughing, she suggests that "in the back of their head, [they're thinking] 'Oh, I might meet my future husband here.'" College organizations cultivate cultural "values," including heterosexual expectations about marriages, and become places to meet potential spouses. Meena's speculations support Sunaina Maira's (2002) assertion that the sexual and gender expectations of desi college youths intertwine with ideas of ethnic authenticity. Like marriage, dating should also be endogamous (although outside the awareness of parents), which regulates female sexuality. Mainstream desis also exclude and question the ethnic loyalty of those who do otherwise. Artists who are gay or had relationships with other minorities were further ostracized. D'Lo was frustrated by attempts to claim a desi identity at the University of California, Los Angeles, as a gay Sri Lankan intent on challenging the homophobia and heteronormativity at desi events.

Second-generation desi youths live within institutional, historical, and racial constraints. The insular social organization of ethnicity on college campuses is one response to racism, and it celebrates unique "cultural" identities that can hide racism. Exclusive cliques predicated on ethnic sameness are important alternatives to assimilation for non-White immigrants. Nazli Kibria highlights the positive ramifications of the ethnic moves by Asian American youth within the constraints of racialization: "We see, then, that the assumption of ethnic authenticity, while constraining in some ways, can also provide access to certain opportunities and resources that are part of a presumably genuine ethnic identity . . . Authentic ethnicity, with its signaling of ethnic capital, was also associated with certain opportunities" (2000: 91–92). Yet, framed by students as a "choice" to "self-segregate," mainstream desis often impose ethnic loyalty upon co-ethnics by demanding insularity. Thus, identity-based authenticity calls upon primordial notions of identity and is dangerously essentialist, despite the sense of unity it provides. Prashad explains that "desis seek out an 'authentic culture' for complex reasons, among them the desire not to be seen as fundamentally inferior to those who see themselves as 'white' and superior" (2000: 157). Thus, as Maira states, "the turn to ethnic identity and the emphasis on certain ideologies of Indianness become a common strategy for Indian American youth in the context of American college life"; through their experiences with co-ethnics, hip hop desis experience how "shifting identifications are complicated by everyday practices of essentialization and boundary marking" (2002: 14). This marriage of multicultural model minorities to ethnic hegemony asserts one way of being desi. Ironically, the "diversity" that multiculturalism hails ends up curtailing and silencing its internal differences.

While some individuals find comfort in sameness, for others it stifles. Prevalent discourses often limit the choices of nonconformists who find it difficult to imagine alternatives. South Asian students who became MCs, DJs, producers, and record label founders critiqued insularity and were disdainful of the "superiority" that mainstream desis expressed through desires to "maintain . . . our cultural purity." The distance of hip hop desis from those whom others assume they would share a natural connection highlights the limitations of ethnicity as the only pathway of culture. Their "surprising" adoption of a culture that does not "belong" to them reveals other sources of identity. While mainstream desis focused on the incongruity of "hip hop" and "desis," the artists questioned presumed ethnic bonds.

Through interactions with co-ethnics in college, hip hop desis came to understand exactly how complicated the ethnic rules were. Not only was one expected to be Indian and Hindu—something out of their control—but they were also supposed to have the capital to participate in pricey desi social events. These expectations taught artists the terms of desiness, but they began to negotiate with them. Their contestations of second-generation expectations about class and consumption reveal one more example of how ethnicity is a bounded yet alterable option.

Middle-Class Norms and Consumption

The guys [college desi] were very materialistic, [they] value materialism to an excess, I should say. And some seemed nice, but they . . . just talked about business and being a doctor. And sometimes it doesn't seem that they followed their own dreams and just talked down about poor people. —Indian American Deejay Bella

The University of California is a public school system, yet many of its students come from wealthy families.[16] Many college desis want to fulfill their parents' hopes of lucrative jobs and high class standing for their children. The purchasing power of college students becomes a defining aspect of desiness that is evident in their youth culture and socializing. Clothing, accessories, cars, and the more intangible aspects of style—having the right hair and body shape—are status markers open to evaluation (Shankar 2008). Notions of ethnicity are classed: Abercrombie and Fitch, a popular brand with Asian American youth, is also widely regarded as "yuppie" and middle class, irrespective of one's background.[17] Yet why can someone wear a yuppie "White" style and still "be Indian," while individuals wearing baggy jeans and the latest kicks are considered sellouts? With their twenty dollar cover charges (not to mention expensive drinks and parking rates) the high cost of Indian student parties excludes even moderately middle-class youth. But even the wealthier hip hop heads who could afford these events did not necessarily wish to because of differing tastes.

In the piece "Part 3: Sri Lankan Boi," D'Lo writes of his/her father as follows: "It never bothered him that I was one of few in my hometown city of Palmdale, California who listened to hip-hop, walked and dressed in hip-hop cultural attire (baggy jeans and t-shirts) from the time of its mainstream birth." People read desis by interpreting their stylistic choices, which, as for many youth, are informed by peer groups and class status. Rawj says that his Indian friends later confirmed that they did not initially think he was "one of them" because of his style. "I didn't dress in Abercrombie and Fitch or [wear] whatever everybody else was wearing. I had baggy-ass pants, my hat backwards, headphones on, and glow-in-the-dark shoes." ("Well," he humorously reconsidered, "they weren't glow-in-the-dark, but you know what I mean!") Desi youths also evaluate gender and ethnic roles based on style, and desi hip hop artists often felt judged by their peers. D'Lo's aesthetic was closer to the hip hop-inflected clothing that Maira (2002) calls "hoodie," which includes baggy jeans in contrast to the skin-revealing and tight-fitting clothes that Maira in turn calls "hootchie." Mainstream desis' complex and close monitoring of self-expression exasperated some desi hip hoppers, thereby challenging their attempts to find a comforting group away from home.

Desi social life may also alienate working-class individuals who cannot afford to participate in events. Some artists from urban neighborhoods argue that the class privilege of mainstream suburban co-ethnics sheltered wealthy desis from the starker realities faced by urban residents and from the harder time those urban desis might therefore have had in adjusting to college. As K B says, "I saw a lot of bad stuff that really gave me a perspective on life." His young friends were moving out of their homes, dropping out of school, and getting jobs to support themselves. "I've seen people get shot," he told me. As a result, "coming to college, I think I had a very different perspective on life than most Indian kids that grew up in the suburbs. A lot of stuff that concerned them that they were worried [about] on a day-to-day basis, I guess was sort of petty." South Asian American scholarship has only begun to respond to these kinds of class cleavages that affect second-generation youth.

Karan, an Indo-Fijian from Hayward, California, abhors the ethnic and class elitism of desis whose parents migrated directly from India (his forceful critiques cross over to attack the crass consumerism of corporate hip hop). While flipping through hip hop magazines (the advertisements fueling his anger) and exchanging witticisms about rap album covers in Telegraph Avenue's Rasputin Records store in Berkeley in the early 2000s, Karan exploded into one of his tirades. He was disgusted that another Indian Berkeley student complained to him about her "meager" starting salary of $50,000. Referring to my status as a social science graduate student, he asked me, "Why aren't there more Indians like you and me out there? They're only concerned with money!" Karan's aversion to materialism and the pursuit by desi students of "stable" (business or medical) careers stems from his own family's material circumstances and his liberal political perspective. Karan expressed the ideas of many Indo-Fijians and Indians who immigrate to the United States from the West Indies who are bothered by Indian immigrants' distain for their diasporic histories and current circumstances. In addition to the triple migrants, the non-Indian artists proud of their ethnic heritage, like D'Lo (Sri Lankan) and Dinesh (Nepali), faced additional challenges finding comfort in mainstream cliques.

Indian Hegemony and Non-Indian South Asians

Everyone who knows a Sri Lankan, knows how much pride we got . . .
But we gotta, cuz ain't no one ever really included us in the South Asian diaspora.

We're a small island with big issues, thus, we come off as having "short-dick" complex.

This is why when someone lists off North and South regions of the motherland, somewhere in the back of the room, one of our people speaks up and says,

"hey, you forgot Sri Lanka."

—D'Lo, "Loving the Fart that India let Off the Side of its Ass . . ."

The numeric and ideological dominance of first-generation Hindu Indians is reflected in the organization of college life, which presents a conundrum for non-Indians. In order to be more inclusive, Indian cultural organizations began changing their names to represent South Asians in the early 2000s. This shift, however, proved to be symbolic rather than actual. These exclusions bothered both non-Hindu, non-Indian artists *and* Hindu Indian artists who refuted the confines of constructed desiness. Their experiences illustrate some of the obstacles to a developing panethnicity.

As a fiercely proud Sri Lankan, D'Lo did not know much about or associate with Indian Americans at the University of California, Los Angeles. "Yeah, this was hardcore: I didn't have any Indian people in my life. When I went to college and was meeting North Indians, I was like, 'Wow. You all are some *com-plete-ly* different people!' . . . I didn't know shit about India until I went to college. I thought that Indians were mostly South Indians: if they spoke Tamil, they were our people. But still there was [this] hardcore [sense that] we were Sri Lankan. I didn't even know that the Sinhalese people were the majority. You know? And that's all that was said. We were Sri Lankan. We were Tamil." Since college cliques encourage separation and restrict cross-cultural sharing, Indians' hegemony obscures South Asian ethnic, migration, and class diversification. Non-Indian South Asians are often invisible and misrecognized. D'Lo, who is sometimes misidentified as Trinidadian, recalls that "people didn't even think that I was Indian. *Occasionally* I would get asked, but it was very seldom." D'Lo wrote in a poem that invisibility might compel one to "return home" to Sri Lanka, or even a substitute, in search of recognition:

She still goes unnoticed walking though city streets
And her silence makes her almost invisible.

And invisibility, she realizes, is the one condition under which
an urge to visit the mother land, or even Cuba, would manifest.

As in this poem, some of the artists eventually went elsewhere, away from a category and their presumed cohort.

Dinesh, a Nepali engineer, highlights the South Asian panethnic tensions in his California college by stating that he "had a choice of blending in as a desi" but "decided not to do that" because he had many nondesi friends. Internal power imbalances that silence some groups make it difficult to sustain panethnicity, yet panethnic identity was one way that desi artists engaged with ethnicity's flexibility. Generations can change the grounds upon which various groups differ as well as find affinity. Yen Le Espiritu highlights the "changing scope of ethnic identities, as linguistically, culturally, and geographically diverse groups come together in the interest of panethnic, or all-ethnic, solidarity . . . We also need to look at the qualitative transformations of what constitutes ethnicity, that is, changes in who belongs to the ethnic groups" (1992: 2). While the first generation finds comfort in their ethno-national identities, the second generation may find an additional shared identity, as South Asians, across ethnic specificities due to their experiences in the United States, the conflation of various subcontinental ethnicities, and the racial lumping imposed upon them. The artists needed to acknowledge rather than smooth over the internal cracks of nation and religion that prevented an even melding across differences.

National differences become more complex in the case of non-Hindus, as desi life in America often takes shape around religion (see Purkayastha 2005; Joshi 2006). Indo-Fijians were even spatially distinct by settling in California cities like Hayward and San Jose and attending community colleges. Non-Indian South Asians and Indians from Fiji and the West Indies are an important component of this project because they form a notable presence among the already small numbers of South Asians in the United States who produce hip hop music. I discuss in later chapters the central appeal that hip hop holds as a voice for the underrepresented and voiceless. In fact, it may be their relative invisibility in the larger South Asian community that accounts for their involvement in and greater identification with hip hop as a vehicle for representation.

As the artists see it, ethnic tensions point both to the importance

D'Lo incites audiences with the content of his/her rhymes and striking image. Photograph courtesy of David Beeler.

of historical, socioeconomic, and racial differences between White and racialized groups (Hall 1991; Leonard 1992) and to differences *within* panethnic categories like "South Asian American" (see Espiritu 1992; Valdez 2009). These intraethnic divisions rooted in naturalistic and blood-based assumptions spill beyond their borders to inhibit the development of panethnic (and, ultimately, racial) identities. Mainstream college desis employ multiculturalism to understand differences across racial categories, which they reformulate as "cultural" distinctions. (However, when pressed, they often fall back on racist stereotypes.) But to explain divisions within South Asian America, desis, including the artists, retreat to the very discourses multiculturalism attempts to hide: biological group distinctions. Dinesh says, for instance, "I am Nepali and there's no way I cannot be Nepali," a feeling that "comes out because of things I talk about naturally." However, as the potentials of panethnicity began to open up for this generation, the artists turned toward other sources of information that would enable them to uncover these processes.

The artists, particularly those who were not Hindu, Indian, and middle class, sensed their position somewhere between "Indian" and "panethnic" spaces. In South Asian and Ethnic Studies classes they learned to theorize racial and ethnic group making within the context of power and history (Palumbo-Liu 1999). This helped them understand their identification as ethnically specific "Nepalis" and "Sri Lankans," for instance, who simultaneously wanted to develop a broader panethnic identity. They began to take part in this dialogic process of category construction by filling in the categories of "South Asian" and "desi" with new meanings.

Maintaining Desiness Outside of Desi Cliques: South Asian American Panethnicity

I'll never say "I'm Indian" but I'll say "South Asian." I say "desi" because I use it as an understanding of a broader community of South Asians but also including Bhutan, Burma, etc. I see it as a second-generation term.
—Dinesh, Nepali American

The desi artists maintained their claim to ethno-national bonds, but they were also taking a central role in crafting an emerging

South Asian, or desi, panethnicity. Their desire to expand ethnicity to become more inclusive of difference was central to their growing articulation of anti-essentialism and the portability of ethnicity—they felt they could "take it with them" rather than having to perform in front of like-minded individuals. South Asian American panethnicity often operates as a racializing category that develops as a result of shared experiences among the United States born (Espiritu 1992); however, the artists' attempts to bridge divides were motivated by external factors (racialization) and internal intra-ethnic dynamics. Their turn outward does not signify a *doing away* with meaningful internal differentiations—those exist simultaneously. They put this model to work by expressing themselves outside of ethnically inscribed social circles; this was a political move as much as it was one of self-preservation.

Dinesh identifies as both a Nepali and a desi because, he says of the latter, "it's also a *political* reality, especially in the days ahead" (referring to 9/11). He feels "that collective self-identity is important, and as a second generation [desi] who's been active in community action, I have a sense of responsibility." He distinguishes ethno-national specificities (i.e., "I am Nepali," "not Indian"), but also finds a panethnic "second-generation" identity useful because these multi-scalar identifications exist *simultaneously*. Thus, difference exists *within*, not *instead of*, a shared overarching identity. This ethnographic finding supplements broad-scale sociological surveys that attempt to quantify the *one* way that members of the new second generation identify (Rumbaut 1994).[18]

Political realities also pushed some artists away from mainstream desis toward a broader "progressive" constituency. D'Lo, who also took college classes on South Asia, nonetheless felt disillusioned and says, "I just feel like, them Indians, I'm cool on them. I was almost equally as racist toward Indians as I was to White people."[19] Having faced racism from Whites, s/he finds desi parochialism equally oppressive. Other hip hop heads submitted to dominant notions of South Asians as apolitical and defined themselves accordingly. For example, in describing an Indian graduate student who, like Karan, enjoyed discussing politics and was aware of world events, the Indo-Fijian stated, "You know, he's not really Indian." "Real Indians" are not invested in politics. Another response was to rearticulate the meanings of desiness to include political activism through the category of "desi." D'Lo who "had been living this reality as this gay woman who really thinks this world is fucked up," and who felt Indians "weren't concerned with shit," expanded his/her social circles and his/her sense of belonging.

Despite "leaving" desi groups, the artists were not rejecting their ethnicity. They realized ethnicity was not simply something to be expressed through identification with others, but it was a knowledge and sense of self located within themselves. They increased this knowledge through their studies by taking comparative social science and humanities classes that informed their thinking. Interdisciplinary ethnic studies courses taught them a range of methodologies for crafting knowledge and provided them with the backgrounds of various minority groups. They learned theories about how racialization works and how people construct categories, like "Latino," in the same way they were constructing the meanings of "South Asian" on campus. D'Lo was "learning more about India finally, [and] I took this class on the South Asian diaspora and it was talking about what was going on in New York at the time, with the rallies around the [South Asian] cab drivers and the protestors against all of that. So [we] had a [course] reader: this was my bible into the world of the Indians." The artists majored in both traditional fields (medicine and business) and "less typical" ones in interdisciplinary studies, political science, and ethnomusicology. Thus, claiming some space away from hegemonic social circles gave them room to explore untraditional majors and career paths. A few have since gone on to postgraduate work: D'Lo went to audio engineering school; one of Karmacy's members attended business school and another went to medical school; Chee received his MFA in 2007 in creative writing and fiction. While the artists all deepened their commitments to hip hop after graduating from college, some simultaneously pursued careers in professional fields (medicine, engineering), while others focused on beefing up their musical skills. These professional decisions enable them to fund their musical careers.

Trips back "home" also fueled their sense of desiness and allowed them to be ethnic without having to socialize just along those lines. As Radhika, who is Bengali, says, "I think what really helped was by going to India. I saw how many million ways you can be Indian and it's okay, you know?" The artists informed their politics and worldviews through classes and travel that pushed them to develop inclusive panethnic groups. By "leaving" the mainstream set, these desis found room to develop their own ways of being. It also motivated them to continue to try to engage with desis, this time *on their own terms* because of the salience that their definitions of ethnicity held for them.

Rather than "looking back" to the homeland for their social location as many first-generation immigrants do, these youths create an identity and a home in the United States that is local and transnational (Espiritu 1992; Purkayastha 2005). As KB says, for example, "I was never really interested in a 'South Asian' identity, but more of a 'South Asian American' identity." He identifies as an "Indian American" but also advocated for a shared South Asian American experience. As he further notes, "The thing is when we come here, we are all sort of in this melting pot. No one cares that I'm from South India, he's from North India, or he's from Maldives: we all look the same." In looking back at college from the vantage point of 2002, he saw his understanding that desis across ethnicities share an identity confirmed in the responses to South Asians after 9/11. A South Asian American identity "in essence, does exist," KB explains, describing the process of racialization "in the sense that people see a picture of bin Laden on TV and they go attack a Sikh man. That's a South Asian American identity."

Racialization may enable panethnicity but hegemonic desiness is exclusive and can block this development. The artists' interactions with co-ethnics in college reinforced their earlier ambivalence toward ethnicity with its cleavages and inequalities. However, they eventually recognized and soon became a part of the processes of meaning making. One response to the insularity and conservatism of ethnicity was panethnicity. As rapper KB states, "Americans created the word South Asian. It never existed before America." Yet they were motivated to engage critically with these ideas, refusing to simply let others do the defining. In college, KB harnessed the political nature of one category to develop a forum for subcontinentals to talk across divides: "I figured, we have this word 'South Asian' that some way unifies us, it encompasses all of us. There's absolutely no question." These reconfigurations are emblematic of hybridity in the sense that "hybridization does not necessarily mean decline through the loss of identity. It can also mean empowering existing identities through the opening of new possibilities" (Laclau in Hall 2000: 236). Thus K B engages with the dialogic process of identity formation through choice and imposition by identifying ethnically and panethnically. College-aged hip hop desis harness the malleability of ethnicity to expand the contours of desiness, thereby making them available to future generations. One of the most potent forums for expressing alternative desiness is through the platform of hip hop music. It was in college, after all, when some of the rappers picked up the mic in public, melding music and activism, to take up the specific challenges of claiming desiness and crafting inclusive and progressive communities across ethnic, religious, and class differences.

"It's Either Us or Bollywood!"
Expressing Ethnicity through Hip Hop

When I got to [the University of California,] Berkeley, I started rapping at [the Indus] culture show and I guess I got a pretty good response. They were all politically oriented rhymes about issues that we were facing in the community . . . Second-generation identity, or first generation, or one and a half—creating a South Asian American identity, appreciating what our parent's generation did. The first year I did it, the name of the song was "Claiming to Be a Nation of Peace." The chorus was,

> Claiming to be a nation of peace
> What did Gandhi die for?
> All we got is a nation of war . . .
> How are our children supposed to learn
> That a temple or a mosque is not a place to burn?[20]
> Down to the ground like they see on TV
> 'Cause that's what they're gonna see
> Believe me.

And that was like . . . halfway in the second verse and the whole auditorium stood up and started clapping. A standing ovation from three thousand people in the middle of a song, and I was just like, "Whoa!" And that was the first time I performed live in front of a very big crowd. I was stunned. I mean that was such an adrenaline rush! When I left college

I always told people that that [show] was what I'd always miss the most: that culture show performance. —KB, Indian American MC

Nearly a decade after the event KB reenacted these lyrics with passion as we sat at a Starbucks in Fremont, California, where he now lived. This story like many others refutes others' interpretation of desis in hip hop as misguided individuals who reject their ethnic communities. Artists like KB who feel a strong sense of ethnic identity used their music before, during, and after college to talk about their distinctive positions as sons and daughters of immigrants. He and his fellow Karmacy rappers later articulated an ethnic identity that spotlighted the unique experience of being South Asian in the United States on their album *The Movement*. In the 2000s, their songs drew on their bicultural knowledge and connection to their parents' homeland and appealed to Asians across ethnicities. They produce what I term "ethnic hip hop" by demonstrating ethnic pride and engaging with South Asian America through a Black art form. Fueled by contentious relations with co-ethnics and dedicated to creating a space in which to express their own take on ethnicity, some desi MCs infuse hip hop music with distinctly immigrant narratives. They express alternative desiness through hip hop, thereby altering South Asian and Black cultural formations.

Hip hop was central to these performers' newly developing panethnic identities, and through it they could illustrate commonalities across bloody religious and national divisions on the subcontinent by quoting Gandhi, for instance. Their conscious lyrics backed by social actions reflect a legacy of South Asian activism framed by the importance of history and political expression through artistic flair (DasGupta and Das Dasgupta 2000). They offer an alternative to naturalized divisions among groups in a nonconformist and unexpected format, all while doing so, in KB's case, at an event that quintessentially represents hegemonic desiness.

The artists sample those aspects of ethnicity they find to be important and express them through hip hop. Ethnic hip hop broadcasts the components of a critical ethnicity: it highlights history and the diasporic migrations of South Asians; it employs tropes of movement and travel that link the MCs to the "motherland"; and the rappers claim membership within transnational communities through linguistic and sonic choices. It is through hip hop, therefore, that they are able to express their commitment to co-ethnics and craft a diasporic sensibility, or a sense of connection to broader communities across national borders. They also use hip hop as a mode through which to transfer their cultural knowledge to the next generation. Thus hip hop is a manifestation of their ethnicity, and through it these artists act as cultural brokers across generations of South Asians.

In contrast to ahistorical cultural explanations of group difference, desi MCs contextualize their present circumstances through copious references to the past, including family, ethnic, and American histories. Whether United States born, like some of the members of Karmacy, or from India, like Chee Malabar of Himalayan Project, these rappers pay close attention to family narratives that appeal to broader immigrant audiences. Within one song an artist may refer to India, to being a South Asian, and to their immigrant parents, thereby revealing their multiple and overlapping identifications that speak to all second-generation youth. They use hip hop to articulate diasporic identities, and thus Black popular culture adapts to reflect the experiences of recent arrivals. The American-born MC Rawj, a member of the Bay Area–based Feenom Circle, describes the metaphoric journey he took to become familiar with his ancestry on the track "Masters Too":

The moon and sun could neither reach my birthplace,
My mother held me in the cold,
Blankets protected my face,
A child born with no knowledge of his blood line,
But in time realized the throne is mine.

Raised by his mother in Richmond without a strong ethnic community, Rawj lacked knowledge about Punjab where his parents are from. However, he learns ethnic pride ("the throne") over time and "returns" to the nurturing fields of his mother's birthplace, signaling his connection to a newly discovered homeland evoked by the falling rain:

The few drops of water fell on my face,
Returning me to my peoples' birthplace,
The dirt embraces me, not pullin' me under,
Barefooting on fields which birthed my mother.

The ties of young desis to their parents' (often unspecified) home-lands is part of an immigrant sensibility that helps them contend with local tensions in panethnic ways. Rawj connects two genera-tions across space and time as he goes full circle, returning him to the subcontinental soil that nourishes rather than drowns him. South Asian Americans draw upon transnational connections as a uniting force against established ethno-national tensions in South Asia and the United States. "Along with their global awareness," Bandana Purkayastha writes, "they use their transnational family experiences to 'mark off' their own versions of difference, and to build mechanisms for rejecting some of the more racist interpre-tive frameworks used to maintain boundaries against them" (2005: 68). Through this learning process Rawj comes to consider people of his mother's birthplace as his own "peoples," thereby reflecting many of the artists' connections to South Asia despite the diasporic conditions of their birth. Gaining cultural knowledge further de-velops this link.

Lyrics such as those about parents' hopes and dreams that at-tend to family and immigrant histories and highlight movement populate ethnic hip hop tracks. Like Rawj, Chee uses hip hop to reflect upon his time growing up between Baroda and Kerala in India before coming to San Francisco. Himalayan Project's track "The Middle Passage," for which the album was named, invokes a bluesy and thoughtful tone with the help of a saxophone's mellow drawl and a slow beat. Chee begins by reflecting back but, unlike many mainstream desis, his is an unromantic nostalgia:

> I came from a gray slum in the earth's far corner,
> Where men are hemmed by superstitions, celestial stars warn ya,
> '89 they was aligned, and we moved, to California.

His immigrant parents placed their hopes and expectations upon him although they may have been complicated by class struggles:

> 11 years old; I was the immigrant poster child,
> diligent, broke, uh, forced to strive,
> in the course of life I've seen dreams through my folk's
> hopeful eyes . . .

Chee's description of immigrant hopes and generational concerns reverberate across time and immigrant communities. Those Latino

HIMALAYAN PROJECT
THE MIDDLE PASSAGE

Album courtesy of Chirag Menon.

and Asian youths from immigrant families can relate to these lyrics, particularly as Chee does not mention exactly *where* that "gray slum" was located. Other artists, like the members of Karmacy, use multilingual raps to reveal universality across categories.

Karmacy performs a unique ethnic identity that samples ethnic and sonic quotations within a hip hop framework. Many young desi fans of hip hop have never seen the actual melding of these forces before attending a Karmacy show. The group's effort in cutting and mixing accomplishes several things. First, it highlights the constructivist processes of meaning making by jarring audiences with the seeming dissonance of ethnic identification through a racialized artistic expression. Second, it encourages audiences to interpret the references, thereby creating a temporary community of South Asian, East Asian, and Latino youths. Karmacy has crafted and offers to the third generation what they, themselves, had been missing. These MCs, like all the artists, came to know themselves better through hip hop. In return, they offer a new, relevant, and fresh image of immigrant ethnicity.

The songs by Karmacy that are multilingual have elicited perhaps the greatest responses by Indians in India on blogs and Web sites. The ability of Karmacy's members to not only rap but do so in their mother tongues as well as in Spanish evokes the strength of their ethnic identifications and their familiarity with Mexicans, who represent a major population in California. Hip hop is not a substitute for ethnic literacy—indeed, it is yet another language they have learned. Karmacy uses multilingualism in the same way that Kid Frost, the members of Cypress Hill, and other California-based Latino rappers who rhyme in Spanglish do to express their multiple affiliations. Karmacy is unique among the desi artists for producing an album that includes lyrics in five languages. Their song "Blood Brothers," performed by Nimo and Swap in English and Gujarati, may resonate with the hundreds of thousands of Gujarati immigrants in the United States; it also strikes a chord with members of other immigrant families who may not understand the lyrics but who identify with bilingualism. Even young people who live in India have accessed Karmacy's music online and have left the group messages about how "dope" their songs are. The themes in "Blood Brothers" and other Karmacy songs reflect the changing demographics of Los Angeles, which is home to some of the groups' members as well as the location of their label Rukus Avenue Records. While some lyrics make broad connections across immigrant groups, others speak to the specific experiences of America's South Asians.

The four MCs of Karmacy "go classically to India and bring it to your room" by rapping in Gujarati and Punjabi and through the use of multiple references of traveling or "going on a passage" to India. The performers mix various cultures in their live shows; the rappers perform alongside a live dhol player and they even incorporate bharatanatyam movements, a South Indian dance mostly performed by women that includes ornate hand and foot movements along with facial expressions.[21] Their incorporation of various performers, instruments, and influences along with their thematic scope is a panethnic and even pan-racial expression of unity across groups that may at first seem distinct but are, in fact, commensurable.

In 2002, Karmacy gave an exhilarating featured performance at Los Angeles's Artwallah in an outdoor daytime concert attended by a sea of South Asians.[22] On that typically sunny day, the mostly young and hip Brown attendees browsed through merchandise sellers' wares exhibited in small tents while others took in the art exhibit. Many had never heard of Karmacy at that time (this has since changed), but those more eager gathered in front of the stage where Nimo, Swap, Sammy, and KB grabbed their mics as the DJ, a young Black man with dreadlocks, a long-haired Sikh drummer, and Gurpreet "the Tabla Guy," warmed up. Casually dressed, the rappers looked like many other attendees of the event, although

Album courtesy of Sammy Chand.

they wore some markers of hip hop style. As usual K B wore a cap, and he wore jeans and a Karmacy T-shirt partially covered by an unbuttoned printed short-sleeved shirt. Nimo, representing Southern California, sported a Los Angeles Lakers' basketball jersey with matching sweatpants and sneakers, while Swap donned baggy khakis and a T-shirt. Sammy, bald with a goatee and earrings, was also informal, dressed in a Rukus Avenue T-shirt and pants. Their clothing suggested that these were artists familiar with hip hop fashions but not in the exaggerated ways that many people interpret wannabe hip hoppers to have. The men's pants were not excessively baggy and they did not smatter their language with Black vernacular or wear oversized gold chains. One could also intuit their (differing) familiarity with Blacks through demeanor, including body language, gestures, and word choice and pronunciation. The rapping intonation and flow of K B suggested his Richmond, California, roots; he was relaxed and rocked his head to the beat. Sammy, who lives in a wealthy neighborhood in Los Angeles, had a rhyming style that, like his on-stage movements, was more staccato as he pronounced each word.

"Passage to India" is perhaps the group's most popular and well-known song, and the crowd began to swell once they began their rhyme. It's a party track, and as soon as the familiar chords of the sitar rang through the speakers followed by a drum beat and the sweet whine of a violin the four rappers had the crowd nodding their heads:

> Passage to India, here come the Rukus for your ears
> Comin' on down, bringin' it to you from this Western hemisphere.
> We come from Californ-I-A through the San Francisco Bay
> Trekking from the Himal-A-Y-A, to I-N-D-I-A!

Standing close to one side of the stage a young Black woman, nodding her head to the beat, turned to me and said as if pleasantly surprised, "They sound *good*!" The chorus alternates between Hindi and English, urging the audience to "come on come on, we're going to Hindustan, we're staying in this country. Passage to India, Passage to India." The second verse begins with classical bharatanatyam beats: "Dha ding, dha dha ding, dha ding da," and in response the audience shouted encouragements as Nimo half-seriously simulated a dancer in mid-turn, his neck shifted from side to side and his hands twirled in an arch overhead and to the side.

The Artwallah festival, along with a similar event named Diasporadics, offer the perfect opportunity for rappers to captivate a South Asian audience. The artists pick up hip hop to take their audiences *with them* on a collective journey to India, thereby reversing the travels their parents once took in the 1960s and 1970s. Karmacy's rappers identify as the children of immigrants (Sammy, a Punjabi, came to the United States via England) and participate in transnational communities through their themes and styles. The video filmed for the song foregrounds the message of travel to and within India by globally linking South Asians.[23] In the video we see the streets and sights of Bharat (India) through the window of a moving vehicle. Interspersed are images of the artists at work in their Los Angeles studio, the process which literally takes them to India. Their images of the homeland are less about untarnished idealizations of the past than they are aimed to signal the ongoing relationship of many of these artists with their ancestral homes.

In transmitting their culture to the younger generation through a Black art form Karmacy talks back to the segmented assimilation scholars and first-generation aunties and uncles who feel that South Asians who affiliate with hip hop and Blacks have "lost their culture." Sammy told me that he and Swap performed at an event hosted by a Sardar Patel organization in Los Angeles in the early 2000s.[24] As soon as their track came on during the sound check, the elderly audience responded quite sourly—telling them to turn the sound down. Realizing that it would not be very effective to jump into a rap song with its booming bass line, Sammy decided to explain their "rap shap" music to the "aunties and uncles in the crowd." Sitting on the edge of the stage, he grabbed the microphone and said, "Listen folks. You know, we are responsible for keeping all the beliefs and all the issues and all the civil rights and everything that you guys preach about. We are, believe it or not, passing it on to everybody else out there. It's either us or Bollywood. Take your choice! That's how it's going to happen." Here and in their music, Karmacy engages South Asian Americans in dialogue by translating first-generation struggles for "civil rights" and other beliefs and issues to "everybody else," including the next generation.

The content of Karmacy's rhymes also has something to teach the first generation—namely, how to articulate their experiences with, and anger about, racism. Their lyrics offer historicized and racialized excavations of South Asian immigrant experiences, thereby providing a different take on ethnicity. In contrast to the "feel good" party vibes that the quartet is most well known for, their song "Outcasted" ponders what emerges once they uncover South Asians' experiences with racism. Produced and recorded by Sammy, the forcefully delivered track rests on a deep, head-nodding bass line and the strumming of a guitar. The female vocalist Saila marks each chorus with vocals reminiscent of the old Hindi records that our South Asian parents play when they miss home.

Following the line "I was outcasted" repeated twice, Nimo jumps onto the track and quickly notifies his audience about the effects of being shunned at the very start of his life. He begins:

I was outcasted, banned by the age of my birth.
From the eyes of this planet I was only worth
2 cents.
Like a dirty bastard that ever fell on this earth . . .

In the next verse, Swap flows along the same vein of racism:

So I grab the mic and pre-medically meditate.
And as you segregate, I contemplate
The meaning of my race.
You delineate a road for me to take
A path for me to follow.

Swap, who at the time was in his residency to become a doctor (he "pre-medically meditate[s]"), might use the term "race" instead of "ethnicity" to refer to his background because it rhymes. But the effect is one that places his struggles within a broader historical context of segregation. Despite their early exposure to discrimination, both Nimo and Swap follow with their own resistance. Nimo explains that, while "banned" from the start, he nonetheless strives by gaining knowledge and unearthing silenced stories. Refusing an ostrich-like strategy of burying these differences, the artists are forthright about their non-White status in revealing how ethnicity is formed through power dynamics that discriminate against others. Coming to terms with unspoken truths leads some artists to adopt ethnic pride in response to their devaluation. In doing so, they turn ethnicity—being Indian, for example—from something that was once the basis for childhood and college racism into a form of empowerment and self-articulation.

> Only in time, within minds,
> Ever learned what I learned.
> That my people and color will rise from the roots of our dirt.
> And all of the gold on this planet's not equal to all that we're worth.

In contrast to mainstream desis, MCs draw upon their cultural roots to explicitly voice rather than deny their interactions with discrimination and exclusion. Their lyrics emphasize the concurrent processes of racialization and the development of ethnic pride. Hip hop, a cultural form produced within the context of racism, provides them with the vocabulary and mode to express these ideas. Gaining pride "as an Indian," Nimo becomes defiant, "deleting everything that gets in my path if it's a nuisance." Nimo's reference to his people rising from the "roots of our dirt" is similar to Rawj's verse about how his newly found self-knowledge returned him to the fields of his mother's birthplace. Through hip hop, these rappers apparently came to grips with previous conflicts they might have faced about their identities. After voicing the egregious nature of the past, they move on to embrace being desis. Swap, for example, resists the expectations others have placed on him, "comin' up" as a South Asian:

> I say, "no, it's crazy." Hard for you to swallow
> The truth because it hurts that I'm comin' up.
> South Asian from my birth,
> Living life on this beautiful earth.
> What you get is what you see,
> But do you get what you see?
> I'm on a quest for the real reality.

Karmacy offers the mostly South Asian audience at Artwallah a well-articulated and nicely packaged ethnic identity that contributes to the range of artistic expressions of desi politics featured at the event, including sculpture, comedy, dance, and paintings (see Mani 2001). Songs from their compilation CD *Passage to India* and debut album *The Movement* make use of multiple languages, instruments, and themes; they use Indian instrumentalists in live shows. *Passage to India* is described by KB as "a very South Asian album," which resulted from "tailor[ing] a lot of the songs . . . to have a more South Asian feel." Karmacy provides listeners with a prideful panethnic identity that is relevant to youth today because it is sampled to incorporate popular desi and American youth references.

Ethnicity is not so plagued a concept that we must do away with it; individuals sample ethnicity just as the artists mix and mash up their identities, and thus we can deconstruct and reappropriate the ethnicity model to speak about "new ethnicities" (Hall 1991). Karmacy's music illustrates theories applicable to understanding new desi identities—identities that are deeply historicized and based on contextual understandings rather than lazy attributions of group difference to culture. The artists are attuned to power and sociohistorical forces and remind us to incorporate these perspectives in our analyses. Ethnicity "acknowledges the place of history, language, and culture in the construction of subjectivity and identity, as well as the fact that all discourse is placed, positioned, situated,

Image courtesy of Sammy Chand and Rukus Avenue Records.

and all knowledge is contextual" (Hall in Hutchinson and Smith 1996: 162).

All of the MCs claim space for alternative desiness by using hip hop to engage in dialogue *within* South Asian America. Ethnic hip hop alters conceptions of desi youth as culturally circumscribed or fully Americanized. Instead, these artists work out their contentious relations to and rightful claims of ethnic identity by creating communities through Black popular culture. Music is central to the cultivation of some new ethnicities and hip hop's desis exemplify a "politics of ethnicity predicated on difference and diversity" (Hall 1992: 258). Hip hop provides a language that can tackle inequality, power, and systematic forms of oppression that shape immigrant youth's American identities. Desi artists use Black popular culture to craft ethnicity that places difference and diversity within, and not outside, the context of history and power. It pushes youth to understand that despite the logic of multiculturalism, "difference *makes* a difference" (Davis 1996: 48; italics mine).

Rewind—Conclusion

Through collaborative *and* contentious relations with co-ethnics, the artists inherited, rejected, and refigured ethnicity. Their sensitivity to racism dissuaded them from aspiring to be White, but their frustrating encounters with desis turned ethnicity into a charged, rather than comforting, option. People often interpret minorities who do not express a "strong" racial identity as oreos, coconuts, twinkies, and other colorful edibles that imply that they are "whitewashed."[25] But what of the troubling intra-ethnic dynamics that can lead to contentious attitudes about ethnicity? Americans have branded South Asians in hip hop who are critical of hegemonic desiness and White racism with even stranger "race traitor" fruit metaphors, such as rotten coconuts and bruised bananas (Sharma 2001). These confused responses emerge from our undertheorization of why relatively privileged individuals identify with those who are considered undesirable.

Hip hop desis confront hegemonic desiness, which emerges among South Asian immigrants contending with their new status as minorities. First-generation immigrants who conceptualize themselves in the context of their country of origin differ from their United States–born children who face more immediate local contexts. Second-generation youth, who are of but not bounded by the United States nation, forge emergent identities by juggling and sampling compelling forces, including their parents' hopes and co-ethnics' expectations of proper desiness. They also reject particular aspects, including social insularity and class and status norms.

Even in the 2000s, years after matriculation, the artists were still concerned about their relations with other desis even if their own paths had moved them beyond the trials of college. In 2001, Rawj explained, "I have this whole issue with Indian identity. Sometimes I think a lot of us really don't know ourselves so we go to the standard protocol, which is to be close minded and we over delve [into our ethnic identity]. But maybe that isn't too healthy to do. I've always had concern over Indians. Like there's actually certain norms that are expected. I could have said it back then [in college], too, 'Yeah, I'm just as Indian as these fools, so what if I do this or that?' But I was probably trying to employ a broader sense of it." It is probably the case that, with some distance, the artists are now able to claim they are "just as Indian as these fools," whereas earlier it was difficult negotiating being an Indian who wished for expanded social boundaries.

College posed old challenges reconfigured and each artist faced rejection by and of mainstream desi groups. Students debate authenticity and rightful claims to ethnicity. In awkward encounters desi hip hoppers produced and contested normative second-generation "Indianness" by reshaping older identities into novel ones just as a DJ mixes two preexisting recordings to create a new track. Co-ethnics rebuffed hip hop desis, who in turn learned to carry their ethnicity within themselves rather than collectively through homogenous social groups. Although the performers felt marginalized at just the time ethnicity and identity appear so critical to youth, their blooming musical and political commitments pushed them to confront ethnic identity politics through direct engagement.

Ethnicity may be both a powerful positive force in the lives of immigrants and a restrictive set of expectations that delimit the possible range of options. One has to socialize ethnically, align with the proper clique, have some knowledge of one's parents' country and language, date within the group, and even wear the "right clothes." Artists did almost none of this by choice or circumstance but dominant discourses inhibited their ability to articulate other possibilities. However, the artists realized that the very development of norms revealed the plasticity of ethnic identity and of categories. The artists, urban and suburban, disrupted ethnicity as the default identity of the new second generation by creating inclusive panethnic communities. In the process, they challenged assumptions of "sameness" and "difference," of alienation and belonging, often through song.

Ethnic hip hop illustrates immigrant stories and diasporic sensibilities. Lyrics detailing family histories within historical and global narratives call forth this sense of belonging to extranational communities. The artists make links across time and space; ethnic knowledge leads to a growing attachment to their parents' homelands that connect to their own experiences as post-1965 American minorities. Through hip hop, these desis name the discrimination faced by South Asians and turn knowledge into a source of pride and empowerment.

The internal group dynamics of ethnicity is only part of the story. The artists' dissociation with central aspects of ethnicity leads to their openness to other communities. How did these desis first come into contact with hip hop and what do their engagements with Blacks look like? How does race and racism operate distinctly from ethnicity and how did the artists negotiate their status after 9/11? The artists found few models within their own communities to help them with these issues, thus they turned to those who could help. In the next chapter, I discuss why the artists choose to affiliate with Blacks, a group that many mainstream South Asians consider most different. These identifications provide an intriguing reconception of race and space of desis in American racial hierarchies.

2.

Making Race

Desi Racial Identities, South Asian and Black
Relations, and Racialized Hip Hop

I was just baffled. I had never thought about politics, I had never thought about race. That [rotten coconut] conversation basically changed my life . . . I totally backed away from the Indian community. I [thought,] "Ah, these people don't accept me. The Indian community is like this, and I'm like this, so I'm an outsider." And so I basically tried to hang out with the Black community . . . because I knew that, and it worked for me. And they accepted me—which the Indian community didn't.—KB, Indian American MC

We often operate with too simplistic a notion of "belonging." Sometimes we are most "spoken" by our attachments when we struggle to be free of them, quarrel with, criticize or dissent radically from them. Like parental relationships, cultural traditions shape us both when they nurture and sustain us and when we have to break irrevocably with them in order to survive. And beyond—though we don't always recognize it—there are always the "attachments" we have to those who share our world with us but who are different from us.—Stuart Hall, "Conclusion: The Multicultural Question"

This book is about the "attachments" that, to paraphrase Stuart Hall, some South Asians in America have to those who share their world with them but who are different from them. Why would some South Asian youths spend their lives producing Black popular culture, loving Black men and women, and living in Black communities, particularly when we expect them to behave otherwise? Ethnicity is just one of several meaningful identities that hip hop desis develop, and their ambivalence toward it leads them to other communities of belonging. They claim racial identities: as people of color undergoing discrimination, they identify with Blacks and form lifelong relationships with Black people. By sampling they recast meanings of ethnicity and race—overlapping yet distinct phenomena—through relations with co-ethnics and other minorities. Thus, instead of imagining ethnicity as a chosen and malleable self-expression and race as a "problem" fixed and imposed by others, they find that race provides a sense of self-efficacy and empowerment. By claiming their non-White status, the artists reconcile their racialization by others with the affiliations and politics that they themselves have elected. They engage in making race: changing the nature and meaning of existing racial categories by producing their own versions.

These South Asians' lack of ethnic networks and opposition to ethnic expectations make the identities and worldviews of some Blacks appealing. As members of relatively voiceless and deracialized communities of South Asians, performers are drawn to the visibility of the dominant American minority, particularly in college. Their experiences with racism and awareness of class and racial differences in the United States left them with questions to which co-ethnics did not provide satisfying answers. Blackness serves as a model of an explicitly racialized response to this void.

Desi artists from urban areas grew up alongside Blacks and together they created hip hop culture, while those from suburban White communities first came into contact with hip hop through an evolving obsession with music. Often calling themselves "not really Indian" or "outsiders," both sets of desis introduce hip hop and Black people to South Asian America at the same time that they attempt to represent who South Asians are to their Black peers. In college, the artists developed a critical awareness of power but they had to form their own curriculum, so to speak, as few discourses explained their sense of cross-racial connection. They learned about the South Asian and Black interconnections that many South Asians gloss over and other Americans hardly know. Sustained interactions with Black male and female peers during the artists' early and college years through which each learned more about the other complemented their artistic development. This perspective of connections across differences informs their music through which they present racial and political identifications.

The artists reflect on South Asian and Black commonalities while they analyze their specificity as Brown, and not Black, Americans. Because neither ethnicity as "Pakistani" or "Indian" nor the racial identity of "Black" can fully articulate their emerging selves, they sample from their peers' cultural practices and worldviews but apply them to their own situations and histories as South Asians. Desi hip hoppers redraw the lines of "sameness" and "difference" that define identity-based communities through their bonds across categories. Ethnicity as sameness obscures internal divisions and can enhance and inhibit a sense of communal belonging; the opposite can be said for communities of difference. Why do these desis find "family" in Black communities and how do they articulate these bonds? I highlight the impacts of Black men and women upon desis' production of hip hop and their solidarities across constructed divides.

The cultural distinctiveness and non-Black status of Asian immigrants allows them to sidestep race, or so it seems. Thus, engaging topics of race and racism appears to be a matter of choice, even if the experience of racism and of being racialized is not. Identifying racially for desis—or acknowledging how one's body becomes marked in ways that are enacted upon by those in power in order to devalue difference to support White supremacist and capitalist gains—can be disadvantageous since it evokes one's non-White status. In the first section of this chapter I analyze the prevalent racial politics of mainstream first- and second-generation desis that frame why some desis turn to hip hop for alternatives. Many desis experience racism, yet few adopt explicit racial identities, so what would lead some to turn away from the relative privilege of a deracialized status?

Although many Americans have thought of South Asians as cultural rather than racial beings, race and racism are central to desi lives. Race organizes social structures in American society in empowering and disempowering ways (see San Juan 1992; Chang 2000). In the second section of this chapter I illustrate how sustained interactions with Black peers and hip hop's messages exposed urban and suburban desi artists to perspectives uncommon in their ethnic communities. Desis use this information to frame their racial self-conception and their unique understandings of South Asian/Black relations as one of linkages rather than as only contentious. I conclude with examples of desis' "racialized hip hop," or traditional-sounding hip hop music, that speak to issues commonly considered "Black" rather than South Asian and that express the artists' negotiation as Brown men and women living in a post-9/11 America.

The cross-racial identifications of hip hop desis are not rooted in ephemeral, theoretical, or romantic notions of connection; instead, they are based on their knowledge of the historical and global forces that have shaped how South Asians and Blacks came to the Americas. Through their critical awareness of power, cross-racial interactions, and hip hop music, these desis engage with difference; they construct communities based on shared interests of music and politics not circumscribed by ancestry. They create racialized hip hop to articulate a global race consciousness that links individuals across time, space, and racial categories. By making race—taking an active part in the process of racialization—individuals stake out new racial meanings that can become the foundation of empowered non-White identities from which individuals build cross-racial alliances.

The Meaning of Racism and the Meaningfulness of "Race"

The identities of desi hip hoppers are paradoxically fixed and ambiguous and they shift from the margins to mainstreams of multiple communities (see Okihiro 1994). Tied to other South Asians as a group marked by sameness, they also bond with Blacks and broader communities of color. Scholarly analyses of the "problem" that South Asians have posed to American legal constructions of race illustrate their racial ambiguity and the fallacy of biological conceptions of race (Koshy 1998; Lopez 2006). Today desis find themselves at a unique juncture. Some harness the productive power of their racial ambiguity—arising from a history of changing census classifications and their status between Black and White—in order to distinguish themselves from either pole, or else align with the privileged, White, position. Other groups occupying "the racial middle" also have these options, but individuals respond to their stations in life heterogeneously, beyond "whitened" or ethnic identities (O'Brien 2008). It is true that many Asian Americans have internalized dominant racist ideas and dissociate with other native-born minorities and their working-class counterparts (Leonard 1992; Singh 1996; Prashad 2000; Kim 2003.) But what of those who tackle the ambiguity of their otherness by attempting to solidify (but never fix) its meaning by evoking race as an empowering identity and racism as a shaping but not determining force? Conceptions and deployments of Blackness and its markers are central to this process. How is it, I ask, that some South Asians strategically deploy their ambiguity relative to "races" that people imagine are more fixed, and how does this allow them to relate to a number of groups? Their liminal position grants these desis the opportunity to shift from being marginal outsiders to central spokespersons within South Asian, Black, and hip hop communities.

These stances highlight another central contradiction: they illustrate, on the one hand, the fixity and "realness" of *race* while, on the other hand, they reveal the slipperiness and potential transcendence of *racial categories*. Decision-making groups have imposed ideas about where South Asians fit in the racial hierarchy of the United States, but desis also inhabit these spaces self-consciously. In employing a double consciousness (Du Bois 1903) they interpret how others read them through their structural understanding of how the powerful have constituted race relations. Like biracial and other ethnically ambiguous people, desis can harness the power of their ambiguity. They engage the malleability of race to construct emergent identities and meanings through strategic essentialism (Spivak 1995) and strategic anti-essentialism (Lipsitz 1994).

Two primary factors lead to the responsiveness of these desis to their Black peers' perspectives on race and class dynamics in the United States: their sense of otherness in American society evident in the racism that they and those around them face, and the rise of hegemonic desiness and discourses of ethnic exceptionalism (itself a response to the former). Problematically, the latter reaction leads to forms of racism *among* minority groups. First-generation race politics frames second-generation options and inspires some to search for alternatives. For some desi youths, including these artists, South Asian anti-Black racism leads not only to their ambivalent relationship to ethnicity, but also pushes them to become anti-racist (see Das Gupta 2006). Hip hop desis learn how and why racism operates and their awareness of global and historical processes that link communities of color leads them to connect the ways that South Asians are racialized to the mistreatment of Blacks. These links encourage their opposition to manifestations of racism that extend beyond their ethnic communities. Blackness would thus appeal to those looking for empowering responses to discrimination without succumbing to assimilation or further advocating racism.

First-Generation Race Politics

You don't identify with people worse off than you are. You make your deals, if you can, with those who have more, because you hope one day to have more yourself. (Russo 2007:13)

Second-generation desi youths come to understand their status by attempting to reconcile Americans' notions of South Asians with their parents' ideas about who South Asians are. In attempting to fit favorably within their new nation predicated upon a Black and White binary, immigrants often align themselves on the side of Whites and maintain a deracialized identity detached from racial concerns. This racial maneuvering sans explicit racial engagement trickles down to their United States–born children who, in their own desires to fulfill their parents' dreams, adopt many of their elders' problematic ideas. Ultimately, desis are ill-equipped to deal with racism while they advocate racialist ideas about non-White others.

The racial attitudes of the first generation toward Blacks and about race more generally stem from their dissonant experiences as immigrants. For postcolonials from elite families in South Asia that were members of the majority group, becoming recast as racialized minorities can be troubling. They often see group difference in biological terms, thereby evoking transported notions of caste, blood, and purity forged within the context of subcontinental histories, including British colonialism. "Such conceptions of race," Nazli Kibria writes, "which are so different from the principles of U.S. racial thinking, have helped South Asian Americans to remain ideologically disengaged from the U.S. racial order" (1998: 72). Immigrants' self-conceptions from their homeland intersect with the Black-White paradigm of race in the United States, which emphasizes the devaluation of Blacks (Rajagopal 1995; Prashad 2000, 2001). Some assert that Asians can access Whiteness because Americans consider them to be culturally distinctive, or ethnic, and therefore potentially assimilable, whereas the position of Blacks in the American imagination is racial and therefore more fixed: "The 'exotic' east lends itself to certain mystifications, whereas the history of slavery in America, while certainly secured in part by ideological imagining, has nonetheless embedded blacks more concretely and determinedly in the material" (Palumbo-Liu 1999: 87).

South Asians focus on what they came for—job opportunities and golden futures—yet class aspirations link with conceptions of race. As Vijay Prashad explains, "Desis realize they are not 'white,' but there is certainly a strong sense among most desis that they are not 'black.' In a racist society, it is hard to expect people to opt for the most despised category. Desis came to the United States and denied their 'blackness' at least partly out of a desire for class mobility (something, in the main, denied to blacks) and a sense of solidarity with blacks was tantamount to ending one's dreams of being successful" (2000: 94). Thus, even on the heels of the race-conscious movements of the 1960s and 1970s, South Asian parents across class lines, like other immigrants, encourage "American" values about work and money among their children. But in agreeing with the foundations of the model minority myth, South Asians comply with White supremacy: "With blacks at the bottom, there is every indication that any migrant has a good chance both of being above the nether end of society and of experiencing some mobility. Recognition of this fact illustrates the acceptance of structural racism against blacks in U.S. society" (163).[1]

"It's hard to live as a negative, positive, derivative," pens Rawj in the rap song "Masters Too" on Feenom Circle's Souled Separately album. The relative wealth of Indian Americans may shield them from the more blatant forms of racism (Kibria 1998: 73; Prashad 2000), but it continues to impact them. "In order to celebrate the triumph of American democracy," writes David Palumbo-Liu, "it is necessary to have a racial other whose success bears witness to the legitimacy of such basic notions as upward mobility. Yet even an assimilation into the elite classes cannot erase the mark of racial difference and the psychic and cultural differences that are assumed to accompany it" (1999: 212). "Positive" stereotypes about Asians as "mysterious" and "mystical" only signify one form of racism (Prashad 2000).[2] Superstudent and computer geek stereotypes reveal that Black and White Americans consider Asians "eternal foreigners" rather than White, despite the presence of Asians in the United States as early as the 1700s.[3] The "eternal foreigners" status is likewise ascribed to Latinos, whose land in what is now the southwestern United States was stolen from them. So although South Asians consider themselves to be "cultural" beings not victims to racism, Orientalist conceptions still rule American minds, existing simultaneously with depictions of Black inferiority.

Racial evasions are striking given the anti-Asian backlash in the 1980s.[4] The general racial politics of South Asians in the United States comprise a complex denial and assertion of racism that second-generation youth must confront. The United States offers non-Black immigrants some rewards that intersect with cultural explanations that deny racism and heighten divisions among minorities. The choices of South Asian parents to not discuss their racial identities and racism undeniably impact the lives of their children.

Impacts upon the Second Generation

It would not be an overstatement to say that most South Asians in the United States consider Blacks to be their antithesis. However, American-born desis comprehend the process of alienation that they and other minorities face, and American racial politics often registers with them more than it does for their immigrant parents (Visweswaran 1993: 307). Discrimination sometimes motivates desi youths who, in Kibria's words, "may find it more necessary than their parents did to confront directly the dynamics of U.S. racial thinking" (1998: 73) in order to develop friendships and coalitions with other minorities (Singh 1996: 98).[5] This is partially due to parents' unfamiliarity with United States–based racisms (Lessinger 1995: 136). But this does not mean that most desis claim racial identities in common with other non-Whites.

Notions of racial difference held by elders have filtered down to desi youth and are reinforced by colorblind, culturalist, and multi-cultural discourses in the 1990s. Some Indian Berkeley students, for example, claim that Indians fare better in school than other groups because of their family values. In the same breath, these students conflate cultural and biological explanations of difference: Blacks, one male student says, have better ball handling ability than others, are "naturally" more sexually promiscuous, and yet lack the cultural impetus for schooling. As such, desis often partake in cultural racism (Balibar 1991), whereby "culture" substitutes for biological notions of difference despite the fact that other Americans subject South Asians to this same form of racism. South Asian youths also call upon their class status as evidence of hard work rather than analyzing the impacts of structural and historical factors. Thus, hegemonic desiness and national discourses about difference in the United States reinforce one another to inform South Asians' racial politics.

The social and geographic distance between South Asians and Blacks has exacerbated desis' misinformation, including in diverse college settings in California in the 1990s. Even where cross-racial interactions may occur—in dorm rooms, classes, and at events—the divide seems so great and the desire to overcome it too little. Most desi youths get their information about Black people from images permeating all forms of information and interpret them through prevailing understandings. For example, Amit, an upper-middle-class mainstream Indian student at UC Berkeley and a self-described "wannabe emcee," explains his blossoming love of hip hop. At Berkeley, he was making impressive dual efforts to become involved in the separate Indus and hip hop scenes. He bravely participated in a freestyle battle and even attempted to start a "South Asian hip hop group" (it never got off the ground). Amit loves hip hop, was raised in the Bay Area (known for its multiracial mix), and attended one of the most diverse universities in the nation. But at the end of our interview, he confided, "Yeah, because, you know, socially and personally, I never knew a Black person. Not one. Not even today." Amit's interests and experiences echo other ethnographic depictions of desi youth.

Many South Asians across generations perceive Blacks to be an uneducated group that is prone to violence and that should be kept at a distance (see Leonard 1992; Singh 1996; Prashad 2000). This may seem like an unduly harsh assessment, yet the prevalence of these attitudes argues otherwise. The MCs' own parents have at times commented on the "undesirable" elements in Black communities. As one artist noted, "I do think a lot of members of my parents' generation have . . . derogatory notions of other races without having firsthand experiences with it, which bothers me." In their childhoods, these Brown MCs would face their parents' prejudices when they brought Black friends into their homes: "Don't bring these people to my house," said one mother. "There was always tension. Always, always," said the rapper Rawj who grew up in a Black community. Despite this pressure, Rawj formed a hip hop group with Black and Filipino peers because he didn't find the anti-Black sentiment to be an "intelligent argument" backed by reasoning. Like other non-Black second-generation youths, the artists chastise their parents' ideas about race, specifically their anti-Black prejudices.

While critical of their elders, the artists generally describe their parents as "relatively liberal," and they are deeply conscious of the sacrifices their parents made for their futures. As KB reflects: "I think they're more scared than anything else. [It has] just got to be so hard [for them] to come over here and make a life for themselves. They've just done so much for the youths' futures." Hesitant to call their parents "racist," desi artists contextualize their elders' choices. In college courses, they learned that South Asians entered the nation in 1965 because of civil rights gains and Black protests that helped enact changes to immigration restrictions. While the artists were more forgiving, I concur with Prashad's (2000: 91) critique of desi anti-Blackness as an attempt to curry favor with Whites by demeaning other minorities despite the fact that some Indians are darker than some Blacks.

These ideas are linked not only to desires for upward mobility but also to colorism, or the practice of favoring fairer over darker skin tones, among Asians and in Black communities. Skin color— just one aspect of racial identity—"remains an inescapable barrier" for diasporic South Asians (Ballard 1994: 299), thus challenging assumptions that middle-class desis are (becoming) "just like Whites." The fact of their racial uniform (Takaki 1989) also upsets some South Asians' desire to disengage from racial matters (Kibria 1998: 72). Min Song says that possibilities "of forming alliances, willingly or unwillingly" between, for example, South Asians and Blacks, arise out of America's confusion between race and skin color (1998: 87). As Sucheta Mazumdar states, "While foreign-born South Asians may be able to overcome color prejudice to some extent, through unusually high levels of professional training typically acquired abroad, they cannot be certain that their U.S.-born sons and daughters will fare as well. Like the dilemma facing the black bourgeoisie . . . they cannot escape identification with people of the same skin color who, as part of the working class, are more directly assaulted by the cruder manifestation of racism" (quoted in Song 1998: 87). In India there is a diversity of shades of skin yet Indians are thought to be one group in a racial sense (Kibria 1998). Thus, color may be separated from race in contrast to the conflation of the two in the United States. A number of Black men and women in the Bay Area felt that South Asians should share their attitudes about America because some are "darker than us," and they were puzzled that desis expressed anti-Black prejudices. Yet race obviously refers to more than skin tone. Racism, too, is not restricted to hue; ruling elites racialize groups differentially, which reaffirms South Asians' sense of cultural uniqueness in contrast to both Blacks and Whites. Still, the non-White racial ambiguity of desis can sometimes be foundational to interminority alliances.

Many first- and second-generation South Asians thus lack a vocabulary for analyzing race within their ethnic communities and are exposed to dominant United States conceptions. As a result, some youth have adopted White normativity that is revealed innocuously enough in their conflation of "American" with Whites and a belief in the Black and White binary. Desi youths impose many of these ideas upon other South Asians in their attempts to understand why some people seem different. So many of the artists recall that they "felt bad" because they seemed to "fail" in college interactions with mainstream desis that were dripping with repercussive expectations. As Richmond's KB says, "A lot of times I'd be on campus and these random Indian guys [would ask], 'Why do you act Black?' Or, 'Why do you talk Black?' . . . Part of me actually felt bad because they were basically saying, 'Why don't you act Indian?'" The accusation stuck. Like his reaction to his being called a rotten coconut, he thought about it, was bothered by it, and flipped the logic of the statement by challenging its thesis. In his senior year of college, KB realized that "they weren't asking me, 'Why don't you act Indian?' They were asking me, 'Why don't you act White?'" In response, he recalls—laughing—he started asking them, "Why do you act White?!"

Desis are bothered both by the racism they face and the anti-Black attitudes of co-ethnics. As MC Rawj rhymes in the song, "Masters Too," "If it's me vs. you, then we all goin' to lose." They learn that racial denials by South Asians stem from an unawareness or unwillingness to see the mutually and relationally constitutive relations between colonized Blacks and Asians (Hesse and Sayyid 2005); they are distinct and overlapping shades of one another (Okihiro 1994). At the same time, it is difficult for immigrant parents to understand how their children's process of becoming "American" can include notions of Blackness. Hip hop desis have to develop a different racial paradigm in order to address the questions that plague them. So, despite cautionary tales against Blacks, both Americans' racism toward South Asians and South Asians' anti-Black sentiments lead some youths away from the designated culture of their ancestry to adopt a culture rooted in the experiences of their other. Sustained interactions with Blacks form the foundation to the performers' re-articulations of race and race relations. Desis who became hip hop artists met Blacks and hip hop at different stages of their lives, depending on their childhood backgrounds.

First Contact with Blacks and Hip Hop: Desis from Minority Neighborhoods

> One question I haven't addressed is how did I end up doing [hip hop]? I think just by personality, or by education, or just my whole consummate being here on earth. I'm just an expressive person and this is probably the only form of expression, the first form of expression presented to me. I didn't have this background of who my forefather was or my culture. So I feel like it chose me.—Rawj, Feenom Circle MC

MC Rawj points to the totality of his being to explain his embrace of Black expressive culture. Along with personality and taste, his family and childhood background in Richmond, California, presented hip hop culture to this desi as a youth. For urban artists like Rawj, their racial otherness in America and relations with co-ethnics intersect with their love of music and interactions with nearby Black peers in post–civil rights America. When, where, and how the artists first met Blacks and encountered hip hop culture depended on where they grew up. Desi artists from less wealthy and more racially diverse urban neighborhoods made strong friendships with local Blacks, Mexicans (in California), and Asians, including Filipinos. The rappers and their youthful posses were part of the hip hop generation born in the 1970s around the time that Afrika Bambaataa learned to spin records, the Jamaican transplant Kool Herc was playing break beats at parties, and the Sugarhill Gang's vinyl "Rapper's Delight" hit the streets. These Black and Brown boys hung out together on the city streets of California and New York, the fertile ground from which the latest in a legacy of resistant Black arts and cultures arose. They played basketball at the park and then played the dozens (or verbally battled in good spirits) on their way home. This environment and its residents exerted their influence on young desis to be hip hop. As a result, these youths began crafting their own rhymes, practicing in private as they spent hours listening to LL Cool J, Eric B. and Rakim, and Doug E. Fresh in the 1980s. These are the desis who grew up to become performing MCs with albums for sale, including Chee, Asad, Fahad, Rawj, and KB, and they join Puerto Rican, Filipino, and Chinese youth in the creation of hip hop.

These atypical desis, like some Nuyoricans, lived among Blacks and, racialized as non-Whites living in neglected areas, felt underrepresented (Flores 2000; Rivera 2003). But the situation of desis differs from that of Puerto Ricans in the South Bronx who are tied with Blacks by "a history of joint ghetto experiences" (Rivera 2003: 114) and by "history and lived experience" (115). They do not claim that "it's almost like we're the same race" (MC B-Unique, quoted in Rivera 2003: 114), as do some Blacks and Puerto Ricans. South Asians do not share the histories of slavery that Puerto Ricans and immigrants from the Caribbean do with American Blacks, and the overall class profile of South Asians is substantially higher than their Latino counterparts. Even the families of less wealthy desi artists faced upward mobility and eventually moved out of Black neighborhoods. Nevertheless, their childhood experiences with

Black boys and girls in their city neighborhoods were too formative to be forgotten.

Urban desi youths, who are often the only desi on their block, found in their local Black communities a surrogate for missing ethnic networks. Instead of identifying ethnically, they were more open to the cultures that surrounded them and thus became part of the hip hop generation (Kitwana 2002). Chee Malabar's San Francisco school teachers, for example, placed him in classes for English as a second language. He decided that he could learn English by listening to rap music "because all the kids around my way, that's what they listened to," and he began rapping with local kids, whom he initially thought were African immigrants. Dinesh, who grew up in what he describes as an "inner-city" area in northern California and whose mother was the sole breadwinner, posits that his lack of an extended Nepali family enabled his desire to identify broadly: "Maybe I don't hate Blacks because we didn't have an extended family to poison us that way." These desis enjoyed the room to befriend Blacks and engage in Black cultural production. Dinesh developed a "connection" with "different cultures" that "overrides race," and Rawj says that by the time he got to college he knew more about Black culture and history than "his own." Black urban youths involved with hip hop did not find their Brown friends' participation in the culture to be odd. Rather, they embraced them as they did later when their desi friends also became performing artists, because they both came from the same 'hoods and shared passions and predicaments.

Interracial contact exposed desi youths to a range of Black residents—young and old, thriving, surviving and struggling, men and women with diverse attitudes toward local issues. This taught these desis an obvious yet often diminished fact of the heterogeneity of "Black America." Black friends' families treated these budding Brown MCs "like a son." They could hang out in Black friends' homes and were privy to domestic banalities and occasional beefs. Desis also brought their friends into their own homes, where they ate and witnessed family dramas translated into other languages, and realized that some Indians came from single-parent homes. These intimate interactions introduced both parties to class, racial, and cultural differences and commonalities. Socializing in this way also exposed youths to things not provided within their own homes.

First, despite being Brown and being aware of their "Indianness," for example, they became part of race-based communities of support where families cared for each others' children. Second, within these families and at family functions at their peers' homes they heard different ways of discussing the world.

These desis lived near Oakland, the home of the Black Panthers, and Berkeley, home to a campus of radicals. Some members of their local Black communities expressed an explicit Black consciousness as they spoke about history and oppression, which contrasted with desi family conversations focused on studies, marriage, and careers. Working-class residents of the Bay Area theorized neoliberal economics, police surveillance, and crack as part of a historical legacy of oppression against Blacks. Minorities in these neighborhoods also did not interact daily with Whites or face the kinds of racism that artists from wealthier and Whiter areas did. These desis grew aware of institutional racism through housing segregation, underfunded schools, and a lack of viable jobs (see Lipsitz 1998). They saw their Black friends respond to racism through expressions of racial pride that engaged with race directly. Urban desis bring these perspectives to college where the exclusionary racial and class admission and enrollment policies cause them to find the concerns of middle-class desi students "petty." In college, they studied South Asia and merged their Black peers' perspectives with their immigrant experiences and transnational ties.

Just before college, however, the desi artists and some of their Black high school friends began to diverge and found that they were "headed for different paths in life." They saw firsthand the ways that police, just one form of institutional and state power, singled out their Black peers.[6] Some close friends began dropping out of school, went to prison, or died. These troubled waters inspired some artists to live life fully. On the track "Misunderstanding," MC Rawj rhymes:

> sending shots to my peoples behind prison doors,
> oppressive gates got our thirst unquenched,
> soul pours out of poisonous containers
> drums and words the only remainders
> starving youths the reminders
> that some of us need to be the truth finders.

This MC sees these realities as the result not of his friends' poor choices but rather due to historical and institutional practices that target people of African descent with a specificity that South Asians had thus far avoided. Rawj says these diverging paths were "all environmental" and were related to the unequal distribution of resources rather than to inherent racial or cultural attributes. In speaking of his transfer from his public high school in Richmond to a wealthy suburban school, Rawj points out, "I'm at this top-notch prep school and they were going to a school that I almost failed [out of, in the] ninth grade, with no funding, no teaching, no opportunity. Really it's the whole nature and nurture thing, I mean but it was all nurture. It was the fact that I was in a stimulating environment and they weren't." They became even more aware of this split in college where these desis became part of an "overrepresented" group of Asians whereas the enrollment of Black students suffered from the neoconservative backlash in the 1990s.

Desis from cities like Richmond sometimes attended community college or summer bridge programs for incoming students before transferring on to a university. In contrast to mainstream desis' difficulties in bridging racial divides, urban hip hop desis seemed to befriend Black students quite easily. "It just so happens that those were folks that I met," Rawj says of the "large group of cats," mostly Black, that he encountered through basketball and classes and hung out with at community college. "I won't be uncomfortable, but I won't make an effort, either. It's just who you meet and how you interact. Maybe I needed help with homework," he says, flipping the model minority myth on its head. Urban South Asian youths signaled to other students their former familiarity with Blacks through cultural references, styles, and interests. This included the way that Chee and Rawj, for instance, interacted and spoke and the way they wore their clothes. Further, their modes of interaction, conversational topics, and interests also communicated their commitment to Black music. Atypical desis already understood that they did not have to be Black in order to develop close friendships with Black hip hoppers. How one represents oneself and one's commitments and interests is critical in hip hop–based communities. Hip hop, with its own set of cultural references, is central to these interactions and the creation of multiracial social groups in college.

Black friends and hip hop culture came together in college for urban desis who found comfort in this set of hip hop heads that encouraged their artistic development. Particularly for some desi men, this was their first time exhibiting their rhyme skills in public ciphers, or circles of rappers, along with Black male students (others had grown up rhyming in public). As one half of Himalayan Project, Chee had been composing poetry since the eighth grade, practicing his rhymes in private. His freestyling debut happened, he says, in his sophomore year in college where "kids from the inner cities and kids who were having a hard time [were] all clumped together, so we're all close." A DJ threw on instrumentals over which other boys were "just reciting shit they had written. I didn't have anything memorized." Inspired, Chee "just started freestyling, and they were taping it." Fellow battle rappers were surprised by his skills and assumed he was rhyming from memory: "Oh shit, when'd you write this!" they asked, when in fact he was just "spitting it off the top" of his head.[7] Submitting oneself to peer evaluation through public rhyming can be treacherous since freestyles can become verbal battles in which non-Black MCs take a tongue lashing as outsiders; ciphers are also male-dominated spaces in which women must work particularly hard to insert themselves.[8] For Chee, however, this paid off and he was validated for his impromptu rhyming ability and masculine boasting. These tests in front of others of the hip hop generation encouraged Chee to develop a thick skin and rhyme excellence, thereby leading to his status as a confident MC who performs across the country.

The musical paths of these MCs are shaped by their childhoods in which they developed diverse social groups bonded by hip hop, which became their culture of identification over ethnicity. In time, these Black and Brown youths became like family and urban desis became members of their local Black communities while also being cognizant of important distinctions. From these stories it makes sense that some desis from urban areas would become attached to hip hop in the 1980s, just as it did for Puerto Ricans in the Bronx. On the other hand, what accounts for the musical obsession of suburban middle-class desis who grew up in predominantly White neighborhoods like many of their second-generation compatriots?

First Contact with Blacks and Hip Hop:
Middle-Class Desis in White America

I hear a lot of these South Asians, and they grew up in the suburban areas, but they identified as White. My reality was different, you get what I'm saying? . . . Already I was experiencing hard-core racism at my school. My high school was 95 percent White but my friends were all the other 5 percent. I didn't know any of the other White kids in high school. I was militant. I hated White people . . . It came from me understanding that something wasn't right.—D'LO, MC, poet, activist

D'Lo is a Sri Lankan poet and performer who identifies, according to the flier of one of his/her shows, as "Gay, Hindu, Hip Hop." While these monikers together make him/her unique among the desi artists, D'Lo's experiences growing up in "SriLancaster" just north of Los Angeles mirror those of the other desi audiophiles from mostly White middle- and upper-middle-class areas. D'Lo was highly aware of racial demographics, experienced "hard-core" racism, created multiracial minority social groups, and had a sense that all these things put together (along with his/her gay and emerging transgender identity) led to D'Lo knowing that "something wasn't right." It is D'Lo's retrospective on White people ("I hated White people") that may seem the most shocking: desis don't often say (or feel?) such things. Yet this view, stated or not, is the key to what leads some musically minded desis away from both Whites and ethnic identification. The hip hop music that came on the airwaves and across television stations in the 1980s and 1990s "saved" these suburbanites by explaining the processes that they were undergoing. Once they were in college they searched out peers who shared their love of hip hop.

Differing sets of discourses about difference, race, and racism circulate within racially diverse urban areas and mostly White wealthy neighborhoods. Where could those from White neighborhoods find articulations of their frustrations if not at home and in their communities? Artists from these areas like Lancaster in the Los Angeles region and Fremont in the Bay Area may resemble the "model minority" image, but racism was a defining feature in their lives, a force that affected their life paths and perspectives (see Radhakrishnan 1994: 223; Purkayastha 2005). In high school, these artists learned the histories of Blacks in America, but it wasn't until college, when they knew Black students in numbers, that they saw this strong minority identity as an appealing response to racism that could adapt to fit their circumstances. Unlike those who grew up around Black youths, suburban desis felt like American minorities in contrast to their neighbors. As one Fremont-raised Gujarati said, "Going to elementary school, it was predominantly White, but I was always with the others: the Asian kids, the Black kids, and that's always been my thing." These middle-class youths attempted to sort out with minority friends the racist encounters that occurred within settings that elided discussions of race in the 1980s. If, overall, South Asians deny the effects of racialization, their children bear the costs of this strategy. In kids' homes and schools, what is discussed is as important as what is assumed and silenced. Desi parents wrestled with their children's growing engagement with Black music and friends and generally did not support their desires for alternative—artistic—futures. Interminority exchanges, some elders feel, may stain the reputations of their children (does that imply that the cultural lives of their children are malleable and fragile?).

Suburbanites like Jonny and Bella came to hip hop through an evolution of musical tastes that ranged from the Cure to Fugazi, and from ska to bhajans (Hindu devotional songs). Hip hop did not initially spring from their suburban streets bordered by well-manicured lawns. It came to those living outside of urban centers powerfully and visually through the television, urban and college radio stations, and their local record stores in the late 1980s and early 1990s. D'Lo had access to only two pop radio stations; s/he found hip hop through Yo! MTV Raps, the premier MTV hip hop showcase that started in 1988. "That was my connection to anything else. Like I always knew about N.W.A.[9] I knew everything about the upcoming West Coast [rap scene], Ice T . . . I knew all that shit . . . I was listening to BDP [Boogie Down Productions]. I was listening to Poor Righteous Teachers . . . Pete Rock. I was listening to Special Ed! Like I loved that shit!" D'Lo and others took hip hop seriously and were home schooled by rappers, their rhyming professors. At home, D'Lo did his/her homework and "became a student of hip hop." These suburbanites, with their reduced access to live, spontaneous, and consistent rhyming as occurred on some city streets, shied away from rapping. Instead, wealthier artists became involved in the technical aspects of music production and went on to become DJs and producers in contrast to the urban artists who flexed the oral skills that required less capital.[10]

A number of researchers outside of the United States have analyzed the appeal of Black music for non-Black youth. In England, Black musical forms help White youths sort out critical class and racial issues where working-class Whites and Blacks sometimes collaborate through musical productions (Hebdige 1979). According to Paul Gilroy, reggae in particular reveals "how popular culture has formed spaces in which the politics of 'race' could be lived out and transcended in the name of youth" (1991: 167). He further notes that a "political relationship between Afro-Caribbeans and Asians on which the future of black Britain may depend is being created in these cultural encounters" (218)—a factor that also bears out in what I see between some desis and Blacks in the United States.

Suburbanites were much like mainstream desis from wealthier families, except that they, like other desi activists and "unruly immigrants" (Das Gupta 2006), were not content to follow the path directed by their co-ethnics. Disturbed by the inequalities they faced, they became avid hip hop heads before commercial interests told them to because they were drawn to its beats, wordplay, and messages. After high school, they made a beeline to the college radio station where they met like-minded individuals, including Black students also into hip hop, and remixed versions of their multiracial childhood peer groups.[11] At the radio station, bonds over musical ideas and hip hop (the students would listen to music for hours) were fortified by shared access to records, technology, and the airwaves. Jonny, who had a weekly hip hop show for three and a half years and became the musical director of two other shows, benefited from these resources. Hip hop, the college radio station, and the social circles comprised of "likeminded individuals" provided a necessary alternative to the racism and ethnic expectations that continued to plague them. Music formed the basis for social bonding and ideological development; the college radio station provided the location. Jonny may have felt like an outsider to other social groups, but "it really clicked with me there" at the station, he says. "Being involved with hip hop gave me my first setting in which I had a lot of Black friends." Jonny, Bella, and Asma, a Muslim Indian radio producer, each bonded at their stations with other music lovers expressing "music as identity," or the notion of how music, rather than race or ethnicity, defines one's peer group (Frith 2007: 10–12). Over time, all of the artists' investments in hip hop culture led to increasing interactions with Blacks, which in turn affected their growing racial consciousness as they examined issues like contentious policing practices.

Black friends, whether from childhood or later in college, became important peers with whom urban and suburban hip hop heads developed a growing and shared understanding of the world. Black peers, some of whom expressed themselves through hip hop music, helped the artists come to better understand themselves as racial beings. Blackness, the "single sign of alterity," modeled one politicized and proud response to their distinctions as minorities (Baker et al. 1996: 5). Not just concerned about "their" people, hip hop desis were indignant about the impacts of racism upon Blacks. Blackness, which rearticulates difference as empowering, connotes neither a free-for-all identity nor the stereotypical and racist images promulgated in the popular media about Black youth. Instead, it partially refers to those political and historically attuned ideologies that resonate for the desi youths who find it applicable to themselves.

At times Blackness means something more expansive, thereby signifying the experiences of all racially marked bodies enacted upon by domination and resistant against it. This sense of the term explains the adoption of Blackness by marginalized populations across the globe, including New Zealand's indigenous Maoris and the Brazilian residents of favelas (Green 1997; Basu and Lemelle 2006). Blackness as racialized political consciousness therefore intersects with but is distinct from the performers' identifications with desiness as diasporic ethnicity. They use their music to rebut mainstream attempts to reduce the meanings of "Black" to racist conceptions. Desi artists model rather than mimic this most visible and vocal resistance to White supremacy through a critical awareness of racism. However, they mix it with a critical ethnicity that addresses their diasporic sensibility and transnational ties.

The artists stand on the margins of ethnically and racially circumscribed communities. Denigrated by Whites, they disagree with national discourses that deny inequalities; but the responses of those Black peers who embrace hip hop do resonate. In college, Brown performers incorporated a racially informed consciousness into their self-conceptions as ethnic beings. Aware of their liminal status in relation to co-ethnics, Blacks, and Whites, they sample the race consciousness and counterhegemonic messages of hip hop lyrics and fuse them with an immigrant perspective. The ambiguity of South Asians is a potentially productive force—one the artists learned to explore over time.

Multiple Racial Affinities:
Outsiders, Slippery Signifiers, and Strategic Ambiguity

At one level, the observation that identity or subject positions are complex and nonfixed is banal. But the important thing is that politics is usually conducted as if identity were fixed. The question then becomes, On what basis, at different times and in different places, does the nonfixity become temporarily fixed in such a way that individuals and groups can behave as a particular kind of agency, political or otherwise? (Dirks, Eley, and Ortner 1994: 32)

Desis in hip hop resemble "sliding signifiers" whereby other Americans consider them to be at times White and at other times Black. The artists negotiate the liminal spaces between groups that are continually changing in membership and meaning. Although ideologically we often consider categories to be fixed, who and what comprises desi or hip hop America are in flux. By staking their claim to hip hop, seen as a Black sphere, and by maintaining distance from other desis despite their ancestry, these individuals disentangle the conflation of blood and ancestry and question automatic and natural senses of belonging.

Hip hop desis epitomize ambiguity, shifting relations, and multiple racial identities. As shifting "insiders" and "outsiders" across communities, their identities are informed by their overlapping yet distinct experiences with Blacks. Desi performers' slippery locations betwixt and between (Turner 1967) emphasize context in the process of identity formation; their lives suggest important distinctions among the concepts of race, ethnicity, culture, and belonging. Their identities uphold theories in Mixed Race studies that advocate the possibilities of belonging to several races at once while simultaneously combating the very logic of racial categorization. Ultimately, they fail—or perhaps refuse?—to provide us with one fixed response to the question "What are you?" According to the Mixed Race studies scholar George Kich, "people without the experience of resolving ambiguity, of moving from marginal status to center, or of expanding definitions beyond traditional constraints in order to really see what in fact exists often cannot adapt competently to marginality or to ambiguity, much less to a person who embodies ambiguity" (1996: 273). And what of the possibilities of those who *are* ambiguous and who draw upon that condition strategically in ways that advance unfixed notions of "race," tied not even to ancestry? Often contradictory and unclear, hip hop's desis draw upon essentialism (Spivak 1995) and anti-essentialism (Lipsitz 1994) strategically to signal their racial affinities.

The artists respect the boundaries between themselves and Blacks not as limiting but as sites where "differences" are meaningful but not absolute. By claiming racial identities as Brown people, these South Asians pry open the hegemony of Blackness as the sole signification of otherness within the United States. Desis identify with ideological aspects of Blackness that emphasize oppositional politics as an alternative to normative discourses, and slavery informs this understanding. But in crafting racialized desiness they supplement this with information about South Asia. This combination encourages them to emphasize the relationality of racial categories (Kim 1999). Yet this unresolved process still leaves open the question of their racial status. This is in part because South Asians do not fit comfortably within existing racial categories, and in part a result of the unrooted way they live their lives.

The ethnic, racial, and hip hop communities across which these artists navigate operate like concentric interconnected circles of separate yet overlapping communities of belonging. Instead of resolving the tensions that arise from rigid norms within each group by planting their feet firmly in one, these performers maneuver across contentious social groups by way of their identifications as South Asians proud of their heritage and as hip hop artists down with disenfranchised groups. Their identities signify shifting and comparative levels of distinction and connectedness, including ethnic specificity, pan-ethnic South Asian identifications, and pan-racial minority identities.

Like multiracial and ethnically ambiguous individuals, desi artists negotiate having race "done" to them as they take an active role in "doing race" by informing people's perceptions of who they are (Williams 1996). In many cases, their performances underscore the inadequacy of existing categorizations. One strategy they use to temporarily tie themselves to another group is through identifications that imply allegiances. For instance, although immigrants come from multiple backgrounds, they can *choose* to share a set of concerns with others. They employ "strategic anti-essentialism" when they take on identities that signify a group seemingly unlike themselves (Lipstiz 1994). In challenging our expectations by playing with their phenotypic and categorical ambiguities in unexpected ways, they push us to investigate their motives for race crossing (Wald 2000). At other times they incorporate essentialism to strategically fix themselves to impact how others read them (Spivak 1995). For example, in being conscious of the way their bodies are read by others (i.e., Du Bois's double consciousness) they take on racial cues of Middle Eastern peoples—shaving their beard in particular ways or wearing *kufis*—to identify with them as a statement against racist policies that harass this newly re-minted racial-religious group. Thus, desis in hip hop employ a range of strategies that put their ambiguity to work in order to belong to and express political allegiances with targeted groups. However, the slipperiness of race also makes it difficult for South Asians to claim one racial category.

The artists often identify as "outsiders," and belonging and alienation describes their social interactions. On the one hand, they argue that they are not desi, based on what they look like and who and what they know; on the other, they assert that desiness resides within them despite outward expressions. They are less ambivalent about being a part of hip hop but still consider themselves outsiders to those circles of Blacks who produce the culture. Nonetheless these performers identify with people across boundaries despite being subjected to evaluations of their authenticity by others.

The artists dislike categories and labels—they do not want to be placed in boxes, and to do so would be a difficult endeavor. As a result, they find it difficult to describe their lives sufficiently using existing categories. Jonny, a Californian Indian who moved to New York, never seems to anchor himself to any one community, and perhaps this is a conscious strategy. As a hip hop journalist he is attuned to the racial politics of the hip hop industry, but his perspectives often contrast with those of the desi rappers. In one of our lengthy email exchanges he explained, "Oddly, I view the Black experience from the classical American perspective, which, I guess, is a White lens. I certainly couldn't understand it from a Black lens, so I think there is no other third perspective." This argument raises at least two immediate points: Why can Jonny and other South Asian Americans have access to a "classical American" (i.e., White) perspective but not a "Black" one? Second, can there be a non-Black minority perspective?[12] Some of the other artists—particularly those who had grown up in Black communities, unlike Jonny—identify as "minorities" whose views contrast with the "White perspective." The Black or White option seems too limiting even in his own analysis as later he distinguishes his experience from that of Whites in the hip hop business. He states that "Indian isn't necessarily the establishment," because most rap artists are young Black men whereas the label owners and executives tend to be White men. Jonny's phenotypic ambiguity (his sense is that he does not look Indian) and his non-Black, non-White identity disassociates *and* associates him with various segments of the industry. At the same time, he employs rigid notions of "White" and "Black" but identifies as neither. He explains that he has "access and flexibility in some ways that aren't afforded White males. In an 'us versus them argument,' because of my non-Whiteness, I can very conveniently side with the 'us.' But it does have its limits in that I'm also not Black, so I can't be absolute in any of my arguments." His inability to be absolute and his references to what he is not signal the incompleteness of existing discourses of race. Jonny may appear to be trapped within the racial categories he finds himself exterior to, and he experiences life liminally.

Jonny deals with a different set of expectations regarding race compared to the other artists in part because many hip hop writers are not Black.[13] But he shares with other desis the sense of in-between sliding. Perhaps Jonny is being evasive by employing a particular understanding of race politics in the United States when he says, "To Whites, I [can] say 'I know more about the Black experience than you do.' To Blacks, I [can] say, 'I'm not the one who oppressed you.'" However, I think he illustrates our American inability to comprehend race as a whole by resorting to racial binaries when that paradigm is incapable of describing contemporary rela-tions. Further, Jonny's conundrum results from both Americans' dis-ease in speaking about race and the ineptness of the categori-zations themselves, which leave South Asians *without* a racial iden-tity (this is why we often hear Asians and Latinos referred to as who they are *not*). Jonny's rationalization illustrates the sliding and constructed nature of racial identities and yet it also relies on es-sentialist notions of what "Black" and "White" *are*. Racial identity is fluid and constructed for all individuals, but the history of race relations in the United States allows some groups greater flexibility. These kinds of slippery and triangulating experiences challenge old binaries and caution against new renditions of a Black/non-Black polarity (Lee and Bean 2007).

Like people who claim multiple heritages, desi artists' identifi-cations are situational (Williams-Leon and Nakashima 2001). Ac-cording to Teresa Williams, "No other social reality than that of racially mixed people questions the one-dimensional racial struc-ture upon which America has founded and built its national iden-tity" (1996: 193). But the conditions and possibilities facing mixed-race people extend beyond this population to include all groups. When the performers reject expected scripts to take on those that appear to be "unexpected," they remind us of the malleability of identity. Thus, seemingly "monoracial" or even deracialized South Asians actually have also, like biracials, "learned to 'do race' with twist and turns, stepping in and out of the racial molds prescribed to [them] by the larger society that projects race onto [them]" (208). For South Asians there is also no single choice to the ques-tion of racial categorization since they may exist within, across, and above United States classifications that do not accommodate shift-ing allegiances.

Individuals who choose to stand at the crossroads of commu-nities challenge the racial and ethnic identity politics of groups. Not only do these artists disavow the narrow expectations of ethnic authenticity while laying claim to desiness but also they battle the commonsense notion that rappers must be Black as they gain repu-tations as credible MCs. In their position as the only desi in pre-dominantly Black events such as at hip hop clubs or at Oakland's Juneteenth celebrations commemorating the abolition of slavery, they confront their difference as non-Blacks. However, their presence also expands the Black attendees' conceptions of who belongs in these spaces because desis' non-Whiteness and engagement with the event can be bonding. In such interactions the artists consider themselves "non-Black minorities," and they relay their perspectives as immigrants to Black peers while feeling comfortable as non-Whites in Black spaces. However, when they rap at concerts that attract college-aged mostly White and Asian American crowds, or when they are harassed by police, they identify as "non-White minorities." These identity acrobatics are complex and contradictory. They disrupt expected associations, such as the idea that prisons and profiling are "Black issues." One Indian American, for instance, who taught in underfunded schools in a Southside Chicago neighborhood, cofounded with a Black friend a hip hop record label with an antiprison agenda that signs conscious Black rappers. Desi hip hoppers also perform markers of Blackness by adopting a particular style or mannerism, such as Chee's hip hop–inflected speech, without claiming to be Black or erasing distinctions. The MC Vivek illustrates another, contrasting, strategy of identification.

Vivek, an MC from Connecticut whose story begins this book, is sometimes (mis)identified as a Black man and his Black peers often treat him like "one of their own." This is due in part to his appearance (his brown skin, closely cropped hair, and clothing), mannerisms (hand gestures and body movements), and long-term social and professional familiarity with Blacks. He exudes positive energy, especially if you catch him on the dance floor of a reggae club like Oasis in downtown Oakland. But even after strangers who are Black "find out" that he is not Black, they accept him as a brother because of his attitudes and commitments. Like one earlier conception of Blackness in Britain, Vivek's Blackness is a political identity that stems from his experiences as a non-White American and his commitments to justice (he has worked with Human Rights Watch) in Bangladesh and Sierra Leone. Vivek is like the British Asian musicians for whom, as Rehan Hyder notes, "the identification of a wider 'political' category of black was something that most of the Asian musicians bought into at various times and was linked to particular contexts; there was no sense of contradiction felt by simultaneously inhabiting black and Asian identities" (2004: 165). As part of being an MC, Vivek's active support and engagement within local Black communities, including his founding of Umoja (an educational organization) and cofounding of Timap for Justice (an organization that provides legal services for poor Sierra Leonians[14]), encourage some Blacks' acceptance of him as Black-as-political.

Vivek's formal political commitments to Black communities at home and abroad are not unique among the artists who use hip hop to express broad ideological worldviews. They comment on race and politics together in tracks like Himalayan Project's "1964," a deep, mature, and well-produced track on the album *The Middle Passage*.[15] In his verses the rapper Chee Malabar performs multiple identities as an immigrant tied to other communities of color. He covers topics traditionally found in message or conscious rap while inserting a new perspective.[16] The song's title refers to the year that President Johnson signed the Civil Rights Act—just one year prior to the Immigration Act of 1965 through which the artists' parents arrived in the United States. Chee begins with a description of poverty in India and moves on to a discussion of race, South Asians in the United States, and social movements in the 1960s, and he concludes on a pessimistic note about the future. The song opens with a soulful low-toned saxophone and is awash with the sound of slow waves coming ashore, a light guitar strum, and a drum beat:

> What's goin' on America, it's your least favorite son,
> You know the one, some beast mixed with East Indian rum,
> Hemmed, condemned to rent slum tents in dense settlements

In an uncharacteristically calm voice, Chee sweeps through a series of social issues beginning with his people's past (and present) experiences of being cordoned off, colonized, and "condemned to rent slum tents."

> See my melanin's akin to a felon's sins in this, civilization,
> Where dead presidents replacing the God's you're praising,
> Jesus? Nah, it's just g's, churches is worthless, it's a circus,
> Clowning around ain't where the work is.

Chee speaks about the plight of Brown people living in this "civilization" that criminalizes people of color (i.e., "my melanin's akin to a felon's sins"). He uses the term civilization ironically by pointing out our enslavement to the prominence of money ("dead presidents" represent dollar bills; "g's" are "grands" or dollars in the thousands). And it is money, he avers, that has replaced the role of religion—even churches have become profit-making enterprises, as Chee once pointed out to me as we drove through Brooklyn.

> We migrant workers, descendents of slaves,
> Ascended to a stage, beyond brave,
> Rendered a plague, civil rights came and went,
> And what's left?
> A few tokens molded hopin' they symbols for progress and for the rest,
> It's stress, no checks, credit debts is societal death,
> So what's bread?
> I ain't gotta tell you that it's kneaded (needed) dough,
> What we even breathin' for,
> Where most of us live, if it ain't the slugs or drugs,
> The air's sure to kill ya.

Chee lists a barrage of stresses that even the Civil Rights Movement failed to assuage, including the elements most urgent among poor urban communities: slugs (bullets), drugs, and debt.

> I breathe the oxygen, cough a lung,
> Sit and think for my people hope my freedom songs get sung.

"My people" is who Chee raps for and hopes for. This phrase denotes an inclusive, broad community—one that arches above distinct ethnic and racial communities. In these moments, hip hop desis envision, cultivate, and perform a global race consciousness. In an almost existential despair, Chee concludes by hoping that his own "freedom songs get sung," over forty years after the signing of the Civil Rights Act.

Using their racial ambiguity, these American desis adopt shifting identifications and allegiances. Despite the seeming fixity of race, Brown rappers alter meanings in their daily practices and lyrics by employing Black as political ideology. Their strategies to contend with race and racism illustrate the dynamics and possibilities open to all Americans, not just ethnically ambiguous or multiracial people, to inspire new theorizations of race. Black peers are central to the emerging self-conceptions of these budding hip hop artists. But it was by historically contextualizing the relationships between South Asians and Blacks that they were able to fully understand the conflicts—and possible alliances—within contemporary inter-minority relations.

Drawing Global-Historical Connections Between South Asians and Blacks

History is rich and complicated and diverse . . . I always see commonali-ties, but also lots of differences. History is the complexity of life.
—Vivek, desi MC and activist

Class and social distance make it difficult for most mainstream desis to grasp the links between South Asians and Blacks. Arun, a New York City DJ who remixes Hindi songs with hip hop beats for desi audiences, is skeptical of the connection between South Asians and Blacks. As he explained to me in an email, "To try and draw a connection between 1) a culture that was brought here as workers/slaves and is plagued by drugs, poverty, lack of educa-tion, etc. and 2) a culture that was brought here as doctors/pro-fessionals/students and is plagued by high incomes, stability, and success is somewhat absurd." Arun diagnoses the model image of Indians as a problem (repeating the term "plagued," perhaps using it ironically the second time) while advancing two of its central and problematic assumptions. First, he homogenizes both groups, erasing nonprofessional South Asians and middle-class Blacks and associating "hip hop" with all Blacks rather than with a particular generation or segment of Black America (or with other groups). Second, he poses South Asian and Black predicaments as incom-mensurably opposite cultures. The multiculturalist logic of these two claims is mutually reinforcing. In contrast, desis who became hip hop artists claim an immigrant-identified minority status informed by Blackness. Four factors shape this conception: first-generation ideas, desis' racial otherness in America (and racism), their inter-actions with Blacks, and their commitment to hip hop. Relatively unknown links between Blacks and South Asians across time and space frame this identification.

While cognizant of important group cleavages, desis express new ethnicities (Hall 1991) through Black popular culture by highlight-ing in their music the historical, cultural, spiritual, musical, and political linkages between South Asians and Blacks. These precedents inform the "surprising" unities that we witness in their lives today. Brown performers harness the power of "Afro Asia," described by Fred Ho and Bill Mullen as "a strategic intersection for thinking through an internationalist, global paradigm . . . as well as an anti-imperialist, insurgent identity that is no longer majority white in orientation" (2008: 2–3). High school history texts cover Black history cursorily; the story of South Asians is virtually unknown. Yet, as Amritjit Singh urges, "South Asians have much to learn from African American history about how they are being acculturated in North America" (1996: 94). Artists unearthed silenced histories through research, self-exploration, and dialogue. As cultural workers, according to Henry Giroux and Patrick Shannon, they "mobilize knowledge and desires that may lead to significant changes in minimizing the degree of oppression in people's lives" (1997: 5).

History helped explain the artists' sense of alienation from the status quo and their attachment to Blacks. Their identifications are founded upon "the mutual influence of and relationships between members of the African and Asian diasporas in the Americas" (Raphael-Hernandez and Steen 2006: 1), particularly the British colonials' displacements of these groups. While many immigrants call upon elitist and lofty legacies in their homelands in order to represent themselves as respectable newcomers, these desis reject such pasts. Instead, they speak of British colonial expeditions in India by linking them *directly yet distinctly* to Whites' enslavement and inhumane transport of Africans to the Americas. These conceptions of exploitation are not fixed geographically ("over there") or temporally ("back then"). In further studies, they uncovered how British colonials indentured the Chinese and Indians as replacements for slave labor; some Chinese even came as "coolie" labor to the southern United States (Jung 2006; see also Yun 2007). Today, Indians and Africans constitute sizable and sometimes opposing populations in some West Indian nations, including Trinidad, Guyana, and Surinam. Artists historicized other connections. Non-Indian performers refer to ethnic strife in South Asia: D'Lo is deeply troubled by the civil war in Sri Lanka, and the Pakistani MCs Humanity and AbstractVision recall the traumas of Partition, the separation Pakistan from India in 1947 when India gained its independence from the British.[17] Further, middle-class artists call upon links to bridge their distance from working-class compatriots. These remembrances reveal race to be historically constituted and forged through power relations but articulated in locally specific ways. Legacies of colonialism, imperialism, and labor exploitation tie them to other minorities, but groups have been *differentially* racialized. Analyzing the overlapping processes of racialization enables a perspective that highlights the relational formation of minority identities. That is, Blackness and Asianness have not only been constructed in relation to Whiteness but also have developed in relation to one another. These theories inform the lyrics of these artists, who use hip hop to advance a global racial perspective that contests multiple racisms and offers a model for solidarity.

Chee Malabar, who along with the Chinese American MC Rainman make up Himalayan Project, presents an especially illustrative persona to his listeners. Chee and Rainman's albums include *Himalayan Project* (1997), *Wince at the Sun* (2003), and *Broken World* (2007). The title of their project from 2002, *The Middle Passage*, refers both to V. S. Naipaul's (1962) scathing indictment of West Indians as colonial mimics and to the legacy of cross-Atlantic slavery. The title choice acknowledges the meaningfulness of slavery to Blacks and expands its symbol (the Middle Passage) to postcolonial non-Blacks. Like Naipaul, Chee lashes out with his words, but his target is the United States and its history of racism, exclusion, and capitalist exploitation of the poor. Over the course of eleven tracks, he articulates a complex self-portrait by positioning himself in relation to former slaves who now inhabit a racist and problem-filled America, a country that maintains power and privilege through a de facto system of exclusion and discrimination. He tackles these topics through both a macrolevel analysis of political and economic corruption and his individual experience as an immigrant who, as noted in the song "Nuttin Nice," "came off a plane, with Brown folks' hopes seeped in [his] veins."

Chee's hyperopic vision attests to several pasts. Some lyrics go back to his personal history ("since [he] leapt from Mrs. Menon's [i.e., his mother's] stomach") while others reach farther back to comment on macrohistorical factors, as in the song "Nuttin Nice": "I stalk the stage, gauge my mood, I came from caged slaves in servitude." Sometimes calling himself a "Tamil Tiger/slash/rap

HImaLayan PROJeCT
WINCE AT THE SUN

Album courtesy of Chirag Menon.

writer," the rhymster identifies with "terrorist" organizations like the Tamil Eelam, a nationalist group in Sri Lanka fighting against the government for an independent nation. Such cross-national recognitions highlight Sri Lankans' migration from India, and he denaturalizes "race" and "nation." Chee links exploited immigrant workers *within* South Asia (the British brought South Indian Tamils as bonded laborers on Sri Lankan tea plantations) to the *global* migration of Indians to the West Indies and the United States ("caged slaves in servitude"). The parallels with the exploitation of Africans are obvious.

Other Asian American rappers have made similar connections, such as the Chinese American rapper Jin who compares the refugee experience and slavery in his song "One Cry." Some scholars restrain from celebrating these cross-racial moves, including Oliver Wang who cautions: "Some Asian Americans romanticize the African American experience and believe that their participation in hip-hop brings them closer in solidarity with African Americans" (2006: 157). Wang rightly argues that hip hop is not the ideal site for positive Black and Asian relations in the absence of actual interactions. But the involvement of these desi rappers reflects years of intimate interracial relations and signifies their appreciation for shared and distinct experiences rather than a wishful desire for such things. These desis are like the young New York Dominican activists who adopt, as Ana Aparicio notes, a "strategic manipulation of historical memory, racial politics, and identity shifts" (2007: 197). Unlike Dominicans, however, the diasporic narratives by desis do not enable them to call upon an African ancestry denigrated over time; they call instead upon denigrated subcontinental identities and pasts.

Despite their distance from colonialism Brown rappers raise its specter by sampling it with critical commentary to make pan-racial and pan-ethnic ties because they find it informs their current status. As the product of an intercaste and religiously complex union, Chee uses rap lyrics to situate the communal conflict between Hindus and Muslims within the context of British colonization and post-independence attempts to modernize India. In "Postcards from Paradise," a poignant, slow-paced song, Chee, who is from South India, utters melancholic remembrances of the slum overlooked by his own housing area: [18]

> So two gods can't live in the same alley, side by side,
> Religious riots, firebrands scar a black night,
> Flashback to a past life.
> Fatehgunj Housing sphere's overlooking thatch and shoddy made
>   dung huts,
> Shantytowns sprout then, stick out like gout.
> Politicians talkin' 'bout "forward progress NOW,"
> So these beautiful folks had their huts burned to the ground

Though developers burned down the slum houses, Chee finds that the residents are resilient, coming up like a "rose grows through cracks of concrete."

But genius lies in all things simplified,
They'd take cow shit, mixed it with grass, a few twigs,
Exposed to the sun, it hardened once plastered to a few bricks,
Add some sweat and you have a makeshift apartment . . .

Poor Indians use an innovative material, dried dung, to re-erect their homes, as is the case with my own paternal family in their village. These gritty images sully orientalist stereotypes, as Chee notes:

Follow the stark stench of humans, fume and disease,
Where my peoples get by simply on ritual beliefs,
It's steeped deep in what the British did before they flee,
Left more than just English literature, cricket, whiskey and tea;
Psychological damage, famines, but we managed,
'Cause even a rose grows through cracks of concrete,
And a lotus floats hope in the stream of the Ganges,
There's love here, but hate too, for that you can blame karma,
And nah, we just ain't Deepak Chopra and our famed martyr,
So why would you wanna travel any place farther?
You can come-leave-reassured, your world's a safe harbor,
So here it is, the picturesque postcard you chase after,
Complete with Taj Mahals, camels, and snake charmers.

Chee flashes back to a less popular British remnant than literature and cricket and the Chopra-like images tourists desire: the colonials left a legacy of conflict, with repercussions among American Hindus and Muslims today. Despite what remains of that day, Chee's India is far more varied and interesting than the one with snake charmers and Taj Mahals, which remain the backdrop of postcards from a "paradise" (or images in *National Geographic*) that this MC does not recall from his childhood.

Just as hip hop celebrates multiple aspects—artistry, creativity, perseverance—of Black life in America despite structural obstacles, Chee celebrates India in nonessentialist visions. His anti-orientalist portrait of the difficulties of daily life foregrounds the causes and consequences of conflict. Hip hop becomes the perfect vehicle for this lyrical analysis by artists who prefer to address national leaders concerned with liberation over the "Indian spirituality" that travelers seem intent on finding (see Prashad 2000). An-

While MC Chee Malabar creates racialized hip hop, he also performs for desi audiences. Photograph courtesy of Preston Merchant.

other MC, Vivek, also speaks of his bond with young and old Blacks by stressing the historical and political moorings of these groups. He simultaneously considers African and African American history as part of his own while also viewing Indian history as distinct.

The artists merge their historical knowledge with samples of political ideologies, including those of Marcus Garvey, Babylon, indentured servitude, imperialism, and Rastafarianism. While many American youths across races are unaware of past Third World radicalism, Martin Luther King Jr.'s visit to India, and international dialogues about liberation, Vivek wrote his senior thesis on the shared political ideologies of Martin Luther King Jr., Malcolm X, and Mahatma Gandhi.[19] Yuri Kochiyama, a Japanese American activist, spoke about the impact of Malcolm X, whose head she cradled when he was assassinated: "I think that most important is the impact he made about the awareness of . . . knowing oneself . . . and to know one's history, one's heritage. And then, to link it with politics" (1994: 131). As she further noted: "Malcolm said 'the struggle of Vietnam is the struggle of all third-world people,' capsulizing that Asian and third-world people's fight was against foreign domination, imperialism, and colonialism. He had great admiration for Mao and Ho Chi Minh" (133). The desi artists sampled Malcolm X's speeches on their albums as he indicted India's colonization by comparing it to slavery: "Excepting the African slave trade, nowhere has history recorded any more unnecessary bestial and ruthless carnage than the British suppression of the non-White Indian people" (quoted in Mullen 2004: xiii-xiv). The desi artists' conversations with their politically oriented Black peers re-create legacies of Afro-Asian dialogue. As Chairman Mao stated in a speech delivered in 1963, "I wish to take this opportunity, on behalf of the Chinese people, to express our resolute support for the American Negroes in their struggle against racial discrimination and for freedom and equal rights . . . I call upon the workers, peasants, revolutionary intellectuals, enlightened elements of the bourgeoisie, and other enlightened personages of all colours in the world, white, black, yellow, brown, etc., to unite to oppose the racial discrimination practiced by U.S. imperialism and to support the American Negroes in their struggle against racial discrimination."[20] Remixed strains of a former global radicalism, popular among Du Bois and Mao and later picked up by civil rights and Black Power activists (Mullen 2004), exist today in the music of desi artists. The artists know that Martin Luther King Jr. was moved by the words of Gandhi, the father of Indian independence. As King stated: "As I read, I became deeply fascinated by his campaigns of nonviolent resistance. As I delved deeper into the philosophy of Gandhi, my skepticism concerning the power of love gradually diminished, and I came to see for the first time its potency in the area of social reform" (quoted in D'Souza 2003: B7). Recounting his trip to India, King said: "We were looked upon as brothers, with the color of our skins as something of an asset. But the strongest bond of fraternity was the common cause of minority and colonial peoples in America, Africa, and Asia struggling to throw off racism and imperialism."[21] Black radicals were also influenced by the ordinary Indians in their lives, perhaps represented today by hip hop's desis. Angela Davis, in her compelling autobiography, writes of her friendship with Lalit, a foreign exchange student: "It was my friendship with Lalit more than anything else, I supposed, that helped me understand concretely the interconnectedness of the freedom struggles of peoples throughout the world." As Lalit described the "incredible misery of his people in India," Davis writes, "I found myself constantly thinking about my people in Birmingham, my people in Harlem" (1988: 120). Some Asian Americans at the turn of the twenty-first century not only learn from and sample these exchanges but also continue the legacy of Afro-Asian activism.

Desi artists also cull diasporic cultural and spiritual crossovers among, for example, Indians in Kenya and Uganda or African Sidis in western India (see Baker, Diawara, and Lindeborg 1996; Hawley 2004). Thrice-displaced South Asian and African migrants to England in the latter part of the 1900s created hybridized music that emphasized Black British experiences (Gilroy 1993; Sharma, Hutnyk, and Sharma 1996; Hutnyk 2000; Hyder 2004). In the United States, this is beginning to take shape in the burgeoning bhangra scene, in desi hip hop, and in mainstream hip hop's appropriation of South Asian styles and songs (see chapter 5). Like their British compatriots some desis are fans of reggae music; these artists find that its sonic resistance parallels that of hip hop. Deejay Bella and, to a lesser extent, Vivek, were entrenched in the Bay Area reggae scene and felt connected to Caribbean Islanders as fellow diasporic peoples with cultures and roots in another homeland. Reggae also represents Indians from the Caribbean who identify with their island nations without affiliating much with Indians from the subcontinent. These various South Asian youths in America have affinity for reggae and Rastafarianism and also find value in strains of Afrocentric thought expressed in nation-conscious rap. The multicultural production of these forms parallels the artists' music- and identity-making processes. Such diasporic knowledges illustrate a broad conception of community that informs new identities and social formations that the rappers, DJs, and producers express through music.

The British Asian performer Apache Indian creates bhangra-muffin music (influenced by reggae and bhangra) and, like hip hop's desis, gives shoutouts to revolutionaries ranging from Gandhi to Bob Marley (Lipsitz 1994: 131). Like Wang, George Lipsitz warns against overly celebratory interpretations of intercultural mixing, but he also emphasizes that "the very existence of music demonstrating the interconnectedness between the culture of immigrants and the culture of their host country helps us understand how the actual lived experiences of immigrants are much more dynamic and complex than most existing models of immigration and assimilation admit" (119). And just as "popular music affirms the positive qualities of the unity forged in part by negative experiences with British racism" (128), hip hop affirms the shared experiences of South Asians with Blacks in the United States. It also affirms their extranational ties. Some of the artists have been to the Caribbean with their friends from the islands and know of the possible links between Indian *sadhus* (holy men) and Rastafarians in Jamaica. Prashad (2002) cites the possibility that it was from Indian workers that Rastafarians learned of dreadlocks and smoking ganga (itself a Hindi word for marijuana). Thus what we commonly know as "Black" is in fact composed of a variety of influences, just as desiness is created through intercultural exchange.

The mixed populations and cultures of places like Trinidad and Jamaica express the artists' own affinities and musical passions and they pay attention to innovative musical crossings outside the United States. Energized by the established bhangra and Asian music scene in London, the politicized rapping of British Asian groups like FunDaMental and Asian Dub Foundation is inspiring to the artists' own processes. Chutney soca, an "Indianized" form of African soca music in Trinidad, is yet another example of what emerges at the nexus of South Asian and Black remixing (see Manuel 2006; Niranjana 2006), and in their own context desis in hip hop elaborate the sonic parallels of hip hop and bhangra music. Sammy, a Punjabi who lives and runs Rukus Avenue Records in Southern California, describes how the bass in hip hop echoes the dhol drum used in his native music (he incorporates both in his musical productions). "Bhangra," says Dinesh, a Nepali whose best friend is a biracial Black and White man, "was so much like hip hop it was great and [it] led to community camaraderie."[22] But as Hyder notes, desis in hip hop, like South Asian bands in Britain, "have not simply transported traditional sounds from the Indian subcontinent and relocated them to the UK but have adapted and transformed them to form part of the array of cultural influences that are experienced and negotiated in their everyday lives." These syncretic musical forms across the South Asian diaspora "reflect and inform the expression of contemporary expressions of ethnicity and identity" (2004: 151; see also Gopinath 1995). Hip hop desis, however, are prone not to create "remix music," or a fusion of hip hop beats with Indian lyrics, and "ethnic hip hop" would not fall under this category either. Instead, it is important to the artists that they maintain the familiar sonic and rhythmic format of hip hop while incorporating multiple influences into their lyrics, thereby injecting desi perspectives into a recognizably Black art form.

Because of this choice, audiences often think that desi rappers like Chee and Rawj "sound Black." The writer Judy Tseng responds similarly to the Chinese American MCs Mountain Brothers because their "lyrics do not explicitly refer to an Asian American identity, but instead present a critique of society from a perspective shared by other people of color" (2007). Desis who share this critique create "racialized hip hop," a subgenre that incorporates rhymes about allegedly "Black" issues, including an analysis of structural and institutional forces that affect minorities, from prison and poverty to politics and policing. In this case, the artists use it to uncover racism and oppression that affects not only "their" (ethnic) group, but also its harm to others they consider family. They arrive at this perspective because the historical, political, cultural, and sonic links I have described impact the artists' *contemporary* identities as people of color.

Police brutality, so rare a topic among professional desis (even since 9/11), fills the texts created by the desi artists (see Omatsu 2000). One such example is D'Lo's poem, "Police Brutality" (1997), which begins with an event with a multiracial cast of characters playing baseball, America's favorite pastime, and joins it to past injustices. A police officer shows up in the midst of the event with another kind of bat in hand. As D'Lo flows:

Listeners heard the screams
and saw in the beams of light
the primary colors of
Red, Blue, Black and White
But no fight was put up,

They shut up.
As they saw Alicia and Rodney and
Poor lil' Abner
Get their bodies massacred.
It occurred to be a helpless situation
Of tribulation.
Scared adults
Protect themselves
From "Peace" officers.

D'Lo strings together the violence faced by Black and Brown, men and women: starting with Alicia Soltero, a Mexican woman beaten by police in Riverside, California, not far from the city where a few years earlier Rodney King was also beaten by police officers. D'Lo then sweeps to the East Coast in New York where the Haitian immigrant Abner Louima was assaulted and attacked by police officers in 1997. In considering these three victims as *a part of* rather than *apart from* those whom s/he considers "his/her people," D'Lo's activist efforts go hand in hand with his/her music. D'Lo was part of the Artists Network of Refuse and Resist and was active in the 911 anti-police brutality organization in defense of the imprisoned Black Panther Mumia Abu-Jamal. This poet has long been concerned about what happens to marginalized groups due to D'Lo's early experiences with racism and homophobia.

The rapper KB's verse in "Outcasted" clarifies how critical thinking about the past inflects the music of today's desi MCs. Further, hip hop is not just a vehicle for exposing hegemonic renditions of history that have become common sense; rather, it is the desis' vehicle to counter prevailing narratives by filling in the blanks and re(w)rapping history. Desi MCs sometimes become the rhyming griots that so influenced them in their youth. As KB firmly raps:

To all the menaces
Kicking their subtle prejudice,
Addressing us with stereotypical references.
And still oppressing us
By filling the syllabus
With lessons of how they got the best of us
In ancient fisticuffs.
Malicious messages taken from history texts

And such, are locked in mental prisons
For unprecedented sentences.
Supposedly what I'm supposed to be and what was meant for me,
Is told through the odyssey
Of my ancestry.
Instead, I choose to separate
Destiny and heredity
And bomb everybody's perception of our identity.
By dropping these intellectual properties
With prophesies
To challenge the traditional inequalities of men.
So, if the world remembers me
Then hopefully they'll let it be my legacy.
You'll have properly pushed pens.

In some ways KB's rhymes are both a lyrical reflection and extension of his critical consciousness. Growing up in Richmond in the
1970s and 1980s, he was aware of "subtle prejudice" and was later
profoundly shaped by the incident in college in the 1990s, related
in chapter 1, of being called a "rotten coconut." He illustrates the
shifts in racism as it changes its skin while its inner workings stay
the same. How other desis read KB and how the media depicts South
Asians make him question the limitation that "what I'm supposed
to be and what was meant for me" is circumscribed by "the odyssey of my ancestry." He took classes in college that taught him of
"malicious messages taken from history texts," which spurred him
to create his own major detailing how strongly the media shapes
"people's perceptions of our identity." The desire by KB to understand the world and its inequalities, the courses he took in college,
and his embrace of message rap are representative of the other artists who also aim to drop "intellectual properties with prophesies
to challenge the traditional inequalities of men," although he does
not include women in this line. Like the others, he "choose[s] to
separate destiny and heredity," squashing master narratives as his
"legacy."

These examples of racialized hip hop aim to build bridges, which
is rare within communities that tend to disidentify with Blacks.
The artists also came face to face with the global events that hardened interminority rifts. The aftermath of 9/11 revealed the struc-

tural links between Blacks and South Asians, but it has also entrenched discourses that naturalize group difference that divide South Asians, Arabs, and Blacks (see Maira 2006). In the realignment of racial politics following 9/11 some Blacks have banded together with other Americans against "Muslim-looking peoples," the new target of racial profiling and unfair detention practices. The artists use hip hop in this changing racial climate to remind others what they have long been stating: that discrimination, racial profiling, and incarceration affect all groups and not just one.

Post-9/11 Links and Racial Realignments: "Soundtrack to the Brown Experience"

Since 2001, Black and Brown people have both reaffirmed and severed their relations.[23] After 9/11 the responses at the state level and more generally to people from the Middle East and those mistaken for them, including the South Asians in this project, reflect the consolidation of the longer-term racial projects (Omi and Winant 1994)—namely, *global* racial projects—that homogenize members of these groups as fundamentalist non-Christians and terrorists. This in effect solidifies their status as different, if not dangerous, foreigners in the minds of many Americans. Hindu Indians in the wealthy suburb of Fremont, California—also home to numerous South Asian computer industry millionaires and some desi artists—responded negatively to their conflation with Muslims by posting American flags on their doorways and by stating, "We are not Muslims, we are not the enemy." The post-9/11 moment also distinguishes South Asians from both East Asians and the category of "Asian American" and has led to the rise of a new and specific Brown referent distinct from that of Latinos. The racial profiling, detention, and hate crimes that targeted these individuals coincided in particular ways with the long-term and well-documented experiences of American Blacks. However, it distinguishes Brown youths from Blacks as the state imputes their bodies with different, but overlapping, meanings.

Although anti-Muslim sentiment has a long history in the United States, South Asians are no longer shielded by their pre-9/11 invisibility and racial ambiguity. Negative responses to Brown people and the wars in the Middle East that now include South Asia have been painful muses for the artists, some of whose lives have altered during this time. Hate crimes and surveillance create dissonance with the formerly "positive stereotypes" of this "model" group, protecting not even those who attempt to distance themselves from Muslims. Orientalism has reared its head to cast those who "look like terrorists" as threats to the nation that must be expelled, "disappeared," and stopped (Fernandes 2006). According to the theory of racial triangulation (Kim 1999, 2003), shifts in the status of one group affect the status of others; we see this in the racialization of "Muslim-looking" people, whereby their demonization reinforces White superiority. It may not raise the status of Blacks in the eyes of White Americans, but their attention is temporarily displaced from Blacks. At the same time, a new (Brown) target may make fervent patriotism appeal to those Blacks who bond with other anti-immigrant Americans.

Since 9/11 and the ensuing wars in Afghanistan and Iraq, the artists have been self-conscious about others reading them as Middle Easterners. Some, particularly those who live in New York City, have had to reckon with police misconduct. These MCs, including Chee, D'Lo, AbstractVision, and Humanity (the latter two of whom are Muslim men), have transformed trauma into fodder for their art. Because they are aware of past histories and the injustices faced by Blacks (i.e., they understand how "race" operates through racism), they attribute their harassment to the same mechanisms of surveillance, incarceration, and state-sanctioned violence.

Himalayan Project's second and third albums, *The Middle Passage* and *Wince at the Sun*, reflect Chee and Rainman's concern with America's wars abroad and the rising anti-Muslim and South Asian xenophobia at home. Generally disturbed by American politics, Chee turns his words into sound bombs "of scuds whizzin' past an Arab's tunic." The song "Rebel Music" is about both targeting politicians and defining commonalities among oppressed groups. In an angry yet earnest voice, Chee responds to naysayers who do not believe in the existence of politicized and informed rappers:

Someone once said, America's a Melting Pot,
The people at the bottom get burned,
While the scum always seem to float to the top,

Ack, send seven shots from glocks at Trent Lott,
They ain't upset that he said it, they mad he got caught,
Might as well use the constitution as toilet tissue,
'Cause ain't shit changed since 1964, duke.
De-facto segregation exists, dissident voices, diluted then muted,
Through the strategic placements of polls and voting booths, and
Since we don't sit, where decisions get made,
I wouldn't piss on a burning bush to extinguish the flames,
Axis of evil, Jihad and crusades, so who's sane? (Hussein),
Saddam got napalm and thangs, while we build nukes, talkin'
    disarmament.
To you my religion is seen as voodoo,
Fuck you, I'll consider Christ when your pope is Desmond Tutu.

As with D'Lo, Chee's community is a broad one—spatially, racially, and temporally. He locates this war within a longer trajectory of global and national racisms against non-Whites. Chee identifies

Album courtesy of Chirag Menon.

with India (the country from which he migrated), crosses religious lines by denouncing anti-Muslim hatred (he is not a Muslim), and expresses his anger through the voices of notable Black figures, such as Malcolm X, on his albums.

The performers' ideological links between the past and present and between global and local politics stem from interactions with the state that link their bodies — resuscitated by historical orientalist stereotypes as dangerous fundamentalist others — to the "War on Terror." Artists like Chee also go a step further to point out racial crossovers, as Chee does in the song "Silent Scream":

> . . . as the cops lurked the station
> Searchin' for a brown-faced cajun
> Baggin Arabs, blacks and South Asians

On his solo rapping project *Oblique Brown*, produced by Zeeb, Chee zeroes in on the harassment he faced in New York City. He recounted to me how his mother urged him to at least place a sticker of the American flag on his car since he would not agree to shave his goatee. She was afraid that the police and others would mistake him for a "Muslim." They did. In the title track "Oblique Brown," Chee draws from the response of one police officer who pulled him over:

> "What! Hold on Osama, don't be so near sighted"
> Before I snatched the ticket, the cop got excited,
> Clutched his glock and screamed, "Don't even budge bitch"
> Thought he'd call Tom Ridge to tell him "flip the color switch."
> A white boy rock a beard, he's considered rugged
> And if I sport one, I'm a threat to the public,
> "What you got in the trunk? Any guns, drugs explosives?"

Sarcastically, Chee responds, "Nope, got some cd's though you can keep as coasters!" The rapper interprets the situation through the framework of racial profiling:

> Yup, guess I'm America's worst nightmare,
> 'Cause I'm young, brown and look Middle Eastern, yea
> "Now get out the car, hands up knees on the floor!"
> I said, "My sister went to Seton Hall I know about the law"
> He's like, "Dude, your face is probable cause!"

The officer assumes that similar-looking people must share characteristics, in this case a penchant for terrorism. Calling upon his educated sister does not help his case. Racial profiling, which usually leads to arrest for the "offense" of "Driving While Black," now targets those "Driving/Flying While Brown."

As the song moves on it links unjust policing to a lineage of migration for exploitable labor and the war in Iraq.

> Wonderin' why, we crossed the dark waters,
> With its past: slavery, exploitation, slaughter . . .
> (Laughin') Laughin' and treatin' us like savages
> But America's built on inhumane pain
> And I bet you felt safe when the FOX news came,
> "Uday and Qusay Hussein Slain"

Mainstream discourses such as those on the FOX news network lump Chee's Brown face with those of Hussein's murderous and executed sons. His identity is slippery both in his self-identification and in how others position him. It means that although he is not a Muslim, institutional power may act upon him on the basis of phenotype as if he were. However, Chee and the others did not have to wait until a particular incident exposed them to these injustices firsthand—they knew this well before 2001 because they saw and heard about such things from their young Black friends. The tentacles of the law enforcement apparently "Protect (some) and Serve (others)," thereby inhibiting the mobility of multiple Americans (see Gilmore 2007), and not just Blacks. And Chee also recognizes how various non-White groups become affiliated with race-specific crimes while Whites grant themselves humanity and heterogeneity despite the terrorists among them:

> If you black you sell crack, if you brown you down buildings,
> Timmy McVeigh did the same shit, Y'all killed him
> But you ain't trample the rights of your white civilians
> Didn't harass 'em or ask 'em for Passports, Visas,
> Didn't freeze their assets, no search no seizures.

Underlying this vamped up state of surveillance was a religious president who conjured the very system of othering: he decried the practices of "non-Christian fundamentalists" while he prayed in the oval office.

While Bush is up on stage, quotin' Jesus,
While the sons of the slums cuffed up on trumped charges,
'Cause we look different, talk different, labeled as Jihadists

Chee's organic intellectualism takes root in a particular world-view that weaves together war, religion, migration, racialization, policing, and capitalism. In his analysis, the interdependence of this ecosystem underlies the global dominance of the United States; White supremacy is the root of inequality. He nestles his individual experiences as a Brown immigrant male growing up with a diversity of friends on the West Coast and living as a Muslim-looking adult in millennial New York within these macro-level processes. They shape his sense of self, as he raps in his song "Malawho": "Brown man in a White world, live it through Black music."

Conclusion

Some desi hip hoppers who grew up with Blacks and lived in Black neighborhoods come to identify as minorities and understand race politics within a White versus non-White framework. They merge aspects of ethnicity that they feel strongly about with models of racial pride expressed among their Black friends that exemplify a resistant response to racism. Yet all of the hip hop desis understand that while they can take on some of the perspectives of Blackness, they do not claim a Black identity. They are drawn to sample from various sources, in part due to the liminality of South Asians as neither Black nor White, which emphasizes to them the fluidity of categories. Some desis harness this ambiguity productively through strategic essentialism and strategic anti-essentialism. Informing these strategies are the multiple global-historical connections between diasporic South Asians and Blacks that the artists actively uncover. This knowledge infuses their rhymes.

Current events, particularly those following 9/11, illustrate the artists' perspectives that the past is implicated in the future. They find that power relations historically produce contemporary practices, such as the policing and profiling of non-Whites and other forms of unjust state violence upon Black and Brown bodies. Desis in hip hop consider Blacks and South Asians as neither oppositional nor distant groups. Past and present historical, cultural, religious, and political connections increase the artists' bond with Black peers and their commitments to broader international communities. While they are committed to their ethnic communities on their own terms, they also continue their work as culture brokers *across* constructed color lines by producing racialized hip hop.

This ethnography highlights the role of racism in South Asian American lives. Race-focused studies analyze power and inequality that powerful groups inscribe institutionally within past and present societal structures. This approach is also a defining feature of the music made by desi hip hop artists, who highlight structural and historical relations. Motivated by racism, the performers understand structural relations due to their study of history and institutional power, and therefore they see their connection and relationality with another uniquely racialized group. They highlight the paradox central to Mixed Race studies scholarship that, in the words of Williams, "identity formation is complex, interactive, and ever-evolving, yet racial designations have been created and employed to simplify, sort, and rank individuals into fixed, exclusive categories" (1996: 202). These desis use hip hop to shift from racial categorization to political identification that transcends insular identities based on identity politics. Alterity, instead of primordial or blood ties, may form the basis of emerging multiracial communities. As Jan Weisman notes: "The continued adherence to such [a nonblood-based] identity by a steady or increasing number of individuals can in fact lead to the societal recognition of such new forms of identification" (1996: 158). Desis who remind us of the interplay of agency and structure actively create new panethnic and pan-racial communities in the United States rooted in social justice.

Biological understandings of race hold that race predetermines behavior, whereas hip hop desis understand race as a social process that they can contest. Race is not so predetermining as to limit or erase agency (Giddens 1984). Given their racial ambiguity, South Asians have room to identify across constructed and material differences, taking advantage of the space between constraining structural forces and their individual agency. They sometimes use essentialist racial conceptions, which can slip into dangerous reifications of the notion of race as real (Lipsitz 2007: 43), in their attempt to offer something more complex in their rhymes. Hip hop's desis harness the productive power of community building through creative and collaborative musical relations. Music is central to identity production and it has the ability to unite seemingly disparate individuals through lyrics and beats that speak to common experiences (Frith 1996: 111). As Hyder states, "Although music arouses a sensual pleasure on the part of both the listener and performer, it is also a means of cultural dialogue; a medium through which issues of politics and identity can be articulated and developed" (2004: 32). Hip hop is the form through which the desi artists shore up alternatives to essentialist and insular identity politics as they perform new knowledges that merge ethnic and racial identifications across time and space. They inform listeners of silenced histories that link Blacks and South Asians and that become foundational to pan-racial identifications.

3.

Flipping the Gender Script

Gender and Sexuality in South Asian
and Hip Hop America

> Because, though I am Tamil,
> I am silver piercings
> Am hip-hop
> Am boy
> Am bald
> —D'Lo, male-identified queer MC and poet
>
> Discourse can be both an instrument and an effect of power, but also a hindrance, a stumbling-block, a point of resistance and a starting point for an opposing strategy. Discourse transmits and produces power; it reinforces it, but also undermines and exposes it, renders it fragile and makes it possible to thwart it.—Michel Foucault, *The History of Sexuality*

America's differential and relational sexualization of Asians and Blacks over time has shaped contemporary gender and sexual politics within desi and hip hop America—communities that frame the everyday dynamics between South Asian and Black men and women. This chapter examines how desi hip hoppers contend with the gender and sexual norms of the various communities to which they belong. Desi performers create new second-generation identities by sampling ethnic and racial influences, and they draw from a range of gender and sexual identities as well. Sex, love, and music are linked in the artists' lives as they evaluate expectations, obligations, and passions: who they love crosses over with what they love; what they love is deeply implicated in who they love. My analysis of the engagement in hip hop by South Asians centers on their intimate and professional relationships with Black and South Asian men and women. The artists' desires and attempts to reconcile professional and romantic aspirations for love and art highlight the undertheorized impacts of Blacks on the formation of alternate desi gender roles and sexualities.

In extending my account of desis' disruption of ethnicity and innovative racial claiming, I analyze in this chapter how desi men and women negotiate the gender and sexual politics of hip hop, of mainstream society, and of their insular immigrant communities. I reveal how, or even whether, these men and women incorporate particular gendered and sexualized aspects of "Black culture" into their self-conceptions, and I show how this is accomplished in ways that may be surprising. I offer alternative interpretations to the existing literature on the appeal of hip hop for non-Blacks through my ethnographic account of non-Black and non-White, female and male, straight and gay hip hoppers. Theories developed about Whites and hip hop do not apply equally to their Asian counterparts. The scholarship is often critical of Whites' desire for a racialized sexuality that expresses distanced and insincere complexes of fear and desire. Using this explanation, many Americans interpret Asian American men's interest in hip hop as a desire to overcome their emasculation. My examination of South Asian masculinity, however, troubles this move and rejects the conflation of desis with both Whites and East Asians.

Female artists, in particular, confront desi and Black notions of respectability along with misogyny and gender double standards (McBride 2005). Hip hop scholarship, in addition to overlooking Asians, has also paid inadequate attention to women, particularly non-Black women (cf. Rivera 2003; Chatterjee 2006; Nair and Balaji 2008). Black female scholars, many of them part of the hip hop generation, have foundationally recounted the presence of women in hip hop and illustrated how female artists, particularly rappers, challenge the sexual stereotypes of Black women. I too depict how women negotiate misogyny and sexism, and I highlight hip hop as a culture with empowering models for women's sexual agency, even for non-Blacks. Two of the desi female artists, one of whom is a gay MC and the other a heterosexual DJ, claim hip hop identities and clear the way for pro-womanist spaces within the predominantly Black, male, and straight world of the music industry, and they do this despite their marginalized gender, racial, and sexual statuses as Brown women in hip hop. Related to this, I address whether or not the male artists also partake in dismantling or maintaining gender hierarchies of oppression.

By culling insights from Hip Hop studies, South Asian American studies, and Afro-Asian studies I highlight in this chapter the role that Blacks play in contemporary sexual and gender formations of Asians in America. Analyses of South Asian and Black relations mediated by Black popular culture expand our understanding of Asian American gender roles, sexuality, and intermarriage with Whites (e.g., Espiritu 1997; Koshy 2004; cf. Hall and Turner 2001; Thornton and Gates 2001). The majority of the artists have been in romantic relationships with Black partners—including African Americans, Africans, and Caribbean Islanders—despite South Asians' anti-Black prejudices and parents' desires for cultural continuity. Racism and a love of hip hop frame the desi artists' professional and romantic choices and these converge in their emerging race consciousness. However, female and male artists reflect different relationship patterns that speak to the differential ways that gender intersects with sexuality among American South Asians.

The artists draw from sexual and gender references provided by their Black peers that are found within hip hop culture seemingly outside the repertoires of mainstream desis. They are often absent in research as well: ethnic studies literature on interracial relations privilege these populations' relations with Whites. The artists, like all Asians in America, forge their sexualities within the nexus of historical processes (e.g., immigration legislation) and ideologies (e.g., conceptions of Asians as sexual deviants). For instance, the desi women in this project are aware of their desirability by men across color lines. Their interactions in hip hop clubs with Black men who orientalize them and compare them with Black, rather than White women, for instance, reorient the factors that scholars have determined shape Asian Americans' and African Americans' self-conceptions of beauty, desire, and competition. However, I also distinguish between the American racialization of South Asians from East Asians as it impacts their sexual lives.

Analyzing the artists' negotiation of interracial relationships and the hip hop industry calls attention to interactions between South Asians and Blacks that, despite historical precedents, scholars have largely avoided (cf. Prashad 2001; Bald 2008). The lack of attention paid to Asian/Black relations, particularly sexual and romantic ones, insinuates their impossibility in our imaginings of racialized sexuality. Yet surely desi artists represent a larger cohort of Asian Americans who find models of sexuality and gender roles within Black popular culture and through their interactions with Blacks. Their experiences confound interpretations of "Asian American sexuality" as emasculated males attempting to access the virile hypersexuality of Black masculinity or as exotic Brown women who embark on rebellious escapades through temporary trysts with Black men. Instead, the complex negotiations between Black and Brown partners attempting to fulfill ethnic and racial obligations while pursuing musical passions highlight the veritable minefield of complex allegiances and expectations that push apart and pull together young Americans in a nation highly conscious of "difference." Ultimately, we find that the influences of Blacks and Black cultural formations upon the emergent identities of Brown youth extend beyond the realms of ethnicity and race, fear and desire.

These Are the Breaks:
Two Brown Women in a Black Male Business

I wanted a male perspective, so I asked a desi MC what he thought about the position of women in hip hop. "Wow," he said, which he followed with "um." He paused, but then stated, "Within hip hop, I think women have a very good place, a very solid place. Very good form for representation." For clarification I asked if he thought that women were already in hip hop or that there was the potential for women to be in hip hop. "I think they're there. The doors are open for them." At the same time, however, he acknowledged that "it's a very tough place for women to be in hip hop." And he went further to add, "I think a lot of women end up selling themselves into the stereotype"—referring to one conception of women in hip hop as sexually available. The women agree that hip hop is a very tough business for them especially when, as in the case of D'Lo, the female-born artist identifies and performs as a male. In our conversations the desi female artists and I ambled through dense thickets of gender, race, desiness, music, and sexuality only hinted at by this male MC. As women familiar with Black urban club culture and passionate about hip hop, we bonded by going together to concerts, clubs, and other events where we faced similar interactions with Black men and women.[1] We navigated and analyzed the complicated gender and sexual dynamics of this highly masculine and heteronormative culture.

Straight and gay South Asian female hip hoppers illustrate how the historical sexualization of Blacks and Asians in America informs the artists' musical passions and progression today. These women's conceptualizations of their range of sexual and gendered choices counter the more "traditional" thinking of fixed options within South Asian communities. While much literature on Asian American gender and sexuality either leaves out or assumes South Asian Americans, femininity within South Asian communities is viewed as something to be guarded and is tied to upholding respectable ethnic traditions and mores. Perhaps more neglected is desi masculinity, which is usually seen as both exceptional of Asian American manhood (i.e., not following the line of Asian American emasculation) or as typical (the emasculated South Asian tech worker or the comedic foreigner like Apu on *The Simpsons*) and tied to economic stability. In fact, hip hop provides sexual roles that resonate with these women who have few models of desi femininity available to them that speak to the United States–based context of their lives. Additionally, being a woman shapes their musical productions and has led to struggles in business interactions.

Their sampling and expressions of gender and sexuality are creative second-generation responses to the limitations of American, South Asian, and Black ethnic and racial politics. Despite the tricky maneuverings required by these dynamics, the strong gender identity and passion for music by Deejay Bella and by the poet-activist-MC D'Lo, the two female-born artists in my study, lead them to use Black popular music—putting their gender politics on the dance floors in club spaces—to intervene in male-dominated places. I intersperse their stories in the text of this chapter to illustrate how some artists negotiate the business while expressing desi gender and sexual identities that sample Black masculinities.

The hip hop industry promotes the commodification and sexualization of women, the idea of women as extraneous accessories, and heteronormativity. These ideas operate in and beyond the videos and lyrics of some kinds of commercial rap to infiltrate the experiences of women in all levels of hip hop. Hip hop historians and the culture's major players have silenced women's contributions by relegating them to a few token paragraphs in the extensive volumes of hip hop production (cf. Pough 2004, 2007; Sharpley-Whiting 2007). We see how gender and sexuality mediate the experiences of non-Blacks in a highly racialized domain; taking part in predominantly Black productions leads to unexpected racialized expressions of desi gender and sexuality. I begin my examination with a brief biography of the musical careers of Deejay Bella and D'Lo before detailing the gender politics of Brown women in a Black male dominant field.

The Technician, Deejay Bella: Marginality, Sexuality, Positivity

No one's listening to me . . . It's not right to work so hard and not go anywhere. Women are not seen as being bomb ass DJs blowing a party up.—Deejay Bella

Bella spins records for music-loving crowds, making them dance until the wee hours. In a phone conversation one night she told me that she wanted to meet more women in the business. She chatted about people's conceptions of DJs: "You think of a guy. I'm not the type, right! I'm sort of petite, right?" She laughed, "Nobody's going to carry my records for me," and then ended with an upbeat, "but it's all good." These devoted artists deal with overlapping and conflicting sets of expectations that are often brought together in their homes. Bella, a manager-level environmental engineer by day and a DJ in every other moment of her life, leads an exhausting schedule. Her home displays the signs of her true calling: there is no TV in her Oakland apartment, just hundreds of records stacked in crates from floor to ceiling across an entire wall of her living room, spilling into her walk-in closet, just as a professor's books might. Where there are no records, the walls are papered with famous reggae artists' autographed posters. Other walls are adorned with family photos, and as a strict vegetarian Bella has cleared a place for a *puja* (prayer) area in the kitchen. How did this suburbanite from Las Vegas become so involved in the Bay Area Black music scene?

Bella likely inherited her audiophilia from her father, a Gujarati immigrant who was a guitarist in a rock band in India. In the early 1970s he created a small studio in their Las Vegas home where Bella would play records as her father taped all his music on a reel-to-reel recorder. They "always had music," she noted, because her father listened to music while he worked. In addition, her mother listened to prayer music on the weekends, and Bella and her sister also danced the *garba* (an Indian dance from Gujarat). Mostly self-taught, she had figured out how to play the organ and then moved on to play the violin in elementary school. Then she began her own record collection with money she earned from babysitting. Bella's interests intersected with those boys at high school who shared her depth of knowledge and penchant for particular artists. After graduating from high school and heading to college in the early 1990s, she was also well on her way to becoming a hip hop and reggae aficionado—a niche that has captivated her interest for almost two decades. The investigative nature of her interest led to the evolution of her musical tastes. Always historicizing music, Bella says, "It's the roots of the music" that are important, as she searched for the original versions of songs not played on the radio, including punk, ska, reggae, and hip hop. Her sense of the power of music eventually deepened to become her life.

Like other artists from mostly White areas, Bella expanded her musical repertoire at the radio station at her Bay Area university. She became the station's promotions director and was responsible for reviewing music, arranging time slots, raising funds, and networking.[2] Venturing off campus, armed with her own pair of turntables, the sophomore began to volunteer at break beat sessions in an alcohol-free Black cultural space in East Oakland. She then became entrenched in the Oakland-Berkeley-San Francisco Black music scene, which was dominated by local producers, promoters, and DJs—most of whom were men.[3] Bonding with some of the prevailing DJs of the time who were doing a lot of "good political and social music work" helped her develop her own sound. As an

Deejay Bella, with a career spanning almost two decades, spins at a 4th of July event. Photograph courtesy of Deejay Bella.

accomplished DJ, who has now also produced and recorded original music, by 2000 Bella was a recognized member of the reggae/dancehall/hip hop scene and her name graced nightclub fliers and the events section of local papers. As she began to book her own gigs, this petite Brown woman had to find her place in an arena enmeshed with gender and racial politics.

D'Lo, the Crossover: Gay, Hindu, Hip Hop

Everything that I've ever done [in music] has been a *stru-g-gle*.
—D'Lo, poet, MC, activist

D'Lo is the only female-born desi artist in this project who produces and performs poetry and music for a living.[4] A mutual friend told me about this "female Sri Lankan MC" who had been the opening act for the political rapper Michael Franti and performed on Russell Simmons's Def Poetry Jam in 2003. I first met D'Lo in 2002 during a visit to New York City when s/he invited me to a spoken-word event organized by the 911 pro-Mumia anti-police brutality organization that s/he worked with ("nine-one-one, not nine-eleven," D'Lo clarified).[5] The MC's invitation, a return of an earlier page I had sent, went as follows: "Hey woman, why dontchu stop by? It's real casual and all. Just meet me there and we can kick it. There'll be some other desis there, too, so don't worry." (D'Lo later confided his/her relief that I wasn't what s/he thought I might be: the [mainstream] type who needed to be around other desis to feel comfortable.) I was surprised by his/her voice—s/he sounded "straight up like a hip hopper dude," I wrote in my field notes. I went so far as to rethink what I was wearing, worried that it might be overdressed and too feminine. But I kept on my dress and Indian wool shawl and headed on foot toward the Baptist church on 31st Street that cold October night. Inside, it was a laidback scene of about twenty people, mostly young and racially heterogeneous, including a few Blacks, a larger number of Whites and Filipinos, and four desis including D'Lo and myself.

Luckily, I had not missed D'Lo's performance. As s/he limped (s/he had just been in an accident) to the front of the audience, I was struck by his/her style: s/he looked like a boy. D'Lo seemed to be influenced by the geographic and racial context of his/her

D'Lo's multiple ambiguities force audiences to check their assumptions about race, gender, and sexuality. Photograph courtesy of Bernie DeChant.

youth, borrowing from the styles of Chicano and African American youths from Southern California. D'Lo wore what I learned was his/her uniform: super-baggy jeans, a T-shirt covered by an oversized plaid jacket buttoned only at the top (or, alternately, a baggy hooded sweatshirt) that hid any trace of his/her female body (or brand names), and black lace-up boots. Over his/her head, shaved bald as s/he mentions in the poem that opens this chapter, D'Lo sported a blue bandana, and s/he also had pierced ears and wore a nose ring. D'Lo claimed the stage, and our attention, with bold gestures and bolder statements. Boisterously cracking jokes with hip hop-inflected slang in a girlish drawl, s/he used sweeping arm gestures reminiscent of male MCs to emphasize his/her points. D'Lo crossed all kinds of boundaries and broke all kinds of expectations — racial, gender, and sexual. But I came to learn that underlying all of D'Lo's identities was his/her commitment to social justice through political activism and art, always infused with knowledge and comedy. With a brilliant smile, D'Lo commenced with an NYPD joke:

"Knock knock!"

We all replied, "Who's th . . . !"

"BAM!!!" s/he yelled before we could finish our response.

D'Lo's reference to the de facto police policy of "Shoot first, ask (questions) later" had the audience roaring with laughter. S/he was just as skilled in bringing his/her tenor of seriousness back to a low rumble. His/her three poems, told in a funktified L.A. drawl that seemed more girly than gritty (an issue s/he often joked about), were about the civil war in Sri Lanka, jazz and the depth of music, and the corruption within the Rampart Division of the LAPD.

D'Lo has been a student of music (and a jokester) his/her entire life: "The only thing in life that was constant was music." Similar to Bella, s/he took piano lessons, sang *bhajans* (devotional songs), and says s/he "loved me some hip hop" before s/he was a teen, in the 1980s. Although s/he lived just seventy-five miles north of Compton, California, where Black youths were producing gangsta rap, his/her access to hip hop in his/her predominantly White neighborhood was limited to watching *Yo! MTV Raps*. By the time s/he was a teenager, D'Lo had compiled a list of over two hundred rap artists. S/he began writing poetry, mostly about music, when s/he was around twelve years old. Modeling Sweet Tee, one of his/her favorite MCs, s/he soon began to write lyrics.

Self-taught like the other artists, D'Lo formed a female hip hop dance crew with South Indian, Pakistani, and Latina dancers who performed at parties and culture shows in high school (at that time, D'Lo identified as a gay woman). For D'Lo, hip hop was "never really a Black thing, or a White thing. It was a cultural thing and it's *youth*."[6] Hip hop helped him/her to contend with the racism that was "hard core" in his/her childhood, and it aided in his/her developing sexuality and gender identity. D'Lo conducted his/her own "cultural analysis" of music—and a new set of race relations—during his/her study abroad at Oxford University where s/he attended video school. Music again drew him/her into multiracial social situations: s/he began to take drum lessons and at night s/he would pop lock and take part in dance battles at hip hop clubs in London. In these venues s/he stood out, "because back then, in '95 even, you never used to see Indian people at hip hop clubs. You never saw Brown faces."[7] There probably were not many female battlers, either, let alone Sri Lankan girls who identified as bois. Heading back to the United States to attend University of California, Los Angeles, for ethnomusicology, D'Lo joined with a White Jewish girl to become the rapping duo Disturbing Silence that "fuckin' tore UCLA apart." As an androgynous-looking Brown woman performing Black popular music with a White woman, D'Lo disarmed audiences with his/her smile. S/he explains that s/he never "played the gay card"; instead, s/he and his/her partner presented themselves as "strong" rather than queer women in front of student organizations such as La Raza and for Black student audiences. Over time, however, D'Lo has crafted shows that force his/her viewers to contend with all of his/her counternormative crossings.

When I first met D'Lo s/he had graduated and moved to New York, where s/he was among the minority of women who had earned a certificate from the School of Audio Engineering. D'Lo became heavily involved with the Artist's Network's Refuse and Resist program against police brutality, as well as with their anti-war Not in Our Name protest. D'Lo was also active as an MC, hosting various South Asian shows such as Artwallah in Los Angeles and Diasporadics in New York. Performing at these festivals alongside desi male MCs like Chee Malabar, D'Lo's non-White queer masculinity diversified the range of desi masculinities performed onstage. D'Lo's presence stretches the options that desi audiences deem imaginable for themselves, as D'Lo claims a "gay, Hindu, [and] hip hop" space for him/herself (see Fajardo 2008). Prior to his/her current success as a solo actor, poet, lyricist, and comic performer, D'Lo had tried to learn the technical aspects of music production from male studio producers who were reluctant to show the trade to a woman. In spite of these difficulties, D'Lo is on the road to attaining his/her goal of working in a studio and producing tracks for hip hop artists.

Brown Women in a Black Male Field

The difficulty that desi women face in infiltrating the business is not solely due to racial dynamics; some of the desi men are able to make a mark by opening studios, starting record labels, and signing artists. Women's knowledge at least equals their male counterparts, and it is evident that sexism pervades these realms. As a product and reflection of the United States, hip hop is a male-dominated culture. The MCs in particular are mostly men; women, even Black women, tend to be rare among rappers, just as they are at freestyle battles and in the hip hop business at large. Hip hop scholars have detailed the challenges that women face as they attempt to make a name for themselves, especially given their relative lack of access to technology and the greater restrictions on their time (see Rose 1994; Kelley 1997; Pough et al. 2007). Additionally, both Black and White men in the industry promote women less, and female artists may lack access to male networks that could advance their careers while they also face sexual harassment. Brown women in hip hop face tensions and articulate contradictions that overlap with and diverge from those of both desi males and Black females in hip hop. In response, D'Lo and Bella act by engaging these groups through dialogue.[8]

Bella confronts a particular set of gender and sexual dynamics as a Brown female DJ in the Bay Area. Since our first encounter in the late 1990s, Bella and I have spent time together hanging out at our homes, attending social events, and going to numerous clubs where we partied and I was able to see her work. When I asked her how people react to her as a female DJ, she stated: "As a DJ period, they listen, they respect." She reflects on the positives and negatives when she remarks, "Nice guys come up to me, surprised, and a lot of good comments, too. Flirted a lot with on the bad side." Sexual politics intersect with gendered dynamics when Bella experiences the paternalism of male club owners, promoters, and other DJs who are surprised that she is technically skilled, knowledgeable about the music, and has such a large selection of records. She feels like she is "constantly proving" herself, and although she tries not to "waste that energy and [instead] focus on playing," it sometimes feels like having a "stack of cards against you." As in many aspects of American business, women in hip hop need not only have the skills of their male counterparts; Bella and other female DJs like Spinderella and Kuttin Kandi also need to work especially hard to gain the respect of and recognition from fellow professionals. According to Rachel Raimist, the creator of a documentary on female MCs, "As a woman in hip-hop you have to struggle that much more, constantly having to prove yourself, fight for respect, and strive to be taken seriously" (2004: 62). The experiences of Bella and D'Lo link them to their predecessors in hip hop herstory, including Roxanne Shante, Queen Latifah, and MC Lyte, all of whom had to negotiate similar dynamics.

Misogyny has a concrete and much contested place in hip hop and takes center stage in academic debates about this culture. However, desi female fans and producers, like Black women, must grapple with misogynist lyrics and sexist attitudes in their everyday work lives and feel silenced and reduced to sexual beings by men in the industry. Bella interacts with a variety of people across genres of music. The Bay Area reggae and dancehall scene, for example, is led by DJs and promoters whose families came from South Africa, Nigeria, the Republic of Congo, and Jamaica, as well as by local White American DJs. In contrast, the hip hop scene is made up of a different set of people, mainly African Americans, but still incorporates a range of styles. The sonicscapes that Deejay Bella occupies exemplify the multidimensionality of Black musical worlds, especially in the multiracial mecca of northern California, yet men still predominate. Many accept Bella, but she still faces solitude. Both in her science and her music work, men sometimes attempt to usurp her authority by reducing her to her sexuality. Men have often portrayed women in hip hop in one of two ways: the sexually available vixen/ho (e.g., Lil' Kim) or the potentially gay artist/dyke (e.g., Da Brat) (Raimist 2004: 62). As Bella says in frustration, "I'm a little person and everyone looks at me and says, 'You're my boss?' . . . People can just think I'm gay, if that's how they rationalize it."[9] The politics of being non-Black and female intersect with the generally progressive sexual politics of the Bay Area and its large presence of gays and lesbians. This nexus places alternative sexualities at the front and center of numerous interpersonal exchanges. I asked D'Lo, who at the time placed his/her identity as a gay woman who identified as a boi front and center of his/her performances, how s/he felt about misogynist elements. D'Lo responded, "Yeah, but that's just one part. I love this shit . . . There has to be changes somewhere, but meanwhile, let's make something new so that there's that alternative."

As Tricia Rose argues: "Rap music and video have been wrongfully characterized as thoroughly sexist but rightfully lambasted for their sexism" (1994: 15). Mark Anthony Neal further notes that "despite popular belief, hip-hip is *not* the most prominent site of

sexism and misogyny" (2005: 146) and, Neal includes, homophobia, given that its producers live in a society that engenders these
same "values." Bella's engagement in the worlds of science, music,
and local desi circles frames her interpretation of sexism, paternalism, and gender dynamics as systemic and societal rather than
defining them as "hip hop" or "Indian" cultural phenomena. After
all, so much of the criticism directed at Black urban youths and
their cultural expressions scapegoat hip hop for societal products
such as sexism, for instance, in place of a sustained and structural
analysis of heterosexual male privilege in a racialized nation (Morgan 2000; Collins 2004; Pough 2004; Chatterjee 2006; Sharpley-
Whiting 2007). This diversion is propped up by media depictions
that reduce "hip hop" to its most commercialized, basest representations, including stereotypical and repeated images of Black
men and women. Mainstream conglomerates profit from pimping
stereotypes and seducing Americans to partake in mindless consumption. This is done partially for sales and to distract Americans
from urgent matters including wars at home (on the poor, for example) and abroad. This is not to say that rappers, from the super-
star to the everyday variety, should advocate sexism and homophobia, or excuse them when they do. But it provides a broader context
within which to read the gender and sexual dynamics in hip hop.

Extending an analysis of sexism beyond the actions of men in hip
hop to hear the voices of women, including desis, whose lives are
shaped through hip hop illustrates the complexities of gender relations (see Pough 2004; Neal 2005). As Neal, a proponent of Black
feminist manhood, remarks, "Rarely do we discuss how women use
hip-hop to articulate their view of the world, a view that may or may
not be predicated on what the men in hip-hop (or their lives) might
be doing" (2005: 158). Beyond this, imagine what we discover when
we listen to non-Black and gay women who use hip hop to form and
express alternative and sampled identities.

Black popular culture imprints upon the emerging consciousness
of Bella and D'Lo, along with the Bay Area radio producer Asma,
who apply the insights they gain from hip hop to their analyses
of American society. Just as they and their desi male counterparts
locate racism as a structural and historical process, these women
understand sexism and patriarchy to be phenomena that are both in
and beyond hip hop culture because of their encounters with these

practices in multiple circles. Radhika is a hip hop fan and organic farmer who has worked on community garden projects with people coming out of jail in the predominantly Black Bayview area of San Francisco. As a woman who is Bengali and White, Radhika indicts the racist scapegoating of hip hop when she states that heavy metal bands "have all the same misogyny and nobody wants to talk about that." These women take hip hop to task for perpetuating negativity while contextualizing antiwomanist sentiments within a societal framework.

Desi women in hip hop come to question its male and masculine norms not only through their relations with Black men but with Black women as well. Black female MCs from the 1980s were formative to the self-conceptions of young desi girls in love with music and learning to love themselves. D'Lo loved "all the female MCs," and his/her favorites include the hip hop pioneers Sweet Tee, Cookie Crew, and MC Trouble. Hip hop fans and foes alike debate in too simplified a manner the role that women play in their own oppression. Desi girls, who often had access to only one generation of female elders, drew from the range of sexpressions among Black female rappers, including the pro-woman, proud Afro-centric Queen Latifah; the hard-core MC Lyte who could lyrically smash any dude; TLC, the safe-sex rhyming trio; and Lil' Kim and Foxy Brown, who proclaim as much right to their sexual liberty as the men who diss or desire them. Those hip hop heads who grew up in multiracial communities were drawn to nondesi and non-White expressions of sexuality virtually absent in the literature on Asian American youth. Just as their ethnic alienation turns them toward race-central worldviews, the gender restrictions within South Asian diasporic communities direct them toward alternative modes of expression. The particular intersectionality of the racial and gender identities of desi women in hip hop marks their experiences as unique from and overlapping with hip hop's other participants (Collins 2000).

Sexism encourages desi women to find allies with Black women and their shared experiences in hip hop. This includes the issue of how to be true to one's minority and female status simultaneously, which leads to the development of female cooperatives or networks that help protect them in the business. Bella, who finds it difficult to meet other women involved in hip hop, creates women-centered networks by hosting events and spinning at parties hosted by female DJs. D'Lo's position, on the other hand, disrupts an understanding of his/her position strictly in terms of being a woman because as a boi s/he sometimes employs a "male" perspective in explaining why s/he enjoys surrounding him/herself with women. "I was a boi. I *loved* women anyway, you know what I'm sayin? I'm gay. I like to have women around me." D'Lo's public presence as a boi-identified gay Sri Lankan pries open hip hop as a male-dominated site of hegemonic Black masculinity, particularly in his/her role as an MC—a role generally occupied by men (Fajardo 2008: 419). At times, D'Lo takes the stage next to male MCs as an embodiment of alternative masculinity, but at other times s/he faces men who treat him/her unlike "one of the boys." Thus, the unconventional gender, sexual, and racial identities of desi female artists also bring them into conflict with other groups.

Some Brown female hip hoppers feel marginalized and treated unfairly by both Black women *and* men in the industry: some do not get paid for their gigs, are dropped from the lineup of performers, or feel that promoters do not communicate fairly with them. Although they usually celebrate other women's achievements and build community with them, at times desi women are frustrated when they compare themselves with their peers whose careers seem to advance. One artist feels that Black women are not inclusive in music, which heightens her sense of invisibility. Some also face harassment—even physical intimidation as other women in the business also face—and in club spaces alcohol can lead to tense encounters. A desi woman was hired by a promoter to spin records at a "party for lesbians" in the Bay Area. Upon her arrival, however, the DJ realized that the crowd was in fact not a gay one (for which her record selection for the night was geared) but rather the regular heterosexual weekend audience. During the course of the event, a young Black patron, frustrated with the music, threw her drink over the DJ's equipment. The desi artist, who said she "dealt with this shit before," felt set up by the promoter and analyzed the altercation as an unfolding drama of the intersection of race, gender, and sexual politics. She pointed to a number of her identities that, within the context of a heterosexual Black nightclub, was reread as nonnormative: "I'm sure part of it is that I'm Indian, I looked gay, I wasn't playing enough rap." The DJ held a relatively "powerful" status as music selector within a setting in which Blacks often set the terms. The DJ interpreted the patron's dissatisfaction with the music choices as a signal of the patron's dissatisfaction, too, with the DJ's "deviant" identities, combining to make desi female artists sometimes uncomfortable in their roles in the hip hop business.

These conflicts are the exception, yet it is nonetheless virtually impossible to be a woman in hip hop and remain unaware of the gender and sexual politics at play. For desi female performers, sometimes the odds seem to be stacked against them. As one artist said in frustration, "I should go for a woman's field. What's a woman's field? Rape counseling, I should work with abused girls." And although the artists do give their time to progressive causes, none can leave music; indeed, above all other identities it is music that defines them. Music moves each artist in ways that cannot be described through words and intellectual analyses. In turn, they each wish to move their audiences.

When young desi women enter the hip hop scene as participants, they enter a predominantly Black social field with few models for understanding their position as non-White, non-Black artists. Over time, DJs and MCs like Bella and D'Lo see that their experiences merge with those of other females attempting to gain distribution and attract wider audiences while contending with sexism, sexual advances, and homophobia. At other points where the racial outsider status of desis subsumes their gender status, Black and Brown women are at odds. Desi artists and the tricky orchestrations that they describe contribute to the conversations in hip hop studies scholarship that thus far largely implies a Black audience and focuses on the relationships between young Black men and women of the hip hop generation. Some scholars and journalists have become attuned to the silencing and mistreatment of women in hip hop. We can reflect even more on the problems and promises of hip hop culture when we understand how non-Black, female, and non-straight participants contend with potent exchanges that play out in clubs and within the hip hop business at large.

These dynamics are part of the game, however, and the artists, having spent a good portion of their lives in these spaces, learn to negotiate them and even carve out spaces in which to voice their own identities alongside the range of their Black peers who cohabit hip hop's social landscapes. In fact, the lessons learned by desis about the implications of gender and sexuality impact their music and their relationships with Blacks, as does their racial and ethnic difference. Tense and productive exchanges emphasize to desis the meaningfulness of differences, and they infuse their music with this sense of commonality and distinction. Artists like D'Lo and Bella, despite their double marginalization as non-Black women, continue to manage their frustrations and work independently and consistently. Because they live for music, they contend with these complexities and occupy spaces "in the middle"—between and across communities, identities, and expectations. However, their membership in ethnic communities often operates under a different set of gender expectations than those in hip hop, thus requiring the artists to expend equal amounts of emotional effort. Hip hop's desis once again check our assumptions of sameness and difference with regard to gender and sexual mores across communities.

Negotiating Gender Roles in Desi America, Expressing Sexuality through Hip Hop

Oh, I know that when Neil will grow older, he will appreciate and he will realize how beautiful our culture is.—Indian mother's voiceover on "Neil," Karmacy Track

But she knew enough not to go . . .
Knew that, over there, bald heads were for
bad people turned pious   or just bad people
and bad people are ugly
coz hair always matters.
And these bald women had to wait   as punishment   to
     slowly become beautiful.
And she? She re-shaved her head once every week   And waiting to
     do it   Was punishment.
—D'Lo, "From Silent Confusion to Blaring Healing"

In his/her performance of the poem "From Silent Confusion to Blaring Healing," a Brown, bald, boyish D'Lo flips the gender script by calling attention to the differential (de)valuation of the bald head in transnational perspective. In Sri Lanka a shaved head is imposed upon outcastes, such as widows, to mark their pariah status; in

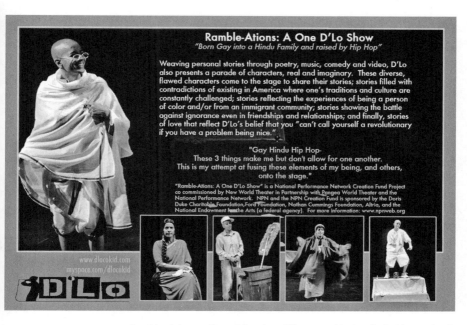

Ramble-Ations, a "one D'Lo show," features skits in which D'Lo embodies a number of roles including Gandhi and his/her Amma (mother). Flier courtesy of Pilar Castillo.

the United States, D'Lo willingly shaves his/her head to represent his/her inner self. Instead of sidestepping the factors that mark him/her as different, D'Lo engages with these dynamics up front through comic and political self-expression. D'Lo has been touring the nation with his/her show "Ramble-Ations: A One D'Lo Show." [10] The subhead on the promotional material for the show reads, "Born gay into a Hindu family and raised by Hip Hop." And the text further proclaims, "Gay Hindu Hip Hop—These 3 things make me but don't allow for one another. This is my attempt at fusing these elements of my being, and others, onto the stage." As a boi born in a woman's body, D'Lo performs complex gender and sexual identifications onstage in what seems to be a direct affront to the norms valued within South Asian communities.

D'Lo, however, wishes no disrespect. Rather, through lyrics and onstage performances the artist encourages audiences to rethink ethnic, racial, gender, and sexual authenticity by enacting alternative desiness as s/he lovingly—even humorously—refutes desi respectability. D'Lo employs call and response—a foundational principle of hip hop—to engage the audience members, who may even perhaps identify with some of the performer's multiple transgressions. This use of hip hop to alter the terms of South Asian Americanness is just one example of the artists' engendering of political participation. D'Lo's visual presence and artistic material expand the range of South Asian sexualities in the diaspora as s/he illustrates to Brown audiences identities, including queer female masculinities, previously believed impossible and certainly deemed ethnically diluted (Halberstam 2000; Chatterjee 2006).

The presumed "invisibility" of South Asians in commercial hip hop underestimates the impact of Black popular culture. Further, desi artists correct the misconception that the "values" of hip hop and South Asian ethnic communities are at odds, like Black and Asian "cultures." But how can a gay Brown male-identified woman find solace in the misogyny and homophobia of hip hop? Black female artists and queer producers of hip hop, some of whom create a genre called "homohop" that is present in the Bay Area, show why those seemingly ignored or even oppressed by hip hop remain committed to the culture.[11] Additionally, some scholars and "hip hop feminists" (Morgan 2000) have also found agentive ways to employ Black culture as a tool for dialogue and self-expression. So, too, have some desis. The explicit sexuality of some aspects of hip hop does not always devalue Black women; instead, it is often a celebration of expressive embodiments of Black women and their bodies (Neal 2005: 130), particularly in a context in which men have undervalued Black womanhood (hooks 1981). The content of hip hop and its characters spark the conversations of desi female artists on relationships, sex, and sexuality. It provides some desis with models of sexuality that they could choose to emulate or challenge, sample or reject. D'Lo's queering of the diaspora may be interpreted as exceptional or as inauthentically desi (how can one be desi and queer?) (see also Takagi 2000; Eng 1997, 2001). Yet D'Lo illustrates what Black sexualities offer American desis in their process of providing (queer) alternatives to hegemonic conceptions of desi gender and sexuality (Gopinath 2005).

Like other immigrant parents, South Asian elders feel it their duty to indoctrinate children with culturally appropriate gender roles and sexualities, an especially urgent task within the context of displacement from their home countries. Thus, not only are "the daughters of their community disproportionately burdened with the preservation of culture in the form of religion, language, dress, food, and child-rearing" but also female chastity and regulations against exogamous relations are of ultimate importance (Dasgupta and Das Dasgupta 2000: 327). American-born children, conscious of filial responsibility to re-create culture through economically stable and reputable careers along with heterosexual, endogamous, and timely marriages, struggle when they see that they might fail to realize their parents' dreams. Intergenerational rifts open because American social norms expose desi youths to new possibilities. These become potential samples for American desi life. Parents attempt to restrain crossovers, however, when they observe their children interacting with Blacks and, worse, see them taking active part in a despised culture. This is not what "coming to America" means. But, parents reason, this is just a phase of youthful rebellion, and it will end with future stability.

Along with the nearly universal assumption that their children are heterosexual, parents from the subcontinent generally hold their sons and daughters to different sets of expectations. To be marriageable, girls should be chaste and not date. In marriage, they should emulate their mother's role as "keepers of culture" responsible for enculturating their children with religious, linguistic, and culinary practices (Gupta 1999; Espiritu 2001; Maira 2002). Parents grant boys, on the other hand, more freedom and less accountability.[12] However, brothers and male cousins are expected to marry appropriately—before which they must attend good schools, major in something useful, and secure a solid and respectable job. When the girl's family looks for a boy in marriage, parents often evaluate all of these factors.[13] "Almost abusive in its consistency," writes a hip hop desi to me about his parents, "is their asking when I'm getting married, usually coupled with the suggestion [that] I should go to India and find a wife."[14]

Second-generation desi youths do not simply mimic their parents' values and perspectives as automatons. Rather, they sort through them and try to balance competing dreams. Desi youths often make the kinds of marriage and career choices that gel with their parents' hopes, partially to fulfill their duties and because it fits well with their own visions of a future. Others dissent, however. In particular, although desi artists want to please their parents, this desire often clashes with their love of Black popular music, a distinctly nontraditional practice. Interestingly, their choices are as gendered as their parents' expectations. Male MCs feel it important as sons to care for their parents, marry South Asian women, and raise desi children to continue the family line. But they understand that their eccentric career paths limit marital choices among desi women who might prefer men in more stable fields. Desi women in hip hop, however, often form relationships with men in the music business, meaning they flout family expectations in career *and* marriage. That is, some of the men feel a tug to choose between love *or* art, but the women's romantic love *and* their passion for music coalesce.

Before attending to the sexual politics of desire I want to clarify the way that desi MCs approach hip hop as a masculine field. Too many times their motivations have been dismissed as simply an eroticized desire and fear of racialized Blackness, though this may be true in the case of many—but not all—non-Blacks (Lott 1993b; Roediger 1998; Maira 2002). To rephrase Bakari Kitwana's observation on Whites and hip hop: "[desi] boys don't necessarily want to be Black. This conclusion is an oversimplification" (2005: 14). Some mainstream desi youths *are* attracted to hip hop for its racialized masculinity, but the artists have other motivations.

"Indian Negroes?" The Racialized Sexuality of Desi Men

We call [Blacks] *kalus*. We kind of have this affection for them, it's kind of funny. We're kind of afrai . . . not afraid of them, but we have so much respect for them. Also 'cause Indians love basketball, right? So we totally have respect for, like, kalus that can dunk. And the general muscular body that they have, we want . . . A lot of Indians are thin . . . So, we all want to be like that: the thick calves and being able to dunk . . . So for the male point of view, the kalu is what we find, like, not the ideal, but . . . first because you know in terms of their mental, or whatever, in terms of how they study, we don't have respect for that in general. It's kind of racist, but, you know. But we want the physical typing. We want to maintain like the Indian goodie-goodie, academics, but we want to have that too. The view is to have the best of both worlds. But in terms of kalu

women, the majority of us don't find them too much attractive . . . I actually find White women more attractive than kalu women . . . Our whole connection to the kalu culture is through the men, you know?
—Rajiv, mainstream Indian University of California, Berkeley student

The idea of a young desi man like Rajiv, in the above quote, attracted to hip hop often conjures images of a model minority who, in the words of Thien-bao Thuc Phi, "take[s] on a racist exaggeration of black manhood to replace the demasculinization placed on [him] by white supremacy" (2008: 303). After all, states Judith Halberstam, "arguments about excessive masculinity tend to focus on black bodies . . . and insufficient masculinity is all too often figured by Asian bodies" (2000: 2). A second interpretation reads the attraction of Asian Americans to Blackness, including the adoption of hip hop aesthetics and slang, to be a response to their devalued immigrant ethnicity. Indeed, the racialized hypersexual masculinity of Black men depicted in some hip hop is a draw for men of all backgrounds. Sunaina Maira explains the sexualized draw of "a particular machismo" signified in hip hop for mainstream desi males who contend with the contradictions of class and race by negotiating "coolness" and "nostalgia": "It may . . . connote a certain image of racialized hypermasculinity that is the ultimate definition of 'cool'" (2002: 336). As such, for Whites Blackness becomes, according to David Roediger, "the object of racialized desire, and simultaneously racialized fear" (quoted in Maira 2002: 336; see also Cornyetz 1994). This is not, however, what motivates desis in this project to produce Black popular culture and live in Black urban communities in New York and California. Desis who become MCs do not learn who Black people "are" through decontextualized media images. Daily, they engage with Black men and women as romantic and business partners alongside their interactions with South Asians in love and art. In this section I examine how the consumption and production of Black popular culture by desi MCs intersects with heterosexual romance to accurately explain how hip hop and ethnic commitments shape their gender identities and sexual choices.

Mainstream desi youths often display a paradoxical relationship to Black men, specifically through their desire for Black masculinity yet distaste for interracial relations. This is partially related to the American sexualization of desi men, who confront depictions of themselves as "lacking" masculinity, particularly in their encounters with other men. An Indo-Fijian I spoke with felt his manhood challenged by a pair of racist White men; he also felt disrespected when the leaders of a basketball pickup game routinely passed him over in favor of a Black man who had less basketball skill. Dru, a young Black student attending a San Jose, California, community college who dated desi girls, describes his male friend as "surprisingly muscular for an Indian," thereby reinforcing Rajiv's conceptions about desi men's fitness. Some desi girls' preferences for "big," "muscular," and "dark" Black men also imply that desi men lack these features.

Most of the analyses of South Asian masculinity, few that there are, draw from theories about Asian Americans despite their differential racialization. Many desis disidentify with the category Asian American because of cultural and phenotypic distinctions. But there are overlaps, such as in media depictions of emasculated Asian men as caricatures, cab drivers, and as nerds and geeks who rarely get the girl. And particularly in relation to Black masculinities, South and East Asian men become lumped in the constructed dualism of Asian/Black. While there is little information on South Asian and Black male relations in the United States, desi men may feel and may be viewed by others as relatively less masculine, thereby accounting for the desirability of Black masculinity (but not mentality) recounted by Rajiv.

While avoiding Blacks, mainstream desi men attire themselves with racial and gendered cues (or samples) of young Black men, thereby turning racialized aesthetics (low-slung jeans, particular brand names, slang, and posture) into ethnic and gendered performances (Maira 2002). They ethnicize or remix these by, for example, incorporating Hindi or Punjabi slang in their speech, calling themselves "coolies," and wearing gold chains with khalsa medallions, the symbol that represents the Indian religion of Sikhism. One desi woman I spoke to, Meena, prefers it when Black men talk to her because the style of South Asian men, who try to "talk like they're Black," seems "forced." "They don't want to mix into that [Black] community," the Berkeley student says, "but they want to take their dialect and music and stuff like that and try to put an Indian face on it." "Indian face" immediately conjures images of "blackface," but does it imply something different than "rotten coconut"? In either case, such interpretations of "doing race" are contradictory because they suggest that individuals *construct* racial identities, which contests the essentialist assumptions of Blackness and Indianness that underlie such comments, including the idea that certain groups "own" certain authentic gendered performances. These reified conceptions bear the imprint of centuries-long discourses that have racialized the sexuality of various groups in the United States in order to "naturalize" — and therefore differentially value and exploit — group distinctions. But perhaps we can also interpret the sampling of urban styles by Brown youths as the expression — possibly troubling, possibly innovative — of a process of cross-racial fertilization symbolizing connectivity.

Urban desi MCs mark their familiarity with Black culture in the way that they carry themselves: the kinds of clothes they wear, the way they don them, and the way they walk and talk. For others, the way the artists inhabit their bodies and their displays of cultural capital, particularly their knowledge of hip hop, can imply that they grew up within this culture. These men do not usually feel compelled to challenge stereotypes of Asian masculinity. However, they are not indifferent to the forms of masculinity expressed through hip hop. Hip hop settings often require performances of normative masculinity and aggressiveness that initially attracted these rappers. "There *was* a masculinity to it," acknowledges the Rukus Avenue cofounder Sammy, "and there's certainly [an] appeal to it in that sense and that's where I fell in love with hip hop after that point." Chee enacts his masculinity as often as he performs race when he battles other MCs in order to help onlookers interpret him. In these ciphers of evaluation, he feels, one needs to represent or else be embarrassed: "If I don't come off here, I'm gonna look like a sucker." But if the consciously cultivated stage personas of desi male MCs are obviously masculine, they are not overstated in the ways that others, upon hearing of "desis in hip hop," often assume. Contrary to some analyses of the adoption of hip hop by non-Black men, these artists do not embody stereotypical conceptions of Black masculinity, and neither does this fully, or even mostly, explain their participation. This is partially because they represent the genre of conscious rather than gangsta or bling rap that earns airplay. Intergroup contact does not always erase conflict, but it often can do so. Because of their close ties to Black friends, girlfriends, and their extended families, desi rappers are conscious of a range of Black masculinities (as there are among South Asians) not captured in stereotypes promoted by the mainstream media. Blacks, too, reflect "heterogeneity, hybridity, multiplicity" (Lowe 1996). Thus, desi men realize that they have options in thinking about how to be a man.

Though there are exceptions, non-Black males who love hip hop are not unequivocally "thugs" who desire Black masculinity to compensate for their emasculation. "That's a stereotype," Rawj said when we were talking in a coffee shop in Berkeley about the appeal of Black masculinity for Asian rappers. He reminded me that when he was growing up in the 1980s, sex did not pervade the image of hip hop and videos (in which "every rapper is hella hard or trying to look sexy," Rawj describes) were not yet widespread. Looking over the press photos for Feenom Circle's latest project, we joked about potential booty pictures and jewelry, highly unlikely given

MC Chee Malabar. Photograph courtesy of Preston Merchant.

their perspective (in the photos the closest thing to bling was a kukui nut necklace). Another Indian MC, Vivek, told me of the time, after rapping at a post-9/11 desi gathering in Oakland for which he was wearing a kurta with the skull cap often worn by Muslim men, he stepped outside for a breather. He was accosted by a first-generation desi man in his thirties who, with cigarette in one hand and beer in the other, exclaimed "Man, I'm glad you're not what I expected, to be all thuggish!" Speaking about this exchange later, Vivek emphasized to me that Indians in hip hop were trying to do something "*positive*," something "*conscious*," and that this is neither about drinking and smoking (which he does not do) nor about fulfilling stereotypes.

Desi men, despite the recent arrival of their families to the United States, find a range of masculinities available to them. More concerned with art than image, their engagements with Black people and hip hop culture differ from desi males who desire and despise Blacks from a distance. Drawing especially from local ethnic, racial, and musical collectives, they sew together various stylistic and expressive cues to perform their masculinity. These MCs enact Brown masculinities onstage that reject problematic images of Black men promoted in commercial hip hop and expand the range of available gender roles for desi men.

Love or Art?

I feel that there's a responsibility attached to making that commitment to somebody in terms of being able to provide, or help provide. And I want to have a family. That's, beyond anything, my biggest goal in life. I would give up everything else for that in a heartbeat. That's not even a question to me.—KB, Indian American MC

Why do some—though not all—desi men dedicate their professional and artistic lives to Black culture and yet marry desi women? Is it the "raja syndrome" that privileges boys (DasGupta and Das Dasgupta 2000: 333), drawing them to their female counterparts? "Indian guys are probably more into the obligation [to family] than the girls. I've heard so many stories where guys just leave their girlfriends because their parents found a wife for them," says Meena. Calling them "mama's boys," Meena says that while desi men will do things in college that their parents are not aware of (dating, for example), they ultimately follow parental advice about majors, and "they'll get a good job and they'll marry who their parents want them to marry, so they usually keep the traditions going." Discussions about South Asian parental constraints often focus on daughters; males are thought to have relative freedom. Radhika, who is Bangladeshi and White and dates a Black male rapper, says: "In general for any culture the men have a lot of freedom to go explore other cultures and the women are the keepers of culture." If this is the case, why don't we see *more* interracial marriages among desi men in hip hop?

Missing in descriptions of the gender double standard is the filial duty and economic pressures that South Asian parents place on sons. "Men are supposed to carry the family," Deejay Bella says. "They have to take care of their parents" as sons do on the subcontinent. The economic achievements of Asian male professionals in America link their masculinity to upward mobility and wealth. "Controlling images" of Asian American doctors, engineers, and professors that abound in television shows and in Hollywood films affirm their association with the mind rather than the body, which tends to be the focus of stereotypes about Black men and women (Espiritu 1997; Collins 2000).[15] South Asians usually expect men to support their families, and as a result desi men "*have to* make money," Bella emphasizes.

Such expectations set up a tension between ethnic obligations and musical passions in the lives of some desi men. "It was more like love or art," says Rawj, and this "actually caused me a lot of inner distress." "It's a tough choice," Karmacy's Sammy concurs. Finding love and art to be oppositional, Rawj decided in his twenties to pursue music with his hip hop group Feenom Circle instead of finding a wife, despite his sense of sacrifice. For him, music was his "dream, but at the same time this is the importance of your culture." Moreover, money is important in finding a wife and supporting a family. As Rawj explains, "I really felt like a Punjabi father wouldn't be really hip to giving his daughter away to a guy who, on the side, does this. You know what I mean? Unless I was successful at it. Successful in monetary terms." As these rappers attempt to fulfill obligations, they contend with people's misunderstandings of their musical choices as a desire for (Black) hypersexuality, which contrasts with the respectable white-collar masculinity praised as an ethnic ideal among desis (Maira 2002: 49). Social status and their elders' views of music as a fanciful vocation is just as important as financial security: "I feel like there's a certain stigma against musicians in general in Punjabi culture. That it's like, of a lower breed," says Rawj. Thus, hip hop may represent a barrier to potential desi spouses who search for more familiar lifestyles. Material realities and their individual passions and obligations cause some rappers to keep daytime careers in computers and law, for example, even if these jobs "drain" them of creativity. Despite such conflicts, a number of performers wed desi women and made albums; they succeeded in both love *and* art by wedding their ethnic and hip hop communities.

Marrying a co-ethnic, the norm among South Asians in the United States, is important, and not only to please one's parents. "I *did* want to marry a Punjabi girl . . . because I thought it was important and it wasn't because somebody put it into my head, either," Rawj asserts. Like Rawj, KB married an Indian American woman and felt that this was not predetermined. Desi women are familiar with the filial expectations that their partners faced; perhaps, too, they may be counted upon to continue ethnic traditions. But the desis whom the artists feel comfortable around are, themselves, not mainstream. As Rawj explains, it would "take a certain kind of woman" in order to "meet [him] at the same point" where he found himself to be. These rappers were looking for "an equal," someone "real deep," "sympathetic" to their music, "someone with culture," and an educated woman who did not expect her husband to be the sole breadwinner. As it happened, Rawj ended up marrying his rap group's Web designer, a desi woman who looked at his career "as a plus as opposed to a minus." Rappers like Rawj, KB, and Sammy are able to bridge divisions between the pulls of art and love because they found supportive women—women who are "completely down" and who understand their choices. These unions discount the "raja syndrome" as the only explanation for desi endogamous marriage and instead point to a less-stereotypical view of American desi women and men who are concerned with more than economic incorporation and cultural preservation.

Hip hop culture impresses upon desi rappers ideas about gender; it is also the mode through which they express their own perspectives on gender relations. Their rhymes on this topic are hetero-normative as they discuss marriage, love, and loss. Sometimes rappers praise South Asian women. Karmacy's four-man Indian crew in their song "Neil," for example, rap about an Indian girl that Neil's mother had been trying to set him up with since grade school, and whom he consciously avoided because he was too busy being an American boy. In college, however, he sees this woman in a new light and ends up with her, praising her as a repository of Indian culture and thereby fulfilling his mother's hopeful prediction quoted in the epigraph. That Karmacy's MCs found and married desi women who respect and support their engagement in the arts may be the ultimate expression of this mother's hopes *and* the artists' own dreams, articulated through hip hop music. This is a prime example of sampling—the artists neither reject fully nor adopt wholly hegemonic desi gender norms.

Desi men who are not married tell a slightly different story. The majority of male artists have dated both desis and nondesis, thereby avoiding their parents' ethnic insularity. "I think [my parents] know I don't play by those rules," said a desi man who prefers "light-skinned bohemian" women of color. It is probably the case that the artists' involvement with a Black subculture with alternative notions of beauty has shaped their preferences. Lara, a Black woman in her early thirties who works in the music business in Oakland, is surprised to hear about South Asian anti-Black sentiment, countering, "But boy, do those Indian men love on Black women!" Yet desi and Black relationships raise the scorn, disappointment, and grief of South Asian parents who are "scandalized" and "cried." In the case of one Indian American man who had married a Black woman, his parents were disturbingly "happy" the marriage ended in divorce. In rare cases parents come around once grandchildren are born, although these elders tend to be triple migrants—Indians from Africa or the West Indies where contact with Blacks is greater.

To some extent, interracial—even interreligious or interregional—marriage is an increasing possibility for diasporic youth. Yet while many South Asians have mixed marriages in their extended families, they still remain the topic of gossip and derision. Desi youths have aunties and uncles who subscribe to "BMW," a witty acronym used by the novelist Gautam Malkani (2006) to stand for "Blacks, Muslims, and Whites," the hierarchy of preferences, from "least" to "most" desired, if one makes the mistake of marrying "outside." Such condemnations have been "extremely traumatic" to some desis in relationships with Blacks.

Almost as a rule, however, desi artists do not date White women, in contrast to most scholarly depictions of Asian American sexuality (Marchetti 1994; Fong and Yung 1995; Shinagawa and Pang 1996). They cite attraction, politics, and compatibility as their reasons. Early experiences with racism may still impact these adults. The politics of attraction during high school made these artists all too aware of their racial difference from White beauty ideals, especially for those who went to White schools and who felt unattractive to White girls. For example, White women were not attracted to one desi rapper until, he says, "jungle fever"—"the movie and the phenomenon" of interracial attraction—came on the scene in his senior year.[16] He reacted to this and, like D'Lo, "wasn't really trying to have too much time for White women or White people in general, you know?" Reflecting back, he reasons that he might

MC Chee Malabar. Photograph courtesy of Richard Louissaint.

have had "too strong of a racial politics" at that point, now that he agrees with Gandhian principles of tolerance. Chee Malabar, who prefers the "Black and Spanish women" who approach him in New York, is not attracted to White women because he feels they would not be able to understand his perspective and experience in life. "I have more on my mind than they can imagine," Chee said soberly. That minority women "understand where I'm coming from and . . . I can be honest with them," is critical to this MC, which reflects the importance of a shared worldview that crosses some color lines but not others. These MCs view Whiteness as a divide that they cannot or will not overcome.

Romantic choices relay something about the racial identities of MCs: "Tell me whom you love, and I'll tell you who you are," notes the epigraph that frames Frances Twine's essay on the "romantic management of racial identity" (1996: 292). In her study of the dating patterns of biracial Black and White youth, Twine argues that the "shifts in racial self-identification were often partially expressed and grounded in romantic choices" (295). The racial identities of South Asians in America are ambiguous and shifting, too, and their decision to date minority women and not White women is an explicit identification as being non-White. The commonality of being a minority—including Whites' deviant sexualization of minorities, which affects conceptions of desirability—is an important component of what they find attractive in non-White women. Hip hop offers South Asians access to an explicitly racialized identity; dating Blacks may similarly offer, as Twine notes, "romantic access to a racialized cultural identity" (301). If, as Milton Gordon (1964) claims, intermarriage (to Whites) is seen as the final stage to assimilation, then what does it mean when one chooses a non-White partner? The artists' views on Whiteness and their tendency to date minorities suggest a relation between their racial politics and the way they conceive of themselves as racial and sexual subjects, thus discrediting the notion of a colorblind or postracial America (Hollinger 1995; see also Moran 2003). That these South Asians in relationships with Black women identify as desis and maintain their connection to other South Asians and certain ethnic practices also means that they are not "becoming Black."

The rappers also date desi women (it would be "strange" not to love Indian women, one commented) who tend to be "like them":

some of these women have also dated interracially, understand the artists' choices, and are willing to go against the desi grain. Another MC's interactions with South Asian women have increased alongside his involvement in the desi music scene. Pointing to cultural and environmental reasons as opposed to shared ethnic background, he says of one West Indian desi girlfriend that they were similar because "she grew up in the Bronx around all Black people, she talks the way I talk, she listens to all the same music I listen to." Hip hop rather than ancestry, therefore, becomes their shared culture.

Desi men in hip hop sometimes represent and sometimes diverge from the broader second generation in their career and marriage choices. They attempt to deal with competing expectations within South Asian and hip hop America, both steeped in particular gender and sexual dynamics. While male artists often consider love and art to be competing realms, some bridge the two, including the married artists, all of whom wed desi women. Indeed the other desi men in hip hop have formed relationships with a range of minority women, thereby finding it important to be with someone who supports their decisions and shares their interests—including hip hop culture—and the concerns they rap about. But what explains what looks like a full crossover into hip hop by the female artists who tended not to date desis at all? Is it because "girls seem more brave in a way," as Meena hypothesizes, and are more willing to take part in particularly those social arenas parents most want to restrict them from? And if so, how do these impact our interpretations of the identities and politics of desis?

Love and Art

I've personally never had a problem dating Black men, and I don't feel like culturally I would have to be with an Indian to do the things that I need to do. I feel like I need to be with someone with the same worldview. There are Black men who clearly approach me for the Kama Sutra thing. But then there are others who approach me and are just open; they respect me and that's all I really need.—Radhika, community activist

Female artists contend with the notions of race and sexuality of both South Asians and Blacks, but their gender and sexual dynamics play out differently than they do for their male counterparts. Historically, Westerners have exoticized South Asian women as desirable albeit devalued partners. The dynamics of interracial heterosexual relations are not limited to interactions between South Asians and Whites; Black men also orientalize desi women. How, or do, female artists interject these fantasies, and how do such perceptions shape the dynamics between Black and South Asian women? Desi women's own sexual preferences highlight the impact of mainstream notions of Black masculinity and the counterweight of sustained interracial contact. Like their male counterparts, female artists do not date White men, but they rarely date desi men either. Desi female performers are aware of the gender and sexual norms among co-ethnics and their Black male and female peers. In staking claims in multiple communities they sample from a range of available options—including tropes of Black masculinity—to present alternative sexualities and lifestyles. They take risks to challenge orientalist stereotypes as well as misconceptions of "women in hip hop." Their choices overlap and diverge from the male MCs, but both sets deal with similar difficulties in achieving satisfaction in love and art.

Desi men and women in hip hop both look for partners who understand and are supportive of what they do, yet the women tend to date Blacks, including African Americans, Jamaicans, and Ethiopians. They do this at considerable risk of ostracism, because South Asian anti-Black sentiments often culminate in anxieties over the particular pairings of desi daughters with Black men. This frustrates many of the female artists who want the freedom to love whom they desire while also keeping their family's affections. Understanding the tensions surrounding these patterned choices deepens our examination of the causes and consequences of romantic relationships between South Asians and Blacks.

Although some of the female artists had wanted to date desi men when they were in college and soon after, they are generally resistant to doing so now, in their thirties, precisely because of the ideas that many desi men, even those born in the United States, hold about tradition and gender role expectations. These women remember all too well their childhood and college experiences within their ethnic communities, and they continue to dislike others monitoring their sexuality and thus critique mainstream desi ideas. As one

Berkeley student told me, "I think Indian guys really have a problem . . . like 'oh my god, she's such a ho!' for doing anything that's not completely covered from head to toe and not touching anyone." For example, a female artist and I, dressed in club attire on our way to go out, ran into a group of desis we knew at a popular Indian *chaat* (or snack) shop in Berkeley. They circled the artist and praised her tight-fitting outfit—attire associated not just as "American" but as Black American (see Maira 2002: 13). Yet once she was out of earshot one man disapprovingly claimed that she was just there "to strut around." In light of this incident, Sunaina Maira's description is apt: "The Indian remix subculture . . . showed little variation in the coding of female style and, more important, an underlying preoccupation with the stylistic coding and regulation of Indianness, and implicitly of Blackness, especially for women" (2002: 46). By contradicting—in fact moving all the way in the opposite direction—of standards set for proper desi behavior, the artists' ethnic authenticity is questioned. If proper desiness is linked with community solidarity, then "women deviating from this idea of traditional Indian womanhood are considered traitors to the community" (DasGupta and Das Dasgupta 2000: 327). In response, desi artists operate largely outside of desi spaces.

Hip hoppers find their co-ethnics' reactions to be hypocritical and close-minded erroneous assumptions of who a person is based on his or her attire. They feel that desi men will "totally judge females that act a certain way, and then they'll try to get with them," laughed Meena, who believes this is "disrespectful." Ironically, mainstream desi men often imagine these very "disrespectful" interactions to be characteristic of desi female-Black male interactions, and this displacement becomes their touted reason for their need to "protect" desi girls. Thus while South Asians often imagine that hip hop spaces are tense with male-male heterosexual competition, patriarchy, and sexism, ethnic communities in fact re-create these dynamics.

Desi female MCs and DJs are subject to a unique expression of anti-Black racism on the part of desis: namely, they become its target. After fending off drunk and groping desi men at parties who assume the "right" to (touch) desi women (the same men who claim it is Black men who "prey" on "their women"), female performers do not agree with mainstream desi men's assumption about the (sexual) motivations of Black men in contrast to the "honorable" motives of desi men. "Black culture is very sexual," comments a desi man. Thus, the artists' attachment to hip hop and Black people—especially the Black men whom desi women artists date—lead mainstream South Asians to glue such stereotypical conceptions to the artists. Meena says that the Indian men in her college circles often link desi girls with darker skin color to (loose) sexuality. In tricky moves, South Asians' biological conceptions (i.e., the imagined hypersexuality) of Black people are contradicted by the plasticity with which they apply these ideas to others: desis—who are not (inappropriately) sexual—who hang out with Blacks (who are inappropriately sexual) therefore become (inappropriately) sexual, themselves! The artists have long encountered such sentiments and their prevalence continues to turn them off from socializing with co-ethnics who do not understand their sense of style and find their access to Black people and cultures mysterious and suspect.

In contrast to desi hip hoppers, countless mainstream desi girls told me that they ended their relations with Black men because they would never marry them. The disturbing ways that some mainstream desi youth relate to Black men and women in their intimate relationships parallels the troubling and anti-Black ways they adopt hip hop culture. Black men relate their own stories of "crazy Indian women," often remarking that their girlfriends refuse to introduce them to their parents, or deceive their parents about the true identities of their boyfriends. Dru, a gregarious biracial Black and German college student from the South Bay, went to a Muslim desi's house (appraised at three million dollars) and his date prepped him to say, in the event that her parents came home, that he was attending community college but that he was transferring to "whatever UC (University of California) you like," in order to elevate his educational status in their eyes. In another case, he says he went out with a Pakistani girl who instructed him to get into the back seat of the car (a Lexus GS300, no less) and duck down as they drove by her parents' house so they would not see him. Dru fully understood the implications of her request: "It's to hide the fact that (a) she's talking to boys, and (b) she's talking to boys who look like me." Such is the extent to which unquestioned racist norms circulate among South Asians and affect those outside its bounds. That desi girls still date Black men does not make them anti-racist, especially when they condone their parents' behaviors by choreograph- ing charades and expecting their Black friends to understand the degree to which the South Asian community devalues them. "I said no," Dru says in response to the girl who asked him to duck down. "I'm not gonna do that for anyone. It makes me feel like a coward, even if it's for her benefit."

The desi artists attempt to challenge these kinds of interactions that frame the general tense dynamics of South Asian/Black rela- tions in the United States. In contrast to other desis' clandestine activities, they usually maintain open relationships with Black men despite community pressures against doing so. Therefore, different kinds of conversations emerge among family members; whether positive or negative, their presence expands the extent to which South Asians across generations have to contend with the influ- ences of Blacks. Just as White racism and beauty norms push desi artists away from dating Whites, desi racism and chauvinism send these women away from South Asian men and sometimes toward Black men.

The situation is a bit more complicated for female performers who, now in their thirties, want to find life partners but find re- lationship choices to be difficult. As Maira explains, "Women who had dated African American men and struggled with parental dis- approval expressed perhaps the most emotional critique of the anti-Black prejudices of immigrant parents" (2002: 71). Like their male counterparts, women think deeply about how to develop per- sonal lives that can support their professional, political, and artis- tic choices. As a result, they weigh the merits and drawbacks of dating South Asian versus Black men. As this is the case, we cannot contend that America is either a colorblind, postracial society or a multicultural haven in which differences matter no longer. Neither can we believe that South Asians are on their way to "becoming White."

One desi in her early thirties—prior to dating her boyfriend, a Black rapper—was becoming anxious about her single status and decided to search for a husband on a desi Internet dating Web site. Pulled by her political and future desires (she wants to remain con- nected to Bangladesh and have her children learn Bengali), Radhika stated, "Well, logically I should find a Bengali guy because I can't give the kids that language." Having dated only one Indian in her life, she had primarily dated Black men over the past decade. But the question arises, "Okay, could he [a Black man] handle India? Could I bring him there?" She believes that a Black man might be mistreated, especially "the darker they are the worse it is." She did meet a desi man whom she "admired culturally and intellectually" (not physically? I wondered), but the relationship failed after a couple of months. When she stated, "I think that no matter which way I go, I'm going to have to give up something" in choosing between a desi or Black man, she describes the same tension voiced by the men I discussed earlier in the chapter. Radhika's conundrum differs from those faced by other Asian American women who choose between the comfort and ethnic continuity assumed in endogamous marriages and the potentially privileged status accessed by marrying White men. This desi was giving up visions of her future that related either to living in South Asia or to continuing her work within a Black working-class community in San Francisco. Her political and emotional futures seem to unzip within the racialized politics of dating and marriage. In what appears to be individual decision making, the artists confront conditions by forces—like racism and immigrant community formation—larger than themselves. And so, they pick their battles.

Generally speaking, desi women in hip hop do not seem overwhelmed by the tension between "love or art," or if they do they try to overcome it. Perhaps they are already living so outside the bounds of their parents' expectations that they feel a kind of freedom to confront certain expectations while conforming to others. But it is nonetheless difficult to control the positive (integrating into an artistic community) and negative (losing ethnic support) repercussions of choosing nondesi partners. But their bonds with men in the hip hop business, men with whom they can share their passion about music, hip hop, and art, also offer support and community. For some of these women, their passion for music overlaps their passion for the men, often Black, who produce the music.

Asian and Black couples garner much public interest: an online article titled "Black Men, Asian Women" alone garnered 555 comments (Sen 2006).[17] Clearly the phenomenon of Asian and Black relationships is not odd or surprising to hip hop's desis. Desi female artists in relationships with Black men will often meet their families, attend holiday events, and share food and music. In turn, the women introduce their partners to Indian food, Bollywood, and South Asian music, the latter of which their male partners sometimes incorporate into their musical productions. But being open about their interracial relationships necessitates the couples' courage as they negotiate which cultural events they attend, especially during important festivals like Diwali, the Hindu festival of lights. Attending a hip hop party, particularly in the multiracial Bay Area, can be more relaxing for a mixed couple than dealing with elders' stares at a desi event. Many desis I spoke with feel more comfortable among Blacks than among desis, although these, too, were spaces rife with complex vibes.

While the intersection of sex and race can lead to a type of "double burden" for women in hip hop, this is not always the case. Gender relations can be even more complicated: South Asian women sometimes have an even easier time entering Black social circles (such as at predominantly Black house parties and hip hop and reggae clubs like Oasis in Oakland) and functions (such as the Malcolm X Jazz Festival in Los Angeles) than do their male counterparts. Being seen by men in the industry as sexually desirable can trump, or integrate favorably (albeit problematically) with, in this sense, their racial difference.[18] Hip hop is of course not only a highly gendered arena but is also a heavily sexualized one, particularly due to the sociality of the events (i.e., going to hip hop shows or clubs is an explicitly social, even sexual, affair aided by alcohol and other drugs, whereas going to school, for example, might not be). But here desis often face remixed politics that characterize South Asian and White interactions.

Some Black men subject desi women to Black Orientalism, a rendition of the exoticization and otherness they experience from White Americans. Afro-Orientalism, with its ability to link Blacks with Asians, can be colonizing and decolonizing. As Bill Mullen notes, "Afro-Orientalism is a counterdiscourse that at times shares with its dominant namesake certain features but primarily constitutes an independent critical trajectory of thought on the practice and ideological weight of Orientalism in the Western world" (2004: xv).[19] Without discrediting the political potential of Afro-Orientalism (the critical contribution of Mullen's work), the sexual dynamics in nightclubs also reaffirms aspects of Western (White) Orientalism. "Where y'all from?" a Black man asked a group of desi girls at a hip hop club peopled with attractive young Bay Area natives working hard not to look too expectantly at potential dance partners. "You all look exotic," he said appreciatively. Black men sometimes describe Indian women as desirable and "beautiful" for having "long wavy hair" and "big butts." We also find hints of both "kinds" of Orientalism in Du Bois's overlooked novel from 1928, *Dark Princess: A Romance*, an anti-imperialist love story about Matthew Townes, a young Black American medical student, and Princess Kautilya, the daughter of a maharaja (king) from India. Mullen focuses on Du Bois's internationalist perspective and on workers of the world, but he also highlights the fact that "Du Bois's conception of orientalism was wedded to a patriarchal or paternal ideology inflected in contemporary debates about female subalterns in the United States and India, in particular, and by Du Bois's own romantic conceptions of the Asiatic" (2003: 218–19). While analysts have argued that Du Bois attempts to fuse the exoticism of Kautilya with "radical politics and love" (232), desi/Black relations in the club are not politically progressive just for being interracial.

Many of the South Asian women I spoke with who frequent hip hop clubs explain that they are a "safe race" for Black men because they are not White and not Black and because they are "exotic" ("the whole Kama Sutra thing"). D'Lo says that his/her Sri Lankan girlfriends often go to clubs where Black men approach them because, s/he interprets, the men like "dark-skinned girls with nice hair." These issues, "especially the effects of skin color and hair texture," impact "Black women's self-images and how others treated them" (Collins 2006: 166); they also shape the self-awareness of desi women who socialize with Blacks. A fair-skinned green-eyed Indian woman from Seattle told me that Black men like her because she is "whitish" but also "not Black." Colorism is yet another link between South Asian and Black communities in which individuals place a higher value of beauty on fair skin (indeed, most South Asian parents warn their children to stay out of the sun). For Meena, being exoticized by a Black man who thought she was Egyptian was "flattering in a way, but it's kind of sad, too. Like, why do they think that someone of a lighter race is so beautiful to be?" These dynamics also affect the experiences of Brown women in hip hop since it may be the case that, as Thien-bao Thuc Phi says, "the growing number of African American men with Asian women has caused some tension between black women and Asian women" (2008: 312).

The sexual and heteronormative dynamics between Black and Brown men and women in Bay Area dance clubs in the 1990s and 2000s fostered competition between heterosexual women of color for (Black) male attention. Women of color can and do forge bonds resulting from their shared experience of gender and racial disenfranchisement in the United States but they have had to overcome obstacles of the patriarchal race-first framing of American society (Lorde 1984; Harris and Ordona 1990; Espiritu 1997). Heterosexual romances in clubs mostly populated with young Black men and women often assume the racial solidarity of Black Nationalism, similar to desi men's "protection" of South Asian female sexuality in the desi remix scene. Despite this parallel, when tensions over courtship arise Brown women in Black social spaces become defined in contrast to Black women, making the former feel "like an outcast a lot of times." However, the female artists also adopt conceptions of physical beauty that intersect with musical interests that draw them to Black men.

Like some mainstream desi girls, some of the female artists feel that Black men are more masculine than desi men, pointing to their musculature. Some highlight physical aspects of their past and present partners, saying that they prefer dark skin. Does this correlate with Eric Lott's characterization of Whites' "fascination with black male potency" (1993b: 57)? The artists certainly claim that their boyfriends are sexy in what may be seen as the reverse flow of Afro-Orientalism. But their desires for Black men are contextualized, and are rooted in more than fantasy and distance: they are also turned on to the men's passion for music and their artistic skills. One woman finds the content of her boyfriend's rhymes — that he's "putting a good message out there" — important: "I'm really drawn to his brain, that he can do that stuff." Another woman ponders whether her obsession with music translates into an obsession for men who make music; by spending time with them she could figure out how their minds work and then apply these lessons to her own productions. Thus, it is not Black men per se that these artists find attractive but rather the individuals, often Black, who make hip hop music. We see from desis' experiences inside and outside of the club that while racialization and sexualization impact South Asian and Black relations, their trajectories are not predetermined. For both parties in the long-term interracial South Asian/Black relationships that I witnessed, their motives for being with one another surpass the stereotypes of either desi exotification or Black sexualization (Sen 2006). They bond over shared experiences as American minorities and as fellow music heads.

Music, love, and sex entangle themselves in cross-racial desires. Desi women who became hip hop artists try to pursue their sexual, social, and career lifestyles without too greatly disappointing their parents. Relative to the male artists, female artists take greater risks of being shunned for their refusal to be proper desi girls in their personal and professional lives. For them, love and art often coincide. Ironically, while female artists may seem like they have crossed over to the "other side," Blacks and South Asians still imbue these women—whom they tie to "culture"—with desi ethnicity and femininity. The gender and sexual choices of hip hop's desis speak volumes about the intraethnic and interracial dynamics between South Asians and Blacks in the United States. And desis cannot resolve these tensions simply by inserting themselves into the Black social, business, and sexual worlds of hip hop.

"In the Middle": Brown Women, Black Masculinities

Girl, I'll be your rebounder.
—D'Lo, Sri Lankan MC and poet

Queer diasporic cultural forms work against the violent effacements that produce the fictions of purity that lie at the heart of dominant nationalist and diasporic ideologies. (Gopinath 2005: 4)

Male and female desi hip hoppers have differing relations to Black masculinity. They disrupt our assumptions of Asian men's desire for a racialized masculinity, and the female artists reveal the underreported desire of some women to embody (not necessarily access) this same Black masculinity. That is, images of Black men in hip hop and other elements of the culture offer women like D'Lo several sexual *and* gender tropes they can emulate to reconstruct their nonnormative identities into an expression of self they feel is true. I was fascinated to learn that desi women risk disownment from their families when they decide to live out extreme decisions that contradict South Asian and American gender and sexual norms. In fact, it is desi women, not desi men, who incorporate tropes of Black masculinity into their own sexuality in surprising ways by adopting the persona of "pimps," "players," and "b-bois."[20]

D'Lo faces extra tension from Sri Lankans for his/her lack of conformity on multiple fronts (see Gopinath 2005). "I had come to the conclusion that I was different, nobody was going to understand me," D'Lo says. Being gay and identifying as a male in adulthood, D'Lo embraces a lifestyle and look counter to Hindu, Sri Lankan, and Tamil femininity. Some members of minority communities in America name homosexuality a "White disease," or as something that exists outside of their groups and is one of the perils of becoming "too Americanized" (Takagi 2000; see also Maira 2002: 47–48). Constructions of non-White sexuality heighten South Asians' reactions to desi homosexuality and transgender identities, which, according to gatekeepers, "harm" the overall image of "the community." This policing recasts South Asian gays and lesbians, who already are targets of multiple vectors of homophobia, as internal threats to the proper images of ethnic respectability of Asian America (McBride 2005). But by no means did all desis choose to live by these terms.

D'Lo's ambiguous racial, gender, and sexual crossings cause anxiety among people whose expectations s/he disrupts. Misunderstood and rejected because people "couldn't understand" him/her, the budding artist "needed to bounce [leave home] in order to search" elsewhere. Music, particularly hip hop, became D'Lo's sanctuary and career, which in turn only contributed to his/her parents' dismay. D'Lo didn't want to become a doctor, and "in fact," s/he says, "there's a piece that I [perform that] says, 'She was supposed to get married and be a doctor / I'm gay and I want to be a rock star.'" In order to pursue his/her passion for music and women, D'Lo was always "running away" in order to find "freedom." Just as Asians in America have been ousted from their home(land)s, queer and transgender Asian Americans are ousted from their familial and ethnic homes (Eng 1997).

Hip hop shaped D'Lo's sense of self. His/her "gay consciousness developed" from the time s/he was little: "Like I felt like I was a male, you know what I'm saying?" Having to become a girl during puberty was difficult because s/he "couldn't do it properly." Then hip hop came as a revelation: "Finally . . . I realized, 'you know what? I can just be true to myself and just take the title of a b-girl.' You get what I'm saying? Because that was truth to me. That was like in the middle." D'Lo's sense of being "in the middle" echoes descriptions of biracial and bisexual individuals. Like ethnically and sexually ambiguous people, D'Lo disrupts reified and pure notions of "male" and "female," "South Asian" and "Black," "immigrant" and "citizen." Indeed, this very ambiguity often creates discomfort and destabilizes knowledge, thereby causing others to ask "What are you?" As in so many other ways, hip hop provides these individuals with the possibility of being "in the middle" and maintaining the "truth" of their racial, immigrant, and other identities. Hip hop provides a flexibility of roles that speaks to the very experiences of these second-generation youths.

D'Lo adopts the b-girl/b-boi persona as a way of being that allows for the expression of his/her queer and masculine identities in forms borrowed from hip hop and expressed through performance. As Sandra Chatterjee writes, "Because D'Lo, a gay performer with a female body, embodies clearly a hip and black masculinity that many young South Asian men aim to sport, her performance destabilizes the heterosexual foundation of diasporic ideologies of domesticity that define hierarchies of authenticity, inclusion, and exclusion" (2006: 451; see also Gopinath 2005). As it does for other queer rappers, hip hop allows D'Lo to showcase his/her sexuality— his/her love of women—while also encompassing his/her racial and dancing identities, which are malleable in his/her hands. D'Lo also expands the repertoire of desi masculinities beyond desi men. Yet despite the trenchant commentary of D'Lo's performative work, his/her experiences still reflect the common United States conception of ethnic dilution through racial contact. Describing his/her more femme days when Black men used to flirt with him/her, in a telling slip of the tongue s/he said, "Even when I was Sri Lankan . . . I mean, even when I was a girl!" Catching this, we erupted in laughter, understanding the fluidity and interconnection of ethnicity, gender, and sexuality (see Johnson 2003). Although D'Lo identifies strongly as a Sri Lankan, s/he has access to *having been* Sri Lankan and a girl, whereas now s/he has transformed into something other than a Sri Lankan girl. B-boying grants this metamorphosis a suitable shape and fulfills D'Lo with its *content*, or message. And in all this flux, D'Lo finds the stability of hip hop to be not only healing but also generative. D'Lo's onstage performances fulfill Halberstam's hope that "masculine girls and women do not have to wear their masculinity as a stigma but can infuse it with a sense of pride and indeed power" (2000: xi).

D'Lo isn't the only female-born desi to appropriate male roles within hip hop. I was with Bella at a hot Oakland nightclub called Sweet Jimmy's where she was hired to spin the backup tracks for a local rapper's performance. She began her set with two records of the commercial Black rapper Ludacris's contagious hit song "Area Codes," one on each turntable. Bella mixed his hook, "I've got hos . . . I've got hos . . . I've got hos . . . ," back and forth, switching from one turntable to the next, with the audience members nodding their heads to the beat. Bella not only switched from turntable to turntable but also switched codified gender roles by taking the rapper's recorded voice as her own as she swayed in her long, form-fitting pink dress. Through mixing and spinning the DJ flips words used to denigrate women and rearticulates them from a female's perspective about heterosexual relations. "See," she said to me one day as we lounged in an African-owned San Francisco bar sipping hibiscus-flavored cocktails, "they have it all wrong. Men are the hos, they are always willing to put out" (be sexually available). These women engage anti-essentialism strategically by identifying with a group against whom they have been defined. This enables the DJ, in Bella's case, to flip discourses of hegemonic Black masculinity to redefine herself as a woman.

Some female artists also identify with pimps or, more accurately, with pimping. To be sure, they identify not with a literal pimp, but with what some members of the hip hop generation have redefined "pimping" to mean (Neal 2005: 137)—namely, calling the shots and having control over one's life in potentially counternormative ways. For example, one artist uses pimping to refer to "trying to get hookups" and gigs, and maneuvering within the music business in general (also considered hustling). Can South Asian women appropriate pimping as part of a feminist consciousness tied to a minority status? "Pimping is a state of mind . . . a movement about no longer being the victim, a movement where women do not have to take some of the crap that men dish out" (Megan Moore quoted in Neal 2005: 138). According to Gwendolyn Pough, Black female artists "have appropriated the language used by men rappers to denigrate women and use it as a means of empowerment in their own lyrics" (2004: 13). Thus, even a desi woman might assert that *she* was the pimp in her relations with men, thereby challenging the idea that these men played her. This counterintuitive framing of gender relations reflects the competitive nature of the music industry as well.

D'Lo and Bella present an intriguing pair of women in hip hop because they seem to contrast in so many ways, including their self-presentation and style. D'Lo's masculinity counters Bella's femininity, for example. But they both sample and weave together Black male tropes of players, pimps, and b-bois, thus flipping the gender script by identifying with Black masculinities. In doing so, they alter both *Black* masculinities, and desi *masculinities*. In the "One D'Lo Show" performances, which include D'Lo's skit as a sari-clad Sri Lankan mother grappling with her daughter's homosexuality, audiences are confused: "Is she a girl? Is that a girl or a boy?" Even offstage, D'Lo confounds norms and expectations altering the terms of masculinity and desi sexuality. D'Lo shines as an MC while Bella flexes her technical mixing skills. In critiquing rappers for their anti-womanist sentiments and also adopting their voices as a "means of empowerment," Bella's dialogue with hip hop not only deeply engages its gender and sexual dynamics but alters the very terms of what is possible.

On occasion, desi women artists adopt Black masculinities—sometimes those very stereotypes that define Black male "deviance"—to position and empower themselves within the complex dynamics of urban popular culture. Adopting models of identity from nondesi sources, they still present themselves and their nondesi partners to South Asians despite repercussions. Ultimately, they identify as women of color who share struggles over sexism and sexuality with Black women in and out of hip hop. These desis negotiate love and business relationships with Black men and women by sharing information and knowledge about how to better their skills and enjoy shared passions. Rather than suppressing their ethnicity, gender, or sexuality, they cultivate these identities through woman-friendly networks and challenge sexism and homophobia.

Deejay Bella. Photograph courtesy of Bilen Mesfin.

Claiming Womanist and Queer-Friendly Spaces

The female desi artists create spaces of positive energy where women can convene as progressive-minded artists within a male-dominant scene. They "bring wreck" (to sample the hip hop scholar Pough [2004]) by bashing stereotypes and forcing women and men on the dance floor and in the studio to recognize exactly who is bringing the beats and busting the flow. Sexual and gender agency expressed through music and enactment becomes politically potent when audiences, drawn into the collaborative nature of hip hop performance, bring closeted identities to light. According to Pough, the actions of some Black women in hip hop "represent a kind of space where they are claiming this public sexual identity in ways that . . . we really haven't seen because of the politics of silence surrounding black women and sexuality" (2006: 808–9). South Asian and Black women are sexualized in differential yet overlapping ways, and desi women, too, contend with ethnic restrictions on their sexual expressions in the diaspora. They emphasize crossovers among minority women by cultivating racially inclusive women-friendly spaces and networks.

To meld political and gender concerns Deejay Bella created Sistrens, a gathering designed for Bay Area "women artists with a social bent." Events sponsored by Sistrens include motivational speakers and home-cooked vegetarian fare. Further, at parties and clubs Bella makes sure to play female reggae and hip hop artists who rarely get airtime with male DJs, and she goes out of her way to support women in hip hop. When asked why she does this, she responds, "I *have* to." Bella has developed subversive techniques to deal publicly with the abundance of homophobic and misogynist lyrics in recorded music. First, she raises these topics when socializing with men in the business. "I don't play any of that homophobic shit. Do you guys play that?" she asked two Bay Area male DJs as we partook in late-night dining after their gig. When one said he played it if he thought the crowd could not understand the patois, Bella offered her own method of dealing with an offensive but popular song the audience wants to hear: she would just play the instrumental version of the record. Other cases call for her to play a verse of the man's song, but she will follow it by mixing in a female "answer track." This creates a dialogue between the two artists and engenders a certain—sexy and equal—vibe on the dance floor. Bella once came across fliers that featured nude women advertising an upcoming Bay Area party. She tore down the fliers and replaced them with new, women-friendly ones she had made. By initiating conversations with male colleagues and making executive decisions, women in hip hop claim a space and maintain dialogues—between men and women, among women, and between Blacks and non-Blacks—that fuel the growth of musical forms and consciousness about music content. In these dialogic relations (Bakhtin 1981), South Asians and their peers draw from their knowledge of dominant ideologies and the ideas and expectations of society in order to denaturalize the terms of the exchange. And although the power of our times is increasingly centralized, it remains unfixed, denaturalized, and not "owned" (Foucault 1976:

210). As such, these individuals may change the very terms that define them—and the consciousness of those around them.

Desi artists are codified, restricted even, by the popular meanings of race, class, gender, and sexuality. But they nonetheless take action, or "decision making power" (Giddens 1984), to shape their lives. They try to work within woman-centered networks, support other female artists, and identify with women of color. "We're really similar," Deejay Bella says about Latina and Black women, "I feel them and what they're saying and the stereotypes Black men have of women." Despite the business-fostered competition, desi women connect across lines and call on hip hop and the men who produce it to be accountable for their role in gender oppression. The performers continue to thrive while taking pro-womanist and anti-homophobic stances against stereotypes that sexualize women of color and silence their presence. D'Lo, for instance, once formed with two Black women a group called WADDAG (or "What a G," perhaps signifying on "G," meaning "gangsta"), based on an acronym standing for "Women Aware Deep Dark and Gay." Black and non-Black women in hip hop can make feminist interventions for social change, despite "finding it hard to claim a space for themselves in the male-centered world of Hip-Hop" (Pough 2002: 9). Through women-centered events and artistic choices that celebrate female artists, female hip hoppers practice their art in ways that aim to equalize gender relations within and beyond the music industry. They remind us of the possibilities of bounded agency and the political potential—the "transformative capacity" (Giddens 1984: 92)—of everyday actions.

Conclusion

The choices of desis in hip hop illuminate the process-oriented dualities of actors' agency and institutional determinants. No one's options are limitless; *habitus*, which creates bodies as bodies create it, is a structure that defines what is conscious and informs a society's members of their available options and active possibilities. Institutional forms, no matter how restrictive, are not determinative and within this concept is the possibility of changing accepted wisdom, or *doxa* (Bourdieu 1977). Hegemony, or the power of societal norms and structures that are expressed through daily practices, interacts with the power of the individual to actively promote or rebel against those very norms. Because they choose a critical consciousness that contests a variety of norms, the desi artists engage in everyday acts of resistance against not only conformity but also oppressive ideals. As members of multiple communities, they contend with sets of competing and overlapping hegemonic norms. They strive to represent a spectrum of sexual and gender expressions in desi America; similarly, they attempt to mark their presence as non-Black men and women in the male, Black dominant industry of hip hop.

Hip hop scholarship must be careful not to reproduce the inequalities of hip hop culture and the sexism of American society writ large by granting airtime to male stars who disregard or speak for women and non-Blacks. Fans and commentators often view Black women's concerns as supplemental to the "real" issues in hip hop, and they are generally asked to comment only on the topics of gender and sexuality. Similarly, non-Blacks are underrepresented and often only enter debates about race and authenticity. Women, non-Blacks, and gays and lesbians must be integrated in dialogues on hip hop as they comprise, along with straight Black men, the hip hop nation.

Some desis interject these conversations, bringing with them some of the concerns of their ethnic communities. So what does it mean when non-Black minorities insert themselves into a culture exploding with Black sexual politics (Collins 2004)? Their engagement with Black popular culture as *bricoleurs* (Hebdige 1979) who cut and mix identities engenders new articulations of desi gender and sexual identities. As samplers, hip hop desis perform the construction of gender and sexuality. Desi male and female MCs deflect assumptions of their desires for Black masculinity by articulating South Asian American masculinities that provide new models for desi youth. At the individual level, desi hip hoppers relate to Black masculinities and femininities, which they try to reconcile with ethnic expectations. While all of the desi artists wish to fulfill their parents' expectations about marriage and career choices, their musical and personal pursuits often run counter to these expectations. Bridging the various communities allows them to fulfill multiple obligations of love and art while cultivating inclusive and progressive communities.

Black masculinities resonate with some desi women in fascinating ways as they negotiate—and sometimes alter—the assumptions of audience members. Reflected in the artists' lives are tense and productive encounters between desi and Black men and women framed by the historical racialized sexualization of these communities. Desis in the business of hip hop and interracial romance uncover overlapping concerns across Brown and Black communities that are obfuscated by divisive discourses. The evidence insists that we consider not only the impact of Blacks upon South Asians but also the power of desis to alter hegemonic notions of Blackness and sexuality.

The artists also contradict hegemonic ideals through their relationships with Black men and women. They embrace the humanity of Black people by challenging anti-Black racism through their musical and personal choices. In exchange, they are rewarded with respect and are accepted by Black peers who offer community outside of ethnic bounds. Although not inherently progressive, inter-minority relationships are part of the artists' racial consciousness and signal their identification as people of color. In this way, love and music are deeply entangled and are infused with the politics of gender and sexuality. Underlying this complex vortex of interactions and identifications is the conscious politics of these hip hop desis.

Hip hop still maintains a space of empowerment and politicization in which unequal gender relations can be worked out, within and even *across* color lines. These dialogic encounters reveal important crossovers with those designated as the "other" of South Asians. Female artists express a race, gender, and sexual consciousness beyond any one form of identity politics. They embrace and enact social change against multiple forms of oppression, including the sexism and homophobia that compound the racism and nativism they experience in America. While these women contend with misogyny in hip hop, they and their male counterparts locate the roots of sexism and homophobia—just as they locate the roots of inequality and class exploitation—within broader historical, structural, and societal factors. This type of critical consciousness enables them—indeed compels them—to continue to produce hip hop music.

4.

The Appeal of Hip Hop, Ownership, and the Politics of Location

> Maybe it was living in the desert that made me concerned. Maybe being one-of-one made me conscious. Maybe being identified as Sri Lankan made me feel concern over the island's plight. Maybe being raised in a strict Hindu household allowed for Hip-Hop to present itself as the ultimate escape and solution. Maybe I wanted to represent the island in the desert like how black folk painted their pride on hip-hop's canvas.
> —D'Lo, "Part 3: Sri Lankan Boi"

"Music is what made me, do you get what I'm saying?" D'Lo insisted to me in one of our conversations. "[People] don't understand that something else can make you besides your reality and your environment," s/he added — particularly if that "something else" is the cultural product of a denigrated people. In this chapter I address the central question of why South Asian Americans are producing hip hop, and I explain how the desi artists came to proclaim that hip hop is their "jewel." I contest traditional interpretations that are superficial at best, racist at worst, for the appeal of hip hop to non-Black youths. Media depictions of urban Blacks in commercial rap music often stereotype Blacks as deviant beings, thereby encouraging the notion that non-Blacks must be drawn to this racialized violence and scatology. It is true that for many desis, as for other young Americans, adopting hip hop is a way to be cool and rebellious (Kitwana 2005). It also helps to resolve particular class and ethnic anxieties (Maira 2002). But these elements are not the only attractions for those who eventually produce hip hop music. D'Lo's poem cited in the epigraph above provides clues for why hip hop becomes the compelling answer to the problems faced by these desi artists.

Some desi youths have trouble with their emerging ethnic, gender, and sexual identities and contend with "being different all the time." In their youth, the artists also felt a more general "void" emerging from the discrepancy among their life experiences, their closeness to young Black peers, and national and community discourses about difference and belonging. But the appeal of hip hop is greater than its ability to help resolve individual problems—problems that the artists have mostly dealt with by adulthood. Indeed, in the long run hip hop enables the politics of desi artists as they become community builders, knowledge producers, and consciousness raisers. From this Black cultural production they adopt the foundational practices that incite reaction, including the communal nature of the form, the practitioners' attention to history, the use of call and response, and, of course, sampling. Brown performers employ these practices to forge inclusive communities and consider themselves legitimate hip hop producers as a result of their awareness of the polyvalent influences that form hip hop. Hip hop is a lifestyle they merge with a global race consciousness.

For these adults, hip hop is a positive and conscious way of life. Yet shifts in its content and marketing over time forces them to contend with the tension between the messages they wish to relay and their audiences' presumptions of "Indian rappers," for instance. Even before they open their mouths, desi MCs are thought by some listeners to be "wannabe rappers" and "thugs," with these assumptions reflecting the images glorified by some mainstream artists, labels, and media outlets.[1] But the artists in this book defy this interpretation, as expressed by Vivek when he insists, "I'm trying to do some positive shit, so [thug] is the last thing you should call me, you know?" Another Indian MC is disturbed by his co-ethnics' fetishization of his presumed "authentic" access to Blackness because of the way he speaks and rhymes. The simplistic notion that fetishization motivates all non-Black hip hop lovers reduces the humanity and diversity of Black people to one genre of one popular cultural production currently in favor with the masses. The goals of hip hop desis are to make music, express themselves, and "do something that's more positive, more conscious," both in their music and in the way that they live. This is the draw of today's Black popular culture.

This chapter analyses, first, the appeal of hip hop for desi artists; second, their perspectives on racial authenticity and Blackness; and third, how they locate themselves within hip hop as legitimate producers of a culture commonly associated with urban Black men. South Asians who dedicate their lives to producing hip hop responded viscerally to the race-conscious rap of the late 1980s and early 1990s. Black rappers' messages of countercultural critique, racial pride, and the emotive and physical pleasure of this culture spur the young desis obsessed with music to action. Hip hop is also the soundtrack to their activism and they create their own music to reflect inclusive race politics. As producers cognizant of hip hop's own race politics, they engage with debates over the place of Blackness in hip hop, including whether or not the culture has transcended race. While at first adopting discourses of Black Nationalism wholesale, they later translate Black Power into Brown Pride. In the process, they alter both established Blackness and desiness.

The roots and ownership of hip hop is one of its most vexed debates. Simply stated, hip hop is a multiracial production of a Black popular culture. There is something undeniably Black about hip hop. It is rooted in the experiences of the descendents of enslaved Africans, and it emerged at a particular socioeconomic and political juncture in the United States during the 1970s. Yet those hip hop historians bent on keeping hip hop a purely Black form, who say, for instance, "Latinos to me is Black" (Davey D), erase other contributors, including women and Puerto Ricans, who lived in places like the South Bronx.² Hip hop neither contains nor expresses the totality of American Blacks nor does it consist only of African (American) elements. Brown MCs and DJs approach this culture as they do their relations with Black friends—with knowledge of context, origins, and politics. The awareness by desi performers of the complex rise of this culture and its incorporation of multiracial and diasporic influences leads to their claims as legitimate artists. Like all cultural formations, hip hop is polycultural, which denies neither history nor its central players. But I am less invested in defining the moment of hip hop's origins or in parsing out to particular participants the copyrights of its innovations, particularly when so much of hip hop contests the notion of sole authorship. Hip hop is a musical and aesthetic form and much more. It is an ideology and, therefore, it is political. Parts of hip hop culture question dominant narratives and value that which is devalued in the United States, including Blackness and other forms of difference. These messages resonate with those politicized desis who are contending with their own distinctions. Counterhegemonic, critical, and resistant ideologies shape hip hop desis' life practices; their thoughts on race shape their participation.

In order to participate as legitimate producers of Black popular culture, Brown youths confront expectations of racial authenticity. They face these tests and make a place for themselves where previously there had been no representation. Their conceptions of hip hop and their reasons for loving it impact the artists' self-definitions as "legitimate" or "authentic" artists. But they apply these criteria not only to their music; they apply equally to an artist's politics and approach. Brown performers reveal a concept of authenticity that is not tied to identity but rests on one's approach to music. As they expand their knowledge of history and the politics of race, they consider the structure of hip hop's own racial politics. Hip hop desis present three perspectives on what hip hop is and their location within it. Instead of sidestepping matters of race and arguing that hip hop is a utopic culture that has transcended race, these South Asians attempt to apply the same explicit race talk found in this cultural formation to their own ethnic identities and diasporic locations. They illustrate the impacts of being an American minority while contesting the biological and hierarchical basis of racial categories, thereby confounding the notion of America as a postracial society.

The Appeal of Hip Hop

For me at that time, hip hop was a context for me to think about life—it embodied all the things I was awakening to and the things I had contemplated for a long time: an alternative artistic sensibility that was radical to what the norms of society urged you to be. It was rebellious; it involved race politics, displayed crafty word play and was very social. It all

The attractions of hip hop are numerous, and for the desis who became producers in the 1990s their reasons overlap. Not finding the appropriate responses to racism within their ethnic communities or in mainstream national discourses, desi youths heard early rap delivering potent, race-conscious reactions. These desi youths were nonconformist, music minded, and open to sonic expressions of politics. Hip hop gave them the vocabulary to understand local conditions and served as the vehicle through which to articulate their global concerns.

Some desi youths are drawn to hip hop because they felt that in their lives "something was missing." Hip hop fills the disjuncture between what these young people see around them and the everyday ways that individuals make sense of their situations. These desis grew up amid two general sets of socioeconomic practices married to racial discourses —first in the 1970s and 1980s when the second generation was young, and later in the decades that hugged the twenty-first century during and after their time in college. The Bay Area was a unique place to experience the Reagan years that represented the first socioeconomic context, as instituted by the cutback policies of Reaganomics and deindustrialization that led to an hourglass economy. Artists from urban and working-class neighborhoods saw the rise of crack cocaine and the heightened policing of their communities —realities that were invisible to many South Asian professionals. The twin racist ideologies of the cultural dysfunctions of Blacks detailed in the Moynihan Report of 1965 and the Asian model minority gained prominence at this time.[3] But few residents could miss the activism of the Bay Area, the land of the Black Panthers and the Yellow Panthers and the first ethnic studies departments at universities. Second-generation Asians may have been too young to recognize that the area was ripe with the Chicano Movement and the American Indian Movement, and many are unaware that there ever was an Asian American Movement. However, as students at Bay Area universities in the 1990s, KB, Rawj, Jonny, Bella, and Asma, a hip hop radio producer, are direct beneficiaries of these movements. But the 1990s also heralded a second set of economic, neoliberal, and globalizing practices that touted "pull yourself up by your bootstraps" ideologies and entrenched cultural (rather than racial) explanations for difference. Many of the desi artists became politicized in college when their studies mixed with hip hop—a combination that spoke to questions unanswered by colorblind or multicultural discourses.

Hip hop desis are attracted to the nonconformist and politically explicit theories of local rappers because of the questions they raise and the responses they give. Hip hop culture provides an important alternative that keeps race and structural inequality central to discussions in the Black—and increasingly national—public sphere, even if it garners negative press (Pough 2004; Iton 2008; see also Lipsitz 1998a). The commercialization and increasing visibility of hip hop, particularly through music videos, has encouraged greater consumption of this culture. This commodification has engendered the racist stereotypes of Blackness and "realness" that the artists resist but that nonetheless inform the responses of audiences and limit the options of non-Blacks in hip hop. But the popularity of this genre has also led to the emergence of Hip Hop studies and town hall meetings around the country about the politics of Black popular culture. If desi artists could not initially find a voice in mainstream hip hop or in these scholarly discussions, they have recently cleared some space and participate in national dialogues on hip hop, identity, and justice (Nair and Balaji 2008).[4] Yet the motivation underlying the efforts of these artists is the pleasure that overcomes them as they listen to the music of their generation.

Robin Kelley reminds popular culture scholars of the "deep visceral pleasures black youth derive from making and consuming culture" (1997: 37); the same can be said for South Asians and hip hop. The pleasure of hip hop for desi artists is equal parts music (or form, i.e., beats and track production) and message (or content, i.e., the lyrics). At first, KB felt that he "[got] into hip hop" from such an early age because he was from Richmond, California. "But looking back," he revises, "when I was in third grade, hip hop music was the only thing that ever really interested me, in terms of music . . . In terms of my creativity, somehow the idea of putting words on the paper, that style always intrigued me—something about the way the words rhymed, the way they flowed." The artists' renditions of this love story portray their connection with hip hop as neither surprising nor puzzling; they echo the reasons given by

Filipino DJs in the Bay Area, Mexican Angelenos, and Asian b-boys and b-girls in Hawai'i (Osumare 2007). Music summons sonic and visceral pleasure that we cannot reduce to technicalities of message and form (see Sacks 2007). Part of the draw is that music is a "universal language" that pulls these youths toward it. The "feel" and "emotion" of hip hop may be considered "noise" to some listeners, but it touches these desis, some of whom say it resonates with forms of Indian music. It "can give a lot of *feel*," says Deejay Bella, stressing hip hop's depth of knowledge and pleasure (Lipsitz 1994; Kelley 1997)—a view that contrasts with John McWhorter's claims in *All about the Beat* (2008) that the beats and rhythm of hip hop *deter* social consciousness.

In his book McWhorter asks, "How many among us really believe there is a meaningful connection between that rap and making people think in new ways—ways so new that the nation's fabric changes?" (143). Indeed, the engagement of mainstream desis with hip hop appear to confirm McWhorter's theory. I asked a number of desi college students what they liked about rap music, and they said that they "liked the beats" or that it was "something to dance to" but they did not really "understand the words." McWhorter and these mainstream desis reflect the perspectives of individuals primarily exposed to commercialized rap music. They may neither contextualize the images and content of mainstream hip hop nor approach the pleasure they derive from commercialized culture through an oppositional viewpoint (hooks 1999). To argue that hip hop is "just music" that is just "all about the beat" evades the depth of pleasure and its link to politics. The range of today's hip hop, including that which is produced by South Asians, reveals hip hoppers across the nation to be embracing various levels of artistic, anti-racist, and political commitments. As Public Enemy in their classic hit from 1989 "Fight the Power" explains, "As the rhythm designed to bounce / What counts is that the rhymes / Designed to fill your mind." This in fact explains why many youths are so drawn to the form *and* message of rap that they take part in its "legacy." In using hip hop as their voice desi artists engage debates on art and politics and their growing presence becomes a model for other hip hoppers and racialized immigrants. Yet form, content, and pleasure do not cover the factors urging them in this direction.

Racism, which I have discussed at length in these pages, compels these youth to embrace hip hop and distinguishes them from Whites. In place of alienation, it offers what Vivek calls "a wider urbanish Black consciousness" that results in "automatic" rather than "intentional" friendships with Black youths. Rocky, an MC from Toronto, has sentiments that echo his United States counterparts; he "quickly related to" the music of N.W.A. and Public Enemy "because they talked about racism, and how they were mistreated by the authority for doing absolutely nothing." Hip hop fills the emptiness with an analytics to comprehend American race politics.

Music is central to the articulation by underrepresented individuals of their groups' presence in America. Like hip hop, punk music "projected a disdain for mainstream society that young Chicanos found useful as a vehicle for airing their own grievances." Chicano fans found they could "gain visibility for their own views by emphasizing their families of resemblance to the alienations aired by punk," as desis do with hip hop (Lipsitz 1994: 85; see also Mahon 2004 on Black rockers). Chicanos and desis are also linked as Brown youth for whom Black and White modes of expression cannot contain their emergent identities. We find examples of Latinos and South Asians turning to Black musical forms to express their racial and American senses of self. According to Deborah Wong, "Identifying African American musics as a source for Asian American expression becomes a way for Asian American musicians to rescue certain possibilities made so difficult by racializations that muffle and silence them" (2004: 179). Specific to the early favorites of desi hip hop heads were those rappers who analyzed the nexus of the individual within societal changes. For instance, gangsta rappers in the 1980s not only glorified (and warned against) the prevalence of drugs and violence in their communities; they also highlighted the economic and political policies that led up to such travesties. Desis are among the Asian and Latino youth who were attending college when Californians passed Proposition 187 that denied social services to undocumented immigrants, voted for Proposition 21 that increasingly criminalized youth (Watkins 2005), and overturned affirmative action. The messages of hip hop helped them contextualize these changes within broader histories of oppression. Thus, while South Asians in Silicon Valley were making millions, other desis rapped their responses to the troubling conservative backlash of the time.

While co-ethnics were hearing hip hop for the first time in college, the artists already found it their "sanctuary" and "savior." By "listen[ing] to everybody else's shit," D'Lo was able to "figure out my shit." When hip hop provided the answer, D'Lo "realized that the only thing in life that was constant was music." Beyond "just the beats," hip hop "fed" the desi artists and became a "lens" through which they understood the world. Serving first as a "secret jewel" that some held tight in private, creating music collectively became "group therapy."

Adopting hip hop is a political choice (Hebdige 1987; Strauss 1999) that enables the desi artists to confront hegemonic ideas and carve their own paths (Mercer 1995). The artists embrace "conscious nonconformity" (Jones 1963: 187) in their world approach and life choices. Ravi, the cofounder of an independent record label, told me that hip hop often appeals to outcasts and misfits. It is true that desi hip hoppers tend to be different, independent, and nonconformist. Not only do they go against family and community pressures to associate with the "proper" people and follow traditional paths; many of them also question the notion of "norms" in the first place.

Hip hop is also attractive because it combines these desis' interests in academics, music, and critical ideology. They were questioning the world as early as high school when music and critical thinking came together with ideological force. For instance, had it not been for two "hippie-ish, really bright counterculture" high school teachers, Jonny would have "stayed on the right track," he says with some irony, and might have become an accountant instead of making the "somewhat adventurous" choice to become a music journalist. Such teachers "armed" their students how to think: "To question authority. To think for ourselves. To believe in something. To discover how all is not what it seems. To really extend our thought process beyond the surface and to make connections amongst various elements." These concepts were "really intoxicating and formed the foundation" of the rest of Jonny's life. Their lessons of critical thinking and challenging authority "all culminated in empowering us as individuals, in having us realize we could think for ourselves and weren't just a cog in the big machine." Indeed, these lessons, later taught by ethnic studies college professors, echoed the ideas of their favorite rappers who were beginning to get airtime. Critical thinking skills developed their social aware-ness, and the sermons of their favorite rappers articulated what such a perspective could offer.

Desi hip hop artists fall within a legacy of non-Blacks drawn to the rebellion in Black expressive forms—including the blues, jazz, and hip hop—that refer to messages of revolt against the mas-ter narratives of American history and meritocracy (Woods 1998). These desis are attracted to hip hop's rebellion as resistance against oppression rather than rebellion as the wild side of life. In this way, hip hop desis sometimes contend with their predicaments in ways similar to earlier White jazz musicians. Jazz offered some Jews and Italians a means through which to work out ethnic ambivalences by enabling them to critique "mainstream" society and by serving as an alternative to a sober middle-class White American lifestyle (Lipsitz 1994: 55). Hip hop's desis, like White jazz musicians and Chicano punk rockers, contest rebelliousness as their primary or only motive. For example, some Whites in jazz ostracized them-selves despite their access to a mainstream or privileged status and chose to identify with Black performers, the nonconformists (Jones 1963: 200). Desis, particularly educated suburbanites, are also non-Blacks with access to a (relatively) privileged identity. And as non-Blacks who turn to a predominantly Black form, they too must assess their status. In his book *Blues People* Amiri Baraka (LeRoi Jones) reveals how White jazz artists "had to face the black Ameri-can head-on and with only a very literal drum to beat. And they could not help but do this with some sense of rebellion of separate-ness from the rest of white America" (1963: 152).

In the process of developing their critical perspectives, hip hop's nonconformity drew the desi artists to its form, content, and com-munity. Beats and rhymes resonate with the performers, but hip hop was not *strictly responsible* for developing their nonconform-ism; instead, their sense of alienation and engagement with criti-cal thinking inspired this move. The need to interrogate the world preceded their engagement with the messages of hip hop in the late 1980s and early 1990s.

According to MC Humanity from Staten Island, New York, "The ability of rap to [express] so much of what's on a person's mind was something that drew me to it. The social messages and the poetic wordplay were elements that made hip hop a part of me."

At a forum across the country in San Francisco, Davey D, a nationally renowned Black DJ and hip hop commentator, confirmed that "hip hop has always been political and reflected the conditions of the people." Hip hop is an ideology, a way of thinking, as well as a way of being. Many fans who are drawn to the beats and images of hip hop may be uninterested in the development of this culture, its messages, or its producers. But its lyrical and overall content claim center stage to its attraction for many minority youth, including the South Asians who become expert rhymers, mixers, and producers.

Unlike some Latinos and Caribbean Islanders, desis do not always share geographic, material, and racial overlaps with Blacks. For instance, some Latino youths, particularly Puerto Ricans in the South Bronx and Mexicans in Los Angeles, also felt excluded from the American mainstream and became core participants in the development of hip hop culture. Filipinos earned a remarkable presence as some of the first mobile DJ sound system crews in the 1980s in Daly City and Los Angeles (Wang, forthcoming). They share South Asians' ambiguous racial status and may feel linked to Latinos as Brown Americans (particularly given their mestizo Spanish and Catholic backgrounds), but their residential patterns place them closer than most South Asians to Black communities (such as Bayview, near Daly City). It is also not surprising that Cambodians like PraCh in Long Beach, California, home to the rapper Snoop Dogg, would go on to become MCs. But it is precisely desis' non-Whiteness that radicalizes them and links them to hip hop.

The messages the artists felt the most were not the images of rappers as gangsters and criminals that became status quo, particularly with the rise of Los Angeles gangsta rap in the 1980s. Neither were they drawn to lyrics that glorified money and the commodities it could buy, even though this theme became so popular in the mid-1990s. Instead, they specifically picked up on the positive messages of politicized rappers and were pulled to the early rhymes of resistance that sonically and intellectually represented a counterhegemonic and anti-racist sensibility. The combination of Black American musicians' "tradition of explaining reality and change" (Woods 1998: 25) and the consciousness "in the air" in the Bay Area and of the music convinced these youth, critical thinkers all, that positive social change could result from their participation. They learned from street intellectuals like Ice Cube, Nas, and Public Enemy why they were treated as minorities and why they felt like "outcasts" and "outsiders."

As they came of age in college in the 1990s, a resistance ideology counter to the status quo became more appealing as both a method and a theory. These aspects of hip hop are similar to *corridos*, or ballads of "poetic symbolic action" created within the context of social struggle (Limón 1992: 170). The artist MC Humanity and his cousin AbstractVision, were moved by the "raw, unrestrained anger" of the Black rapping duo Dead Prez and the "South Asian perspective" of England's Asian Dub Foundation (ADF), who "had a socially conscious message in all their music." As a Pakistani Muslim living in New York, MC Humanity says that he "related to the racism [ADF] felt as South Asians, as well. They talk a lot about the racial oppression felt by our communities and other communities of color," thereby echoing the global race consciousness that these artists would later proclaim. The song "Colour Line" by ADF illustrates this appeal:

Today the colour line/is the power line/is the poverty line
Racism and imperialism work in tandem
And poverty is their handmaiden
Those who are poor and powerless to break out of their poverty
Are also those who by and large are non-white, non-western, third world
Poverty and powerlessness are intertwined in colour, in race
Discrimination and exploitation feed into each other today, under global capitalism

American rappers articulate how racism works in the United States, and politicized British Asian music expresses how racism operates across transnational communities. But analyses of oppression by American desis are neither nation- nor race-bound. One lesson these artists share with their British and American counterparts is that in order to critique racism one has to uncover its historical workings. Thus, they evoke "history" and "ancestry" once they turn their knowledge to action and produce their own rhymes.

Rappers like Chuck D and Queen Latifah taught listeners that it is important to call out inequality and to see that the past imprints the present. Politicized desis incorporate this lesson in their studies of subaltern colonialism and displacement, and it also informs their approach to music and identity formation. In contrast, Dick Hebdige emphasizes the aesthetics of style in bringing together multiracial groups in Britain as it "displaces attention away from the question of ethnic origin onto the question of how to build affinities on a shared cultural and aesthetic ground" (1996: 141). Additionally, Oliver Wang believes that some Asian American rappers attempt to use skills to trump race as a way to obviate the need for a shared past; instead, they seem to embrace the popular rapping veteran Rakim's famous line, as quoted by Wang, "It ain't where you're from, it's where you're at" (2007: 48). Desis diverge in their compelling need to excavate the histories they see playing out in contemporary relations and identifications.

Crates of records speak to Deejay Bella in the same way that an archive speaks to a historian: "So, instead of a book or a TV show, or a documentary or film about a period of time in history, you know, listening to a series of music is the same for me . . . [It's] musical knowledge and it's history . . . 'Cause it's the history of the way that music is recorded [and] reflects the times." These look backs that emphasize context reject ahistorical discourses of the 1990s. Hip hop as the Black CNN became a boisterous and informed response to new coded forms of oppression. Rhymes that uncover how "*culture can also function like a nature, and it* [i.e., culture] can in particular function as a way of locking individuals and groups a priori into a genealogy, into a determination that is immutable and intangible in origin" (Balibar 1991: 22) allow desis to engage strategically their newly unearthed knowledge of South Asian pasts.

The artists harness the political potential of hip hop not only as an ideology and response to racism but also as a methodology for acquiring and relaying new forms of knowledge. Such practices evoke Michel Foucault's genealogical methodology of illuminating hidden histories to challenge master narratives that naturalize power and group identities in his examination of discourses, hegemony, and self-discipline (see Foucault 1990, 1995). And while Foucault may take issue with the artists' quest for "truth," the desis' process of becoming expert artists embodies his knowledge/power nexus. Historicizing cultural norms and discourses, such as hegemonic desiness, allows them to understand the power and production of knowledge, such as "race," and its metamorphosis into "common sense." It was the rap group Public Enemy that put together these messages: to recognize and decode racism, to pay attention to the past and illustrate broader contexts, and to articulate a race-conscious and resistant ideology.

From Black Power to Brown Pride

I learned a lot about the Black experience and saw that as the defining framework for ANY race discussions in America.
—Jonny, hip hop journalist

"When I first heard Public Enemy," D'Lo says, "I was blown away. I was like, finally. It wasn't like, 'whoa, this is some cool shit.' I was like, FINALLY. I felt finally that it was like (pause), somebody was finally gonna give me the space to say what I needed to say. I was like, 'oh, this is exactly what I was looking for.'" Every artist in this project was influenced by Public Enemy—the Black Nationalist rap group initially formed by Chuck D and friends at a college radio station in Long Island, New York—which rose to prominence in the late 1980s and early 1990s.[5] "Fight the Power," one of their most potent and popular songs, incites consciousness:

What we need is awareness, we can't get careless

. . . .

My beloved let's get down to business
Mental self defensive fitness

. . . .

Make everybody see, in order to fight the powers that be
Lemme hear you say
Fight the Power!

"I'm Black and I'm proud," this music exclaims, thereby filling the artists with a deeper sense of self. D'Lo "thought it was so dope that they were saying something. Public Enemy. To just even talk about Black people and what they were gonna do for their people." Many Americans had never before confronted the fast-pitched, highly energetic sonic manifestos found on the album *Fear of a Black Planet*. Chuck D's lyrics proved that the past wasn't past: "Most of my heroes don't appear on no stamps / Sample a look back you look and find / Nothing but rednecks for 400 years if you check."

The Black Nationalism of Public Enemy was also expressed by

other artists of that time, including Ice Cube and Grand Puba, and among more recent rappers like Boots Riley of the Coup, and the deceased Tupac Shakur, who have roots in Oakland. While many early hip hop tracks were party music, a good segment of late 1980s and early 1990s rap took up where the Black Power Movement left off, articulating disenchantment with static economic opportunities.[6] Compton's Ice Cube, in the song "A Bird in the Hand" (1991), laments the slim job options for young Blacks without college degrees: "I didn't have no money so now I have to hunch the / back like a slave, that's what be happenin' / but whitey says there's no room for the African." Some desis welcomed these California rappers since they addressed local concerns that echoed the "Black noise" of New York's Public Enemy (Rose 1994).

Some young Black men and women who witnessed the disappointments of the post–civil rights era in their cities called upon hip hop to voice their anger. California's rappers, including the so-called gangsta rappers of L.A., pointed their fingers at the fiscal conservatism of Ronald Reagan and George Bush Sr., the policies of Republican Governor Pete Wilson, and the increasing police brutality and incarceration of young Black and Latino men under the LAPD's Chief Daryl Gates (who helped create Special Weapons and Tactics [SWAT] teams). Young desi teens heard these indictments in the rhymes of Ice T's "6 in the Mornin'" (1987) and, of course, N.W.A.'s notorious "Fuck tha Police" (1988). These messages may have bypassed those Asian immigrants who wished to close ranks against the increasing volume of rap music, not expecting that this music might appeal to some of their own children.

In this context, it may be surprising that the cries to "fight the power" spoke to middle-class South Asian Americans who had benefited from "the system." Not all of the artists were privileged, as I noted earlier, and many witnessed these structural changes firsthand. Despite their youth, these South Asian artists were like the Asian American jazz musicians who saw "their own activities as an expression of an important political moment" linked to the activism of the 1960s (Wong 2004: 179). Chuck D and his group expressed a politically oriented understanding of the United States. And for these desis, the call to "fight the power" reflected not only American racial dynamics but also anticolonial struggles abroad. Hip hop's desis agreed: "don't believe the hype" of South Asian stereotypes and the purity and exceptionalism of desi culture. As Jonny explains, "I think hip hop's anti-establishment sensibilities resonated with the general feeling I felt about me—reveling in being different and 'un-mainstream.' Hip hop at that time was really political, whether it was obvious (Public Enemy) or not (De La Soul)." These youths were politically committed to understanding and critiquing the system, and Public Enemy shouted that there would be repercussions.

At first the performers adopted, wholesale, Public Enemy's message as their own. The artists were not exposed to a sufficiently critical narrative of the desi experience with regard to race and discrimination. Thus, their initial reaction was to align themselves with Blacks and to see how they fit into the Black American experience. Jonny says that, "for a short time, I think I became seduced with Black culture and I used the politics to justify my seduction after the fact." In time, however, they realized that in order to apply Black Power ideologies to their own contexts, they needed to resolve how hip hop could address their own experiences.

Musical desis sampled these powerful messages and mixed them with their awareness of the South Asian histories and immigrant processes that shaped their lives. As D'Lo notes, after hearing Public Enemy for the first time "I immediately started claiming 'Brown Power' out my mouth." D'Lo later relayed this distinction to his/her cousin from Toronto (home to a population of Sri Lankan wartime refugees) who wore a Malcolm X cap. "Why are you wearing that?" D'Lo asked him. "You can't touch that, that's Black people's thing," D'Lo schooled him. "We got to reclaim something for ourselves." But, looking around, where were the corresponding desi-based articulations? Before they could produce it themselves, the desi artists translated Black Nationalist sentiments by racializing their ethnic identities through addressing power and history. D'Lo epitomizes how individuals can cultivate interminority and international relations when non-Blacks identify *with* Blacks without confusing themselves *as* Black. I was curious how D'Lo developed a perspective that recognized racial crossovers while maintaining a sense of difference. "It's just like you couldn't be stupid," s/he responded. Also, it came with D'Lo's choice to disidentify with Whites, unlike many other middle-class desis. Jonny and D'Lo were attempting to sort out a racialized self-conception not provided in mainstream discourses of how individuals come together in groups rooted in both "sameness" and "difference." The distinctions between the experiences of immigrants and native-born minorities, between Brownness and Blackness, mattered, and yet these individuals could come together as minorities concerned about social change.

In a seemingly ironic twist, Black Nationalism inspired the artists to develop Brown Pride. At this point, some of them realized that through this move they could maintain their identities as desis without having to claim a Black identity. Thus, their worldviews did not *transcend* racial distinctions; rather they took into account how racialization operates upon different populations. Brown Pride emphasizes that race cannot be forsaken for some utopian and transcendent humanism or other category of sameness. The identity politics of Black Power limited the legitimacy of non-Black claims to it, which encouraged the young desis' processes of remixing Black Nationalist rap messages into ethnic awareness in their own lyrics. D'Lo, for instance, who was facing homophobia as well as racism in his/her youth, was also concerned about the civil war in Sri Lanka and the political, social, and nation-conscious nature of rap helped him/her make sense of this.

Thus, the desi hip hop producers drew on the messages of the 1990s to politicize and racialize their ethnicity, and they examined their relationships with Blacks at home and South Asians abroad. Jonny explained that "it was through [Black popular culture that] I then discovered my own politics . . . I started to gain pride in being both Indian and contrarian," and in his reworking this view was not a contradiction. Jonny in fact was able to develop both of these aspects of his identity—his Indianness and his being against the desi grain—in college through Black music, which became the "lens" through which he viewed the world. Being "Brown" and being a hip hop head did not define Jonny's identity so much as express a worldview: being a critical thinker, questioning the norms of society, delving into race politics, and cultivating an appreciation for aesthetics.

Hip hop's desis didn't respond to Public Enemy as either Blacks or Whites—as *their* call to Black Power, as an attack (feeling that Public Enemy was shouting *at* them), or as a stylistic choice. They responded as non-White youth, the Brown children of immigrants, and as minorities. Public Enemy and other influential rap groups cultivated among desis an explicitly racialized, politicized conception and vocabulary for racial pride as Brown people, the very identity upon which Whites have enacted racism against them. But political rhymes also compelled them to create more inclusive visions of the oppressed. In his/her poem "When You Have no Choice," D'Lo recites:

We hear the stories
Of Mothers getting caught in the crossfire between gun and son
Of young girls getting raped
with sticks and poles
Of men tortured to death by fire
Of children snatched and sliced open
for the whole world to see . . .
In Kwanju, In Sri Lanka, In Newark, In the Philippines, In Mexico
We banded together to fight
ignorance and arrogance
We had no choice but to take up arms

D'Lo's connection is a global one to peoples at war for a freedom that "Comes with a price / And no one questions whether it's worth it." Although s/he loves Sri Lanka, D'Lo also criticizes the corruption and laments the situation of children who have never lived in a nation of peace:

Regardless, we are an alcoholic nation run by alcoholics
who fail with the militants thru negotiations to bring on peace for
    the nation.
Don't think I'm lying . . .
But besides all the bullshit,
we all love our island even if it is still in political turmoil

Hip hop has also always been, and continues to be, a voice of resistance—a critical interrogation of the "establishment." However, through D'Lo's loving criticism we also see the artists take part in a hip hop conversation of internal community critique, and therein is another powerful reason for why it appeals to some South Asian Americans. By listening—*really* listening—to rap lyrics, especially those created before the mid-1990s, desis in hip hop reflected on how rappers' articulations about being Black, and the conditions of Black men and women in America, related to their own experiences. In many ways it confirmed their developing race consciousness. But they also used it to speak back to those things they found problematic within their ethnic communities, including those outside the United States, thereby expanding diasporic dialogues through Black music. Hip hop was an appropriate vehicle for their immigrant perspective on global and local matters of inequality. And what they did with it, like the Spanish-infused rap music of the Nuyoricans and the Mexican Angelenos, encourages other hip hop heads to look beyond both the nation and racial categorization.

Like the blues, hip hop provides epistemology (Woods 1998: 29); desis, in turn, improvise upon it. If America's most oppressed group can celebrate and express such fierce resistance and pride through the blues, jazz, and hip hop, perhaps overlooked desis can also adopt this form to articulate their developing voice. Often the artists do this by forging communities with individuals who share "like ideology" rather than by bonding within exclusively defined categories. Counterintuitively, the message of Black Nationalist rap has taught some artists that ideology, rather than identity, is critical to advancing an anti-racist, critically aware perspective of the world. Their Third World race consciousness, articulated by Malcolm X as I show in the beginning of this book, melds Chuck D's racial outrage with Gandhian principles of tolerance and love. These sons and daughters of formerly colonized people create a global race consciousness that is particularly attentive to the international and cross-racial impacts of White supremacy and United States hegemony.

Desi artists who make diasporically attuned hip hop feel the solo and the social draw of hip hop. Chee, for instance, often says that through hip hop he came to understand himself better. And while music production, rhyme writing, turntabalism, and mastering a track are often solo endeavors, the artists also turn outward in making hip hop their life. The sonic appeal of the music leads them to cultivate multiracial communities of interest centered on a shared lifestyle. According to Deejay Bella, "When you meet other people who are interested in [music] as well . . . it just deepens your knowledge and just keeps you in that realm." And beyond their love of hip hop ("because, frankly, a lot of people like hip hop," admits Jonny), shared values and perspectives brings together hip hop heads.

The artists' musical and activist commitments reinforce one another: some teach in public schools, trace the effects of environmental racism, and hire young Black men and women in their companies to try to counteract the unequal playing field for minorities in education and employment. Others have worked for Amnesty International and Human Rights Watch, and have created their own social justice organizations. Asma, a Muslim Indian woman from Richmond, California, became a radio producer of a popular urban radio talk show and a radio news director. Her interest in public and youth-based programming for the masses emerged from dinnertime conversations with her parents about illiteracy in India. D'Lo was able to explore why things in the world were not right through women-centered collaborations and antiwar performances. Hip hop is a form that decries racism and other issues these artists have faced by giving them substance, form, and a platform for expression.

Desi artists revel in hip hop's "capacity to challenge the old racial politics" (Kitwana 2005: 4). Latinos, South Asians, and other Asian Americans also change the old racial politics, and thus move beyond Black and White conceptions of racial identifications and community. Public Enemy gave D'Lo the opening to articulate his/her fears and frustrations about the war in Sri Lanka, and then s/he made it his/hers: "Because I so strongly identified with Sri Lanka and what was going on there," s/he says, ". . . that sort of set me apart in a way where hip hop became mine. . . . Because that was the vehicle, the culture, that I even had a platform to talk about the injustice. 'Cause nothing else in this world would. And [if] I can talk about shit that's going on in my life, then that allows for other people to talk about shit in their life, do you get what I'm saying?" The artists took part in a dialogic process of give and take, learning about the experiences of some young urban Blacks and making hip hop a voice for some young South Asians, thereby contributing an important perspective to hip hop (Rose 1994). They are like the Cambodian rapper PraCh, for instance, who creates a "transnational hip hop nation" by drawing parallels between America's genocide of Southeast Asians with "Whites to the Blacks" (Schlund-Vials 2008).

Desi performers, too, inform audiences, including Blacks, about South Asian pasts and predicaments. These are political acts at the level of everyday action rooted in informed sampling and dialogic exchange.

A central draw of hip hop for these performers is its give-and-take nature; or, as the African art historian Robert Thompson describes, "Black music *communalizes*" (quoted in Cosentino 1992: 54). Participants are joined not only by shared experiences but also shared references, or "public secrets" (Jackson 2008), that help define a community. Beyond this, desis do not just join with like-minded individuals but instead take an active role in giving back to audiences those things that hip hop has so critically given them. The rapper K B emphasizes the social aspects of hip hop as community building, as follows: "People. People have things to say. And when people are talking about something they care about and put so much emphasis into it, it's beautiful." But in order to "break down barriers," as artists like D'Lo and K B do, they must express their *messages* to audiences, who are often quite stuck on either their images (an Indian rapper?) or their deep bass lines. The message is primary; the music is the vehicle of delivery. "I'm a lot more about the words than the music, myself," K B says. The messages they offer are positive as they perform new models of desiness.

The artists' international lens and incorporation of South Asian samples also calls to mind the fact of the cross-Atlantic continuities evident within hip hop music, including the storytelling of West African griots and the percussive-based music and Jamaican toasting that influenced rapping (Thompson 1983). Cyclical, rooted in community, the use of call and response—the kinds of sociality that Brown artists foster on the dance floor are grounded in practices that are foundational to Black music but expand beyond African-descended communities. Thus, perhaps even more than they are aware, the deployment by desis of traditionally Black practices alters the meanings and representations of ethnicity and race in the United States. Sammy, cofounder of Rukus Avenue Records, describes how desis elevate their standing in the United States by harnessing hip hop's potential: "It's always been about a social consciousness . . . Here we are and we're standing between our culture and everybody else saying, 'here, come on up to our world and this is how we choose to do it.'" Jonny felt the same tug from earlier rappers: "It felt like you were playing for the team that was just beginning to rise to the top." This is about more than the camaraderie and sociality of producing music with a message that moves the crowd. Despite the obstacles they face, the artists are nourished by expressing themselves, being heard, and connecting with their audiences. Deejay Bella relays with a huge smile the joys of giving back: "When you love music so much, you want to keep playing it. And when you can play it in a flow, in a continuous flow, it makes the whole emotion that much heavier, that much deeper . . . Music is a collaborative thing." And, in response, she gets back what she gives: "It's amazing. It's *amazing* that somebody you've never met before, who's never met you, actually *felt* what you played, and would actually tell you that." Hip hop emerges from these intangible links between music, visceral responses, and the bonds among collaborators.

As these individuals invest their time and money, becoming experts and professional performers, they explain that hip hop *made them*, rather than the other way around. One DJ says that "having a lot of music around, talking about music all the time" is very necessary. For an MC, music is "always on my mind. I'm always thinking about this." They listen to it, think about it, talk about it, read it, write it, make it. Constantly. Music is at the center of their lives. And just as hip hop was a voice for disenfranchised Blacks, it has become a voice for this range of middle class desis who feel compelled to express their experiences and understand the world around them. For these youths hip hop is not a "phase" in response to generational conflicts and the difficulties of adjusting to life as immigrants. They have spent the majority of their lives in and around hip hop culture, whether producing, writing, and rhyming in the studio or at home, clubs, or shows. They are drawn to the counterhegemonic messages and the sonic force of this culture still rooted in resistance against oppression and the status quo. It is "good music" that appeals to critical thinkers because it is filled with politicized vocabularies that theorize and claim witness to race, difference, and inequality in America.

There are no straightforward or clear-cut distinctions of how South Asian Americans entered hip hop and what they did once they became established artists. Some of them, like KB (Karmacy), Rawj (Feenom Circle), and Chee (Himalayan Project), are drawn to lyrics and performance. The accessibility and "practicality" of the technical aspects, like mixing and producing, draw others, like Bella and Sammy. Nonetheless, the desi artists love and dedicate their lives to this culture for almost identical reasons. It draws those who "go against the grain" and are nonconformist. It is also a culture that accepts many people who are rejected by their ethnic communities. Hip hop is a way for them to remain true to self through a racially conscious but not race-exclusive approach; after all, it enables their transnational identities and ethnic expressions. They say it best expresses their worldviews and their social locations and commitments. Rap music speaks to these desis and it is their ultimate hope that their own carefully crafted messages reach the ears of others. But how do these individuals conceptualize who owns hip hop culture, what its relation is to Blackness, and how non-Black producers earn a rightful place?

The Blackness of Hip Hop: Whose Is It, Anyway?

Maybe Blacks cling to rap because it is ours. Hands down. Period . . . It coincides with the slang, "secret culture" that Blacks use to relate to one another . . . that common bond, which is the underlying principle of what culture really means. Heck, you're an anthropologist, you know what I mean.—Anthony, Black hip hop fan from Oakland, California

A coolie that can spit some lyrics? Oh, you're going to be a star!
—a Black rapper to a desi MC

I asked Anthony, an old college friend of mine who first introduced me to both hip hop and his friends and family in Oakland, what hip hop meant to him. Like D'Lo, Anthony, who did not have an easy life, found hip hop "therapeutic"—a way to "express yourself about your anger." But now, over a decade since I asked him this question, I must reconsider seriously whether or not Blacks still *own* hip hop, "hands down"? And even whether *Blacks* still own hip hop. Who is included in this "secret culture," and is there something "Black" at its core? These debates force Brown hip hoppers to deal with their position within a Black art form, which they do by reconceptualizing the culture in a way that includes them. The debates are deeply contested ones and it is not my intention to provide the ultimate answers. Instead, I analyze what the explanations by South Asian artists of their place in hip hop tell us about Blackness, representation, the politics of location, and the ownership of culture. Surprisingly, although these desis consider themselves legitimate hip hop artists, they do not all agree that hip hop is multiracial. Ultimately, these non-Black performers highlight not only the racial politics of culture, but the fact that popular culture is a highly political field in which transformative action *around* race (rather than "above" it) can take place. Debates that loom large—including contests over ownership and authenticity—often obscure these facts.

Ironically, the very principles and practices foundational to hip hop, including its community-based and populist grounding, have given rise to some of the most debated topics among fans about what—and who—constitutes "real" hip hop. "There's always been a yin and yang in the community and what comes out is what the community allows," Davey D says of hip hop. "Hip hop is what the people is . . . Hip hop is all of us." But Davey D tends to agree with Imani Perry's explicit statement that "hip hop music is black American music" (2004: 9–10). What is at stake in the Blackness of hip hop? Analyses that reduce "the community" to Blacks, even for strategic reasons, are problematic because they reify both Blacks and hip hop and render Black expressive forms static. And because the artists draw from these conceptions, they have a difficult time describing both the Blackness of hip hop and their own locations.

Hip hop is rooted in practices of other Black musical forms, including the oral tradition (going back to African griots), call and response, and improvisation, all of which work to cultivate and define the parameters of community along with pleasure and self-expression (Thompson 1983). With changing technology and the particular historical juncture in which hip hop arose (Rose 1994), sampling, new forms of cutting and mixing, and rhymers' messages relayed in ciphers combine to make hip hop not only parallel anti-essentialist identity formation but also open to adoption by ever-expanding communities. In fact, these aspects are generative of the political adoption of hip hop by individuals across color and national lines. Still, perhaps the biggest issue surrounding disputes over racial authenticity in this area are the effects of corporate capitalism and the problematic and profit-driven links that corporate leaders make between racist stereotypes of Black men and women with "real" hip hop. It is profitable for businesses to sell the images of Black masculinity and femininity, including notions of sexuality and criminality, that emerged during slavery (Collins 2004). Companies wanting to reach larger (i.e., White) audiences turn commercial forms of hip hop consumption into voyeuristic fetishizations of the other that naturalize the status quo. Thus, while hip hop practices encourage its adoption, the stakes of some businesses and individuals in claiming hip hop reify it as a Black-only enterprise, even as these stakes work at cross-purposes.

The common perception that "real" hip hop is created only by urban Black males is molded by corporate White interests. The process of cultural development intersects with its commercialization by global and local capital that reifies both hip hop and the producers of this culture. The process of commodification decontextualizes objects by transforming its content and producers into something palatable for mass consumption. Reified forms of Blackness thus become consumed by those who are unaware, unconcerned perhaps, of its producers and the context of cultural production. The heterogeneity of members of the African diaspora, crisscrossed by ethnicity, gender, sexuality, political views, immigration status, and a host of other factors that critically define individuals, becomes lost in translation. Mainstream desis, for instance, substitute this reality with static one-dimensional images perpetuated in the media and by politicians because it accommodates their perspectives.

The historical appropriation of Black music by Whites has understandably made "ownership" a central concern about power, representation, and recognition (monetary and otherwise). So where do Asians stand? Shall we flip Davey D's example about Latinos and say, "Asian to me is White?" The communal nature of hip hop confuses the question of authenticity: hip hop culture, itself, questions the concepts of purity and individual authorship through sampling and remixing, thereby complicating the idea of copyrightable intellectual property (see Sharma 1999). So can South Asian Americans not be authentic rappers? Its cutting-edge and rapidly changing nature highlights the ephemeral, rather than static and pure, character of symbols, signs, and commodities, and of culture itself (Gilroy 1993b). If we apply these same concepts not only to expressive forms but to *race itself*, the political potential of hip hop expands. Nonetheless, the meanings and representations of "Blackness" and Black people must remain at the center of conversations about the ownership and authorship of hip hop. This expressive culture is unequivocally rooted in Black aesthetic forms and comes from the perspectives of this particularly racialized and disenfranchised population.

Hip hip is not *either* a multiracial art form *or* a Black one. Rather, hip hop is a multiracial production of Black popular culture. This conception differs from that of Perry, who asks, "Why can't something be black (read *Black American*) and be influenced by a number of cultures and styles at the same time" (2004: 10)? In my formulation, hip hop is undeniably tied to the experiences of Blacks and to a lineage of Black musics, but it is more than *influenced by* a "number of cultures and styles." Blacks represent a variety of cultures and styles and non-Blacks have contributed centrally to this creation, illustrated in recent historical studies, although none have dealt with South Asian Americans. Debaters often overlook the diverse and diasporic roots of Blacks in America; post-1965 immigrants from the Caribbean—particularly from Jamaica, homeland of the legendary DJ Kool Herc and second-generation islanders such as Busta Rhymes and Biggie Smalls—infused early hip hop with the sounds of reggae and dancehall. Jeff Chang's *Can't Stop, Won't Stop* (2005) details the participation of Latinos on the East and West Coasts. The Chicano Angeleno Kid Frost and the Cuban, Mexican, and Italian MCs that comprise Cypress Hill were popular and influential artists in the 1990s. The more recent fame of Nuyoricans like Big Pun, Fat Joe (RIP), and Angie Martinez, along with the global phenomenon of reggaeton, only hint at the overall presence of Latinos that has inspired Spanish rhymes among even non-Latino Blacks.

Mentioning these revisionist histories often provokes unproductive debates about "real" or "diluted" music, concepts that Baraka (LeRoi Jones 1963) applies to his interpretation of Whites in jazz and the blues, which trap music as an unchanging pure form. How much more productive would it be were we to reorient the ownership/authenticity debate by focusing on an artist's *approach* to hip hop, rather than on an artist's *identity*? This anti-essentialist approach evaluates the artists' motives, skills, and locations within urban culture without erasing hip hop as an American Black cultural formation deeply attendant to the politics of race that also extends beyond those commonly considered "Black." Centering our analysis on artists' approaches to hip hop displaces hegemonic Blackness (and maleness and a working class status) as the requisite(s) for "real" hip hop. As a result, diverse representatives of hip hop can become antidotes to the monotonous and flattened depictions of commodified Blackness. This perspective does not "take away" hip hop from the young urban Black males who create it; rather it represents the membership and concerns of an expansive hip hop nation.

Some non-Blacks are grabbed by this culture because of their race consciousness that emerges from their experiences as American minorities. The investment of these desis in hip hop is a political act of race-conscious identification. They "sincerely adopt hip hop," which includes "their embrace of both the aesthetic and political location of blackness" rather than deracializing Black cultural formations (Perry 2004: 27).[7] The hip hop nation is indeed multiracial and transnational, but this is not to say that it has transcended the import of race. Hip hop culture, in fact, can provide the platform for expanding racial matters beyond people of African descent precisely because of its attention to racism. It enables multiracial conversations among individuals who articulate their linked fates. American desis who become artists engage with Blacks who shape their awareness of the politics of hip hop. As producers, they contend with being non-Blacks in a highly racialized field. Their strategy is to call upon the race-conscious vocabulary of hip hop to explain themselves while they expand the parameters of mainstream rap music—and perhaps of Blackness, itself—by their presence and perspectives.

Desi Artists Locate Themselves in Hip Hop

Two central issues shape desi performers' conceptions of hip hop: its racial dynamics as a culture rooted in the experiences of Blacks in the United States, and the influence of White corporate interests in depoliticizing and commodifying stereotyped "Blackness." When a Black countercultural form marries major capitalist interests marketed to mainstream consumers, fans question the "real-ness" or "authenticity" of the form. Mainstream consumers, who are mostly but not all White, determine and want hip hop to be like the rapper 50 Cent—Black, male, and from the 'hood. As a result, this rapid commodification pushes debates about the racial membership of the hip hop nation into a global conversation. Musicians are deeply implicated in and often torn by the constraints and dynamics of capital as they try to produce, promote, and distribute their art. The artists agree that commodified hip hop is inauthentic (c)rap. They universally dislike the commercial marketing of rap music because they see media representations as neither Black culture nor hip hop, but rather the peddling of racist stereotypes and the (uncool) sale of coolness. The corporations' disinterest in explicitly political rappers who criticize big business and capitalism at large for advancing racism and economic oppression further dissuade the identification of desis with commercial rap—similar to their disidentification with other hegemonic forms. Therefore, none of the artists locate themselves within commercial hip hop, first because it is closed to them as non-Blacks, and second because they feel commercial rap is about neither the message nor ideology of hip hop. This explains why all of the desi MCs produce socially conscious music along with party tracks, battle raps, and nostalgic looks back, which they usually self-produce and promote out of their backpacks and the trunks of their cars.[8]

Although the artists detach themselves from mainstream rap, their conception of hip hop's racial politics often contradicts their sense as legitimate MCs and DJs. Some call upon the transcendent multiracial quality of hip hop today; these artists tend to create ethnic hip hop. A second perspective, held by those who create racialized hip hop, believe that hip hop is, at its core, Black. Neither perspective accounts for their identification as artists—a shortcoming of how we speak about race in the United States. Despite their varying viewpoints on this matter, in their socializing and music making their lives resemble one another more than they differ. Neither hip hop as racially transcendent nor hip hop as strictly Black suffices. Ultimately, their theorizations reveal a movement toward a third perspective, which can be characterized by Vivek's conception of a "wider Black consciousness."

> Originally, it was a Black art form, but it's not anymore. It's transcended all those boundaries. And it applies to people now. Hip hop is about people. It's about unity, about fostering equality among people. It gives people a voice. —KB, desi Karmacy MC

Nearly half of the artists share KB's notion that hip hop is a voice of the people, and that hip hop has transcended the boundaries of race. These proponents argue that although hip hop stemmed from the Black experience of oppression in America, it has now expanded to become universal, much like other Black musical forms. As a result, non-Black artists can partake in its creation. According to KB, "Hip hop arose out of the struggle of oppressed people . . . It was a way to express those emotions that couldn't otherwise be expressed."[9]

Artists espousing this transcendent view of hip hop argue that fans erase its multiracial history in order to emphasize hip hop as a culture for, by, and about Black people. The multiracialists challenge my college friend Anthony's insistence that hip hop belongs to Blacks, "Hands down. Period." Asian Americans may be hard pressed to claim to have been a sizable presence in hip hop's earliest renditions, but Asian cultural formations, including martial arts films, were influential. Thus, some non-Black artists within the hip hop community contend with their non-Black status by pointing to hip hop as a culture of change, now open to non-Blacks.

A contradiction emerges, however, when we notice that the artists who stand by this perspective often feel placeless in mainstream hip hop where the record label owners tend to be White and the artists they sign are most often Black. Although these desis want to use hip hop as a platform, they feel they have to create a distinctly South Asian space outside the mainstream. One producer, for instance, worked for a major music company but felt there was no room to express himself as an Indian. This inspired artists like Sammy to alter the recognizable form and sound of hip hop and fuse it with South Asian instrumentals and immigrant themes in order to target desi audiences. This ethnic form of hip hop epitomizes their concept that hip hop is a "multiracial creation." Perhaps music tran-

Karmacy rapper KB performs at the House of Blues.
Author's photograph.

scends boundaries, but hip hop has not transcended racial politics within the United States, which inflects hip hop, thereby making some desis feel marginalized.

Some who share this perspective link the inclusive nature of hip hop to what they deem to be the positive aspects of the culture's increasing ties to global capital. Sammy says that hip hop "is growing now. Hip hop is not only growing through power structures, but also through cultural and social structures." He says that as hip hop has exploded as a business, what was once limited to a "Black struggle for [their] minority environment" has now changed and has begun "to go in a different direction." The commodification of Black popular culture has taken troubling forms, yet the waves of global capital also carry the voices of formerly silenced populations around the world. Also, the Internet supplants some of the music monopolies and exposes audiences to a polyvalent array of music. The increasing accessibility and conspicuous presence of hip hop is representative of a generation. Whereas Bakari Kitwana (2002) uses "the hip hop generation" to describe Blacks born between 1965 and 1984, Sammy argues that "*we're* known as the hip hop generation. I think that it's the voice of an Indian generation." Thus, in this view, as the United States has changed so, too, have groups' experiences and their place in the world.

The perspectives of these South Asian record label owners and MCs are telling in light of how youths locate themselves in America, but they may advocate popular discourses that leave them politically, if not culturally, voiceless. A "multiracial" conception of hip hop borrows the logic of multiculturalism, in which all differences are seen to be equal without particular attention to the power differentials across groups (see Wang 2007). Yet, the artists' own attention to history and power alleviates ahistoricism, and it is voicelessness rather than a desire for equal representation that inspires their lyricism. Sammy and KB express themselves because of their sense that South Asians have lacked a voice in America; a sense that also drew Black and Puerto Rican youths to develop this expression in the first place. Second-generation desis are often disenfranchised socially, rather than economically, due to their invisibility in social and political arenas. And the position and vocalization of Blacks who reject their own disenfranchisement leads desi performers to a culture they interpret to be open to the multivocality of its members. Although hip hop is entrenched in racial politics, it offers tools to bridge differences by discussing universal issues and desires. The way that artists like KB, Sammy, Swap, and Nimo use Black popular culture challenges people's stereotypes about "Asian rappers" and also denaturalizes the link between Blackness and hip hop by claiming space in hip hop *as* South Asians.

True Rap Is Black at Its Core, the Underground Is Multiracial

True rap and hip hop is about and for Black people. Mainstream hip hop is commercial crap that just exemplifies everything that is wrong with the racial structures that exist in this country. Although I don't have a problem with non-Blacks producing hip hop (including South Asians!), to define the genre, you must polarize your perception and the genre itself—so hip hop must remain Black music because it must remain hip hop.—Arun, desi remix DJ

The second perspective on the racial dynamics of hip hop, at times subject to the circular logic employed in Arun's words above, states that "hip hop is essentially Black, but there's room for us in the underground."[10] Nearly half of the artists in my study articulate this view, many of them MCs who produce racialized rhymes for hip hop heads rather than ethnic hip hop targeting desi youth. "Hip hop is still based in the Black experience because race matters so much," says a Nepali fan who married a multiracial Black woman. Some of these advocates also argue that hip hop remains by and for Black people and that Black youths' tastes determine what hip hop "is." So in order for one to produce "legitimate hip hop," Blacks need to purchase one's music. But does one have to be Black to create hip hop? If so, who is Black? The artists' responses are contradictory because it is difficult to maintain that hip hop is by and for Black people and yet account for one's deep participation as someone who does not consider oneself to be Black. Like Jonny who argues that the immigrant experience is framed by the Black experience in America, these writers, DJs, and MCs consider themselves to be "people of color" whose experiences are parallel to but not conflated with those of Blacks.

As hip hop artists, some South Asians move in primarily local, social, and musical settings where Black peers often set the standards. These peers, according to the South Asian rappers, unequivocally accept them because these desis do not attempt to portray themselves as Black. "It's never been an issue," Rawj explains. "I've never once felt like [people thought], 'Oh my god, look at them!!'" He laughs, "I've always felt part of the whole movement. I was in a group that was 6/7ths Black. Nobody ever said, 'how are we going to sell music when we have this Indian kid?'" Many of the MCs express that while they do not face censure from Black friends, they still feel subjected to a double standard. Rawj acknowledges that Indians are visual outsiders but does not hold a grudge because "it's still African American music." Chee, of Himalayan Project, battles in ciphers and at open mic events where he displays aggressive wordplay and rhyming skills—both of which he can employ to address or counter the crowd's skepticism of seeing an Indian rapper; his male status is expected. Doubters have approached Chee and have called him out by referencing his Indianness derogatively in their freestyles. Chee responds to this challenge by coming on strong and sticking to the tenets of battle rapping—the diss (disrespect)—while also holding fast to its racial rules: "I don't diss them as a race or a people. But I'll be like, 'yo, your style is wack.' If you got wack clothes on, you got a fucked up haircut, I'll say some shit. That's what battling is about, you know?" Then, like Rawj, he adds, "But I understand. Because I'm an Indian in hip hop, so I expect that. But I'm not going to give it back because that's not the way to handle it." Like White musicians who pay homage to the roots of jazz in Black culture, the approaches taken by these MCs come from their comprehension that slavery and the legacy of disenfranchisement shapes the content and form of hip hop as well as its politics of exclusion and inclusion. Amiri Baraka (LeRoi Jones 1963) explains that Whites who identified with jazz music and its creators, in recognizing the humanity of Blacks in a nation that did not, found themselves outside the mainstream. And in the case of both the midcentury White jazz musicians and the millennial desi rappers, their cross-racial identifications are a choice as opposed to the situation for their Black counterparts.

During a lengthy discussion at a busy café near the Berkeley campus, Rawj, casually dressed in jeans and a T-shirt, related his thoughts about race and the rights to hip hop. In his husky, Bay Area–inflected voice, he stated: "Okay, here we go. I've thought about it a little more. Regardless of how you try to spin it, since we are doing hip hop, we're in a certain capsule. And our expression is molded in the Black voice, because the art form originated there, right? And it's not even [just that] the art form originated there, but the other art forms that contributed to hip hop being made were all Black as well. Funk, jazz, rock 'n' roll, whatever you have . . . So it came in the lineage of Black music. So it's all been molded in the Black voice, right?" "Right," I answered. "But what about the folks who say, 'no, it was multiracial from the start?'" "Hey," he rebutted, "none of those guys or girls were part of it enough to the point where public perception of what it is, is, 'oh, here we are, this is a rainbow coalition'! I think that [it was] just like what it is now—it was a certain body of people with sprinkles of other people. And I think that other argument was erected probably to make somebody else feel legitimate. You know what I mean?" Although Rawj locates the development of hip hop within a legacy of Black musics rather than stemming from a specific pure and original moment, in a move similar to that of Perry (2004), he refuses to overemphasize the contributions of non-Blacks, *despite* his racial status. Thus, much like mainstream Black/White racial discourses that neglect Asians and Latinos, some South Asians accept a racially marginal subjectivity vis-à-vis the position of Blacks as America's major minority.

Conceptions of ownership and racial authenticity—often determined by hip hop's consumers—limit the artists' scope of what is (im)possible for their musical careers. The "hip hop is Black" artists mostly accept the improbability of widespread recognition because the prevailing notions of racial authenticity and marketing priorities neglect Asian rappers. They situate themselves within these terms as insiders within the "underground." That way, D'Lo can claim that Blacks "*own*, [really] own hip hop" and also identify as a hip hopper. Because it tends to be independent rather than corporate, underground music does not reach as many fans (although this is changing with new technologies, including YouTube). Sidestepping mainstream channels often means forgoing dreams of getting signed to a major label or achieving financial success through music. As a retired rapper who is now a label owner says of his role as an MC, "I had to let it go *because* I respected the game [of hip hop] too much. And it was too confusing *as* an Indian. I wanted to prove a point." At the same time, the artists consider the

Album cover courtesy of Roger Kahlon.

underground more multinational, multicultural, and multiracial. It is a site for creative acts of fusion.

These theories remind us that "hip hop" refers to many things, including a form of music, culture, business, and lifestyle, and that recognizing its multidimensionality and that of its members is analytically productive. Their references to "hip hop" include various *kinds* of hip hop music, such as conscious, underground, mainstream, southern bounce, and so forth. Seeing the multiple layers, genres, and voices of hip hop—its polyvalence—leads to D'Lo's anti-essentialist and multiracial perspective on the culture that reaffirms the primacy of the Black experience. In conceptualizing hip hop as a multilevel phenomenon including but not limited to "commercial" and "underground" parts, s/he deconstructs the idea of hip hop as a monolithic expression of "Black culture" as it is promoted through mainstream channels.

Comprised of multiplicity, hip hop culture—like the artists' multiscalar identifications—changes over time and can become inclusive of non-Black artists. The artists' self-positioning in the hip hop business also gives them space relatively free from those commercial aspects of the industry they critique. Thus, artists who share this second perspective find independent arenas to be empowering sites where multiple perspectives and styles can flourish. The artists highlight the complexity of hip hop culture by categorizing their music differently and shattering the notion that "all hip hop sounds alike." (Indeed, despite journalists' desires to report on this topic, there is no one "desi hip hop" sound or scene.) Some are "for the underground," others are "fusion hip hop," and only one may be considered "strictly Feenom."

Vivek's "Wider Black Consciousness": A Global Race Consciousness

Usually, I'm not so impressed with Indian kids trying to rap 'cause it's a [told in a reverent voice] Black tradition, man. . . . You know, once in awhile it happens well, but usually when you're coming from the outside. . . . Hip hop to me is Black music and now it's become worldwide . . . but I feel like if you're doing it and you're listening to it, it has to be something that you respect for that tradition. . . . I feel it's real important to respect those [traditions] and try, to what extent you can, to understand them in order to start flipping it yourself. I feel like that's significant.
—Vivek, Indian American MC

I began this volume with a description of Vivek because he articulates most precisely the kinds of racial identifications and everyday cross-fertilizations that exemplify the thoughts and practices of hip hop's desis. While his words are unique, they apply to all of the artists. In contrast to the multiracialists advocating the first perspective, Vivek agrees with the second view that hip hop is primarily Black culture. However, instead of locating himself within the multiracial and underground pockets of hip hop as D'Lo does, Vivek deliberately considers himself to be a part of a "wider Black consciousness." This approach to understanding the world and one's place within it traverses racial categories, time, and space. This context-driven perspective explains and encourages cross-group identifications without denying the specificities of racialization. The artists share this global race consciousness; it is the political perspective at the heart of this project.

Shortly after 9/11, I attended an arts event that provided a safe space for fearful and concerned young South Asians and Middle Easterners held at a nondescript Bay Area community center. I walked into a smallish first-floor room filled with children's drawings, filled out the sign-up sheet, and bought a glass (or rather plastic cup) of wine—a weak substitute for the sold-out standard fare of chai, samosas, and chutney. About thirty South Asian young adults, including Deejay Bella who also lived in Oakland at the time, were milling about, chatting with friends. After a few men and women had performed and Deejay Bella sang her song, a slender Indian man, perhaps in his mid-twenties, was called to perform. The man, Vivek, was wearing chappals and a long, flowing white cotton kurta pajama similar to that worn by Kashmiri men in northern India. He introduced himself, saying that he was new in town. His unaffected yet distinctive cadence and accent of his voice hinted the possibility that he socialized with Blacks.

Instead of taking on the expected rhythm of a spoken word delivery, Vivek partially rapped and partially sang an a cappella piece. What caught my attention (and, apparently, that of a giddy group of young women who beset him at the end of the show) was not so much the delivery as the content of the rhymes in his song, "One Struggle." Over time, I learned that Vivek's global, political, and linked perspective in this song represented his thinking about the world. In it, he gave his rapt audience an ethnographic account of the parallel lives of two women living across the globe from one another. The women represent both of the places where Vivek is from—Sarabai comes from a village in Kutch, Gujarat, in India and Denise Saunders is a working-class Black single mother from New Haven, Connecticut, near Vivek's hometown. His dynamically executed delivery in English and Kachchie (or Kutchi, the language of Kutch, India) shifted the focus of the previous performances away from the effects of 9/11 on South Asians and Muslims. He accented the links among minorities by pondering the intersections of race,

Vivek mesmerized desi women at an emergency post-9/11 event in Oakland, California. Author's photograph.

class, and gender with particular attention to "unlikely" transnational and nonancestral ties.

In the song "One Struggle," dedicated to the women in his life, Vivek provides a thick description (Geertz 1973) of the hardships of the daily lives of two women who are continents apart yet united in their struggle for multiple ends. It is a material struggle for basic survival, as well as a fight for superstructural factors of "dignity" and "equality." When he gave me a tape (yes, a cassette tape) of his songs, I found that "One Struggle," roughly produced, was accompanied by a strumming guitar and a woman's deep humming that created a bluesy, earthy feel to the song. The song starts with Sarabai's daily tasks, which begin early—before the sun has risen. Sarabai lives in the westernmost desert region of Gujarat where she needs to fetch water because there "ain't no tap in this village." She must also collect firewood so that she can cook food "at the smoky stove for the fam[ily]." Simultaneously, Sarabai is responsible for teaching her daughter, whom she takes along with her, the daily routine in order to socialize her for a future role as a wife, mother, and daughter-in-law. In addition, she has a "baby on her hip" and "another in her belly. More work to be done"—or, one could argue, "more (productive and reproductive) work to be done." Her labor is strenuous and continuous, yet Vivek points to the music of Sarabai's anklets that "begin to clank" as she walks back and forth on her daily tasks. He zeroes in on the grace of her movements as she sways from side to side with three pots of water resting on her head. The song leaves the listener with both a sense of the laborious nature of Sarabai's day and her almost Sisyphean perseverance within the context of village life, familiar to a number of the artists.

Denise, seemingly in stark contrast, lives in one of the most "developed" countries in the world; yet she performs work that is similarly routine, necessary, and arduous: she stitches button after button in the sweatshop as her health deteriorates ("her fingers be stubbin'") and her mind closes down from a lack of stimulus despite reading Franz Fanon (whom Vivek studied in college). Denise is located at the bottom of the production ladder—a position now occupied by cheaper labor in foreign countries such as India and by Mexican immigrants in the United States. The hollowing-out of United States manufacturing, such as Denise's sweatshop, in the 1970s and 1980s has also led to the erosion of rural life in places like Gujarat. The globalization of corporations and foreign invest-ment into "less developed" countries has spurred on rural-to-urban and then international migration, as the need for female labor has increased (Hondagneu-Sotelo 1994; Chang 2000). The connected-ness of these women's lives, therefore, is just a thread in the inter-national yarnball of a global, capitalist economy.

Denise and Sarabai are also connected as "Black women" in their ideological struggles for "immaterial" things, such as dignity and equality. And Vivek is linked with them by history, displacement, and his overall identification with people who struggle. As we were discussing the potentials of racial crossings, he said:

> Sometimes it's funny style how these crossovers, [these] "perpetra-tions," happen . . . I try to be humble and calm about [my familiarity with Black people]. It's not a big deal. But socially, the places I roll, the music I do, those kids are all Black people. I started an organiza-tion called Umoja, which is in New Haven—which is primarily people of color but South Asian teachers in there, too. [And] the political work I do, a lot of that relates to Black Liberation. And actually, that song ["One Struggle"] is exactly about this, in a way. Not talking about myself, but just saying, "here's a woman from Kutch and here's a woman from New Haven and here's how [I'm] considering them to be similar." Exactly that—the wider Black consciousness. 'Cause I say, "two Black women, one struggle." That's like, I'm sneaking in that wider Black consciousness.

To explain his belonging, Vivek offers a host of examples that stra-tegically call upon an "unlikely" set of actions and commitments to Black people by an Indian American (Lipsitz 1994). South Asians in hip hop do not only rap about their associations with Blacks but their daily lives and the lives of all desis are structured by them. In this song, the women's bond is an expression of Vivek's ideol-ogy that advocates unifying agendas, a global perspective, and a woman-centered viewpoint.

Vivek perhaps cannot experience, firsthand, the life of a poor woman, but his *choice to identify* with that struggle as part and parcel of his own is a step across gender lines that parallel other kinds of links. By crossing color lines, for instance, Vivek becomes a legiti-mate producer of Black popular culture. In "One Struggle," the Indian MC extends the meaning of Blackness past biology and uses his own racial ambiguity strategically to embrace a broader collective. This advances his political goals to forge alliances in order to ease the suffering of others and it opens up communities and conceptions of Blackness. His Black friends have jokingly called him an "Indian Negro" and his Jain mother half thinks her son was an African in his previous life. Through his emotional, political, musical, and professional work, does Vivek *become Black*? Who determines whether or not this is the case?

The strategies and ideologies of desi artists who work toward pan-racial alliances straddle strategic essentialism and strategic anti-essentialism. From an external perspective, these crossings may appear surprising. However, a major contribution of desis through hip hop is their insistence not only on links between South Asians and Blacks but on transnational ties that connect these groups to one another across arbitrary divides. They reveal these connections to be less unlikely or surprising, and they use music to encourage this perspective. For now, it appears that all the artists struggle with the limitations of prevailing discourses in describing their lives and ideas. Is there a way to speak about the impacts of racism that respects the particularity of Blacks without marginalizing other racialized groups? Vivek's efforts to describe Blackness as a consciousness or a political ideology and his act of sometimes referring to himself and his community as "Black" allows him to say that hip hop is Black and that he is in hip hop, because he is, in some sense, Black. His ideas defy commonsense perceptions of race and culture and they step on some toes. But communities rooted in consciousness may be more open than those that define themselves along categorical lines. Like race, this consciousness is also ambiguous and open to difference and therefore to its adoption by non-Blacks who feel that although race is important, racial categories are fabricated. Vivek's perspective encourages us to rethink who and what Black is and Black is not.[11]

Conclusion

Hip hop desis call upon their critical consciousness of the world to assist their negotiation of the politics of hip hop culture. They understand that hip hop is a Black culture, art form, and ideology both in the past and present, and that race carries critical implications. The ability of early hip hop music to articulate these concerns is central to its appeal to these Brown youths. They were inspired to put their thoughts into action and they became early participants. This necessitated a direct engagement with the politics of authenticity, and they located themselves within this culture in multiple ways. True to the dialogic nature of identity formation, their positions are informed by identity politics in hip hop and by the industry itself.

How is it that hip hop is a Black expressive form while many of its consumers and producers are non-Black? Some scholars and music producers state that hip hop can be a utopian culture transcending race (Gilroy 1987). Proponents of this view often focus on its multiracial roots and the incorporation of non-Black influences. By illustrating the hybridity of hip hop as a "heteroglot science" (Potter 1995: 105), artists like K B and Sammy assert that membership is "open" and not based along racial lines (Dyson 1993; Lipsitz 1994; Toure 1999: 1). The multiracial attendees of hip hop concerts and clubs seem to support this view. The remix DJ Arun seems to concur with the scholar Neil Strauss who argues that since no one "owns" rap, rap music is "for everyone" and the appropriation debate is moot (1999: 28). But of course history has taught us to be wary of over-celebratory readings of hybridity (Roediger 1998: 361–62; see also Hutnyk 1999–2000; cf. Mercer 1995.) And, if it were true that hip hop is now a voice for all people, why does Karmacy's identity as an "Indian rap group" limit and define its audiences and promotional strategies, and why does this label stand in the way of their wishes to be seen as "MCs who happen to be Indian"? Rather, hybridity is like appropriation; it is embedded in power relations and has multiple meanings and outcomes. This does not, however, imply that we can or should transcend race.

Another primary concern among fans is the increasing corporatization of hip hop and the loss of its original anti-establishment messages. Through the process of commercialization, hip hop is now a global, multibillion dollar phenomenon. Nonetheless, corporations have broadcast the multiple, complex, and contradictory messages and images of hip hop across the globe. The marriage between Black popular culture and global capital illustrates just one of capitalism's central contradictions—that the increasing commercialization of hip hop exports new tastes and "needs"—including racist ones—to new markets. These consist of new audiences who might well pick up on messages that are found between the lines and, therefore, learn more about Blacks, and themselves, than they previously had. While rooted in the Black American experience, it is undeniable that others are producing this art form as it has become globally adopted as a voice of representation in places like Cuba, Puerto Rico, Japan, and India.

The diasporic flows of Black practices are not new; in fact they are constitutive of hip hop. Desis harness the potential of these resistant and resilient practices, including call and response, communalism, counterhegemonic ideologies, and attention to history to create political-artistic worlds. Non-Black actors have also been central contributors to the rise of this culture. A polycultural look back at the early days better contextualizes debates about authorship. This does not displace the Blackness of hip hop, a multiracial creation of Black popular culture, but rather emphasizes the resonance of Blackness for other communities of color attempting to forge identities. Some desi artists find that hip hop in its "essence" is Black. In order to reconcile this notion along with their own identities as participants, those artists like D'Lo and Jonny conceptualize hip hop not as a multicultural mecca but as a culture with multiple levels, arenas, and genres; therefore, as non-Black, non-White participants they see themselves in the underground. At the same time, some scholars engage strategic essentialism in their interpretations of Black culture to encourage racial harmony, protect Black people from criticism, and preserve Black cultures (Reed in Farley 1999: 178; see also Dyson 1993). The failings of contemporary analyses of race do not mean we should do away with race; instead, we should continue to theorize it. We need *race-centered*, not race-only, analyses (see Dyson 1993)—a view captured in Vivek's perspective that takes into account *disenfranchisement* as the centripetal force of hip hop culture (Potter 1995: 10; Gray 1997; Rivera 1997; Poulson-Bryant 1999). "Rap music," states the journalist Scott Poulson-Bryant, "is the language of the disenfranchised, a slang speech of outrage and anger from a people who don't have mainstream ways of articulating themselves" (1999: 180). Desi youths are, as Russell Potter notes, among the "many other groups [that] now share with black folks a sense of alienation, despair, uncertainty, loss of sense of grounding, even if it is not informed by shared circumstance" (1995: 9).

What lures these desi youths to hip hop is the fact that hip hop, particularly in its early stages, articulates the structural positions of Blacks in America and expresses resistance against such limitations (see Woods 1998 on the blues). These desi artists are attempting to sort out their own experiences within a nation that has difficulty positioning them. Some South Asian Americans are keenly aware of their individual positions as racial outsiders to the nation and also in the predominantly Black spaces they occupy. The racially explicit nature of hip hop gives them the vocabulary to make space for themselves within these multiple arenas. The counterhegemonic messages, form, and sonic appeal of groups like Public Enemy in the late 1980s and early 1990s propelled desi performers to use hip hop as their own vehicle and platform to discuss issues, some of which overlapped with Blacks and some that were unique to the South Asian and immigrant experience. They "give back" by translating Black Power into Brown Pride and expanding the range of identities that comprise the hip hop nation and by highlighting diasporic sensibilities so central to Black American cultural formations.

Cultivating lifelong cross-racial relationships and voicing racial attitudes through hip hop music develops fertile ground for communities of empathy (Potter 1995; see also Gilroy 1987; Hebdige 1994; Rivera 1997) or a politics of identification. The *politics of identification* is an alternative to identity politics since it bases interests in a scope beyond or across constructed categories. From this perspective, hip hop neither transcends nor is limited by racial categories. The ability of hip hop to possibly unite disparate and disenfranchised groups may be seen as a threat to the dominant race-class system: "Hip hop is threatening precisely because it can't be *contained*" (Potter 1995: 105). Naysayers who believe that hip hop has become totally co-opted by corporate interests need only open their ears to the thriving and motivated masses of artists who may not yet have gained mainstream exposure. Hip hop represents a viable community of interest and affiliation that serves as an alternative to the limitations of identity politics that often reaffirm the constructed categories used to divide and dominate American minorities.

5.
Sampling South Asians
Dual Flows of Appropriation and
the Possibilities of Authenticity

> I respect those [individuals] who are really, deeply into [hip hop]. How-
> ever, those that just spin it because it's cool or because it gets the crowd
> going or who like to MC so that they can look cool are just appropriat-
> ing.—Arun, Indian American remix DJ
>
> Music thus occupies a domain at once between races but has the poten-
> tial of embodying—becoming—different racial significations.—Ronald
> Radano and Philip Bohlman, *Music and the Racial Imagination*

It was three AM on a Saturday night in 2003. Along with Stacy, a
Black friend of mine who works in the music business, I was helping Pierre, a Bay Area reggae DJ from the Republic of Congo, carry
his records. Our feet were tired from dancing all night long and we
were waiting to cross the street to pack up my car and ride across
the Bay Bridge to our homes in Oakland. We were euphoric from
a good night of partying (good music *and* good-looking people)
hosted by DJs who mixed dancehall songs with Indian beats. Celebrating the pleasure that emerged from these kinds of sonic overlaps, we were pleasurably aware of the fact that the music spoke
to the very multiracial and typically Bay Area configuration of our
group. As we began across the street, a young Black man from the
club attempted to get Stacy's attention, the gold grill in his mouth

reflecting the streetlight as he tried to holler at her. From across the street, I quipped that she was impervious to his very last-ditch attempt to close out the night. "Fuck you, you terrorist assassin bitch!" he yelled. I placed the record crates on the ground, turned around, and was ready to fight. As quickly as it took us to cross the street, our temporary South Asian and Black celebration was halted in the face of the troubling racial realignments that pit these groups against one another in post-9/11 America.

The power dynamics of South Asian/Black relations in the United States are similar to those in other nations in that they are not clearly defined and have, at the first decade of the twenty-first century, become increasingly complex. Here, they are framed by United States imperialism, global capitalism, and international East-West relations. If desis were seen in a positive light in the 1990s, Americans' conceptions of them changed drastically in the early 2000s. Post-9/11 discourses and images have solidified and realigned interminority race relations. On the one hand, new racial projects (Omi and Winant 1994) lump together Middle Easterners, South Asians, and other "Muslim-looking" people as enemies as well as highlight their distinction from "Americans," including Blacks. On the other hand, police and governmental surveillance, profiling, and detention of "potential terrorists" link South Asians with Blacks as populations subject to intertwined systems of oppression. This seesaw of (dis)identification appears in the ways that South Asians and Blacks adopt aspects of each others' cultural expressions. In some cases, actors engage hip hop in ways that are complicit with state-sanctioned and everyday forms of racism that portray South Asians as foreign others and Blacks as a native-born devalued group. Yet there are others in America who grasp this as a moment of possibility and who work collaboratively to forge new alignments of antiracist solidarity. Hip hop thus becomes an arena in which these intergroup relations play out in collaborative and divisive ways. It also becomes the platform taken up by individuals to enable the kinds of future relations they wish to see.

Racial fault lines shift in unpredictable rather than inevitable ways. Global historical processes that connect South Asians to Brown and Black people around the world in overlapping diasporas explain current realignments that frame the choices of individuals. Many aspects of hip hop culture today—particularly those with strong links to global capital—comply with a host of "isms," including ideologies that demonize Black *and* Brown people through sonic and visual representations of stereotypes. But popular culture is also the site where potential formations not yet possible in formal politics can be tested out and aired (Iton 2008). This project focuses on those less-apparent aftershocks that alter the seemingly immoveable armor of American exceptionalism and domination. A post-9/11 framework enables us to examine American race relations within a global rather than nation-bound context; popular culture is one lens through which to analyze such broad-scale movements and to enact change at local levels.

The fluctuating visibility and invisibility, belonging and otherness, of these non-White groups in the American imaginary and in the realm of hip hop play out in the dynamics of South Asian/Black appropriations. How do we interpret the adoption of Blackness by non-Black minorities as well as the incorporation by American Blacks of South Asianness in their hip hop products? Shifting and ambiguous race relations spill into cross-cultural appropriations, distinguishing them from those depicted in the literature on Whites' appropriation of Black cultural forms. Because South Asian and Black power relations appear especially unstable—they shift between being lateral (Wong 2004: 189) and hierarchical—their appropriations do not fit unidirectional top-down theories. Instead, I illustrate the *dual flows* of cultural adoption between South Asians and Blacks.

This chapter foregrounds the post-9/11 context that brings sharp relief to new, dangerous and optimistic, kinds of crossovers. Global political events like 9/11 impact transnational capital and United States race relations. The contradictions inherent in capitalism emerge within debates about race, ownership, and rights when "identities" become increasingly commodified. The worldwide availability of commodified artifacts that represent "culture," "ethnicity," and "race," for instance, affects and reflects American race relations. Thus, in a global marketplace "difference" is viewed paradoxically as threatening and desirable. As Jonathan Rutherford notes: "Otherness is sought after for its exchange value, its exoticism and the pleasures, thrills and adventures it can offer" (quoted in Giroux 1994: 58). These political acts of the corporate commodification of difference (racialized sexuality or ethnic chic, for example) in fact serve to depoliticize and naturalize difference. Commercial hip hop plays an important role in expressing national fears and anxieties about Black as well as Brown people. Yet its less commodified forms are the preferred tool for some members of these groups to express their disdain for state practices that exploit and then scapegoat minority populations for a variety of social ills. As the artists' communities become new targets, it becomes particularly urgent to comprehend how their consciousness (which preceded 9/11) to see minorities' oppression—and thus liberation—as linked led to their politicized adoptions of a globally commodified Black expressive form.

Americans invested in the ownership and legitimate production of hip hop too easily dismiss *all* appropriative acts to be inspired by racist images of Black promiscuity, criminality, and inferiority (see Tate 2003; Kitwana 2005). But while some non-Blacks appropriate Black culture because of its perceived "hipness" and style, others, including some Asian American musicians, "want coalition and connection," and their love of Black music is a direct expression of their political ties with Blacks (Wong 2004: 179). Sampling offers another way to think about these exchanges. In the field of hip hop, I focus on two forms of South Asian/Black appropriations: first, the attraction by mainstream and hip hop desis to Black culture, and second, the incorporation of South Asian sounds, styles, and women in mainstream Black hip hop culture in the early 2000s. In drawing from these examples I distinguish between "appropriation as othering" and "appropriation as identification." This dichotomy, like many, is constructed, yet it reflects the general patterns among these various groups despite exceptions. Multifaceted interpretations of appropriation caution against reducing it to a form of colonization or disempowerment of those whose cultural objects one appropriates. For instance, analyses of non-Blacks' appropriation of Black expressions do not pay enough attention to the cross-fertilizations that inform the very production of Black popular culture. Not all cross-cultural exchanges are progressive, but neither is appropriation always the "stealing" of another's culture.

Agents who appropriate to their signal cross-group identifications or dis-identifications model the cultivation of inclusive communities and help explain how people use culture to divide. Appropriation implies differential access by groups to power (Ziff and Rao 1997: 5); as a result, appropriative acts—and charges of appropriation—are always political. "Listening to music is listening to all noise," writes Jacques Attali, "realizing that its appropriation and control is a reflection of power, that it is essentially political" (quoted in Wong 2004: 272). Even in relations between Blacks and Whites it is inaccurate to codify all Whites as "powerful" and all Blacks as "dominated" (Roediger 1998; Strauss 1999). Increasing numbers of Blacks own the means of production, especially in popular culture, and help define the conditions for inclusion. Black ascendancy in American popular culture, if only at particular levels, may invert traditional racial hierarchies (Gilroy 1987; Strauss 1999). These (un)equal exchanges signal racial fault lines (Almaguer 1994) and strategically deploy culture to bridge them. Not all appropriative acts are equal, and our interpretations of them should not rest on the actors' (racial, national, etc.) *identities* but rather on a contextual comprehension of their *ideologies*.

Appropriation as Othering

We were just surrounded by [hip hop]. Whereas now, it just kinda makes it seem less genuine, like, when you go and choose it, you know?
—MC Rawj

Style is a matter of not being "too ethnic" or "authentic" because it's a matter of taking something and making it your own. If you wear it as is, it looks like you're trying. And that's what White people do—take it as is— and you can almost empathize with them. Whites are in search of soul. Blacks and Latinos don't [appropriate] because they just are.
—Maurice, Black spoken-word artist and hip hop fan

Many desi youths can afford to *buy* Black and not *be* Black. Anyone who strolls across a college campus at lunchtime today will notice the popularity of hip hop styles—baggy jeans, particular brand names, postures, and vernaculars—among youth of all races. Desi students are no less subject to these trends, and hip hop, usually mixed with bhangra beats, is the most popular music among them. But South Asians who produce hip hop claim that their mainstream counterparts are more concerned with the "wrapping" (the latest fads in designer wear and jewelry) than the "rapping" (the messages of hip hop).[1] Mainstream desis love hip hop and can afford the expensive clothes and cars that rappers rap about, yet the extent of their engagement with Blacks often stops there.

There are copious examples of Asian American youths who latch on to Black expressive forms, but not enough has been said about its impact on their emergent identities, affiliations, and politics. Americans have attempted to understand Asian Americans and hip hop through the paradigm of what I term "appropriation as othering." Theorists often note the harm that people who appropriate cause to the object and its subordinated culture; therefore, hip hop scholars focus on the intentions of non-Blacks who adopt Black identities (White 1996; Roediger 1998; Kitwana 2005; Watkins 2005). These studies often center on the appeal of Black arts (particularly music) for Whites and highlight the role of Blackness in the construction of Whiteness, appropriation, and the question of cultural ownership. They interpret Whites as once again denigrating, consuming, and stealing Black culture, pointing to iconic figures like Elvis Presley and Eminem—the "great White rapper." As a result, scholars and other observers tend to be critical of these "racial crossings" (Wald 2000) as minstrelsy and "theft" (Lott 1993b; Cornyetz 1994) fueled by the desire to have and own (even temporarily *be*) the despised other and thereby reassert one's position of dominance. Like Whites who adopt Black culture but who do not interact with Blacks, middle-class desis often feel they "know" Blacks through media sources (Roediger 1998). In adopting Black vernacular and aesthetic styles they are like those Jiggers and Wiggers who have the protection of *not being Black* in an anti-Black society (Wood 1998: 43–47). Yet, while some of the insights on Whites' appropriation of Black cultures apply to South Asian and Black crossings, distinct dynamics shape interminority relations.

The appropriation by individuals of "an other's" culture and identity generally elicits reactions to these practices as either "positive" or "negative." According to the latter view, some argue that it does not lead to empathy with Blacks "at the human level" (Ledbetter 1992: 15; e.g., Perry Hall in Ziff and Rao 1997), particularly when individuals do not interact (although, of course, interactions do not necessarily signal identification). Mainstream desis in New York City, for instance, adopt essentialized and negative ideas of Blacks that inform their own masculinity, violence, and sexuality (Maira 2002; see also Murray in Roediger 1998: 358). Some of the writing on Jiggers, or Japanese in blackface, who literally darken their faces and crimp their hair, concurs (see Condry 2006 for a rebuttal). Jiggers in Japan, according to Joe Wood, "consume black culture with only a fantastically vague sense of what it might mean to do so, and no appreciation of the ironies involved." As is the case for deracialized desis, "Whiteness rules their minds in stealth" (1998: 46).

Non-Blacks' adoption of stereotypical and exaggerated notions of "Blackness" marketed by media conglomerates illustrates appropriative acts that others and distances groups, thereby resembling the logic of minstrelsy. In fact, the adoption of racialized identities can advance racism rooted in the principle of bounded groups defined by difference. Othering practices occur when individuals consume decontextualized and uninformed notions of an other in ways that reinforce essentialist and totalizing notions of difference that are hierarchically valued. Yet, Eric Lott reveals how these actions also rupture the seeming fixity of race: "Blackface performance . . . was based on small but significant crimes against settled ideas of racial demarcation." As such, cross-racial appropriation is about both "love and theft," and is mired in contradictions and the liminality of border crossings (1993b: 4). Appropriation as othering can work through positive stereotyping, such as in the idealization or exotification of the other, or through demonization.[2] Prior to 9/11, Blacks represented the racial other not only to Whites but also to "model minority" South Asians, who marked their distance in verbal and nonverbal ways.

Appropriation as Othering: The Use by Desis of the "N-Word"

Black cultural critics heavily debate the use of the n-word because it is adopted so copiously by less-than-well-meaning individuals.[3] Unfortunately, these debaters have framed this issue as a Black and White one, and in so doing have lost important nuances in interminority exchanges. Mainstream college desis' adoption of urban styles and slang is the most common form of their appropriation of Black culture, and it is often accompanied by racist conceptions of Black people. I often heard young South Asian men use the term "nigga" to refer to themselves and to their friends, particularly when there were no Black people around. In the event that they wanted privately to refer to a Black person in their presence, they would refer to him or her as *kalu*, an uncomplimentary alteration of the Hindi term *kala*, for "black"—potentially the equivalent for "nigger," depending upon the context. A desi Berkeley student, recounting her weekend, exclaimed that she and her friends had seen "real ghetto kalus" during their trip to the neighboring city of Oakland as they peered out of the windows of their locked car doors. These desis literally cannot *speak* about race. Such elisions reinforce segregated and distant social relations and the anxiety and desire that frame some desis' relationship to Blackness (see Lott 1993a). Yet Black youth culture has become so popular that non-Black youths have crafted their own spins on Black slang to use among themselves. Mainstream desi youths have flipped the use of the n-word as a form of camaraderie to fit their own conditions by calling one anther "coolie." These interactions reveal the motivating factors of fear and desire, attraction and domination, closely examined by others (Lott 1993a; Cornyetz 1994; Wood 1998; Roediger 1998). Blackness is not only constituent of Whiteness but also frames the conceptions of Asians and their self-positioning vis-à-vis other groups. Desi youths, too, may be drawn to rap music for its violence, scatology, and explicit nature (Roediger 1998: 661) and their desire for Black racialized sexualities as they come of age. But members of a group do not act in concert. Attending to the distinctions of appropriation fleshes out the multivalent stances by desis toward the members of Black communities.

Desis who produce hip hop are often bothered by co-ethnics whose racial distancing, misinformation, and adoption of Black stereotypes comply with anti-Black racism. Some artists disparage the way other desis consume Black styles because they feel they are based on ill-informed notions of Blacks. The MC Rawj is irritated by the vicarious thrill of many young Indians who do not know Blacks but who think they should "listen to this music so we can visit the ghetto and visit all this crime and lawlessness and activity, but at the end of the day, we'll be alright." These mainstream desis are like others who substitute the content of controlling media images for actual information about who Black people "are," and therefore believe that hip hop represents the totality of Black people in America. When it comes to music, MC Chee explains, "a lot of people, they like the beats, but they're not really paying attention to what they are saying . . . There's a difference between people that listen to rap and are actually involved with it and understand what it's about, or try to understand." Like Vivek, Chee insists that "the attempt would be good enough for me." The Karmacy rapper KB agrees that the popularity of hip hop and Black styles among other desis is often decontextualized: "You get these kids who don't understand the underlying foundation, they don't understand *why* hip hop is, or what the issues are, or even *why* some of the artists in hip hop are talking about some of the negative stuff they are." In response, mainstream desis simultaneously glorify these images and "marginalize what these people in these ghettos and housing projects are going through," which makes KB "feel bad personally." Although KB and Chee can choose now where and how to live, they know that this privilege is not equally available to all people. Their investment in positive race relations urges them to shed light on these issues, including the n-word, in their musical productions and everyday conversations.

Controversy surrounding the n-word centers on the questions of who can say it and whether or not its reclamation as a sign of affection among Black youths is empowering or signals internal colonization (Asim 2007). Michael Eric Dyson doesn't intend to ban the term, but he clarifies that "nigger has never been cool when spit from white lips" (1999: 107); perhaps he would argue the same goes for other non-Blacks. Desi artists agree. But instead of focusing on Black-White race politics, they emphasize their knowledge of context, respect for the music, and their position as non-White "outsider" contributors. Most of those who pen rhymes do not use it in their lyrics because, based on conversations with their Black peers, they feel it is neither positive nor appropriate. "I mean," says Chee, "coming from my point of view, even from your point of view, we're seen as outsiders. I can't say I fully understand that Black experience, but I think I have enough *knowledge* of it where I know that it's not right." The exception to this view was in the event that an MC wanted to highlight interlocking racisms. For example, in "Everything" from Himalayan Project's *The Middle Passage*, Chee raps, "The first son of some / immigrants who ain't learn quicker / This land and all in it / ain't for niggas, spics, gooks, kikes and sand niggas." Although some people close to the rapper wanted him to take this line out of the song, Chee felt that this strategic use of derogative words made his point about the discriminatory and exclusive practices of the United States. And by including "sand nigger"—a racist term used against people of Middle Eastern and South Asian descent—Chee connects the experiences of his family to that of other oppressed groups, and he makes the point that racists do too.

These adoptions by mainstream desis often mirror forms of White appropriation; as a result, their actions, including their use of the "n-word" while referring derogatively to Blacks as kalus, exemplify an othering process of decontextualized "interaction." Yet, even among Whites, not all White musicians are insincere in their love of jazz and hip hop, nor do all attempt to use their art to access racialized stereotypes; this is also the case with desis and hip hop. The artists' method and awareness of the multivalent politics of Black cultural adoption distinguishes them from their co-ethnics. Distance shapes peoples' conceptions of other groups and thus their motivations for appropriating cultural signifiers. Events like 9/11 can drastically alter groups' perceived social distance. Curiously, while in the first decade of the millennium many Americans, Black and White, distanced themselves from "Muslim-looking" others, it has also been the time that mainstream hip hop culture produced by Black artists elected to incorporate South Asian sounds, styles, and women. These actions may connote new crossovers as well as solidify contentious relations.

Appropriation as Othering:
Images of the Middle East and South Asia in Mainstream Hip Hop

Increased public awareness of Arab music and corporate profit . . . offers certain opportunities, as well as pitfalls, for political activism. (Swedenburg 2002: 44)

For Chee, as for the other artists, part of comprehending the context of hip hop is his awareness of his position within it. On one of his visits to California he met me for beers and an interview in a San Francisco bar just south of Market Street. Over the course of the afternoon, he pointed out the circularity and multidirectionality of appropriation and the power relations that underlie them. Like power, culture flows in multiple directions. The goals of mainstream hip hop artists to continue to capture the imaginations of global audiences sometimes also reinforce national political interests in, for instance, the Middle East. Ironically, the mainstream hip hop music and videos by Black artists that aired on urban radio stations, BET, and MTV inundated global audiences with orientalist images of the very region with which the United States was at war in the early 2000s. Like desi artists, Black hip hoppers stand on slippery ground, at times identifying with national concerns as Americans and, at other times, identifying with the exotica and otherness of Asia. The commodification of "over there" sounds and styles in mainstream hip hop exemplifies appropriation as othering.

Shifting the focus to how some Blacks take on and refashion—or sample—non-Black styles and signifiers bears on the debates over the authenticity and "purity" of hip hop culture. Decisions made by contemporary producers reveal the polycultural processes of appropriation that comprise—and sometimes compromise—this expressive form. Analyzing inter-minority appropriations in popular culture is similar to revisioning hip hop history: it neither dilutes nor dismisses the Blackness of hip hop. Rather, we come to see how political cultural formations emerge dynamically through negotiations that enable emergent and progressive social formations.

Since 9/11 the West has increasingly demonized Middle Easterners, Muslims, and South Asians, at home and abroad. Americans have simultaneously witnessed the rising popularity of South Asian and Middle Eastern commodities that are emblematic of foreignness. This Indo Chic or New Asian Cool includes henna tattoos, belly dancing, Indian fabrics, and rap songs infused with Indian music and videos featuring South Asian women (Hutnyk 2000). In the case of belly dancing, Sunaina Maira describes these "Arabface" practices as a cultivation of "whiteness" in a post-9/11 context (2008: 334). Yet how do we interpret non-White Americans' participation in these kinds of imperialistic fantasies? Two trends have drawn consumers' attention to appropriation in commercial rap music: American popular culture and media have glorified, demonized, and conflated the Middle East and South Asia; at the same

An image of an "exotic woman" that was common in hip hop videos, like R. Kelly's *Snake (Remix)*, in the early 2000s.

time, some mainstream rappers, like Jay-Z, have voiced their political perspectives about the "War on Terror" through widely distributed music. I address these issues in the following paragraphs.

Popular representations of cross-racial interactions reflect and shape broader group dynamics. Perhaps mainstream Black artists and producers include South Asian elements in their products because they interpersonally mix with desis, but this is unlikely. After all, like mainstream desis' adoption of hip hop, the producers neither translated nor contextualized the South Asian languages and props they adopted. Some Black rap acts replicate White American women's fascination with belly dancing: "Belly dance performances detach Orientalized femininity from the bodies of Arab women themselves so that it becomes a form of racial masquerade" (Maira 2008: 334). The Afro/Orientalist depictions of exotic women, poorly translated Hindi, and harems in post-9/11 mainstream hip hop videos express American nationalism aligned with Western imperial projects in the Middle East. Thus the contradictions of appropriation surface in popular American forms that reflect and inform the concerns and hopes of a nation's citizens. Mainstream hip hop in the 2000s, much like the mainstream news media, displaced Brown people from the United States by locating them in exotic and distant lands.

In 2001, a critical year in global history, a number of American hip hop songs hit the airwaves that featured the choruses of old Hindi songs and *tablas* (an Indian percussive instrument), while videos highlighted belly dancing and *mehndi* (henna) wearing women. I was surprised that year to hear a man yell "atta mujhe ko" ("I know" in Hindi) on the hit rapper Missy Elliott's song "Get Ur Freak On." Created by the innovative producer Timbaland, the video also featured tablas and a male East Asian martial artist. Following this hit, I saw the MTV video "Addictive" by the R&B singer Truth Hurts (the album was released in 2002) who, in the video, adopts belly dance type moves over a sampled Hindi film song. The following year, how was I to interpret the R&B singer R. Kelly's video

The R&B singer R. Kelly holding a sitar while sitting with a Middle Eastern-inspired woman in a desert for his video *Snake (Remix)*.

R. Kelly enters a lush tented harem in the midst of a desert and enjoys a fighting scene.

"Snake (Remix)"? He trudged through the desert on a camel, was surrounded by "exotic" women inside a lush harem, and then, after changing into American military gear and singing in front of an American flag, left with his boys in a military cavalcade (*see page 248*). Another crop of South Asian–influenced hits was also released just after Britain's Panjabi MC garnered heavy rotation for his song "Mundian to Bach Ke" a couple of years later.[4] On July 10, 2003, BET even aired "Indian Spices"—a countdown show that featured music videos with "Hindi sounds" or, rather, South Asian influences. These trends marked the rising visibility of *representations* of Brown people—now signifying the Middle East and South Asia, linking them to Latinos as foreigners—that could open up space for desi rappers. But desis could not yet compete with the influence of mainstream Black artists and video producers.

On June 25, 2002, Truth Hurts' album *Truthfully Speaking* hit the stands and sold 105,000 units, primed by the smash success of the record's hit single "Addictive." Featuring the prolific old-school rapper Rakim, with identifiably Indian instrumentals and lyrics,

At the end of the video R. Kelly and a dancer, wearing camouflage and representing Chicago, sing in front of an American flag that is unfurled over the desert backdrop.

"Addictive" reached the number three spot on the R&B/hip hop singles list to become a summer dance club hit less than a year after 9/11. I first heard about it from Beni B, a Black Oakland-based DJ and record label owner, who had quickly gotten his hands on the wax single. Indeed, no sooner than a weekend after he mentioned it I attended a party in San Francisco with several desis — my friend Anita, along with her friends visiting from India — where he played the track. Standing around with drinks in our hands, we stopped in mid-sentence when we heard its opening bars:

> Kaliyon ka chaman jabu lantha hai
> Thoda resham lagta hai,
> Thoda shisha lagta hai,
> Hire moti lar the hai, thoda sona lagta hai.
> (The garden of the buds looks like magic,
> Looks a little like silk,
> Looks a little like glass.
> Diamonds and pearls together, looks a little like gold.)

Was Beni B playing a Bollywood soundtrack? "Oh!" I remembered, "this is the song he was telling me about!" We moved closer to the speakers to try to translate the lyrics.

The song is based on a four-minute sample of Lata Mangesh-khar's song from 1981 titled "Thoda Resham Lagta Hai" ("Seems a Little like Silk"), which was produced by the renowned Indian composer Bappi Lahiri. Mangeshkar's original lyrics fill the introduction as well as the chorus, while a young Truth Hurts (nee Shari Watson) sings the body of the song, relaying how much she enjoys her man's lovemaking. In his rap verse Rakim expresses his appreciation for his woman's devotion through the rough times when he was just a small-time drug dealer. Juxtaposed with this raunchy duo is the Hindi film singer's voice floating in the chorus. For many listeners, Mangeshkar's contribution to the song is what made it a hit. Her chorus is good sounding yet unfamiliar to non-Hindi speakers. Lifted straight from the original, the lyrics describe the "beautiful" but "bittersweet" flower garland exchanged during an Indian wedding ceremony. Despite the different topics and languages deployed in the song, the slightly sped-up sampled track is what turns it into a coherent, danceable whole. "Addictive" has lived up to its name by generating much attention, from club goers who want to know what the woman is saying to South Asian Americans who finally feel represented in mainstream hip hop. And most of the attention has centered on the timeless yet unresolved debate in hip hop: the politics of sampling.

One of the most interesting aspects about the debate over the producers' use of the Hindi song is the contradiction it illuminates about who borrows what, how it is interpreted, and the light shed on these dynamics. Much of this depends upon the awareness a listener has of the histories of these songs and artists. Some observers distinguish between the practices of Indian composers like Lahiri, who produced the original track, and the actions of DJ Quik and Dre, the producers of "Addictive" who sampled the Hindi song.[5] As we will see, Lahiri's career and the desi party remix phenomenon, in which South Asian DJs play Indian hit tunes over the latest hip hop beats, complicate such a neat binary.[6] Bappi Lahiri sued the producers of the song (DJ Quik, Dr. Dre, and his company Aftermath) and its parent companies (Interscope Records, Universal

Music, and Vivendi Universal) for $500 million.[7] In the lawsuit, La-hiri accuses the world-famous hip hop producers of "cultural im-perialism" for taking the sample from Third World artists without permission and without giving credit to the owners of the original track, while further describing the act of appropriation as an unfair theft of which he was a victim. Lahiri won the suit when a Los Ange-les judge ordered the record off of the shelves "unless and until" the producers credited Lahiri on the album, which they later did. This case is relevant for several reasons.

First, Lahiri's accusations of cultural imperialism are important. Dr. Dre's counsel reported that they were unable to find the owners of the original track. But many listeners, especially those even re-motely familiar with Indian music, concur with the sentiments of DJ Rekha, of New York City's famous Basement Bhangra at SOBs, who said, "It seems hard to believe they could not locate the song's original composers." Rekha felt that Dre and Quik should have ob-tained permission for the song. Their failure to do so suggests an underlying attitude about the relative worth of South Asian music (i.e., cultural imperialism). While United States–based artists have found it important to clear samples of recognizable (i.e., West-ern) sources when they produce an album, particularly in the face of lawsuits, they seem to hold different standards for music from other, non-Western, parts of the world. Many Westerners may find "foreign-sounding music" from places like South Asia to be an un-identifiable sonic lump that can be sampled, pillaged, borrowed, appropriated, or plagiarized (see Miller 2004). Thus, despite being American minorities—in this instance, Black producers—Dre and Quik embody "American" imperialist notions and practices about culture and ownership.

Native-born Americans across color lines can realign themselves against those imagined to be foreign, including people from Asia, particularly when they have fought numerous wars against East and West Asian nations. During World War II against Japan, the Korean War, Vietnam, and now the global "War on Terror" in Af-ghanistan, Iraq, and Pakistan, politicians and the media picked up on stereotypes of the "foreign" and "untrustworthy" nature of the Oriental while American styles and products have become increas-ingly popular in Asia. These various knowledge producers have cir-culated discourses that temporarily consolidate American Whites

MC Chee Malabar and DJ Rekha at a radio interview.
Photograph courtesy of Richard Louissaint.

and Blacks against Asians—and Asian Americans—through the rubric of the patriot. Attention to the multidirectional flows of sampling in and of hip hop and the flows of global capital balance perspectives in debates over the "theft" and "purity" of cultural expressions. This paradigm highlights the larger politics embedded within hip hop, for example, as a culture rooted in the specificity of Blacks' experiences in the United States, which come to frame those of every other group.

In another twist, many desis know Lahiri as the Indian producer who, without giving credit, remakes songs that turn into hits. As the India Abroad journalist Jeet Thayil remarks, "Most observers in the music business find it interesting that Lahiri, who has been accused of lifting hit songs from all over the world and making Hindi versions of them, has now taken an American producer to court for exactly the same deed" (Thayil 2003). On top of that, Harry Anand did an Indian (re-)remix of Truth Hurts' "Addictive" called "Kaliyon Ka Chaman." These cycles of appropriation complicate—but they do not eradicate—Lahiri's charge of cultural imperialism. And in the end, DJ Rekha opined what Lahiri's lawsuit is all about—namely money. "If 'Addictive' had been some hip hop song that made no money," Rekha told Thayil, "they wouldn't be wasting their time." After all, like many sampled artists who have passed their prime, Lahiri was enjoying renewed airtime because of the lawsuit publicity and the popularity of the Truth Hurts song.

Cultural productions are embedded in a field of racial power dynamics that is itself mediated by the profit motives of global capital. The marriage of global capital to American multiculturalism has led to the rise of consumers who purchase their "authentic" identities—and those of others—through the commodity form that detaches itself from the bodies and contexts they signify. Thus, Madonna can take on and off a variety of Asian wardrobes, including kimonos and saris; similarly, youths consume Blackness through their engagement with hip hop. It is precisely because so much is at stake in connecting floating representations to actual bodies and contexts that debates rage over appropriation.

Desis expressed a range of reactions to the lawsuit by Bappi Lahiri. Fabian Alsultany, a DJ and the CEO of Globesonic, said that "Addictive" "is a straight-up rip-off of Bollywood. Hip hop is a kind of musical thievery anyway, they sample everything." Some hip hop critics, who called pilfering what others have called innovative practices, have made the same argument. One online writer, Suhel Johar, upheld the concept of the copyright law and argued that Dr. Dre and DJ Quik illustrate a case of "shameless plagiarism." As he wrote on an online Indian forum: "The way things are going, more and more American rap stars may use bits from old Hindi songs. As long as it's done through proper channels—wherein the right permissions are taken, credits are given and payments made—it's fine. But to blindly use pieces of old songs without crediting the source is unpardonable . . . In the case of Hindi film songs, they [rap stars] just pick up some tune given to them by the album producer and incorporate it without bothering [to find out] who originally created it and who owns the rights" ("Choli Ke Peeche Kya Hai" Sampled, www.smashhits.com, accessed June 17, 2009).

Johar highlights the double standard applied to South Asian artists by Black rap producers in the United States who do not feel compelled to give credit or make payments to foreign sources. Although he calls it a "different matter" when Indians sample, his next comment nonetheless highlights the dual flows of these practices: "Surely, it must be made compulsory for any western artiste to seek permission of the Indian creator before using even the tiniest sample. *It's a different matter that some Indian composers need to be again reminded that blindly lifting western songs is probably the sickest thing for any creative artiste to do.* One simply cannot justify shameless plagiarism" (my emphasis). This writer conflates mainstream Black popular icons with the West, and thus with imperial power, in relation to the East (Indian creators) because he analyzes race relations through a global lens. American Blacks are not always seen by all people as non-White others; they are also considered African *Americans* in relation to non-Western others. Again, the positions of Blacks, including mainstream rappers, shift according to the scale of analysis, and a global scale can link Blacks to the hegemony of America (just as, in other contexts, it links Black and Brown people). This global conversation on sampling with specific reference to the debates inspired by Truth Hurts's song expands debates about sampling and appropriation beyond the argument that what is happening to hip hop is part of the history of Whites stealing jazz and rock 'n' roll. As a result, we cannot interpret desis' multiple practices of appropriation of Black cultural forms in the same way we do that of American Whites.

Through Hindi-inflected hip hop songs, Black popular culture unknowingly provides desi youths with a new set of "shared secrets" that they deploy to define their communities. Identifiably South Asian elements in hip hop have enabled second-generation youths to claim a part of hip hop as their own. For them, as for Blacks and South Asians in the West Indies, "music was not simply entertainment: it served socially and emotionally to nurture and show one's sense of belonging" (Guilbault 2001: 435). The impact of Indian musical forms on traditionally African diasporic music has had a longer history in the Caribbean as expressed in chutney soca and some dancehall music (Manuel 2000, 2006). In the United States this came to light earlier in jazz and in hip hop at the turn of the millennium. As the children of immigrants familiar with both the Hindi *and* hip hop songs, desi youths, including the artists I discuss in this book, felt their varied opinions on hip hop, art, and culture were warranted since Hindi samples provided them an opening.

Many desi youths, including the artists, responded favorably to the slew of hit songs. Young desis in the Bay Area mostly liked Missy Elliot's "Get Ur Freak On," for example, because they finally felt represented in the music they had loved for years. Desi artists usually evaluated songs on a case by case basis because music means so much more than "just beats" (McWhorter 2008). They tended to disagree with Johar's interpretation of sampling as "stealing" by arguing that it was justified. However, they debated over how "well" artists sample, especially since most of their own track productions (like their identities) included samples of all kinds. Some enjoyed songs that incorporated Hindi while others were disappointed by the lack of originality when producers simply lifted entire prerecorded tracks without manipulating their content as soon as South Asian samples became a trend.[8] Overall, they appreciated musical samples that were "done correctly" — that is, ones that sounded good, were original, and represented the cultures from which the samples came. Others were upset that Blacks in the industry silenced South Asians in most other contexts, arguing that any representation wasn't better than none. For instance, some youths argued that the videos that used Hindi voices as props stripped desi self-representation by keeping them as invisible in the United States as they have been historically. For example, Karan, an Indo Fijian from Hayward, California, was upset at the use of the Hindi speaker in "Get Ur Freak On." "What the hell is he saying?!" the feisty student shouted over the phone. "They don't even let him finish his sentence!" He was not upset that an individual South Asian singer was being silenced but rather that it was an allegory for the silencing of an entire people. Those who shared Karan's perspective were not fans of songs like "Addictive," or Erick Sermon's song "React," that borrowed or "ripped off" unadulterated samples without (they felt) matching them artistically with the rest of the song. The desis did not all agree about the meanings of the sample and the lawsuit, but they did all notice the difficulties of applying copyright law, based on the assumption of a single author, to a constantly shifting, internally referential, digital, and communal culture.

Sampling often upsets those who feel they have been misrepresented and who also often forget the multiple influences upon their "own" cultures. While hybrid collaborations are so evident in the Caribbean, in the United States the monoracial logic sometimes leads individuals to read racial mixing as suspect and obfuscates syncretic realities and emergent possibilities, particularly between minority groups. Despite the ascendancy of Blacks in United States popular culture, neither they nor South Asians have full access to the power of dominant groups that set global and national agendas. Nonetheless, the context of war often impels individuals to pay close attention to the representations of their communities. Black hip hop producers do not unequivocally represent "the establishment," but in some instances agendas overlap. When we move from traditional sampling debates to analyzing the video of "Addictive" within the political climate of 9/11, we find that Dre, Quik, and Truth Hurts represent a type of Western cultural imperialism over the East, shaping and reflecting national perspectives not limited to Blacks, music, or the present moment.

The "Addictive" music video expresses the creators' ideas of the possible origins of its sampled music. The camera is set on the singer's hennaed hands swaying over her head in an attempt to match the "over there" vibe of the song. It takes place in a lush harem surrounding; its interior is laced with vibrant and intricate sari-like fabrics. The effect is sensual and the beauty of the women and the decor draw the viewer into its aura. Staring at us, Truth Hurts sings seductively on a plush bed, "He breaks me down, he builds me up, he fills my cup, I like it rough." During the Hindi chorus, the camera pans across a series of Black women mixing belly dancing with hip hop moves. The harem and dancers represent a feminized projection of "that region" that hides Brown men and sexualizes heterosexual interracial contact, which is pursued by America represented as dominant, male, and Black. The dancers' clothing complements the decorations; they wear Indian-inspired embroidered tops and colorful scarves tied on to their tight-fitting jeans, shimmering with each movement of their hips. Then the scene changes to an American nightclub when rapper Rakim enters the video sporting 100 percent American urban wear—a leather jacket and baggy jeans. As Rakim walks down a set of stairs and into our sights, the set transports viewers back to the United States from a foreign and remote region. In his deep New York accent, he raps, "Thinking of a master plan, you know anything you need, baby, ask your man"—taking part of this line from his old-school classic "Paid in Full." This layered history of sampling extends further across time and race: the remix of Eric B and Rakim's song "Paid in Full," by Coldcut, sampled the Israeli singer Ofra Haza, whose singing echoed an "other worldly" addictively danceable sound that may have inspired this latest pairing.[9]

The video producer Phillip Atwell presents to viewers a fictitious yet compelling place where South Asia and the Middle East fuse. The Hindi lyrics along with the belly dancing and harem scenario filled with gyrating Black (not Brown) women tell a thousand and one tales about the American cultural imagination of "that region" of the world as one filled with beautiful women who are highly sensual and expert dancers available for the male gaze. While Blacks may occupy a particular position within the racial politics of the United States, these kinds of new videos reveal a shared yet ambiguous imaginary of the Middle East and South Asia held by mainstream Americans, Black and White. But conflating these regions is especially dangerous above and beyond the fact that the producers did not gain permission to sample the song. In fact, although music fans have expressed a renewed interest in sampling, copyright, and the ownership of culture because of "Addictive," they have devoted less attention to why these songs are popular while

In the same "Addictive" music video, the old-school rapper Rakim descends into an American hip hop club setting.

America is at war with the real nations that inspire these fantasies (cf. Fitzpatrick 2002). The videos, including R. Kelly's harem escapade in "Snake (Remix)," employ othering practices of appropriation by conflating and exoticizing this "region" and its objects outside a historical, social, or geographic context (Wolf 1982; Fabian 2002). Producers erase actual Middle Eastern and South Asian *bodies* and replace them with Black performers from the West who nonetheless take on the cultural markers of the missing (indeed, *disappeared*) peoples. This appropriation as othering may be read as a strategic use of anti-essentialism (Lipsitz 1994, 2007), whereby individuals take on "unlikely" identities in order to disrupt differences and highlight commonalities. But it seems more likely that the draw to the Middle East and South Asia is a decontextualized allure that underlies othering practices that are less bent on knowing the other than on temporarily donning trappings of exotica. This exotic, yet attainable, depiction implies a desire for the other or, more accurately, the desire for a new global playground devoid of its original inhabitants. Yet the effects become particularly pernicious—and possibly ironic—within the context of American foreign policies (recall that this song debuted in June 2002, less than a year after 9/11).

The events since the collapse of the World Trade Center prompted the sudden growth of interest about that "region" of South Asia and the Middle East among many Americans; colleges offer more courses, stores sell more books, and people are actually having conversations about the Middle East, Islam, and the expansion of American empire. Yet much of the George W. Bush government's agenda had focused on a programmatic demonization of Islam. For example, in collaboration with the mainstream news media, Bush and his aides represented areas far beyond Afghanistan as home to Islamic fundamentalists who were bent on destroying the American way of life. These depictions, in conjunction with many Americans' lack of knowledge about the Middle East, allowed the government to rally the support of a majority of Americans in the "War on Terrorism." Were these enormously popular videos, which were made by Black producers and singers and which often represented who groups "are" to viewers, another mouthpiece for this mission? Is their timing just coincidental, or is there some other explanation?

The few journalists who have analyzed the Truth Hurts video

within the current political context argue that these forms of popular culture were complicit with the government's goals. In an insightful article in *PopMatters*, Chris Fitzpatrick connects the sampling South Asia trend to the invasion of Iraq and comments on how the "Addictive" video alleviates for viewers the actuality of war and death in the Middle East. With regard to Afghanistan, he writes: "Such heightened interest has created a strong market for the sounds and sights of these regions, so it is not surprising that U.S. music producers are finding ways to pillage the 'third world' for material. . . . By collapsing [the Middle East and India], 'Addictive' convolutes and expands the boundaries of 'evil' by making India part of an 'anti-American terror network.' After all, expanding 'boundaries' is what the War on Terrorism is all about, as Ashcroft and Bush know all too well" (2002; see also Miller 2004). It should come as no surprise that the American panopticon has shifted its gaze toward Iran and Pakistan.

While Fitzpatrick rightly points to the danger in homogenizing various regions, as Orientalism does, he is equally guilty of conflating all of "America" into a unified whole. He incorrectly asserts that the producers of hip hop represent the imperialism of the First World outright, unmediated by the politics of race. For instance, while Fitzpatrick concedes that "this is not to say that Truth Hurts is some secret agent for the United States government, but that representation is always political," he still makes a strong connection between the video and the War on Terrorism. He concludes, "In such an ugly, war-ridden reality, 'Addictive' provides a reassuring sedative to the average American viewer, conveniently leaving out mutilations by landmines, refugee camps, resurfacing warlords and drug lords, suicide bombers, occupations, and those current and imminent wars in these regions that could destroy them completely." Yet attention to the variations in the positions of groups, which are not static and shift according to scale of perspective, affects how individuals view group relations. Interpreting popular culture through race relations at the national and international scale prevents the inaccurate slippage between the government's demonization of the Middle East and Truth Hurts.

Truth Hurts along with her music and video producers and video dancers are members of a racial group that is historically overrepresented in the United States military in comparison to the size of their national population.[10] Americans may gather that the decreasing number of Black recruits reflected a growing sentiment against the war in Iraq by some individuals whose more immediate concerns included the wars here in America against the poor and Black. To speak of the effects of this video on "the average American viewer" without locating the producers of the song—or its audiences that include South Asian and Middle Eastern Americans—within America's internal politics too simply ignores the inequalities and differences of perspective that exist within our nation's boundaries. Yet it is true that even if popular artists do not intend to make political commentary, ultimately the effects of these songs reaffirm Americans' geographic misperceptions. As such, as Fitzpatrick comments, these mainstream songs and videos represent a broader lack of both the awareness and desire to adequately represent South Asia and the Middle East.

(Negative) representations of "Muslim-looking" people and the relations between South Asians and Blacks before and following 9/11 represented not so much a distinct shift as they did a magnified continuation of the complex and shifting images and past processes that ebb and flow according to geopolitical events. They also reveal the repercussions of the decisions by the mainstream media, including news outlets, politicians, and popular culture, to cast its attention upon previously ignored populations. Consciously or not, hip hop superstars shape and reflect national—and even international—concerns and play a central role in advocating both hegemonic and counterhegemonic discourses. As a result, understanding the history of hip hop is as important as locating this massively influential popular culture within contemporary political, economic, and social contexts. We need to unpack hip hop as an art form that is interpreted through a social lens and is informed by past and current events. However, it is important also to read hip hop on its own terms in order to understand that the creation of these texts takes place *both* in the marginal and subcultural arenas of society (as in underground hip hop and the spaces occupied by desi rappers) *and* in the smack-dab center of corporatized (popular) culture by multimillion dollar and globally renowned artists like Jay-Z and Sean "Diddy" Combs.

In fact, the strongest explanation for Black sampling of South Asian music since 2000 is that South Asian sounds were just the next big thing to hit hip hop, following the immense popularity of East Asian influences. The latter include the kanji tattoos in Japanese and Chinese that frequently adorn rappers' bodies, as well as the martial arts elements and the "exotic" East Asian women featured in hip hop videos. "Addictive," in fact, came on the heels of a song that initially set the stage for a series that was to follow: namely, Missy Elliott's "Get Ur Freak On." The album *Miss E . . . So Addictive* hit stands on May 15, 2001, *before* the World Trade Center collapsed. Hip hoppers are ceaselessly able to remain relevant by consistently changing their sounds through the incorporation of difference. In this way differences can be crossed *over* without regard to context and history similar to the obfuscation of real differences by multiculturalist ideologies in which representation is depicted as apolitical and equal.

There were earlier signs of mainstream hip hop's "Indian" turn. For example, South Asian women performed in MTV music videos in 2000. Veena and Neena, the Indian "bellytwins," produced belly dance workout videos and collaborated with the West Coast producer Dr. Dre.[11] In 2001 on the album *The Blueprint* another famous rapper, Jay-Z, rhymed in his song "Girls, Girls, Girls":

I got this Indian squaw the day that I met her,
Asked her what tribe she with, red dot or feather . . .
Now that's Spanish chick, French chick, Indian and Black,
That's fried chicken, curry chicken, damn I'm getting fat.

In these lyrics Jay-Z runs through a list of conflated sexist and racist descriptions not, it seems, in order to critique them. Drawing upon the homogenizing logic of race in the United States, Jay-Z's verse muddies distinctions between Indians (indigenous Americans and people from India) by substituting "tribe" for "caste." That Jay-Z remarks upon Indians could signify the prevalence of East Indians in New York, where the MC is from, or it might have been a rhyming convenience. But it was a reference that desi fans and producers took seriously as they were invested in how mainstream hip hop incorporated South Asians.

Some mainstream desi women took unkindly to the reference to "red dots" in "Girls, Girls, Girls," but they also felt rappers like

Jay-Z sits in a room with an "Indian" woman and "asked her what tribe she with, red dot or feather," in his song "Girls, Girls, Girls."

Jay-Z and Tupac were three-dimensional and "real" precisely because they were contradictory and controversial. Yet can we not love *and* critique popular artists like Jay-Z for advocating sexism, racism, and homophobia *across* and *within* racial, gender, and sexual groups, precisely because of their influence? Jay-Z's list of culinary women urges Americans to reconsider advocates of racism and sexism beyond the White male subject. Blacks engage in realignments of race that trouble South Asians' status as model minorities. Jay-Z feminizes Indians as women by lining them up with other desirable women while leaving out representations of Brown men and depicting all of them as foreigners. Indeed, his chauvinism mirrors attitudes of mainstream South Asians toward Blacks and of other Black rappers toward immigrants. The trend of South Asian women also inspired a host of other rappers.

The music video "React" features a song by the old-school Black rapper Erick Sermon that immediately followed the success of "Addictive." In it its producers literally dubbed trivial English captions over the Hindi chorus as women unfamiliar with the language attempted to lip-synch the words. As Erick begins rhyming:

Ay yo, I'm immaculate,
Come through masculine,
Wide body frame, E Dub's the name

. . . .

Come through, storm the block like el nino,
Scoop up an Arabic chick before she close,
She goes:

And the sampled and unrepresented singer responds in Hindi: "Kisi ko / kuch pucheka / to kaho to / kya kare to?" The green-eyed rapper makes explicit his ignorance about the meaning of the chorus by rapping, "Whatever she said, then, I'm that." In the video, he replaced the singer with a green pet hand sock to highlight the alleged humor of the chorus. But in the full version of the original song, the woman is singing about a life and death situation: suicide.

Some desi artists saw "React" as the worst kind of sampling—sampling with complete disregard to context and without the smallest effort to find out where the sample comes from and what the singer is saying. It represents a decontextualized representation of South Asian music literally devoid of the mouth and person from which the voice emanates. Additionally, Sermon's description of the woman as "Arabic," along with the use of Hindi lyrics from India, illustrates a general American ignorance of both geography and non-European languages. Of course there may in fact be no "deep meaning" to the mismatching of his lyrics ("Arabic chick"), the racialized stereotypes of convenience store owners, and the sound of the chorus. Further, I am not certain that these references were tied to the increasing visibility of the Middle East in the news or whether the sample sounded cool and the reference was an attempt to "match" it so that the rapper and singer created a kind of "conversation." It relays the message, though, that artists who have become commercially viable do not need to do their homework—in contrast to the pressures that Blacks and desi artists themselves put on non-Blacks and women attempting to make it in the business.

Sampling South Asians is nothing new and should come as no surprise given that borrowing is foundational to hip hop production. Astute fans could even predict this phenomenon, as South Asia was the next *unexplored* region in hip hop. The racial politics of the hip hop industry demand a cautionary rather than over-celebratory interpretation of the incorporation of *actual* South Asians. But they did not remain voiceless or faceless for long. Mainstream hip hop produced increasing representations of South Asian people and elements just as the underground desi hip hop artists featured in this book were attempting to break new ground in the business.

There are proper and improper ways of appropriating—or borrowing and fusing—identities, aesthetics, and ideas. On the one hand, acts of appropriation can come out of racism and exacerbate group tensions. So-called Jiggers and Wiggers who fetishize Blackness are like some mainstream desis who emulate yet misunderstand Blacks. Such practices embody appropriation as othering; like other forms of appropriation, this is a two-way process. That is, we also see this phenomenon in mainstream hip hop artists' appropriation and exotification of South Asian and Middle Eastern sounds, commodities, and women. With racial politics geared toward questioning the motives of non-Blacks, less attention has been paid to Black hip hoppers' sampling of non-Black forms. Analyzing how Black megastars adopt Asian signifiers reveals their actions as part of a larger, multidirectional flow of sampling among individuals whose statuses are uneven and shifting in a culture rooted in intertextual citation and informed by global events.

At the same time, producing music in a time of war has given some popular artists a venue to voice their political opinions about Iraq *through* studio collaborations with South Asians. Just as desi hip hop artists work with Blacks in their productions, some collaborations reflect appropriation as identification. This occurs when an individual identifies with another group's cultural products through a contextualized approach that takes history, power, and inequality into account. Mainstream hip hop artists including Timbaland and Jay-Z collaborate cross-racially with South Asians to produce informed polycultural expressions.

"Culture cannot be bounded and people cannot be asked to respect 'culture' as if it were an artifact, without life or complexity," writes Vijay Prashad. "Social interaction and struggle produces cultural worlds, and these are in constant, fraught formation. Our cultures are linked in more ways than we could catalog, and it is from these linkages that we hope our politics will be energized" (2001: 148). South Asian American hip hop artists, too, enact appropriative acts of identification with Blacks by fusing Black cultural and racial identities with ethnic, gender, and sexual ones. These processes are rooted in varied and individual approaches, contexts, and ideologies not fully grasped by existing interpretations. Indeed, in reframing our criteria to evaluate cross-cultural appropriations and interracial exchanges through the lens of global and historical processes we come to a clearer understanding of the shifting terrain of race relations and identifications.

Appropriation as Identification

Hip-hoppers have done more to create a common culture for kids of different backgrounds than the integration movement. (Reed quoted in Farley 1999: 178)

While mainstream hip hop has incorporated South Asian elements into its repertoire, the artists in this study have been busy working through their local communities to gain access to broader audiences. The intersection of Blacks and South Asians can reveal not only the problems but also the power of popular culture to engage populations and the possibilities of sampling as political acts of identification. Not all cross-cultural borrowings are racist actions; not all appropriation is "theft" or "colonization" (Lott 1993b; Lipsitz 1994). White men enamored with jazz (and the larger than life personas of Black jazz greats and their alleged wild lifestyles) in the first half of the twentieth century often dedicated their lives to learning and producing this music.[12] Certainly, some were drawn to what they interpreted was its "primitive" aspect of Blackness and the "rawness" expressed in some forms of bebop and later in free jazz, much as many are drawn to hip hop today. But some of these White musicians also inserted themselves into "the scene," spent time with Black players, and took part in desegregating club spaces (Jones 1963). These examples speak to some, but not all, of the motivations of Asian Americans in hip hop who simultaneously attempt to express minority identities.

Racially explicit music, according to Deborah Wong, "speaks to the uneasy position that Asian Americans negotiate between Blackness and Whiteness" (2004: 272). Wong emphasizes the importance of the racialized components of listening to and making

Black music for individuals who find few models of Asian American expression. The appeal of Black music to Asian American jazz musicians parallels hip hoppers one and two generations later. Japanese rappers also challenge audiences' assumptions of, in the words of Ian Condry, the "misappropriation and misunderstanding" of Black expressive forms (2006: 25). The lyrics of MCs in Japan reveal "an affinity between African Americans as disenfranchised citizens in the United States and Japanese youth unable to see their concerns adequately addressed in their own political system" (206). South Asians in America also feel voiceless within larger structural processes. Their lives abound with examples of appropriation as identification—in fact, for many of them hip hop is their culture.

Context is central to analyzing how and why individuals appropriate. Cross-cultural exchanges dialogically inform the artists' identifications. Like the rappers in Japan who use hip hop to comment on immediate global events, some Americans use hip hop to articulate their post-9/11 concerns. The increased sampling of Hindi film songs in mainstream rap during a period of heightened Brown visibility coincided with a number of hip hoppers—desi, African American, Puerto Rican and White—using their art to express their views on the "War on Terror." During this period, some Blacks in the industry have collaborated with actual South Asians, thus helping pave the way for greater desi representation. It is no coincidence that these exchanges have increased since 2001 and that the music they create provides glimpses of new social formations.

Collaborations: Mainstream Black Hip Hoppers and South Asians

Jay-Z is among the commercial rappers who first incorporated South Asian music into hip hop tracks. In some cases, his producers sampled Hindi music without apparent knowledge of its context. In other cases, he worked with South Asians to create cross-cultural, cross-national, and cross-racial musical products. One of the hottest club hits in summer 2003 was the remix of the England-based Panjabi MC's "Beware of the Boys" and his collaboration with Jay-Z. This cross-Atlantic effort marked a turning point for the presence and representation of South Asians in Black popular culture: hip hoppers had now officially moved past sampling Hindi songs for their rap hooks (choruses) to produce an English and Punjabi rap song recorded in real time, though not in the same studio. Jay-Z, a member of the Musicians United to Win Without War coalition, even used the remix of this song (and others to follow) to air his views about the United States occupation of Iraq:

We rebellious, we back home
Screamin,' "Leave Iraq alone."
For all my soldiers in the field
I will wish you safe return.
But only love kills war
When will they learn?

This was not the only reference to the war by Brooklyn's Jay-Z. Indeed, he later collaborated with Raje Shware, a Philadelphia-based Indian American singer. Raje Shwari was "discovered" by a top producer Timbaland, who billed her as the hottest new hip hop act. She was the featured singer on the hits of some hip hop heavyweights: she recorded with Missy Elliot and 50 Cent, for example, and she provided the Hindi hook in "Nas's Angels" on the *Charlie's Angels* soundtrack.[13] I recall seeing her dressed in traditional Indian clothing sitting in the back of a cab in Slum Village's hip hop video "Disco" (why are South Asians always associated with cabs?). The desi hip hoppers I talked with were not aware of Raje Shwari when Timabaland commissioned her to re-sing an older popular Hindi song on Jay-Z's track (thereby avoiding any copyright lawsuits), especially since her voice could have been yet another sample (Americans picture Hindi speakers occupying space in South Asia rather than in American music studios). However, when radio stations played "The Bounce," young desis recognized the chorus as the Hindi original "Choli Ke Peeche," an award-winning song from the Bollywood hit film *Khalnayak*.

In the original song the demure yet teasing voice of Alka Yagnik suggestively asks, "What is beneath your choli?" (the blouse that South Asian women wear with their saris). This song, deemed "vulgar" by censors in India, was popular among diasporic South Asians in the early 1990s. Gayatri Gopinath describes the empowering potential of this song and the pleasures its viewers gain from the disruptive and queer sexuality of the dance sequences that contest heteronormative state discourses (2005: 100–11). In the hip hop song Raje Shwari provides her own rendition of the same words, although her collaboration with the male producers reinscribes a heteronormative, albeit cross-racial, reading. Timbaland's use of "Chole ke Peeche" also advances his sampling practices beyond using tablas and Hindi one-liners. He employs an "actual" South Asian American woman (who had worked for years on her own R&B—not Indian—music) to sing the sample in real time. And she has a face—namely by appearing in the video for the song (although still conforming to ideas of what Indian women "look like"). Timbaland pushes hip hop forward by incorporating new sounds and styles and exposing them to mainstream audiences. The increasing representations of South Asians in popular culture, who themselves change the looks and sounds of hip hop, is one by-product of this. These cross-fertilizations, including Black rappers' commentaries on current events, encourage hip hop's openness to the contributions of South Asians, especially if desi artists make aggressive claims to their presence.

Jay-Z does not limit his references to 9/11 to his remix with Panjabi MC. In "The Bounce" he raps:

> Rumor has it "The Blueprint" classic
> Couldn't even be stopped by bin Laden
> So September 11th marks the era forever
> of a revolutionary Jay Guevero.

Here Jay-Z adorns his persona with the revolutionary aura of Che Guevara; and he infuses bin Laden, the Muslim in hiding, with the power to stop most things but not Jay-Z's album (the audio CD of *The Blueprint* came out on September 11, 2001). Like some desi rappers, Black artists too use hip hop to express their beliefs about the war with specific reference to bin Laden. They also refer to historical parallels to expose the structural processes that underlie America's wars in non-Western nations. Some rappers refer to bin Laden in their rhymes by demonizing him as an enemy of the state or, alternately, identifying with him as America's most wanted. Lyricists also use bin Laden as a foil against which to (re)prove that the state has chosen Blacks as its "worst enemy," thereby critiquing Bush who "hates Black people," as the rapper Kanye West succinctly put it. The song "Bin Laden" by Immortal Technique, along with the Italian/Puerto Rican DJ Green Lantern and with appearances by Mos Def and Eminem, updates and echoes the Muslim convert Muhammad Ali's antiwar sentiments that it wasn't the Vietnamese that oppressed him.[14] On the controversial track that says that Bush was responsible for the World Trade Center attack and that Americans sold chemical weapons to Saddam Hussein after the election of Ronald Reagan, the Peruvian-born Harlemite Immortal Technique raps:

> All they talk about is terrorism on television
> They tell you to listen, but they don't really tell you they mission
> They funded Al-Qaeda, and now they blame the Muslim religion
> Even though bin Laden, was a CIA tactician
> They gave him billions of dollars, and they funded his purpose
> Fahrenheit 9/11, that's just scratchin' the surface

The chorus "Bin Laden didn't blow up the projects / It was you, nigga / Tell the truth, nigga / (Bush knocked down the towers) / Tell the truth, nigga / (Bush knocked down the projects)" illustrates a relatively common interpretation of the war in Iraq, the hunt for bin Laden, and the war on terrorism. Rappers, including those who are Muslims, connect justifications for overseas wars to the same logic that undergirds the government's closing and policing of low-income housing (the projects) populated by working-class minorities in American cities.

There is no single way that American hip hop artists have sampled Middle Eastern and South Asian references, and these actions reflect the diversity of sentiments across mainstream and less commercial hip hop. And, although we all face the repercussions of presidential policies, even artists at the center of American popular culture distance themselves from the decisions of politicians. Even if these explicitly political statements do not get picked up by major labels more invested in decontextualized representations of otherness, the new technologies of YouTube and MySpace spread these messages far and wide. New software also makes it possible for increasing numbers of people to become music producers in their home studios. They contribute to hip hop's critical commentary on current events by sampling from and analyzing news broadcasts and politicians' speeches, for example. Many of the themes — such as the antiwar perspectives of the rappers mentioned above, on one hand, and the patriotism and military bent of R. Kelly and Mystikal (who served in the military) on the other — reflect its multiple perspectives. Hip hop culture simply cannot be reduced, and neither should all appropriative acts be deemed inappropriate.

Perhaps both sets of artists—Timbaland and Raje Shwari; Jay-Z and Punjabi MC—were motivated to work together because of business, aesthetic, or political and social considerations; who knows whether or not they expressly sought to advance positive interracial relations in the United States? Nonetheless these sonic collaborations prove hip hop's openness to South Asian sounds, styles, and people. Within the parameters of our capitalist system, there is still room for new, individual voices and the effects, however unintended, that accompany them. Desis are slowly, yet actually, "on the radar" of hip hop. For example, an Indian American rapper, the1shanti, signed on to Rawkus Records, a well-known hip hop label that also signed the Japanese rapper Kojoe. In fact, Afrika Bambaataa, "the godfather of hip hop culture," named the1shanti the "India Bambaataa": "You have our blessings (Afrika Bambaataa and The Universal Zulu Nation) as long as you use your name in the good of your people and the good of yourself."[15] Other diasporic subcontinentals are also finding their niche in the hip hop business. Chee Malabar was approached by a subsidiary of one of the largest record companies as a potential artist on their label. And while the emergence of desi rappers may not change existing social, political, and economic structures of inequality, they are nonetheless more and more able to self-represent with the music they love. Mainstream hip hop's sampling of South Asia may be a short-lived trend, but the integration of South Asians' music into hip hop proper may prove to have a longer, more lasting impact on Americans' perceptions of desis.

Desi Hip Hoppers:
The Appropriation of Hip Hop as Identification with Blacks

The cross-racial identifications of hip hop desis reconfigure racial boundaries in ways that connect South Asians to Blacks at precisely the moment when global events restructure these relations. They draw from the models of Blackness and hip hop culture to craft politicized Brown identities that are hip hop while reconfiguring what hip hop is. For some non-Blacks, rap music heightens their awareness of Black history and the lives of people struggling with economic disenfranchisement, and it can foster cultural understanding despite their social distance (Bernstein 1995; Roediger 1998; see also Gilroy 1987). Polycultural sampling may give rise to positive interracial interactions that lead to deep friendships (Arlyck 1997: 272; Rivera 1997). It may in one example lead, as Zaid Ansari suggests, "to whites 'becoming X'—that is, losing that quality in whiteness that 'keeps them accepting oppression,' including their own oppression" (quoted in Roediger 1998: 363). The sampling practices of hip hop desis model some politicized uses of Black popular culture that resist disabling processes.

As non-Whites, desis can understand and unite with Blacks in the struggle for equality without forgoing their ethnicity. D'Lo engages music, for example, to show desi youths how to sample and meld influences in informed ways that reject nationalisms and identitarian politics. When D'Lo was young, s/he studied South Indian Karnatic music, and every Friday s/he attended a bhajan (Hindu devotional songs) session where s/he loved to sing. Even as s/he became increasingly involved in hip hop, D'Lo returned to the bhajan sessions on his/her visits home from college:

> But every time I came back home I'd go to bhajan and there were kids and we'd sit around and you know how you go double-time? Like you'd sing a bhajan and then you'd do your second round in double-time, you know? [S/he does a sample and laughs]. So, when I did that, I used to play hip hop beats, and either I'd bring my DV 7 Yamaha with pads in it [laughs] or I'd go syncopated on their off beat. So . . . they'd be like here: [clap, clap], and I'd be like [clap-clap clap, clap-clap clap]. So, my mom would be like, "Stop it!" and all the kids would be edging toward me, and we'd all be having a dope time with the double-time! Everybody loved coming to bhajan whenever I was there! We'd all go nuts, it was dope! [Laughs]

D'Lo's lively narrative expresses a process of polycultural (and polyrhythmic) fusion that is foundational to hip hop and that makes it open to adoption. These practices also reflect how, as Fred Ho and Bill Mullen note, "African Americans and Asian Americans have mutually influenced, borrowed from, and jointly innovated new forms in culture . . . and politics" (2008: 3), just as Asians and Blacks have done in other diasporic locations as well.

South Asian American performers eschew the myopic focus by audiences on the racial status of non-Blacks in hip hop. They see their musical identities through more intangible paradigms—using "authenticity," for example, to discuss, maneuver among, and bridge (although not transcend) meaningful boundaries. They want to be known as "authentic artists," not as "Indian rappers." Authenticity separates them from those who simply "appropriate." But they do not consider authenticity to be a color blind or reified ideology. Rather, desis identify with hip hop in explicitly racialized ways by recasting constructed divisions of race. Invested in distinctions between good and wack music, they concur that to be authentic one needs to "come correct" and make *good music*. Thus, they deploy authenticity as an anti-essentialist "realness" that is not tied to being Black or South Asian, being poor or wealthy, being straight or gay, or being male or female. They recuperate authenticity from an essentialist trap by defining an authentic artist as one who has the right *ideology and approach*, rather than a particular *identity*.

Anti-Essentialist Authenticity:
Knowledge, Respect, and Dedication

The bottom line is that we just be ourselves. I don't try too hard to "act like" them. Meaning in terms of slang, using the n-word. Talking about their culture and race. And still I'm accepted. This is all because of talent.—Rocky, a Canadian Punjabi MC

Rap is based on sampling. It's a way of giving back to the community. Say you sample off Aretha Franklin or Diana Ross—it's like it's acknowledging their past. It's like if me or you were doing hip hop and we sampled Ravi Shankar because that's what our parents listened to.—Chee, Himalayan Project MC

Capitalist interventions in art and cultural production often deploy essentialist authenticity in dangerous ways (Jackson 2005). Corporate interests sign a pact with dominant racist discourses to sell their products and ideas that maintain the status quo. They do this by linking "authenticity" to particular identities, including the idea that authentic rappers are Black, or that women (i.e., their body parts) should be seen and not heard. Reductive and stereotyped concepts of race and gender are in the vortex of capitalist com-modification of difference and sameness. In light of these claims, what are these desis' notions of being "authentic artists," and how do they employ them in anti-essentialist ways in their approach to identity politics? The answer lies in their approach of knowledge, respect, and dedication to life and music rather than appeals to a pure or necessary racial or gender identity. Anti-essentialist au-thenticity as an approach is an alternative to identity-based evalua-tion and resists corporations' attempts to hijack the full humanity of minorities through the commodification of racism.

In taking my clue from desi artists I dislocate authenticity from the body and instead use it to refer to an individual's context-based perspective. The artists' global race consciousness is one example of this, and the way they sample is another. Although individuals may belong and hold firm to their identifications with preexisting categories, this political understanding of difference emphasizes the constructed and divisive nature of racial categories. These art-ists are neither interested in doing away with race, nor feel that they can transcend its impacts. Rather, they are bent on artistic integrity and attend to hip hop as a racialized field of possibility. But can they speak up to corporate interests that profit from the more dangerous conceptions of authenticity? If an artist's biggest aim is to be heard, how do desis negotiate the constraints of corporate interests that create the very reductive and essentialist conceptions that the art-ists wish to challenge?

Maintaining Artistic Integrity within the Constraints of Capitalism

If maintaining integrity, or being real, means staying true to one-self and is central to the artists' definition of authenticity, then desi artists can almost by definition not seek corporate support. Inde-pendent labels may take risks on new artists and offer them con-trol over their product, but they provide little distribution. On the other hand, larger labels offer bigger budgets and vast networks of promotion, but push their artists to craft particular sounds and images. Indeed, almost all of the desi artists are unsigned or else have signed to their own independent labels such as Rukus Avenue Records, Karmacy's label. The politics of race infuse this situation, of course: because the mass consumer base seems to accept the idea that only Black artists are authentic, non-Blacks face a difficult time attracting attention and legitimacy.

As the artists see it, commodification spreads culture, including music, to new markets while tying it deeply to local and, when popular, global capital. It often reduces the complexities of people and their products to palatable packaged essences (of "soul," "coolness," "exotica," etc.) that line the shelves of stores and cyber markets. Some artists comment that tastes and production technologies, hostage to consumer demands, have oversimplified more complex sounds. And they criticize some successful Black artists for aligning with big business. As a writer for popular hip hop magazines, Jonny has seen how the artists he grew up listening to have changed. In an email to me, he wrote: "Hip-hop is a business, not an art. And when groups you thought would make music just for the art of it—for example, De La Soul—start tailoring it for the business, it makes you lose some faith."

These issues come into play as the artists weigh the pros and cons of artistic integrity and authenticity over mass distribution. At one point I spoke with Karmacy's K B about whether or not signed artists still have responsibility for the content of their music. His response emphasizes the power plays between record labels and their artists: "The responsibility is on the artist, but the artists get their arms twisted by the record labels because the labels have the power." He concedes that artists *choose* to make albums, but once that decision is made they enter a business in which "it's about selling albums." Someone who lacks backing may be a "phenomenal artist," but the "problem is, you're just standing on a soapbox, [and] nobody hears you." Ultimately, "there's a trade-off that the artist has to make" between having "something important to say and wanting people to hear it." In the final analysis, rather than feeling trapped, he argues that "artists definitely have the ability to maintain their artistic integrity." But, according to these performers, judgments about their authenticity emerge from their *own* assessment of the consistency of the messages in their music and their choices in the market rather than from listeners' evaluations. This does not mean they let themselves easily off the hook; their self-appraisal as "real" hip hoppers rests upon a complex web of factors: how they negotiate their identities; their dedication; their musical knowledge, content, and quality; and their promotion and distribution choices.

Perhaps most central to their definition of authenticity is the consistency of integrity and image in performance *and* in one's everyday life outside the expressly commodified music world: Do your lyrics express who you are and do you live the way you say you do? If hip hop becomes your life, that disjuncture between being a hip hopper and just being does not exist. Self-proclaimed "conscious rappers" who act in not-so-conscious ways signal inauthenticity. "My problem," Jonny says, "is not in [their] contributing to corporate culture but in [their] waxing revolutionary in their personas . . . It's hard to be the people's revolutionary when you're contributing to promoting a shoe company that uses sweatshops." Rappers who sold fans on hip hop in the first place through their focus on revolutionary change now appear to only sell superficial revolutionary personas. In the eyes of many, hip hop seems to have lost its potential for social change specifically because of corporate co-optation that demands—and will pay for—particular and oppressive enactments. At this point these issues remain largely theoretical for these desi artists: of course they want to remain independent to make executive decisions over their product, but often they remain independent because major labels have not yet approached them (see Wang 2006). South Asian rappers and producers are still marginal to the big business side of hip hop, and they produce and promote their products with limited funding. It is difficult at this point to state definitively how desi artists deal with the constraints of big business except to say that they often critique capitalism and conspicuous consumption while trying to make music and live lives that reveal who they are *and* gain a fan base (Sharma 2007). Throughout this process, they do not constrain themselves by or conform to a particular *image* or *identity*. Authenticity is not about identity or essence at all; rather, it defines an approach of knowledge, respect, and dedication.

Authenticity Equals Knowledge, Respect, Dedication

You know, I feel like [one needs to approach hip hop] just as a Black child who grows up needs to learn his history, read, actively look out, you know. It's also talking to people and chillin' with people, you know, but it's also taking it seriously: studying . . . Doing work, social justice, whatever . . . So, yes, being with people, associating, relating, like being a part of a community is one way . . . Or at least interacting with [people]. And then another part is more active: read a book! Or seven!! [chuckles]— Vivek, MC, activist, lawyer

The desi artists frame their understanding of authenticity in hip hop within broader United States racial politics. Their approach to hip hop based on knowledge, respect, and dedication also reflects a perspective on life that deflects attention away from privileged identities in favor of critical ideologies. Their process of becoming legitimate music producers parallels the process of academics as they become experts: they work to learn the historical genealogy of their particular topic, and they gain membership to a community by cultivating the cultural capital that reflects their dedication and respect. And, of course, they must be good at their craft. Respect for people and the variety of their expressions defines for artists the line between the appropriate and inappropriate forms of borrowing. Sampling means that no identity is pure, and authenticity in this sense rejects the concept of an essentialist identity in favor of the sincere representation of one's thoughts. As a result, the artists do not erase, denigrate, or overly celebrate particular cultures over others in order to experience Blackness or seek soul.[16] These ongoing practices of respect enable desi artists to sample and appropriate while they remain authentic. They reveal how individuals create identity dialogically and how groups socially construct racial meanings through power relations, but always with the caveat that racial identity is not so fluid as to be unimportant or disregarded.

Authenticity is a beleaguered term; it is so tied to dangerous notions and oppressive economic forces that some argue against it. However, like race (an even more contested term), it is a concept that frames Americans' comprehensions; it is also a concept that people can choose to infuse with new meanings. "What happens," John Jackson asks in his ethnography of race in America, "when we think of race in terms of sincerity and not just authenticity" in order to pull apart these two terms? (2005: 13). One of the limitations of racial authenticity is that it tends to reduce people to particularized and static racial scripts. For instance, were they to assign authenticity as a barometer of following expected scripts, these artists would certainly be—and in fact have been—deemed "inauthentic desis." But because they have so often pushed up against the inadequacies of older definitions, desi artists hold on to the concepts of authenticity and race by remixing their meanings into empowering ones. "Realness," so loaded a term in hip hop, both ridiculed and worshipped, is among those concepts that the artists find useful. Rather than being singular and scripted, realness to them is the value of an individual who is consistent in their ideologies (thoughts), practices (actions), and articulations (words). The artists do not reclaim and rearticulate these almost-orphaned terms to claim that skills trump race or that race is irrelevant: rather, they argue that acknowledging race and difference is critical, but one's race is not deterministic (see Condry 2006; Wang 2006). Appropriating authentically and knowledgably is the key.

The artists use the same criteria of their self-evaluations to examine the practices of others. "Now," MC Rawj pontificates, "the originators [of hip hop] aren't all Black. And it's just like jazz. It's basically what's happening to hip hop: it's been removed from its original nest, regardless of who makes it . . . And other people are starting to cultivate it." He continues by stating, "I think it's just like religion. When you're lower and lower on the ladder of spirituality, you start debating over small shit and miss the big picture. But any true believer of one religion could sit down with a true believer of another and there won't be any issues between them. There's a certain plane, that as soon as you cross a certain line, it's not an issue anymore." Rawj's example of religion is instructive as it shifts the discussion from music and race to beliefs and values. Being a "true believer" unhinges belonging and production away from identity politics and the body and bolts them to ideology—how one thinks, one's perspective and worldview.

Knowledge, respect, and dedication—as private and social practices—explain these desis' claims as legitimate artists. Jonny asserts the importance of his musical intelligence above all else. Social capital, or expressing one's knowledge of culture (Bourdieu 1986), and hustling to create and spread one's message is highly valued within a culture that to outsiders seems like coded terrain. One desi DJ from New York discussed with me how these values define an approach to cultural ownership: "I think that nobody has a place in composing any kind of music because everyone has a place in composing all music. I don't care if a Ugandan decides to start producing Punjabi folk giddha if that's what he or she feels a passion for." Emphasizing historical knowledge, the DJ continued by stating, "I would have an issue if he or she was doing this without knowledge or respect for the history of that music, but the notion of 'place' or 'right' doesn't apply here." Desi artists adopt the principles of hip hop culture as a value system that frames their lives.

Chee echoes and adds to the New York DJ's sentiments. He asserts that in order to understand and respect hip hop one must know the context from which it came: "It's supposed to build on the past. It's supposed to build on the culture." Chee first heard hip hop in the late 1980s and as he became interested in becoming an MC he knew he had to go back and pick up albums that were out before he came to this country because, as he says, "I understood that for me to understand hip hop, I'd have to know where it came from"—just as we need to understand where these desis came from in order to fully appreciate their music. Regarding desis who just fuse music for beats, he remarks that "they don't know where it comes from. I understand that Indians are trying to form an identity based on something else and add on to it. But a lot of that is disrespectful to Black culture. If you want to build on anything, you have to appreciate [it]. That's where it goes back to sampling, you have to understand the time frame, when it was recorded, why it was recorded, what was going on socially." Like Deejay Bella's connection between music and history, Chee's work "builds" upon cultural knowledge, much like the concept of research in the academy. He finds that sampling can build community when one privileges an informed awareness. The performers' definitions of an authentic being challenge the central arguments against such an idea—that authenticity presumes original and untouched origins. Shifting authenticity to a matter of values rather than preordained identities reveals the constitutive role of polycultural sampling and appropriation in the everyday practices of all peoples. Sampling also plays a role in group relations by reflecting the dialogic and relational processes through which actors cross divisions to form alliances rooted in a shared sense of belonging. Music, as global histories reveal, has been the basis of such intersections and is the foundation upon which new sonic and social formations are being built.

Excavating the roots of both music and people is critical for those who plan to create lasting impacts with their own cultural expressions. "Music is a legacy," Chee announced while we were discussing Bob Marley's musical genius. "When an artist does something, records something, that's going to live on. The recorded word is going to live on, regardless, long after the artist is gone." Marley's authenticity to this MC stands on the fact that "he actually lived what he believed" in the face of capitalist and colonialist interventions. Chee celebrated the fact that Marley "didn't do it for the radio, he didn't do it for the money." The desi MC's respect for the reggae musician led to his close scrutiny of how others have sampled Bob Marley. What matters is not the background of any artist appropriating Marley but whether or not the ideology of the sampler or the product is in line with what they sample. For this reason, many of the artists disagreed with sampling religious songs on tracks that feature hedonistic lyrics. Chee applies these criteria to his own productions of music. He uses jazz music *and* his father's Malayali prayers on his album; he raps about the legacies of colonialism *and* slavery in his lyrics; and he speaks of being an Indian immigrant *and* a minority in America. In doing so, he enacts the processes of sampling—adapting and changing hip hop as people do to all cultures.

This parallels Chee's process of identity and community formation, as he samples from his Malayali, Djibouti, American, and hip hop cultures, just as D'Lo and Vivek do. Thus, according to their own definitions, these artists are also authentic *desis*. Even those who most often rap about racial matters—including Chee, D'Lo, AbstractVision, Humanity, and Vivek—they all use hip hop to reframe their commitments to other South Asians. They adopt Black popular culture as a complement to, not a replacement of, their new identities as American minorities.

Yet and still, the relative invisibility of Brown faces in hip hop tells us that South Asians and Blacks still have a long way to go in the development of broad-scale positive interracial relations. It also points to the central role of sampling and polycultural formation in taking us there. The lives and lyrics of desi artists help explain why these individuals would identify with a group that many consider to be their inferior. We see why they find hip hop to be the appropriate platform for the expression of racialized identities and political perspectives. How they go about making music, forming their identities, and moving across seemingly bounded communities is one model for *how* to develop such cross racial alliances. They act based on their awareness of how global histories—particularly those that have lurked in the shadows—create both meaningful and meaningless group differences. Hip hop desis illustrate what putting knowledge to work looks like and they call upon authenticity to critically assess how one thinks, lives, and articulates one's position in the world.

Conclusion

The desi artists did not bring South Asians and hip hop to the mainstream. This was accomplished, instead, by the emergence of commercial hip hop hits that incorporated Hindi film music and Indian-inspired styles and women in the early 2000s. Pop culture's unlikely marriage of those who have been constructed as model and not-so-model minorities reminds us how individuals exert agency by pushing back on imposed identities and narrow expectations. In their collaborations with Blacks and their coproduction of one kind of Black culture, these hip hop desis turn oppressive racial categories into empowering paradigms to forge coalitions that the logic of race aims to dissuade. Brown performers encourage scholars to re-formulate debates about essentialism, authenticity, and identity politics. Sampling is widespread, and the goal of this analysis is not to strictly condemn or condone it but rather to understand how and why individuals sample and how this practice might be constitutive to the formation of all individuals and social formations—including emergent ones.

The artists' lives illustrate sampling and the cut 'n' mix practices of hip hop. Hip hop, Jonny says, is "a mentality that goes against conformity, taking material things and objects that are around you and re-doing it." Similarly, Vivek's "strange position" as an agent who pulls together disparate groups in dance- and music-filled celebrations also illustrates the art and politics of appropriation. These adult performers warn us against strictly negative interpretations of such cross-fertilizations. Other Americans may see such choices as "unnatural," when, in fact, they illustrate phenomena applicable to all Americans who also sample as a kind of intercultural citation. When MC Vivek was asked to present the principle of collective work for a Kwanzaa celebration of family, community, and culture, he chose to draw on an Indian parable about the figure of Birbal. He disrupts our assumption that the Birbal story is "his" and that the holiday created by Maulana Karenga for African Americans is "not his." Who and what constitutes a group that "owns" culture? Where do individuals and groups draw "their" culture's boundaries? Through the time and commitment that Vivek puts into his membership in multiple communities, he disregards commonsense divisions. The way he moves his body in dance epitomizes sampling as he melds Puerto Rican and Black break dancing techniques from the United States with moves from Gujarati *dandia raas* and West African dance, all the while claiming these new productions as expressions of who he is. "Race" and "culture" blur in these instances of cross-pollination that also express the identities, lives, and consciousness of desis like D'Lo, Chee, Bella, and KB. Their experiences and interpretations disrupt biological and social notions of Blackness, desiness, culture, and difference. And their life-long commitments reveal a "level of sincerity and emotional legitimacy" that frames these choices (Jones 1963: 151).

Intercultural borrowings are external representations of deeper political exchanges. The desi artists' attitudes about race expressed in song and speech differ from those of Wiggers and Jiggers who take on fantastic and stereotypical conceptions of the other in order to reassert their difference. In such cases, cultural transgressions are "dangerous" (Lipsitz 1994) and reassert White supremacy (or "multiracial White supremacy" [Rodriguez 2006]) and Black inferiority. This occurs in the appropriations by some mainstream desis who draw upon Black cultural signifiers. Blacks also take part in the process by, for example, orientalizing Asia and Asians. That I contrast mainstream desi appropriation as othering with the way that desi artists approach hip hop is not a convenient contrast; in fact, it often defines the difference between these sets of desis.

Through a nexus of ideologies and practices, these artists claim membership across cultures in ways that replicate their cross-boundary identity and cultural formations. Desi hip hoppers act upon their ideologies by cultivating interracial peer groups and engaging in political activism. In sampling from other communities and cultural legacies they also claim a culturally relevant ethnic identity. Hip hop does not lead D'Lo or Vivek away from their sense of desiness. D'Lo enjoyed and remade bhajans into a relevant second-generation context by replaying them in his/her own style.

His/her literal fusing of bhajan and hip hop beats and Vivek's hybrid dance productions mirror how hip hop itself arose; the multitude of these cultural formations destabilizes hegemonic projects promoting race, ethnicity, and culture as stable categories.

When "culture" is considered to be "owned" by a demarcated group it is rendered static by trapping individuals within fabricated categories that reaffirm the logic of racism based on naturalized differences. The anti-essentialist views of South Asian American artists unlink Blackness from authenticity in the realm of hip hop. While disrupting accepted conceptions of ethnicity and race, Brown performers actively create themselves by growing and "building" as they (re)make music and American culture. Sampling, the musical "version" of intertextual citation or quotation, is one method they employ to re-fuse new ways of being in the world. In the process, they offer new generations new samples to choose from.

As hip hop exemplifies, creating culture is a communal rather than individual process. The desi artists also adopt the foundational ideologies of hip hop that eschew the notion of a single author; as a result, one can argue that there is no pure ownership of hip hop or, indeed, any culture. Taking part in Black popular cultures also means participating in a historical legacy that one should be informed about. Appropriation and sampling potentially express identification because they acknowledge those who have helped create the art form. Shout outs (to recognize or pay tribute to someone) and intertextual citations are a routine aspect of hip hop music. In calling upon history and context in their lyrics, desi artists perform historically constituted and emergent identities embedded—but not trapped—within a set of power relations. Rather than claiming hip hop as theirs to own, we can perceive of these rappers and DJs as participants within larger cultures—of hip hop, of diasporic South Asians, of America—in which they themselves are constantly in the process of becoming, always growing, always changing (Hall 1996a).

The artists recuperate authenticity as a non-identitarian anti-essentialist ideology and approach. Knowledge, respect, and dedication are part of their critical consciousness and worldview that include thoughts on race and inequality. Their lives and lyrics challenge the purity and meanings—but not meaningfulness—of race. They acknowledge confining structures while pushing across constructed historical barriers that define and limit identifications across difference. Desis in hip hop contest the politics of identity centered on ethnicity as narrow, and on the same grounds they also contest the racial politics of the hip hop industry. In presenting themselves as authentic artists who have a legitimate place in Black popular culture, the performers in this project have earned the respect of fans across color lines.

Polyculturalism is useful for understanding the impurity and cross-fertilization of culture and race and sampling as a way to interpret the formation of identities (Kelley 1999; Prashad 2001). The obvious role of sampling in the formation of desi identities and hip hop culture offers a strong, but not singular, example of these processes. South Asians and Blacks must expand existing conceptions of race, culture, and ownership by reconsidering how we are to frame what constitutes identity, community, and politics. The artists are committed to forging political communities based on shared interests that concern people across a range of categories, and they do this through appropriative acts that signal identification. Hip hop's desis have not only crafted and expressed unique and individual identities informed by multiple processes but also have reshaped daily interactions between Blacks and South Asians. What they offer is a politics of interest—an alternative to identity politics—rooted in identification across consequential differences.

Conclusion

Turning Thoughts into Action through the Politics of Identification

> Political intention adheres to every cultural production.
> —Richard Iton, *In Search of the Black Fantastic*

> This is about people of color. It's something that's a lot about being a Black person in America, but it can also transfer over because the politics transfer. So it's not an imitation. It's the politics.—Ravi, hip hop record label founder

> Someone told me to remember.
> To archive the past
> to witness the present
> and speak to the future.
> —D'Lo, "When You Have No Choice"

The Black experience is foundational to race relations in the United States, where it affects the choices and lives of American desis. South Asians in America, despite our collective unwillingness, must look to and learn from the perspectives of America's racial other. From these lessons South Asians not only come to better understand ourselves but also learn how to advance social justice agendas that benefit all people. Creating solidarity, Vijay Prashad reminds us, depends on commitment, sacrifice, and identification across sameness and difference (2000: 193). In learning the histories of other groups, communities can form longitudinal and structural understandings of the processes that shape our lives. This book emerged from my concern over the gaps between Asians and Blacks at precisely the moment in post-9/11 America that these groups should unite against systemic processes that cross over to affect multiple populations. As an ethnography it represents a model of contemporary productive Black and Asian relations forged through popular culture.

As atypical South Asian Americans, hip hop's desis challenge ethnic expectations by pursuing nontraditional choices in careers, politics, and love. In the 1980s and 1990s they were moved by the messages of rap music as they struggled to find a place in their neighborhoods and schools, whether they lived in a predominantly wealthy and White residential area or as the only desi family on a mostly Black block. Hip hop educated them about how to speak up on the issues they faced, and it enabled them to cultivate relations across color lines. It also reaffirmed their nonconformist and critical ideologies by urging them to question the status quo to articulate strong identities and claim space in a nation still unfamiliar with them. They approach hip hop's tricky race politics just as they daily negotiate their minority status—namely, by learning their own history as well as that of those whom they consider kin. As part of the hip hop generation these young adults express new racialized gender and sexual identities through their own performances of hip hop in the 1990s and 2000s. Hip hop becomes for them the perfect vehicle through which to articulate their multiscalar identities as South Asians, as the children of immigrants, as minorities, and as Americans. Their excavation of hip hop parallels scholarly methods of critical analysis. As Brown producers of a Black art form, they understand why, when, how, and where hip hop was created and, in the process, they are able to articulate various paradigms of hip hop culture that make room for them—most often on the margins, sometimes known as the underground. From this position, desi rappers and DJs dispatch their own messages of ethnic pride, race consciousness, and a desire to rock the crowd. Despite numerous obstacles, the majority of these artists are well into their third decades of producing a form of Black popular culture that is as old as they are.

Hip hop is and has always been more than "just music," and

this is a central draw for the participants in this study. As an expressly racialized form, hip hop culture is necessarily political and deeply implicated in—and not just reflective of—power relations in America. The desis addressed in this book attempt to harness the political potential of Black popular culture, including the foundational practices of hip hop, to express and enact social change. Their multiple forms of social action align them with both the struggles of older generations and the activist members of their generation (Das Gupta 2006). While many have posed the hip hop generation to stand in contrast to the civil rights generation (which in both conceptions most often neglect Asian Americans), these young adults have learned of these pasts and see their consciousness-raising efforts as part of this legacy. They have learned about the ideologies of the Chinese American activist Grace Lee Boggs (1998) and her African American husband James Boggs. Their perspectives mirror that of Yuri Kochiyama, a Japanese American woman who was inspired by Malcolm X. Their rhymes not only sample Malcolm X but also update critiques of capitalism and racism. These desis studied historical political crossovers and use this knowledge to craft their own forms of cross-racial activism.

Desi artists understand their engagements with hip hop to be as explicitly political as their social activist work. Blurring the line between art and politics, their activism crosses racial, class, and national boundaries and is an extension of the racialized political identities that they forge through hip hop. Vivek's music, such as the song "One Struggle," articulates the ideological groundwork that frames his work as a Human Rights Watch researcher on populations at risk of contracting HIV in Bangladesh. His written report on this topic reflects the same global race consciousness and desire for social justice that he articulates in rhyme: he argues for collaboration with disenfranchised populations, speaks truth to power, and indicts authority figures for their counterproductive responses.[1] Vivek's efforts in cofounding a number of organizations inside and outside the United States, including in Sierra Leone, form a more recognizable "political" expression of the "wider Black consciousness" that he already expresses in a musical form that some scholars have erroneously deemed apolitical (McWhorter 2008).

Hip hop's desis do not appropriate hip hop only to fight their own battles; through music they build community and use their art to fight battles alongside Blacks. Motivated by compassion, these artists extend their identifications with disenfranchised people on a national and global scale through multiple modes of political activism that include hip hop performance. Explaining his decision to move to Sierra Leone, Vivek told Gulati, a writer for *Little India* magazine: "I know there are people suffering everywhere, even in America . . . but the suffering in Sierra Leone is so acute that I feel compelled and actually privileged to be able to make a difference." [2] Vivek says he is "addicted" to social change, and other desi hip hop artists share his compulsion; it is also what draws them to hip hop as the most effective tool for expression.

Deejay Bella was inspired in 1988 by the Human Rights Now tour, where she was drawn to a graphic poster that asked "Do you want to stop torture now?" In response the fourteen-year-old Bella began to work with Amnesty International, at a time when she was already deeply drawn to music. She wanted to do "actual political work, and it had to do with the worst issues. The ones that people don't talk about, that are real," and much of Amnesty's work at that time incorporated music. As part of running the chapter at her junior high school in Las Vegas, in collaboration with the University of Nevada, she assisted in organizing concerts and hosting speakers. The governor of Nevada even proclaimed an official Human Rights Day in response to these efforts. Her education on the connections among minorities paralleled her development as a DJ. In high school she visited *maquiladoras* (exploitative factories on the United States–Mexico border) as well as prisons housing immigrants along with the criminal population—experiences that motivated her to continue her work. "It educated me," she said. "To me it just educated me about reality about political suppression . . . It could get you upset about how our government is, by far. But it also motivates you to do something about it and it just keeps you in your fire to be an activist and work for those issues." She provided pro-bono work, as Vivek did, for an organization that aided Latino refugees seeking political asylum. Chee's music and his "day job" also overlap, as he works on behalf of disadvantaged populations through organizations like the Posse Foundation in New York and Youth Built in Los Angeles, which prepares minority youths for college. As adults, the majority of the desi artists live and work in Black neighborhoods in Oakland, Brooklyn, Los Angeles, and Chicago. They take part in anti-prison demonstrations by creating albums whose profits go to educating people about the prison industrial system, and they support affirmative action. These individuals who work abroad and across communities are motivated by the connections they have formed with Blacks through hip hop culture.

Most of the desi artists have come to terms with the sense of ethnic ambivalence that marked their earlier years. Hip hop culture, in fact, has brought them back to their ethnic communities and becomes the mode through which they engage younger and older generations. For example, K B, the South Indian M C from Richmond, California, was disturbed by the divisions among desis on the Berkeley campus and created a South Asian panethnic organization along with a fellow student, a Jat Sikh from northern India. The Hindu-Muslim riots in Mumbai, India, in 1992 — the same year that the Los Angeles riots took place — especially motivated K B and his cofounder to "create a healthy forum" for representation that countered divisions and highlighted commonalities among desi men and women. In this effort K B wanted to foster the idea that South Asians in America should not be motivated by the same divisions apparent in India, especially as desis from across the subcontinent are "all South Asian Americans, whether we want to be called that or not." Similar to the goals of K B's group Karmacy, the organization "was basically the empowerment of creating a voice. I look at creating a voice as the first step in having an identity." Thus K B's fight for a South Asian voice through his campus efforts mirrors his goals for Karmacy to be another form of panethnic representation of its members' South Asian American experiences.

The events of September 11, 2001, politicized sectors of the American populace that had been among the most invisible. Some South Asians, including middle-class Hindu Indians in Silicon Valley, took this opportunity to shore up historical rifts by distinguishing themselves from Muslims, just as Koreans in the United States had distinguished themselves from Japanese during World War II. The rising anti-Muslim sentiment dovetailed with some Hindus' own longstanding anti-Muslim animosity, thereby highlighting the complexities of a post-9/11 panethnic identity. Nonetheless, the subsequent violent targeting of Sikhs and Indians as well as Arab and Muslim Americans revealed how quickly a group that had been under the radar of American society could become racialized and deflated into all-encompassing stereotypes (Omi and Winant 1994). Yet some desis had already been expressing these ideas, notably in arguing that as racialized American minorities South Asians must engage with race and racism. The experience of 9/11 provided them with another opportunity to seize upon national and global events to illustrate further connections with other groups across time, space, and race.

South Asian and Black relations were also impacted by 9/11. The desi artists in solidarity with Blacks were troubled by racial realignments, and they used their music to critique George W. Bush and the wars in Afghanistan and Iraq, to align South Asians with Blacks in the United States, and to express their understanding of oppression and inequality. In forums held in the Bay Area about the impending war in Afghanistan, local Black youths pointed to the wars on their blocks that they fought (against police brutality, crime, violence, and poverty)—ones that nobody cared about—so why should they support or care about a war abroad? Some Blacks also felt that the attention paid to Brown people—the racial profiling, detention, and racism—offered a temporary if bitter relief to America's most wanted who had routinely been victim to these practices (Hassan 2002). The shared experiences of Brown and Black people with racial profiling and incarceration might have made some South Asians aware of how quickly a model group can turn into America's enemy within, but their overall responses revealed their privileging of distance from Blacks, and vice versa.

D'Lo had been involved in mainstream desi activism but felt it replicated many of the limitations and expectations that s/he experienced with other mainstream desis in college. As an active anti-war protester, D'Lo was frustrated by others' inaction—a view s/he addresses in his/her performance piece "Eyes Closed in America":

We all livin' in fear of detainment
Tears constipated
Every move pre-meditated
Watching the shit get worse while we wait and
Still choosing to remain complacent

But we know from D'Lo's story that 9/11 was not his/her wake up call. D'Lo had already been performing for numerous organizations, including Diasporadics, South Asian Women Creative Circle

(SAWCC), and the now defunct Desh Pardesh in Canada. In finding the insular politics and gossip within these groups distressing, D'Lo expanded his/her work to include anti-police brutality campaigns. S/he used his/her poetry as part of his/her work with Artist's Network of Refuse and Resist as well as with Desis Rising Up and Moving (DRUM)—an organization whose efforts aim to better the conditions of working-class desis. As D'Lo rhymes:

Paranoid over phone's being bugged
Revolutionary thoughts tug
Constantly
Though we scheme harder at keeping
those thoughts at bay
Wondering what it would take
With the atrocities of Bush's campaign
Bringin' memories of Hitler's reign
Seem in vain
Any efforts for change
Futile attempts at breaking the chains
And shackles on ankles
Of slave mentality
Meanwhile
Muslims in modern day internment camps
Meanwhile
bombs on Afghanistan n Iraq
Meanwhile
New York's rebuildin' on burial grounds
Meanwhile
Palestine's still on lock down

While growing up, D'Lo was drawn to action because of the racism and homophobia s/he faced; witnessing police brutality against American minorities and growing anti-Muslim sentiment pushes him/her to draw increasingly broader systemic connections among oppressed peoples. In echoing many of the connections made by other artists, D'Lo joins the struggles of people across the globe by linking their domination to similar structural processes that intern, lock down, and enslave our mentalities. This is the artist's expression of a global race consciousness.

Hip hop culture is formative to the investment of these artists in local and global Black and South Asian communities. It is also the vehicle through which they provide alternatives to discourses of difference that divide Asians and Blacks as distant and competing groups. Music and formal political action infuse one another to form a solid basis for turning a critical consciousness into social action. The cross-fertilization that constitutes the lives of hip hop desis also challenges reified conceptions of race, ethnicity, and belonging. By critiquing new forms of racism, including the substitution of "culture" for "race" in discussing group difference in America, desi artists also recuperate other uses of cultural formations that are not rooted in shared ethnic and racial ancestries. Hip hop is not a culture in the traditional sense used by anthropologists to refer to groups with common ancestry that share values and common practices. But, barring shared ancestry, hip hop communities consist of individuals who do share common practices, references, and values. Culture, particularly historically and race-conscious popular culture, plays a powerful role in articulating the possibilities of interracial coalitions.

Because the foundational practices of hip hop are expressly political as resistant forms of community formation in the face of disenfranchisement, these artists understand its relevance and political potency as a vehicle for social change. As a result, many of the MCs exclaim that they are speaking "prophesies," and they believe in their art as a starting point for a revolution through spreading the (counterhegemonic) word. They particularly draw upon the theme of *revolution* in their lyrics as a way to wage war with a militarized racist state. Their songs not only expose master narratives of the past but also offer knowledge and "conscious lyrics" as an alternative to contemporary discourses of history, belonging, and capitalism. On the song "Bridge Techniques" (originally recorded in 1997), we hear Chee's trademark upbeat staccato rhyming style telling listeners who he is and what he is ready for:

Rhyme excellence, mixed with intellect militance,
To kill 'em since, rap city citizens don't pay dues,
Guerilla grammar, straight from Kerala to Beirut . . .
. . . Chaotic elements is melanin with terrorist adrenaline,
To set the revolution, like V. I. Lenin,
Pennin' manifestos signed Chirag Menon.

His lyrics, replete with violent metaphors of war and aggression, cunningly highlight Chee's personality and his critique of America's foreign policy. In this lyrical battle with the powers that be, Chee most often takes on the persona of the enemy of the (nation) state—which is later how the government and mainstream society positioned many Brown people following 9/11. On one track Chee critiques the hypocrisy of America toward immigrants of color by asserting that the letters "U.S.A." stand for "U Shouldn'ta Arrived."

To battle oppression, the artists also evoke militarized metaphors in their lyrics by calling upon *their words* as true knowledge with revolutionary potential, just as early rappers used rhymes as metaphorical bullets. They elucidate how their music contributes to a counterhegemonic discourse of "truth," whether addressed to ethnic, immigrant, or broader communities. Indeed, MCs such as KB, Chee, AbstractVision, Humanity, D'Lo, and Rawj do not just uncover the inner workings of power in society but also offer their words of wisdom as "conscious knowledge" by telling their audiences what time it is. In fact, theirs is a rising voice of subaltern histories that articulate the processes of hegemony, consent, and resistance. Yet MCs are not just using their voices to reveal conspiracies and boast about MCing skills. Ultimately, for many of these artists, rapping is a form of social action in which they articulate a clearly counterhegemonic viewpoint based on knowledge and political consciousness. In "Passage to India," KB raps that he and his fellow MCs

Seem like prodigies, we ought to be put up on pedestals,
We're bringing mental foes to challenge the status quo.
Yo, perceptually we're flexing in a brand new direction,
We're here to question the whole basis of your perception.

One may critique the MCs for presenting their perspectives as "truth" (coming from the mouths of "prodigies" and "prophets," no less). But perhaps we may interpret this strategy both as a sign of the strength of their beliefs and the power of the spoken word. AbstractVision and Humanity, the Pakistani cousins from Staten Island who formed Abstract/Humanity, illustrate this erudition of "consciousness exhibited through rhymes" more eloquently than any thesis.

These two MCs, along with another cousin, DJ Ali, infuse hip hop with the unique perspectives of young Muslim men in New York. According to the inside of their CD jacket, they are two "MC's fighting indirect oppression." On their now-defunct Web site they explain what it means to be mentally enslaved: "Our debut album, *Politrix*, is about how slavery is not limited to just the physical aspect. People out there think they are liberated just because they have freedom of their own life. However, that freedom is largely manipulated and distorted by higher powers to work in their favor. The point is that commercialism, consumerism and patriotism can heavily distort one's perception of the world. They can also prevent one from finding their own beliefs by settling for ones given to them."[3] In the song "Mental Slavery" the rappers argue that we must seek a counterhegemonic understanding and reclaim (previously silenced) histories from within and expressed through hip hop:

> They be makin' the lives of the masses somethin' to hate
> Crime, hate, murder and the women they rape
> Make my strong mind lose track of time
> I sit and wonder, how could they be so blind?
> Well, it's all in the name of makin' that dollar
> But I sit here to write so I can holler
> The feelings that need never be ignored
> We'll give em' something that they ain't never explored
> The torture we feel each and every day
> Will be displayed for the establishment
> The ravishing—feelings of hurt and despair
> Will become bare as I ride on top of these snares
> My rhymes manifest the rare
> Art that is revolution
> At times, it's the only solution
> Sacrifices made, and some lives lost
> But to get ahead, yo, you gotta pay the cost

When the rappers state that "Art is that revolution / At times, it's the only solution" we are reminded of Chee's signature as he attempts to "set a revolution" through "pennin' [lyrical] manifestos." Humanity and AbstractVision rap about reclaiming power; but their lyrics are conspicuously raw and filled with death and blood, thereby signaling the difficulties of what they are up against. These rappers are among the numerous MCs who assign hip hop—and their own voices—a critical role as the tool for bringing about necessary change. It is not a coincidence that the desi MCs have chosen conscious rap as the form through which to articulate their politically charged perspectives. They echo the way that many Black rappers have turned microphones into swords as rhymes morph into verbal and metaphorical battles against the powers that be.

From these examples it becomes clear that theories are clearly inadequate, such as those on contemporary blackface that assume that youths unequivocally map Black identities upon their own racialized bodies without a process of translation (see Lott 1993a, 1993b; cf. Lhamon 1998). The artists' activism may be the most recognizable political expression of a global race consciousness, but it has infused their music from the start. In fact, hip hop has led them to this worldview. My concept of a broader race consciousness incorporates a conception of Blackness applicable to people of African descent and to non-African peoples, without the intent of either erasing the importance and particularity of Blackness to people descended from Africa or negating how formative their experiences are. Instead, this concept disrupts racial categories by revealing the fabrication of homogenized conceptions of Blackness and desiness. In paying attention to and acknowledging the distinctions among various racialized groups, these Brown artists do not deny or attempt to transcend race, or conflate all difference as equal. Recognizing how important these identities are but also finding nodes or meeting points at the crossroads (Lipsitz 1994) nurtures cross-racial collaborations that come together for shared purposes. A global race consciousness enhances our thinking of race, community, identity, and politics in inclusive, and thus stronger, ways.

The artists are all aware of these racial politics, and macro-level structural paradigms do not leave desi MCs feeling helpless. Instead, they call upon their words to expose these processes for what they are. These MCs assert that we are not simply cogs in the machine; instead, we have the *agency* to develop our own understanding of the world. As Humanity raps:

But there ain't no length long enough to measure my strength
Unlimited powers I hold

They call me strong and they call me bold
Ain't no lies, deceit or deception
Gonna challenge my direction

. . . .

Ain't no surprise
Why I choose to use my views insteada'
Bein' deceived by crews
Of corrupted policies
Pervasive fallacies

This young MC decides to draw upon his own resources and experiences to craft ideas that challenge powerful corporate and political groups aiming to keep Americans locked in "mental slavery."

Music is the medium through which some desis claim space in the United States and make race for South Asian Americans. Hip hop is a powerful lens through which to examine Asian/Black relations not only because of its enormous popularity as a global form but also because hip hop culture is explicit about race, difference, inequality, and power. In the desi artists' range of lives and lyrics, documented here for the first time, we see alliance building across race, class, gender, sexuality, and immigrant status that models how to develop and sustain solidarities across differences that matter. Sampling is central to this process; Brown artists craft new identities and communities by drawing from a range of available sources and crossing over multiple community boundaries to weave together influences of disparate groups.

Hip hop—a polycultural production based on fusing and melding various influences into cohesive yet ever-changing expressions—encourages individuals to knit together their own identities. Throughout this book, I have used the trope of sampling to describe how some individuals manage, contest, and construct ethnicity, race, gender, and sexuality (as well as, of course, their music). It also applies to their political consciousness, as it is informed and expressed through relations with Black peers, hip hop, and social action. These potentially political cut 'n' mix technologies can provide an anti-essentialist approach to authenticity, community formation, and identity expression. Sampling practices forge identities, cultures, and communities, including hip hop, in a way that highlights historical and collaborative formation and eschews the notion of a single author or original moment of creation. Brown hip hoppers must nonetheless contend with existing racial politics.

The desi artists are individuals who take action to locate themselves within—and alter—existing hierarchies of race in the United States. They must also attend to their locations within Black popular culture—and do so with knowledge, respect, and dedication. The relevance of *context* in understanding not only Black people and their cultural formations but all people across time and space becomes evident in this approach. By calling upon connectivities—historical, political, sonic, cultural, and racial—some members of the new second generation deal with difference explicitly by challenging co-ethnics' desire to sidestep racial matters. Together their lives and lyrics illustrate the politics of identification, in which they cross *sui generis* categories in order to come together to advance shared goals not restricted to one group.

Hip hop is indeed still a political counterhegemonic voice of resistance and an agent for social change. The participants in this study prove this clearly. Neither their small numbers nor the corporate co-optation of much of hip hop is grounds for discounting their voices. I specifically look at the role of Black popular culture in developing alliances across difference because that is where we can find models of cross-racial organizing for social justice through resistant cultural forms. The seeds of theories of action can be found here—in their articulation of power, history, and inequality. In challenging divisive and incomplete culturalist theories of difference—biological notions of difference in drag—the artists study and further elaborate upon macro-level structural processes that explain migration, community formation, and racialization. America is founded, they rap, on inequities inherent in capitalism and the exploitation of particular groups on the basis of "race." These processes continue today, albeit in disguise, through colorblind discourses, multiculturalism, and the more explicit anti-immigrant nativism and the ongoing exploitation of minority and poor workers. Hip hop's desis draw upon the power of rap to convey and excise these structural inequalities.

Corporate co-optation cannot fully dilute hip hop's political potential. AbstractVision reveals that he has made it through the murky waters of corporate global domination and omnipresence by choosing "the spirit" instead of the dollar. His song is in essence a call to the masses for revolution, to "liberate the nation":

> My style is rare
> Consciousness exhibited through rhymes
> Of bare
> Tell all stories of injustice—don't trust this
> It's monopolization—mental slaves gotta liberate the nation
> These corporate conglomerates act like high-tech armaments
> And abuse their power
>
> . . . .
>
> Their lies received by the millions of fools all over the globe
> Seen through consumerism they be destined to fold
> They choose the dollar while I choose the spirit
> Realize the truth in my conscious lyrics

In putting pen to paper these lyricists become the kind of educators that they found in some of the first rappers they listened to in their youth. Like the old-school veterans, this new school of hip hop continues the tradition of unpacking how power works, how systems oppress, and how knowledge empowers.

This is an emerging face of Asian American youth whose collaborations balance out the scholarly attention paid to conflicts between Asians and Blacks. Revealing the grounds upon which different groups can come together while acknowledging specificities is how any broad-based alliance can become even more inclusive. In our increasingly diverse nation, appropriation is not simply a Black and White debate or a top-down imposition. South Asian youths adopt forms of Blackness in problematic and promising ways—the reverse is also true. The multiple flows of cultural cross-pollination between two American minorities destabilize essential identities and caution against celebrations of both hybridity that assumes pure origins and unequivocal claims to individuals "owning" culture. It also disrupts race, and in contending and not transcending it desis remake race. They alter the contours of both desiness and Blackness and of desi sexualities and gender roles, thereby freeing race, gender, and sexuality from the grasp of biology, stereotypes, oppression, and disempowerment.

Although these desis contend with the politics of hip hop they are more bent on expressing hip hop *as* politics. Hip hop is political because it produces and encourages activisms; hip hop, as KRS-One says, is also knowledge. And, as Michel Foucault (1980) reminds us, knowledge is power. This culture is so expansive that it affects the ideologies and affiliations of youths and adults; it also shapes their actions—how and whether they vote, who they become, and to what issues they commit themselves. Yet books that try to grasp the fullness of hip hop—its past, producers, messages, politics, multiple constituencies, and futures—continue again and again to reduce it to the same debates and major players. Hip hop has expanded, as has the political voice of its producers—Blacks, non-Blacks, men, and women. Hip hop creates activists by giving youths their first lessons in alternative thinking, challenging the master narratives they learn in school, making them multilingual, and tightening their poetic and artistic skills. The politics of hip hop is not just in the official arenas of voting or running for office; the kinds of politics we see these artists partaking in and advancing is everyday politics, detailed ethnographically, in living change that is as much Public Enemy as it is Gandhi.

In standing up to normative discourses within the United States and in their ethnic communities hip hop desis represent just a few of the many hip hop soldiers who have fought for representation and pushed for social change throughout the world. Hegemony is never total, Antonio Gramsci (1971) reminds us: ruling ideas and relations of power face ongoing resistance from below. Unequal relations and constructed group differences that appear static are neither natural nor inevitable. Neither must we reproduce such conditions inevitably, particularly between two minority groups. As non-White immigrant groups enter the United States it is possible that they, too, will experience racism that could lead newcomers to form alliances across color lines based on their shared status as non-Whites. That some have chosen hip hop to articulate these feelings should come as no surprise. South Asian Americans employ hip hop to make their voices heard and to engage in something that brings them and others intense pleasure. They also use it to do what this Black popular form has always done: envision alternative futures and express hope as a youth culture. In order to use their consciousness, lyrics, and lives as one model for coalition building, it is important to consider other crossovers among divided groups.

Comparative racial studies beyond Black and White that uncover collaborative and conflictive relations between groups, particularly non-White groups, enable us to envision new communities of belonging. Similarly, additional research on comparative diasporic studies outside of the nation can only provide global, and therefore more accurate and significant, information on historical parallels and processes that help explain patterns across nations, including why divisions between Asians and Africans seem so profound. Analyzing other racially ambiguous groups through Mixed Race studies, for example, is yet another critical arena for advancing racial theory and accounting for the current potency that race continues to hold for people across the globe.

These studies are critical in light of the increasing gaps and conflicts among communities of color in the United States. The growing social science literature on Black and non-Black participants in hip hop culture attests to the increasing significance of Black popular culture as the arena in which youths across races come to know one another. It is true that many of these interactions are not fueled by well-informed progressive politics. Yet, the maintenance of inequality, the persistence of structural racism, and the continued gaps among and within communities of color all compel me to foreground the counterhegemonic ideologies and worldviews that can push forward broader interracial progressive politics. Members of these social movements are not grounded in narrow identity politics that limit the range of their concerns but rather on broader conceptions of identification. South Asian American youths who fit uneasily within America's Black and White binary are drawn to the innovative and creative processes of hip hop production because it parallels in many ways their own process of identity formation. Having created identities and cultural products anew, they present remixed ideologies and ways of being that allow both South Asians and Blacks to reconsider what race, community, culture, and belonging stand for and look like—both now and in the future. Finally, the experiences and perspectives of these artists, like this study, resist conceptions of a colorblind, race-neutral, or post-racial America. Race is central to South Asian Americans and the development of new second-generation identities. The ever-hopeful D'Lo, who always looks forward, reminds us what we work toward:

But Finally . . .
Falling into deep sleep
Behind eyes closed we CAN'T be blinded no more
Envisioning a new world for us all
Where poor ain't a word no more
Where
all the colors of race would be revered as gold
Where class only means the school you go
Where
the only wars would be against discrimination
Where there's free education
Coz as a community
We kept on resisting
To the point where we were all running things.

Notes

Introduction: Claiming Space, Making Race

1. The first generation refers to adult immigrants; the 1.5 generation generally refers to individuals immigrating before the age of thirteen; and the second generation is the first United States–born generation.

2. My cohost was Samip Mallick at the University of Chicago. The participants included MC Abstract/Vision and DJ Ali, MC Kabir, MC Chee Malabar, DJ Rekha, and the United States debut of the Malayali hip hop group from Malaysia, Yogi B and Natchatra, featuring Yogi B, MC Jesz, and Dr. Burn. See the Hiphopistan Web site, http://hiphopistan.uchicago.edu. And see YouTube (http://www.youtube.com) "AAS Roundtable" Parts 1–4 for the panel presentation, which was co-chaired by Bakari Kitwana and me.

3. The artist MC Rawj now goes by his proper name, Roger.

4. D'Lo, who identified as gay and later as a male, prefers to disrupt gender pronouns "he" and "she" in order to remind others of the flexibility of gendered identities. I agree with disrupting naturalized links between gender and sex, and for purposes of clarity in my references to D'Lo, I will refer to D'Lo by the pronouns "s/he" and "his/her."

5. Bella goes by the name Deejay Bella; in other references to individuals who spin records, I refer to them through the alternate spelling, "DJ."

6. Dandia raas is a traditional Gujarati stick dance performed on Navratri, a celebration of the god Rama and the goddess Durga.

7. Segmented assimilation addresses the influences of Black and White Americans on second-generation immigrants by describing how a range of variables (skin color, socioeconomic status, access to a strong ethnic network) leads to "upward," "linear," or "downward" pathways of as-

similation. In highlighting multiple outcomes this theory corrects the notion of a monolithic nation and a one-way path of assimilation. This theory takes racialization into account and posits that ethnicity plays a central role in the "assimilation" of non-White immigrants. However, in addition to its troubling interpretations of United States–born Blacks, these scholars also assume that the children of immigrants will adopt an ethnic identity when they in fact may not.

8. The album was produced in the United Kingdom where rapper Slick Rick, also on the record, is from.

9. In the 1960s and 1970s predominantly English-speaking and highly skilled Hindu Indian men and women from urban centers across India arrived in a booming postwar American economy (Prashad 2000: 4) and settled in suburbs and cities across the United States. For more on the second wave of Indian immigration, see Saran 1980; Knoll 1982; Jensen 1988; Helweg and Helweg 1990; Hing 2004.

10. In the early 1900s the first wave of Indians, mostly Sikh men with farming and military backgrounds from Punjab, arrived on the West Coast. They settled in Washington, Oregon, and California and worked in agriculture and in the fishery and lumber industries. Their numbers were small compared to immigrants from other Asian nations, but with the rising anti-Asian fervor on the West Coast they were ineligible for citizenship and remained aliens, unable to legally own land or vote. Barred from marrying White women and accompanied by few Indian women, some of these men married Mexican women whom they met while laboring in the fields (Leonard 1992). In the 1980s the third wave of immigrants, many of whom entered through the family reunification policy written into the Immigration Act of 1965, included men and women from across South Asia who entered a troubled American labor market without the safety net of professional skills. They diversified South Asian America and often became domestic helpers, cab drivers, and workers in newspaper stands, convenience stores, and gas stations (see Khandelwal 2002; Das Gupta 2006).

11. The assault by cultural critics on the misogyny, scatology, violence, and drugs in hip hop followed its mainstream popularity in the 1990s. Concerned suburban parents and prominent politicians blamed young Black men for debasing the Black respectability of an earlier generation (see McBride 2005). C. Delores Tucker called rap music "pornographic smut" and, along with Tipper Gore, aimed for censorship (Kelley 1996; Lipstiz 1998a).

12. The combination of a recession, middle-class flight, and heightened police surveillance increasingly confined urban Blacks to communi-

ties without resources. Crack cocaine affected members of these communities in the 1980s, which the government used to justify the increasing criminalization of nonviolent offenders who were housed in growing factories: American prisons. For more on the rise of the prison industrial complex, see Parenti 1999; Davis and Dent 2001; Rodriguez 2006; Gilmore 2007.

13. Examples include the Bay Area rappers Paris, Boots Riley of the Coup, and Oakland's hip hop-based pro-education, anti-prison youth movements in the 2000s.

14. Incidentally, Bodhi Dharma, a monk from India, introduced Shaolin kung fu to China. Although Buddhism is commonly ascribed to East Asia, it originated in India.

15. This ethnography extends into the 2000s, when technological advances in music production, promotion, and distribution gave these artists considerable freedom from the need to be signed.

16. For more on rotten coconuts and rotten bananas, see *Format* magazine, http://formatmag.com/fashion/hoodman/.

17. Copyright law tends to be based on the notion of a single author. The communal formation of hip hop has continually been challenged by, and challenges, this restriction on sampling practices (Sharma 1999).

18. Those who support the thesis that South Asians are honorary Whites point to their structural and economic integration; their apparent model minority trappings; conceptions of the Aryan or Caucasian roots of Indians; and their anomalous categorization as White in the 1970 census.

19. The literature on South Asians contends that "socio-economic repression has stimulated political involvement and opposition while middle-class or elite status has abated it" (Clarke, Peach, and Vertovec 1990: 22). This interpretation posits that working-class people are at the front lines of racism and are therefore the ones to develop progressive identities and alliances (Das Gupta 2006). The class status of wealthier minorities may shield them from the severity of racism, but it does not "whiten" them. For a discussion of Asian Americans in relation to Whiteness, see Okihiro 1994; Tuan 1999; Wu 2002; Zhou 2004.

20. *Girmit* is a metaphor Prashad draws from the contracts that Indian indentured laborers signed on their way to Trinidad and Fiji. See Ghosh 2008.

21. Celebrating all identities as hybrid (e.g., Gross, McMurray, and Swedenburg 1996) can elide both power differences and the fact that, at particular times and places, individuals present their identities *as* fixed (i.e., Hall's "positional identities" 1995: 66).

22. Indians and Africans are the two largest populations in the former British colony of Trinidad. Their post-independence relations have been tense and even violent as they jockey for economic and political power.

23. I had fruitful conversations about these global connections with my Northwestern colleagues Richard Iton and Barnor Hesse, along with Rhoda Reddock at the University of the West Indies in Trinidad.

24. We also see this in the United Kingdom (see Hall 2000: 221–25).

25. The political songs of British Asian bands like Asian Dub Foundation and FunDaMental piqued the interest of Cultural Studies scholars on both sides of the Atlantic. See Vivek Bald's documentary *Mutiny*; Sharma, Hutnyk, and Sharma 1997; Hutnyk 2000; Bakrania 2004.

26. Sam Rao, director of the Indo-American Community Service Center in Santa Clara, was an invaluable resource who introduced me to important members of the South Asian community and invited me to special events.

Chapter 1: Alternative Ethnics

1. In 2004 Richmond was ranked California's most dangerous city, according to a report by Morgan Quitno (http://www.morganquitno.com). Just north of Berkeley, Richmond was, according to the 2000 census, 36 percent Black and just over 12 percent Asian, of which only 1.2 percent were "Asian Indian." In 1980, when the artists were preteens, Asians were just under 5 percent of the city while the Black population was approximately 48 percent ("A Community Transformed: Richmond, California," University of Virgina Faculty Webserver, http://faculty.virginia.edu.

2. "White identified" is a term that some of the artists used to refer to mainstream desis who say they do not "see" race or feel impacted by its effects and who identify as "American." Scholars have also suggested that individuals may turn away from ethnicity to attain a higher status (De Vos 1975). Palumbo-Liu (1999), however, reminds us that the class status of Asians who experience socioeconomic mobility does not mean they have gained equal social acceptance by Whites *as* White. Attention to the effects of non-White status has been one of the most critical contributions of the literature on "new immigrants." Leonard (1992) uses the concept of "ethnic options" to explain ethnicity among Punjabi-Mexicans in California to be flexible, socially constructed, and affected by social structures and history. More recent scholarship has offered "hybrid" and "third spaces" to explain the lives of, for example, Asian American youths. Their Asian and American lives are not considered discrete or pure, and both the individual, particularly youths, and their social formations are considered culturally hybrid (Chaudhry 1998). This literature

portrays South Asian subjectivities that are aware of and that occupy the margins and peripheries rather than conceptualizing two bounded and distinct cultures or "worlds."

3. "Reactive ethnicity" theorizes one immigrant response to racism and one's new minority status by turning inward, thereby highlighting a particular invention of tradition that emphasizes praiseworthy narratives. It helps explain the ethnic insularity of South Asian immigrants (Portes and Rumbaut 2001).

4. During the 1990s, Californians witnessed the rise of anti-immigrant and anti-Black policies including the oversized military industrial complex, the banning of affirmative action, the cutting of welfare, the militarization of the border, and Pete Wilson's Proposition 187 that withdrew social services from "illegal" immigrants. Due to their legal, class, and racial status, many Asian Americans, including South Asians, were shielded from these policies and often supported discourses that justified this backlash.

5. In 1990, more than 45 percent of Indians in America spoke English, even within their homes (Lessinger 1995: 15). A few families owned rental properties or small businesses.

6. I assessed class status based on family income, property ownership, and the artists' descriptions of their quality of life. Fremont is home to an increasing number of Indian and Chinese professionals, while just over 3 percent of the city's population is Black. In 2000, 37 percent of Fremont was Asian, of which 10 percent were Asian Indian (Geography at Berkeley, Fremont Project, http://geography.berkeley.edu). Fremont is fifteen miles from Santa Clara, the home of a number of large computer companies and The Indus Entrepreneurs (TiE) (cofounded by Kanwal Rekhi of Silicon Valley fame). Unlike the younger third- and fourth-generation members now living in Fremont, the artists grew up in the 1970s and 1980s when only 7 percent of Fremont's population considered themselves Asian according to the 1980 census; indeed, they were often the only South Asian children on their blocks—just like those from Black cities.

7. For additional histories of transposed epithets, see Prashad 2000: 24; see also Purkayastha 2005: 28.

8. Over the course of a decade, D'Lo shared with me his/her poetry, sending me individual poems and collections of poems, which I could then draw from for this book. In addition, if I was interested in incorporating a particular piece I heard during D'Lo's live or online performances, s/he would email me the transcription of the poem. I did not transcribe any of D'Lo's lyrics and they are kept in the original formatting. I had access to the other MCs' recordings and either transcribed

them myself, checking the accuracy with the individual artist, or asked them for their written transcriptions of their songs.

9. Some Muslims may be more willing to forge cross-national affiliations in response to their marginalization by Hindus. These tensions also emerge among desi youths who attempt to create panethnic communities. For more on Muslims in America, see Abraham and Abraham 1983; Mohammad-Arif 2002; Mamdani 2004; Schmidt 2004.

10. Included in this scholarship are illustrations and critiques of the development of essentialized and hybrid ethnicities through consumption and nostalgic re-creations of "the homeland" in the remix club culture of desi youth (Maira 2002). Others examine the internal class, gender, and sexual politics of ethnicity within South Asian cultural organizations in colleges (Purkayastha 2005) and political organizations that serve the needs of exploited workers, women, and queer desis (Das Gupta 2006). These new studies explore transnational networks and diasporic settlements, gender and sexuality, and the politicization of underrepresented groups. See also Singh 1996; Prashad 2000, 2002; Shankar 2008.

11. Rawj is referring to the television sitcom *The Fresh Prince of Bel-Air*, in which the rapper and actor Will Smith plays a Black urban youth from Philadelphia who moves in with his wealthy uncle's family in the suburbs.

12. According to an analysis of the 1990 census by Ghasarian and Levin (1996), 3.2 percent of "Asian-Indian" women and 2.9 percent of "Asian-Indian" men were separated or divorced. The rates are even higher for United States–born South Asians; second-generation Indian Americans have the highest rate of divorce among all United States–born Asians (see Gupta 1999: 32). While divorce is rare among South Asians, as are most discussions about this taboo topic, Gupta (1999: 218) argues that divorce rates are increasing, especially among the second generation and particularly among women.

13. Caste, too, is an important (albeit changing) identity linked to religion in India, but it is essentially irrelevant to the artists' self-conception and did not factor into their relations with others. Rarely did the topic arise during fieldwork, even in the context of marriage, possibly due to the precedence of racial, ethnic, and religious differences.

14. In his discussion of Deepak Chopra as the embodiment of United States orientalist ideology, Prashad expounds on the ideology of capitalist accumulation that Chopra advances by stating that "capitalism and New Age orientalism embrace each other" (2000: 62).

15. It is also the case that many desis, hip hoppers or not, did not befriend co-ethnic peers because of their smaller numbers and concentra-

tion in the 1970s. The situation is quite different for the third generation that is coming of age in neighborhoods where South Asians are sometimes the largest Asian population.

16. For statistical information by campus, see the University of California Office of the President, http://statfinder.ucop.edu.

17. Abercrombie and Fitch caused a furor among Asian Americans in 2002 by selling racist T-shirts showing images of slant-eyed "oriental" men wearing rice-paddy hats accompanied by the offensive words, "Two Wongs Can Make It White." Although company spokesperson Hampton Carney stated "We personally thought Asians would love this T-shirt," numerous student protests across the country forced Abercrombie and Fitch to pull the line.

18. Rumbaut draws from a broad-scale survey on second-generation immigrants from Asia, Latin America, and the Caribbean, whom he groups into four categories of self-identification in response to the open-ended survey question, "How do you identify, that is, what do you call yourself?" Such survey questions have difficulty assessing the context of the respondents' answers and do not allow for multiple and situational responses. The four overall responses to this question were as follows: 27 percent identified by national origin ("Jamaican"); 40 percent as hyphenated Americans ("Filipino-American"); 11 percent as unhyphenated Americans; and 21 percent as racial and panethnic categories ("Hispanic," "Asian"). See table 2 in Rumbaut 1994: 764.

19. By "cool on them," D'Lo means "thanks, but no thanks" to the idea of socializing deeply with Indians on campus. His/her description of racism highlights the power of interpersonal and group dynamics to shape individuals' sense of self and relation to others. D'Lo racialized and distanced him/herself from Indians as a group like Whites due to his/her negative experiences.

20. This may refer to the demolition of the Babri Masjid and the subsequent Hindu rioting against Muslims.

21. The dhol, popularized in bhangra music, is a drum used in the Punjabi music of northern India.

22. Artwallah is a four-day annual South Asian diasporic arts festival in Los Angeles in which a number of the MCs in this book have taken part.

23. See the video on YouTube at http://www.youtube.com.

24. Sardar Patel was a principal figure in the Indian nationalist movement and a close friend of Mahatma Gandhi.

25. Food metaphors such as "rotten coconut" are commonly used by students to refer to particular people as "race traitors." The more com-

mon ones include "oreos"—black on the outside, white on the inside; "bananas"—yellow on the outside, white on the inside; "coconuts"—brown on the outside, white on the inside. Surprisingly, young Asian Americans have begun to use these metaphors to describe themselves.

Chapter 2: Making Race

1. They may be similar to Korean immigrants in New York City, who "are not detached bystanders but rather are profoundly implicated in the American racial order from the moment they arrive in the United States—not because they wish to be but because each group's position is invariably defined in relation to those of other groups" (Kim 2003: 12).

2. Asians often signify the rational, mental part of the mind/body distinction made during the Enlightenment. Whites, in constructing themselves in relation to Blacks, also consider themselves to be rational, whereas Blacks signify physicality (sexuality, the threat of violence) and other excesses of the body.

3. Filipinos were in Louisiana in the second half of the eighteenth century. See Bautista 2002; see also Renee Tajima-Pena's film *My America . . . Or Honk if You Love Buddha* (1997).

4. The murder of the Chinese American Vincent Chin by two White auto workers from Detroit who blamed Japan for unfair competition and job losses and the Dotbusters attacks in New Jersey mentioned in chapter 1 are just two examples. See the documentary *Who Killed Vincent Chin?* by Christine Choy and Renee Tajima-Pena (1987).

5. See Parker 1995 for a similar case in Britain.

6. See Marquez, forthcoming, for the case of Latino and Black parallels.

7. A battle rapper is one who freestyles in competition against another rapper. During the competitions they are evaluated for innovative and clever rhymes about their opponents.

8. One can see this phenomenon on the videos posted on YouTube of Jin; see his song and video "Learn Chinese."

9. N.W.A. (Niggaz with Attitude), is a late-1980s Los Angeles rap group comprised of some of the most famous West Coast "gangsta rappers," including Eazy-E (who has since died of AIDS), the prolific producer Dr. Dre, Ice Cube, DJ Yella, and MC Ren.

10. This divide became less prominent as their artistry developed. Today, Bella buys and spins records but also writes and sings; others, like D'Lo and Sammy, produce musical tracks and rhyme on stage.

11. College radio stations took off in the 1980s and gave rap music some of its first air time. The stations tended to be run by students and

offered programming alternatives to mainstream or corporate-controlled stations.

12. Dr. Jinah Kim posed the question in this intriguing way.

13. Many, in fact, are Asian American, including Jonny's fellow writers Jeff Chang and Oliver Wang.

14. See www.timapforjustice.org

15. See the listing provided on the Web site CD Baby, http://cdbaby .com/cd/Himalayan.

16. See the rappers Jin, Mountain Brothers, and The Pacifics for other Asian American examples.

17. Reaching a crescendo in 2009, the Tamil Tigers have been fighting the Sri Lankan government for an independent state in this island nation off the southeast coast of India. Tamils are outnumbered by the Sri Lankan Sinhalese, a mostly Buddhist population. See chapter 4 for D'Lo's application of hip hop to express concern about the war.

18. You can find the online video to this song on YouTube, http://www .youtube.com/watch?v=5QocPeO4s_s.

19. There are other precedents: Ho Chi Minh, leader of the communist revolutionary forces of North Vietnam, lived in New York where he attended the Universal Negro Improvement Association (UNIA) and was introduced to the influential ideologies of Marcus Garvey (Abdul-Jabbar 2007: 79).

20. This quote is from his speech "Oppose Racial Discrimination by United States Imperialism," delivered on August 8, 1963. *Peking Review*, Volume 9, no. 33, Aug. 12, 1966, pp. 12–13.

21. From "King's Trip to India," the King Papers Project, Stanford University, http://www.stanford.edu/group/King/.

22. These musical crossings also influenced jazz artists, such as John Coltrane's collaboration with Ravi Shankar. South Asian remix DJs and music producers have discerned and used these percussive overlaps by layering discrete musical traditions to produce new diasporic sounds that form the basis of desi subcultures in England and the United States (see Sharma, Hutnyk, and Sharma 1996; Maira 2002).

23. This section heading, "Soundtrack to the Brown Experience," is a line from Chee Malabar's song "Thoroughbred" on his solo album *Oblique Brown* (2006).

Chapter 3: Flipping the Gender Script

1. When I attended hip hop shows and clubs with other desi women, men often sexualized and exoticized us, saw us as sisters, or lumped us in some other form or fashion.

2. Jonny, a hip hop journalist who attended another branch of the University of California, also worked at a college radio station and experienced a remarkably similar musical evolution.

3. Hip hop was very popular in the Bay Area in the 1990s, while reggae and dancehall followed at mainstream clubs the following decade.

4. England's M.I.A. is perhaps the most famous Sri Lankan songstress who incorporates hip hop sensibilities into her global sound. See also the British Asian female MC Hard Kaur.

5. Growing up and in college, D'Lo identified as a gay woman and as a boi. Over time, D'Lo has begun to identify as a male who loves women. Therefore, I speak about many of D'Lo's past experiences growing up and in the music industry as a woman. Now a transgender male-identified artist, D'Lo aims to disrupt fixed gender categorizations and, with that in mind, I use the pronouns "s/he" and "him/her" to refer to D'Lo.

6. For more on youth cultures, see McRobbie 2000; Lee and Zhou 2004; Maira and Soep 2004.

7. Popping and locking, or pop locking, is a dance style that emerged on the West Coast in the early phases of hip hop. It features sharp robotic movements combined with waving limbs. Some dancers combine movements from both break dancing and pop locking. The Twilight Players, which consists of three Punjabi brothers in England, are perhaps some of the most well-known pop lockers: www.twilightplayers.com.

8. See Rivera 2003 for an analysis of Puerto Rican women in hip hop, and see Rose 1994 on dialogues between Black men and women in hip hop.

9. A number of strong women in hip hop have faced speculation about their sexuality, including Queen Pen, Queen Latifah, and Da Brat, whom some hip hop audiences have presumed were lesbians; the latter two have undergone feminizing makeovers, possibly in response.

10. Note how the show's title smartly refutes gender and sex attributions as D'Lo replaces the more traditional "one man show" with a "one D'Lo show."

11. Oakland's Deep Dickollective is among the well-known groups of homo hop, or queer hip hop, and the PeaceOUT World Homo Hop Festival took place in the early 2000s in the same city. See the documentary *Pick up the Mic* (dir. Alex Hinton, 2006).

12. Countless sisters have bemoaned this "old school" or "traditional" gender double standard that favors boys.

13. Elders call potential brides and grooms "girls" and "boys" despite their age, especially before marriage.

14. DasGupta and Das Dasgupta 2000 discuss similar American desi gender dynamics in which desi girls seem too Americanized to make

proper wives for Indians boys with the "raja syndrome." Young desis in the Bay Area widely discussed the phenomenon in the late 1990s of United States–born men going to India to "import" a wife because they were "unable" to find "proper" wives in America. See also Gupta 1999.

15. Illustrating the dangers of a "positive stereotype" of Asian Americans as model minorities who are associated with brains and not brawn, the Democratic campaign against Republican Bobby Jindal's successful run for governor of Louisiana (the first non-White governor since Reconstruction) included ads that stated: "Bobby Jindal: Big Brain. No Heart."

16. "Jungle fever" refers to Spike Lee's movie from 1991 about interracial relationships.

17. See Sepia Mutiny, http://www.sepiamutiny.com/sepia/archives/003575.html (site visited on February 3, 2009).

18. I am not saying that this form of acceptance is either "good" or "bad." It is, however, something that allows women easier access to and acceptance among Black men.

19. Du Bois's internationalist lens on race and decolonization linked Blacks in America to the experiences and (sometimes idealized) models of Asians in Asia; scholars who focus on the United States–based implications of his work may overlook this.

20. The term b-boi is a spin on b-boy, or break boy.

Chapter 4: The Appeal of Hip Hop

1. Speaking of polycultural influences, Vijay Prashad explains the Indian etymology of the word "thug" to Michael Eric Dyson (2001: 113–14).

2. "Is Hip Hop Black Culture?" Davey D's Hip Hop Corner, www.daveyd.com (site visited on January 9, 2009); see also Perry 2004.

3. Reagan granted reparations and Bill Clinton signed a formal letter of apology to those Japanese who had been interned during World War II. This begs a comparison with the lack of reparations granted to African Americans for their enslavement.

4. See, for example, the Hiphopistan event described in the introduction.

5. Wang (2007) discusses the influence of Public Enemy on other Asian American hip hop artists. Note once again the generative importance of the college radio station. Additionally, while some critics question the "authenticity" of college-educated desi artists, they do not apply the same doubt toward college-educated Black rappers, including the members of Public Enemy.

6. Consequently, *Party Music* (2001) is the name of one of The Coup's albums.

7. Armond White's assertion that "it is impossible for any White rapper to achieve originality" (1996: 194) is not only wrong but rests on arguments about "essence," sensuality, and ethnicity that cannot hold up to the evidence provided in hip hop culture.

8. Undoubtedly there is a younger generation of desis who rhyme and who may be more concerned with posturing than positivity. The artists I met reflect a segment of a particular generation, most of whom are influenced by the Bay Area culture. These artists have produced and performed for nearly twenty years, which led to their visibility and my learning about them. Those who contributed to this project contend with changes in the hip hop business that have accompanied its increasing popularity and capitalist incorporation. Today's youth will, of course, be drawn to different aspects of hip hop because hip hop, itself, has changed.

9. This analysis by K B is curiously countered by some of his own lyrics, discussed in previous chapters. I suggest that the marketing priorities of Karmacy and the larger label Rukus Avenue Records to attract desi audiences may have impacted this divergence.

10. Although these definitions are highly contested, hip hop is sometimes distinguished as either "commercial hip hop" or "underground hip hop." Commercial hip hop is that which is played on major radio stations. "Underground hip hop" may not reach broad audiences, may be independent or signed to smaller record labels, and is sometimes synonymous with today's "conscious hip hop" (hip hop with politically conscious lyrics). Technological advances have made music production and promotion more democratic, thereby allowing artists alternatives to lobbying for a major record label deal. Thus, desi rappers feel a sense of increasing autonomy and may face less pressure to alter their image or content.

11. See the film *Black Is . . . Black Ain't* by Marlon Riggs (1994).

Chapter 5: Sampling South Asians

1. A desi founder of an independent hip hop record label company made this clever distinction between "wrapping" and "rapping."

2. Aaron Bobrow-Strain helped me clarify these two concepts.

3. The radio shock jock Don Imus's infamous racist comments toward the Rutgers women's basketball team in 2007 compelled hip hop entrepreneurs, including Russell Simmons, to protest the use of the terms "nigga," "bitch," and "ho."

4. Among the hits was "Nas's Angels," a rap song with a Hindi chorus.

In addition, Lil' Kim's *La Bella Mafia* featured at least three tracks with identifiably South Asian music.

5. The song was from the Hindi film, *Jyoti*, starring Hema Malini and Jeetendra. According to Kevin Miller (2004), DJ Quik first heard the song while watching the film on television. Another story says he accidentally bought the record.

6. Many DJs in fact sell remixed tapes featuring commercial hip hop beats without any sample clearances.

7. The same Indian company, Saregama, filed another suit in 2007 against the use of samples on The Game's rap song "Put You on the Game," produced by Timbaland.

8. Fans also expressed this kind of ire in reaction to the early productions of Sean Combs.

9. My thanks to Richard Iton who pointed out this history to me.

10. Some argue that this is due to a "racial draft" that targets minority and working-class Americans while safeguarding middle-class Whites from fighting our wars; additionally, some Blacks without economic means may feel that their ability to afford college and travel the world is limited and the military offers these incentives. This racial profiling is also reflected in the past recruitment tactics used by the American military to appeal to young urban minorities by advertising on Hummers on high school and community college campuses.

11. Born and raised in northern California, the Punjabi bellytwins have danced (along with their snakes) in front of Hillary Clinton and Arnold Schwarzenegger and have performed with Michael Jackson and Ricky Martin.

12. White women were also enamored with these same jazz greats, but they often entered the scene through intimate relationships with them. See Jones 1963; Monson 1995.

13. Timbaland hired the Indian American Raje Shwari to re-sing many of the Hindi choruses used in his songs. Her Web site (accessed November 28, 2008, now defunct), featured a picture of the Taj Mahal accompanied by classical Indian music as the following statement appeared on the computer screen: "Every once in a while, someone totally different and innovative comes along to change the face of music forever." A new screen emerged with the same backdrop of the Taj Mahal during dawn or dusk: "Only because what this particular artist proposes to offer the music world is something that has never been done before." In the final touch, a personalized message from Raje Shwari signs off with a causal, "Get with you later!"

14. Green Lantern, in collaboration with Russell Simmons, released a Barack Obama "Yes We Can" mixtape. The Bay Area rapper Paris refers to

Muhammad Ali on his track "Bush Killa," in which he raps: "Yeah, tolerance is gettin' thinner / 'Cause Iraq never called me 'nigger' / So what I wanna go off and fight a war for? / You best believe I got your draft card!"

15. See www.the1shanti.com for more on the collaboration with Afrika Bambaataa.

16. My thanks to Laura Helper-Ferris for sharing this interpretation with me.

Conclusion: Turning Thoughts into Action

1. Vivek's full report, "Ravaging the Vulnerable," can be found at Human Rights Watch, http://www.hrw.org/reports/2003/bangladesh0803/index.htm (site visited on November 12, 2009).

2. Richa Gulati, *Little India*, http://www.littleindia.com/news/134/ARTICLE/1461/2007–04–03.html (accessed November 30, 2007).

3. http://www.webdust.net/abstracthumanity (Web site no longer accessible).

References

Abdul-Jabbar, Kareem. 2007. *On the Shoulders of Giants: My Journey through the Harlem Renaissance*. New York: Simon and Schuster.

Abraham, Sameer and Nabeel Abraham, eds. 1983. *Muslims in the New World: Studies on Arab-American Communities*. Detroit: Wayne State University Press.

Almaguer, Thomas. 1994. *Racial Fault Lines: The Historical Origins of White Supremacy in California*. Berkeley: University of California Press.

Anderson, Benedict. 1983. *Imagined Communities*. London: Verso.

Aparicio, Ana. 2007. "Contesting Race and Power through the Diaspora: Second-Generation Dominican Youth in the New Gotham." *City and Society* 19 (2): 179–201.

Arlyck, Kevin. 1997. "By Any Means Necessary: Rapping and Resistance in Urban Black America." In *Globalization and Survival in the Black Diaspora: The New Urban Challenge*, ed. Charles Green. Albany: State University of New York Press.

Arnold, Eric. 2006. "From Azeem to Zion-I: The Evolution of Global Consciousness in Bay Area Hip Hop." In *The Vinyl Ain't Final: Hip Hop and the Globalization of Black Popular Culture*, ed. Dipannita Basu and Sidney Lemelle. London: Pluto.

Asim, Jabari. 2007. *The N Word: Who Can Say It, Who Shouldn't, and Why*. Boston: Houghton Mifflin.

Bahri, Deepika, and Mary Vasudeva, eds. 1996. *Between the Lines: South Asians and Postcoloniality*. Philadelphia: Temple University Press.

Baker, Houston, Manthia Diawara, and Ruth Lindeborg, eds. 1996. *Black British Cultural Studies: A Reader*. Chicago: University of Chicago Press.

Bakhtin, M. M. 1981. *The Dialogic Imagination: Four Essays*. Edited by M. Holquist. Translated by C. Emerson and M. Holquist. Austin: University of Texas Press.

Bakrania, Falu. 2004. "Negotiating Art, Ethnicity, and Politics: Asian Underground Artists and the Commercial Public Sphere." *Subcontinental: The Journal of South Asian American Public Affairs* 2 (2): 11–18.

Bald, Vivek. 2008. "Indian Radicals and Sailors in the Overlapping Diasporas of 1920s New York." Paper presented at Diasporic Counterpoint: Asians, Africans, and the Americas, Northwestern University, April.

Balibar, Etienne. 1991. *Race, Nation, Class: Ambiguous Identities.* London: Verso.

Ballard, Roger, ed. 1994. *Desh Pardesh: The South Asian Presence in Britain.* London: Hurst.

Barth, Fredrik, ed. 1969. *Ethnic Groups and Boundaries: The Social Organization of Culture Difference.* Boston: Little, Brown.

Basu, Dipannita, and Sidney Lemelle, eds. 2006. *The Vinyl Ain't Final: Hip Hop and the Globalization of Black Popular Culture.* London: Pluto.

Bautista, Veltisezar. 2002. *The Filipino Americans, from 1763 to the Present: Their History, Culture, and Traditions.* Farmington Hills, Mich.: Bookhaus.

Bernstein, Neil. 1995. "Goin' Gangsta, Choosin' Cholita." *Utne Reader,* March–April: 87–90.

Bhabha, Homi. 1994. *The Location of Culture.* New York: Routledge.

Boggs, Grace Lee. 1998. *Living for Change: An Autobiography.* Minneapolis: University of Minnesota Press.

Bonilla-Silva, Eduardo, and David Embrick. 2006. "Black, Honorary White, White: The Future of Race in the United States?" In *Mixed Messages: Multiracial Identities in the 'Color-Blind' Era,* ed. David Brunsma. Boulder: Lynne Rienner.

Bourdieu, Pierre. 1977. *Outline of a Theory of Practice.* Cambridge: Cambridge University Press.

———. 1986. "The Forms of Capital." In *Handbook for Theory and Research for the Sociology of Education,* ed. John Richardson. Westport, Conn.: Greenwood.

Brah, Avtar. 1996. *Cartographies of Diaspora: Contesting Identities.* London: Routledge.

Chan, Sucheng. 1991. *Asian Americans: An Interpretive History.* New York: Twayne.

Chang, Grace. 2000. *Disposable Domestics: Immigrant Women Workers in the Global Economy.* Cambridge, Mass.: South End.

Chang, Jeff. 2005. *Can't Stop, Won't Stop: A History of the Hip-Hop Generation.* New York: St. Martin's.

Chang, Robert. 1995. "Toward an Asian American Legal Scholarship: Critical Race Theory, Post-Structuralism, and Narrative Space." In

Critical Race Theory: The Cutting Edge (A Reader), ed. Richard Delgado. Philadelphia: Temple University Press.

Chatterjee, Sandra. 2006. "Impossible Hosting: D'lo Sets an Undomesticated Stage for South Asian Youth Artists." Women and Performance 16 (3): 445–64.

Chaudhry, Lubna. 1998. "'We Are Graceful Swans Who Can Also Be Crows': Hybrid Identities of Pakistani Muslim Women." In A Patchwork Shawl: Chronicles of South Asian Women in America, ed. Shamita Das Dasgupta. New Brunswick: Rutgers University Press.

Chen, Carolyn. 2008. Getting Saved in America: Taiwanese Immigrants Converting to Evangelical Christianity and Buddhism. Princeton: Princeton University Press.

Clarke, Colin, Ceri Peach, and Steven Vertovec, eds. 1990. South Asians Overseas: Migration and Ethnicity. Cambridge: Cambridge University Press.

Collins, Patricia Hill. 2000. Black Feminist Thought: Knowledge, Consciousness, and the Politics of Empowerment. New York: Routledge.

———. 2004. Black Sexual Politics: African Americans, Gender, and the New Racism. New York: Routledge.

———. 2006. From Black Power to Hip Hop: Racism, Nationalism, and Feminism. Philadelphia: Temple University Press.

Condry, Ian. 2006. Hip-Hop Japan: Rap and the Paths of Cultural Globalization. Durham: Duke University Press.

Cornyetz, Nina. 1994. "Fetishized Blackness: Hip Hop and Racial Desire in Contemporary Japan." Social Text 41 (winter): 113–39.

Cosentino, Donald. 1992. "Interview with Robert Farris Thompson." African Arts 25 (4): 53–63.

DasGupta, Kasturi. 1997. "Raising Bicultural Children." In Asian Indian Immigrants: Motifs on Ethnicity and Gender, ed. Brij Khare. Dubuque, Iowa: Kendall/Hunt.

Das Gupta, Monisha. 2006. Unruly Immigrants: Rights, Activism, and Transnational South Asian Politics in the United States. Durham: Duke University Press.

DasGupta, Sayantani, and Shamita Das Dasgupta. 2000. "Women in Exile: Gender Relations in the Asian Indian Community in the United States." In Asian American Studies: A Reader, ed. Jean Wu and Min Song. New Brunswick: Rutgers University Press.

Davis, Angela. 1988. Angela Davis: An Autobiography. New York: International.

———. 1996. "Gender, Class, and Multiculturalism: Rethinking 'Race' Politics." In Mapping Multi-Culturalism, ed. Avery Gordon and Christopher Newfield. Minneapolis: University of Minnesota Press.

Davis, Angela, and Gina Dent. 2001. "Prison as a Border: A Conversation on Gender, Globalization, and Punishment." *Signs* 26 (4): 1235–41.

de Leon, Lakandiwa. 2004. "Filipinotown and the DJ Scene: Cultural Expression and Identity Affirmation of Filipino American Youth in Los Angeles." In *Asian American Youth: Culture, Identity, and Ethnicity*, ed. Jennifer Lee and Min Zhou. New York: Routledge.

Derrida, Jacques. 1982. *Margins of Philosophy*. Chicago: University of Chicago Press.

De Vos, George. 1975. "Ethnic Pluralism: Conflict and Accommodation." In *Ethnic Identity: Cultural Continuities and Change*, ed. George De Vos and Lola Romanucci-Ross. Palo Alto: Mayfield.

Dirks, Nicolas, Geoff Eley, and Sherry Ortner, eds. 1994. *Culture/Power/History: A Reader in Contemporary Social Theory*. Princeton: Princeton University Press.

Dolhinow, Rebecca. 2010. *A Jumble of Needs: Women's Activism and Neoliberalism in the Colonias of the Southwest*. Minneapolis: University of Minnesota Press.

D'Souza, Placido. 2003. "Gandhi's Influence on Martin Luther King." *San Francisco Chronicle*. January 20, B-7.

Du Bois, W. E. B. 1903. *The Souls of Black Folk: Essays and Sketches*. Chicago: A. C. McClurg.

———. 1928. *Dark Princess: A Romance*. New York: Harcourt, Brace and Company.

Dyson, Michael Eric. 1993. *Reflecting Black: African-American Cultural Criticism*. Minneapolis: University of Minnesota Press.

———. 1999. "Niggas Gotta Stop!" *Source*, June: 107.

———. 2001. *Holler if You Hear Me: Searching for Tupac Shakur*. New York: Basic Civitas.

———. 2007. *Know What I Mean? Reflections on Hip-Hop*. New York: Basic Civitas.

Eng, David. 1997. "Out Here Over There: Queerness and Diaspora in Asian American Studies." *Social Text* 52–53: 31–52.

———. 2001. *Racial Castration: Managing Masculinity in Asian America*. Durham: Duke University Press.

Espiritu, Yen Le. 1992. *Asian American Panethnicity: Bridging Institutions and Identities*. Philadelphia: Temple University Press.

———. 1997. *Asian American Women and Men: Labor, Laws, Love*. Thousand Oaks, Calif.: Sage.

———. 2001. "'We Don't Sleep Around Like White Girls Do': Family, Gender and Culture in Filipino American Lives." *Signs* 26 (2): 415–40.

Fabian, Johannes, and Matti Bunzl. 2002. *Time and the Other: How Anthropology Makes Its Object*. New York: Columbia University Press.

Fajardo, Kale. 2008. "Transportation: Translating Filipino and Filipino American Tomboy Masculinities through Global Migration and Seafaring." GLQ: A Journal of Lesbian and Gay Studies 13 (2–3): 403–24.

Farley, Christopher. 1999. "White Out Alert." *Source*, June.

Fernandes, Deepa. 2006. *Targeted: Homeland Security and the Business of Immigration.* New York: Seven Stories.

Fitzpatrick, Chris. 2002. "Boom Go the Bombs, Boom Goes the Bass." *PopMatters* (January 14): www.popmatters.com/music/videos/t/truth hurts-addictive.shtml (accessed on August 2, 2003).

Flores, Juan. 2000. *From Bomba to Hip-Hop: Puerto Rican Culture and Latino Identity.* New York: Columbia University Press.

Fong, Colleen, and Judy Yung. 1995. "In Search of the Right Spouse: Interracial Marriage among Chinese and Japanese Americans." *Amerasia* 21 (3): 77–98.

Forman, Murray, and Mark Anthony Neal, eds. 2004. *That's the Joint! The Hip-Hop Studies Reader.* New York: Routledge.

Foucault, Michel. 1976. "Two Lectures." In *Power/Knowledge: Selected Interviews and Other Writings, 1972–1977*, ed. Colin Gordon. New York: Pantheon.

———. 1980. *Power/Knowledge: Selected Interviews and Other Writings*, ed. Colin Gordon. Hassocks, England: Harvester.

———. 1990. *The History of Sexuality.* New York: Vintage.

———. 1995. *Discipline and Punish: The Birth of the Prison.* New York: Vintage.

Fricke, Jim, and Charlie Ahearn. 2002. *Yes Yes Y'all: The Experience Music Project Oral History of Hip-Hop's First Decade.* Cambridge, Mass.: Da Capo.

Frith, Simon. 1996. "Music and Identity." In *Questions of Identity*, ed. Stuart Hall and Paul du Gay. London: Sage.

———. 2007. *Taking Popular Music Seriously: Selected Essays.* London: Ashgate.

Fujino, Diane. 2005. *Heartbeat of a Struggle: The Revolutionary Life of Yuri Kochiyama.* Minneapolis: University of Minnesota Press.

Gans, Herbert. 1996. "Symbolic Ethnicity." In *Theories of Ethnicity: A Classical Reader*, ed. Werner Sollers. New York: New York University Press.

Gaunt, Kyra. 2006. *The Games Black Girls Play: Learning the Ropes from Double-Dutch to Hip-Hop.* New York: New York University Press.

Geertz, Clifford. 1973. "Thick Description: Toward an Interpretive Theory of Culture." In *The Interpretation of Cultures.* New York: Basic.

George, Nelson. 2005. *Hip Hop America.* New York: Penguin.

Ghasarian, Christian, and Michael Levine. 1996. *Asian Indians in the United States.* Washington: U.S. Bureau of the Census.

Ghosh, Amitav. 2008. *Sea of Poppies.* New York: Farrar, Straus and Giroux.

Giddens, Anthony. 1984. *The Constitution of Society: Outline of the Theory of Structuration*. Berkeley: University of California Press.

Gilmore, Ruth. 2007. *Golden Gulag: Prisons, Crisis, and Opposition in Globalizing California*. Berkeley: University of California Press.

Gilroy, Paul. 1987. *Ain't No Black in the Union Jack: The Cultural Politics of Race and Nation*. London: Hutchinson.

———. 1993a. *The Black Atlantic: Modernity and Double Consciousness*. London: Verso.

———. 1993b. *Small Acts: Thoughts on the Politics of Black Cultures*. London: Serpent's Tale.

———. 2005. *Against Race: Imagining Political Culture beyond the Color Line*. Cambridge: Belknap Press of Harvard University Press.

Giroux, Henry. 1994. *Disturbing Pleasures: Learning Popular Culture*. New York: Routledge.

Giroux, Henry, and Patrick Shannon, eds. 1997. *Education and Cultural Studies: Toward a Performative Practice*. New York: Routledge.

Glazer, Nathan, and Daniel Moynihan, eds. 1975. *Ethnicity: Theory and Experience*. Cambridge: Harvard University Press.

Gooding-Williams, Robert, ed. 1993. *Reading Rodney King/Reading Urban Uprising*. New York: Routledge.

Gopinath, Gayatri. 1995. "'Bombay, U.K., Yuba City': Bhangra Music and the Engendering of Diaspora." *Diaspora* 4 (3): 303–21.

———. 2005. *Impossible Desires: Queer Diasporas and South Asian Public Cultures*. Durham: Duke University Press.

Gordon, Milton. 1964. *Assimilation in American Life: The Role of Race, Religion and National Origins*. New York: Oxford University Press.

Gramsci, Antonio. 1971. *Selections from the Prison Notebooks*. New York: Lawrence and Wishart.

Gray, Obika. 1997. "Power and Identity among Urban Poor of Jamaica." In *Globalization and Survival in the Black Diaspora: The New Urban Challenge*, ed. Charles Green. Albany: State University of New York Press.

Green, Charles, ed. 1997. *Globalization and Survival in the Black Diaspora: The New Urban Challenge*. Albany: State University of New York Press.

Gross, Joan, David McMurray, and Ted Swedenburg. 1996. "Arab Noise and Ramadan Nights: Rai, Rap, and Franco-Maghrebi Identities." In *Displacement, Diaspora, and Geographic Identity*, ed. Smadar Lavie and Ted Swedenburg. Durham: Duke University Press.

Guilbault, Jocelyne. 2001. "Racial Projects and Musical Discourses in Trinidad, West Indies." In *Music and the Racial Imagination*, ed. Ronald Radano and Philip Bohlman. Chicago: University of Chicago Press.

Gupta, Sangeeta, ed. 1999. *Emerging Voices: South Asian American Women Redefine Self, Family, and Community*. Thousand Oaks, Calif.: Sage.

Halberstam, Judith. 2000. *Female Masculinity*. Durham: Duke University Press.

Hall, Christine Iijima, and Trude Turner. 2001. "The Diversity of Biracial Individuals: Asian-White and Asian-Minority Biracial Identity." In *Sum of Our Parts: Mixed Heritage Asian Americans*, ed. Teresa Williams-Leon and Cynthia Nakashima. Philadelphia: Temple University Press.

Hall, Stuart. 1983. "The Problem of Ideology: Marxism without Guarantees." In *Marx: 100 Years On*, ed. Betty Matthews. London: Lawrence and Wishart.

————. 1990. "Cultural Identity and Diaspora." In *Identity: Community, Culture, Difference*, ed. Jonathan Rutherford. London: Lawrence and Wishart.

————. 1991. "Old and New Identities, Old and New Ethnicities." In *Culture, Globalization, and the World-System: Contemporary Conditions for the Representation of Identity*, ed. Anthony King. London: Macmillan.

————. 1992. "What Is This 'Black' in Black Popular Culture?" In *Black Popular Culture*, ed. Gina Dent. Seattle: Bay Press.

————. 1995. "Fantasy, Identity, Politics." In *Cultural Remix: Theories of Politics and the Popular*, ed. Erica Carter, James Donald, and Judith Squires. London: Lawrence and Wishart.

————. 1996a. "The New Ethnicities." In *Ethnicity*, ed. John Hutchinson and Anthony Smith. Oxford: Oxford University Press.

————. 1996b. "Introduction: Who Needs 'Identity?'" In *Questions of Identity*, ed. Stuart Hall and Paul du Gay. London: Sage.

————, ed. 1997. *Representation: Cultural Representation and Signifying Practices*. Thousand Oaks, Calif.: Sage.

————. 2000. "Conclusion: The Multicultural Question." In *Un/Settled Multiculturalisms: Diasporas, Entanglements, "Transruptions,"* ed. Barnor Hesse. London: Zed.

Hall, Stuart, and T. Jefferson, eds. 1976. *Resistance through Rituals: Youth Subcultures in Post-war Britain*. London: Hutchinson.

Harris, Virginia, and Trinity Ordona. 1990. "Developing Unity among Women of Color: Crossing the Barriers of Internalized Racism and Cross-Racial Hostility." In *Making Face, Making Soul/Haciendo Caras*, ed. Gloria Anzaldúa. San Francisco: Aunt Lute.

Hassan, Salah. 2002. "Arabs, Race and the Post–September 11 National Security State." In *Middle East Report: Arabs, Muslims, and Race in America* 224 (fall): 16–21.

Hawley, John. 2008. *India in Africa, Africa in India: Indian Ocean Cosmopolitanisms*. Bloomington: Indiana University Press.

Heath, Scott, and Charles Rowell, eds. 2006. "Hip-Hop Music and Culture." Special issue of *Callaloo* 29 (3).

Hebdige, Dick. 1979. *Subculture: The Meaning of Style*. London: Methuen.

———. 1987. *Cut 'n' Mix: Culture, Identity and Caribbean Music*. London: Comedia and Methuen.

———. 1994. "After the Masses." In *Culture/Power/History: A Reader in Contemporary Social Theory*, ed. Nicholas Dirks, Geoff Eley, and Sherry Ortner. Princeton: Princeton University Press.

———. 1996. "Digging for Britain: An Excavation in Seven Parts." In *Black British Cultural Studies: A Reader*, ed. Houston Baker, Manthia Diawara, and Ruth Lindeborg. Chicago: University of Chicago Press.

Helweg, Arthur, and Usha Helweg. 1990. *An Immigrant Success Story: East Indians in America*. London: Hurst.

Herzig, Pascale. 2008. *South Asians in Kenya: Gender, Generation and Changing Identities in Diaspora*. Berlin: LIT.

Hesse, Barnor, ed. 2000. *Un/Settled Multiculturalisms: Diaspora, Entanglement, 'Transruptions.'* London: Zed.

Hesse, Barnor, and S. Sayyid. 2006. "Narrating the Postcolonial Political and Immigrant Imaginary." In *A Postcolonial People: South Asians in Britain*, ed. Nasreen Ali, Virinder Kalra, and Salman Sayyid. London: Wm. B. Eerdmans.

Hing, Bill Ong. 2004. *Defining America through Immigration Policy*. Philadelphia: Temple University Press.

Ho, Fred, and Bill Mullen, eds. 2008. *Afro Asia: Revolutionary Political and Cultural Connections between African Americans and Asian Americans*. Durham: Duke University Press.

Hollinger, David. 1995. *Postethnic America*. New York: Harper Collins.

Hondagneu-Sotelo, Pierrette. 1994. *Gendered Transitions: Mexican Experiences of Immigration*. Berkeley: University of California Press.

hooks, bell. 1981. *Ain't I a Woman? Black Women and Feminism*. Boston: South End.

———. 1999. *Black Looks: Race and Representation*. Boston: South End.

Hutnyk, John. 1999–2000. "Hybridity Saves? Authenticity and/or the Critique of Appropriation." *Amerasia* 25 (3): 39–58.

———. 2000. "Culture Move: On Asian Dub Foundation." *Ghadar: A Publication of the Forum of Indian Leftists* 4 (1): www.proxsa.org/resources/ghadar/v4n1/hutnyk.htm (accessed June 28, 2005).

———. 2006. "The Nation Question: Fundamental and the Deathening Silence." In *The Vinyl Ain't Final: Hip Hop and the Globalization of Black Popular Culture*, ed. Dipannita Basu and Sidney Lemelle. London: Pluto.

Hyder, Rehan. 2004. *Brimful of Asia: Negotiating Ethnicity on the UK Music Scene*. Aldershot, England: Ashgate.

Iton, Richard. 2008. *In Search of the Black Fantastic: Politics and Popular Culture in the Post–Civil Rights Era*. New York: Oxford University Press.

Jackson, John. 2005. *Real Black: Adventures in Racial Sincerity*. Chicago: University of Chicago Press.

———. 2008. *Racial Paranoia*. New York: Perseus.

Jayasuriya, Shihan, and Richard Pankhurst, eds. 2003. *The African Diaspora in the Indian Ocean*. Lawrenceville, N.J.: Africa World.

Jensen, Joan. 1988. *Passage from India: Asian Indian Immigrants in North America*. New Haven: Yale University Press.

Johnson, E. Patrick. 2003. *Appropriating Blackness: Performance and the Politics of Authenticity*. Durham: Duke University Press.

Jones, Andrew and Singh, Nikhil Pal, eds. 2003. "The Afro-Asian Century." Special issue of *Positions: East Asia Cultures Critique* 11 (1).

Jones, LeRoi. 1963. *Blues People: Negro Music in White America*. New York: William Morrow.

Joshi, Khyati. 2006. *New Roots in America's Sacred Ground: Religion, Race, and Ethnicity in Indian America*. New Brunswick: Rutgers University Press.

Jun, Helen. 2006. "Black Orientalism: 19th Century Narratives of Race and U.S. Citizenship." *American Quarterly* 58 (4): 1046–66.

Jung, Moon-Ho. 2006. *Coolies and Cane: Race, Labor, and Sugar in the Age of Emancipation*. Baltimore: Johns Hopkins University Press.

Kato, M. T. 2007. *From Kung Fu to Hip Hop: Globalization, Revolution, and Popular Culture*. Albany: State University of New York Press.

Kelley, Robin. 1996. "Kickin' Reality, Kickin' Ballistics: Gangsta Rap and Postindustrial Los Angeles." In *Droppin' Science: Critical Essays on Rap and Hip Hop Culture*, ed. William Perkins. Philadelphia: Temple University Press.

———. 1997. *Yo' Mama's Disfunktional! Fighting the Culture Wars in Urban America*. Boston: Beacon.

———. 1999. "People in Me." *Utne Reader*, September: 79–81.

Khan, Aisha. 2004a. *Callaloo Nation: Metaphors of Race and Religious Identity among South Asians in Trinidad*. Durham: Duke University Press.

———. 2004b. "Juthaa in Trinidad: Food, Pollution, and Hierarchy in a Caribbean Diaspora Community." *American Ethnologist* 21 (2): 245–69.

Khandelwal, Madhulika. 2002. *Becoming American, Being Indian: An Immigrant Community in New York City*. Ithaca: Cornell University Press.

Kibria, Nazli. 1998. "The Contested Meanings of 'Asian American': Racial Dilemmas in the Contemporary U.S." *Ethnic and Racial Studies* 21: 939–58.

———. 2000. "Race, Ethnic Options, and Ethnic Binds: Identity Negotiations of Second-Generation Chinese and Korean Americans." *Sociological Perspectives* 43 (1): 77–95.

Kich, George. 1996. "In the Margins of Sex and Race: Difference, Marginality, and Flexibility." In *The Multiracial Experience: Racial Borders as the New Frontier*, ed. Maria Root. Thousand Oaks, Calif.: Sage.

Kim, Claire Jean. 1999. "The Racial Triangulation of Asian Americans." *Politics and Society* 27 (1): 105–38.

———. 2003. *Bitter Fruit: The Politics of Black-Korean Conflict in New York City*. New Haven: Yale University Press.

Kim, Jinah. Forthcoming. "Japanese American Internees and Mexican American Braceros at the Crossroads of WWII." In *Transnational Crossroads: Reimagining Asian America, Latin@ America, and the American Pacific*, ed. Camila Fojas and Rudy Guevarra Jr.

Kim, Kwang Chung, ed. 1999. *Koreans in the Hood: Conflict with African Americans*. Baltimore: Johns Hopkins University Press.

Kitwana, Bakari. 2002. *The Hip Hop Generation: Young Blacks and the Crisis of African American Culture*. New York: Basic Civitas.

———. 2005. *Why White Kids Love Hip-Hop: Wankstas, Wiggers, Wannabes, and the New Reality of Race in America*. New York: Basic Civitas.

Knoll, Tricia. 1982. *Becoming Americans: Asian Sojourners, Immigrants, and Refugees in the Western United States*. Portland, Ore.: Coast to Coast.

Kochiyama, Yuri. 1994. "The Impact of Malcolm X on Asian-American Politics and Activism." In *Blacks, Latinos, and Asians in Urban America: Status and Prospects for Politics and Activism*, ed. James Jennings. Westport, Conn.: Greenwood.

Koshy, Susan. 1998. "Category Crisis: South Asian Americans and Questions of Race and Ethnicity." *Diaspora* 7 (3): 285–320.

———. 2004. *Sexual Naturalization: Asian Americans and Miscegenation*. Stanford: Stanford University Press.

Kurashige, Scott. 2008. *The Shifting Grounds of Race: Black and Japanese Americans in the Making of Multiethnic Los Angeles*. Princeton: Princeton University Press.

Lal, Brij, Peter Reeves, and Rajesh Rai, eds. 2007. *The Encyclopedia of the Indian Diaspora*. Honolulu: University of Hawai'i Press.

Ledbetter, James. 1992. "Imitation of Life." *Vibe*, September: 114.

Lee, Jennifer. 2002. *Civility in the City: Blacks, Jews, and Koreans in Urban America*. Cambridge: Harvard University Press.

Lee, Jennifer, and Frank Bean. 2004. "America's Changing Color Lines: Race/Ethnicity, Immigration, and Multiracial Identification." *Annual Review of Sociology* 30: 221–42.

———. 2007. "Reinventing the Color Line: Immigration and America's New Racial/Ethnic Hierarchy." *Social Forces* 86 (2): 561–86.

Lee, Jennifer, and Min Zhou. 2004. *Asian American Youth: Culture, Identity, and Ethnicity*. New York: Routledge.

Leonard, Karen. 1992. *Making Ethnic Choices: California's Punjabi Mexican Americans*. Philadelphia: Temple University Press.

Lessinger, Johanna. 1995. *From the Ganges to the Hudson: Indian Immigrants in New York City*. Boston: Allyn and Bacon.

Lhamon, W. T., Jr. 1998. *Raising Cain: Blackface Performance from Jim Crow to Hip Hop*. Cambridge: Harvard University Press.

Light, Alan, ed. 1999. *The Vibe History of Hip Hop*. New York: Three Rivers.

Limón, José. 1992. *Mexican Ballads, Chicano Poems: History and Influence in Mexican-American Social Poetry*. Berkeley: University of California Press.

Lipsitz, George. 1990. *Time Passages: Collective Memory and American Popular Culture*. Minneapolis: University of Minnesota Press.

———. 1994. *Dangerous Crossroads: Popular Music, Postmodernism, and the Poetics of Place*. London: Verso.

———. 1998a. "The Hip Hop Hearings: Censorship, Social Memory, and Inter-Generational Tensions among African Americans." In *Generations of Youth: Twentieth Century America*, ed. Joe Austin and Michael Nevin Willard. New York: New York University Press.

———. 1998b. *Possessive Investment in Whiteness: How White People Profit from Identity Politics*. Philadelphia: Temple University Press.

———. 2004. "Noises in the Blood: Culture, Conflict, and Mixed Race Identities." In *Crossing Lines: Race and Mixed Race across the Geohistorical Divide*, ed. Marc Coronado, Rudy Guevarra Jr., Jeffrey Moniz, and Laura Szanto. Santa Barbara: Multiethnic Student Outreach.

———. 2007. *Footsteps in the Dark: The Hidden Histories of Popular Music*. Minneapolis: University of Minnesota Press.

Lopez, Ian Haney. 2006. *White by Law: The Legal Construction of Race*. New York: New York University Press.

Lorde, Audre. 1984. *Sister Outsider: Essays and Speeches*. Trumansburg, N.Y.: Crossing.

Lott, Eric. 1993a. "White Like Me: Racial Cross-Dressing and the Construction of American Whiteness." In *Cultures of United States Imperialism*, ed. Amy Kaplan and Donald Pease. Durham: Duke University Press.

———. 1993b. *Love and Theft: Blackface Minstrelsy and the American Working Class*. New York: Oxford University Press.

Lowe, Lisa. 1996. *Immigrant Acts: On Asian American Cultural Politics*. Durham: Duke University Press.

Mahon, Maureen. 2004. *Right to Rock: The Black Rock Coalition and the Cultural Politics of Race*. Durham: Duke University Press.

Maira, Sunaina. 2002. *Desis in the House: Indian American Youth Culture in New York City*. Philadelphia: Temple University Press.

————, guest ed. 2006. *Journal of Asian American Studies* 9 (2).

————. 2008. "Belly Dancing: Arab-Face, Orientalist Feminism, and U.S. Empire." *American Quarterly* 60 (2): 317–45.

————. 2009. *Missing: Youth, Citizenship, and Empire after 9/11.* Durham: Duke University Press.

Maira, Sunaina, and Elisabeth Soep, eds. 2004. *Youthscapes: The Popular, the National, the Global.* Philadelphia: University of Pennsylvania Press.

Maira, Sunaina, and Rajini Srikanth, eds. 1996. *Contours of the Heart: South Asians Map North America.* New York: Asian American Writers' Workshop.

Malkani, Gautam. 2006. *Londonstani.* New York: Penguin.

Mamdani, Mahmood. 2004. *Good Muslim, Bad Muslim: America, the Cold War, and the Roots of Terror.* New York: Pantheon.

Mani, Bakirathi. 2001. "Destination Culture: A Critical Look at South Asian Arts and Activism Festivals in North America." *Samar: South Asian Magazine for Action and Reflection* 14 (fall–winter): 11–14.

Mani, Lata. 1993. "Gender, Class and Cultural Conflict: Indu Krishnan's *Knowing Her Place.*" In *Our Feet Walk the Sky: Women of the South Asian Diaspora,* ed. Women of South Asian Descent Collective. San Francisco: Aunt Lute.

Manuel, Peter. 2000. *East Indian Music in the West Indies: Tan-singing, Chutney, and the Making of Indo-Caribbean Culture.* Philadelphia: Temple University Press.

————. 2006. *Caribbean Currents: Caribbean Music from Rumba to Reggae.* Philadelphia: Temple University Press.

Marable, Manning. 1994. "Building Coalitions among Communities of Color: Beyond Racial Identity Politics." In *Blacks, Latinos, and Asians in Urban America: Status and Prospects for Politics and Activism,* ed. James Jennings. Westport, Conn.: Praeger.

Marchetti, Gina. 1994. *Romance and the 'Yellow Peril': Race, Sex, and Discursive Strategies in Hollywood Film.* Berkeley: University of California Press.

Mathew, Biju, and Vijay Prashad. 2000. "The Protean Forms of Yankee Hindutva." *Ethnic and Racial Studies* 23 (3) 516–34.

McBride, Dwight. 2005. *Why I Hate Abercrombie & Fitch: Essays on Race and Sexuality.* New York: New York University Press.

McRobbie, Angela. 2000. *Feminism and Youth Culture.* 2nd ed. New York: Routledge.

McWhorter, John. 2008. *All about the Beat: Why Hip-Hop Can't Save Black America.* New York: Gotham.

Mercer, Kobena. 1995. "Black Hair/Style Politics." In *Cultural Remix: Theories of Politics and the Popular,* ed. Erica Carter, James Donald, and Judith Squires. London: Lawrence and Wishart.

Miller, Kevin. 2004. "Bolly'hood Remix." *Institute for Studies in American Music* 33 (2): 6–7, 15.

Modood, Tariq. 1994. "Political Blackness and British Asians." *Sociology* 28 (4): 859–76.

Mohammad-Arif, Aminah. 2002. *Salaam America: South Asian Muslims in New York*. London: Anthem.

Monson, Ingrid. 1995. "The Problem with White Hipness: Race, Gender, and Cultural Conceptions of Jazz Historical Discourse." *Journal of the American Musicological Society* 48 (3): 396–422.

Moran, Rachel. 2003. *Interracial Intimacy: The Regulation of Race and Romance*. Chicago: University of Chicago Press.

Morgan, Joan. 2000. *When Chickenheads Come Home to Roost: My Life as a Hip-Hop Feminist*. New York: Simon and Schuster.

Morris, Rosalind. 1995. "All Made Up: Performance Theory and the New Anthropology of Sex and Gender." *Annual Review of Anthropology* 24: 567–92.

Mullen, Bill. 2003. "Du Bois, *Dark Princess*, and the Afro-Asian International." *Positions* 11 (1): 217–39.

———. 2004. *Afro-Orientalism*. Minneapolis: University of Minnesota Press.

Mullen, Bill, and Cathryn Watson, eds. 2005. *W. E. B. Du Bois on Asia: Crossing the World Color Line*. Jackson: University of Mississippi Press.

Naipaul, V. S. 1962. *The Middle Passage: Impressions of Five Societies — British, French and Dutch — in the West Indies and South America*. London: A. Deutsch.

Nair, Ajay, and Murali Balaji, eds. 2008. *Desi Rap: Hip Hop and South Asian America*. New York: Lexington.

Neal, Mark Anthony. 2005. *New Black Man*. New York: Routledge.

Neckerman, Kathryn, Prudence Carter, and Jennifer Lee. 1999. "Segmented Assimilation and Minority Cultures of Mobility." *Ethnic and Racial Studies* 22 (6): 945–65.

Niranjana, Tejaswini. 2006. *Mobilizing India: Women, Music, and Migration between India and Trinidad*. Durham: Duke University Press.

O'Brien, Eileen. 2008. *The Racial Middle: Latinos and Asian Americans Living beyond the Racial Divide*. New York: New York University Press.

Ogbar, Jeffrey. 2007. *Hip-Hop Revolution: The Culture and Politics of Rap*. Lawrence: University Press of Kansas.

Okihiro, Gary. 1994. *Margins and Mainstreams: Asians in American History and Culture*. Seattle: University of Washington Press.

Omatsu, Glenn. 2000. "The 'Four Prisons' and the Movements of Liberation: Asian American Activism from the 1960s to the 1990s." In *Asian American Studies: A Reader*, ed. Jean Wu and Min Song. New Brunswick: Rutgers University Press.

Omi, Michael, and Howard Winant. 1994. *Racial Formation in the United States: From the 1960s to the 1990s.* 2nd ed. New York: Routledge.

Ong, Aihwa. 1998. *Flexible Citizenship: The Cultural Logics of Transnationality.* Durham: Duke University Press.

Ongiri, Amy. 2002. "'He Wanted to Be Just like Bruce Lee': African Americans, Kung Fu Theater and Cultural Exchange at the Margins." *Journal of Asian American Studies* 5 (1): 31–40.

Oonk, Gijsbert, ed. 2007. *Global Indian Diasporas: Exploring Trajectories of Migration and Theory.* Amsterdam: Amsterdam University Press.

Osumare, Halifu. 2007. *The Africanist Aesthetic in Global Hip Hop: Power Moves.* New York: Palgrave Macmillan.

Palumbo-Liu, David. 1999. *Asian/America: Historical Crossings of a Racial Frontier.* Stanford: Stanford University Press.

Parenti, Christian. 1999. *Lockdown America: Police and Prisons in the Age of Crisis.* London: Verso.

Parker, David. 1995. *Through Different Eyes: The Cultural Identities of Young Chinese People in Britain.* Aldershot, England: Avebury.

Perry, Imani. 2004. *Prophets of the Hood: Politics and Poetics in Hip Hop.* Durham: Duke University Press.

Portes, Alejandro, ed. 1996. *The New Second Generation.* New York: Russell Sage Foundation.

Portes, Alejandro, and Min Zhou. 1993. "The New Second Generation: Segmented Assimilation and Its Variants among Post-1965 Immigrant Youth." *Annals* 530: 74–96.

Portes, Alejandro, and Ruben G. Rumbaut, eds. 1990. *Immigrant America: A Portrait.* Berkeley: University of California Press.

———. 2001. *Legacies: The Story of the Immigrant Second Generation.* Berkeley: University of California Press.

Potter, Russell. 1995. *Spectacular Vernaculars: Hip Hop and the Politics of Postmodernism.* Albany: State University of New York.

Pough, Gwendolyn. 2004. *Check It While I Wreck It: Black Womanhood, Hip-Hop Culture, and the Public Sphere.* Boston: Northeastern University Press.

———. 2006. Interview by Faedra Carpenter. *Callaloo* 29 (3): 808–14.

Pough, Gwendolyn, Elaine Richardson, Aisha Durham, and Rachel Raimist, eds. 2007. *Home Girls Make Some Noise: Hip-Hop Feminism Anthology.* Mira Loma, Calif.: Parker.

Poulson-Bryant, Scott. 1999. "Fear of a White Planet." *Source,* June.

Prashad, Vijay. 2000. *The Karma of Brown Folk.* Minnesota: University of Minnesota Press.

———. 2001. *Everybody Was Kung Fu Fighting: Afro-Asian Connections and the Myth of Cultural Purity.* Boston: Beacon.

———. 2005. "How the Hindus Became Jews: American Racism after 9/11." *South Atlantic Quarterly* 104 (3): 583–606.

Pulido, Laura. 2006. *Black, Brown, Yellow, and Left: Radical Activism in Los Angeles.* Berkeley: University of California Press.

Purkayastha, Bandana. 2005. *Negotiating Ethnicity: Second-Generation South Asian Americans Traverse a Transnational World.* New Brunswick: Rutgers University Press.

Radano, Ronald, and Philip Bohlman, eds. 2000. *Music and the Racial Imagination.* Chicago: University of Chicago Press.

Radhakrishnan, R. 1994. "Is the Ethnic 'Authentic' in the Diaspora?" In *The State of Asian America: Activism and Resistance in the 1990s,* ed. Karen Aguilar-San Juan. Boston: South End.

Raimist, Rachel. 2004. "Interview with Rachel Raimist." *Velvet Light Trap* 53: 59–65.

Rajagopal, Arvind. 1995. "Better than Blacks? Or Hum Kale Hain to Kya Hua?" *Samar: South Asian Magazine for Action and Reflection* 5 (9): 5.

Rajan, Gita, and Shailja Sharma. 2006. *New Cosmopolitanisms: South Asians in the U.S.* Stanford: Stanford University Press.

Rana, Junaid. 2002. "Muslims across the Brown Atlantic: The Position of Muslims in the U.K. and the U.S." *Samar: South Asian Magazine for Action and Reflection* 15 (summer/fall): www.samarmagazine.org (accessed December 2003).

Raphael-Hernandez, Heike, and Shannon Steen, eds. 2006. *AfroAsian Encounters: Culture, History, Politics.* New York: New York University Press.

Rios, Victor. 2004. "From Knucklehead to Revolutionary: Urban Youth Culture and Social Transformation." *Journal of Urban Youth Culture,* http://juyc.info (accessed May 12, 2006).

Rivera, Raquel. 1997. "Rap in Puerto Rico: Reflections from the Margins." In *Globalization and Survival in the Black Diaspora: The New Urban Challenge,* ed. Charles Green, ed. Albany: State University of New York Press.

———. 2003. *New York Ricans from the Hip Hop Zone.* New York: Palgrave Macmillan.

Rodney, Walter. 1969. *Groundings with my Brothers.* London: Bogle-L'Ouverture.

Rodriguez, Dylan. 2006. *Forced Passages: Imprisoned Radical Intellectuals and the U.S. Prison Regime.* Minneapolis: University of Minnesota Press.

Roediger, David. 1998. "What to Make of Wiggers: A Work in Progress." In *Generations of Youth: Youth Cultures and History in Twentieth-Century America,* ed. Joe Austin and Michael Willard. New York: New York University Press.

Rose, Tricia. 1994. *Black Noise: Rap Music and Black Culture in Contemporary America.* Hanover, N.H.: Wesleyan University Press.

Rudrappa, Sharmila. 2002. "Disciplining Desire in Making the Home: Engendering Ethnicity in Indian Immigrant Families." In *Second Generation: Ethnic Identity among Asian Americans*, ed. Pyong Min Gap. Walnut Creek, Calif.: Alta Mira.

———. 2004. *Ethnic Routes to Becoming American: Indian Immigrants and the Cultures of Citizenship*. New Brunswick: Rutgers University Press.

Rumbaut, Ruben. 1994. Crucible Within: Ethnic Identity, Self-Esteem, and Segmented Assimilation among Children of Immigrants." *International Migration Review* 28 (4): 748–94.

Rumbaut, Ruben, and Alejandro Portes, eds. 2001. *Ethnicities: Children of Immigrants in America*. Berkeley: University of California Press.

Russo, Richard. 2008. *Bridge of Sighs*. New York: Vintage.

Sacks, Oliver. 2007. *Musicophilia: Tales of Music and the Brain*. New York: Alfred A. Knopf.

San Juan, E., Jr. 1992. *Racial Formation/Critical Transformations: Articulation of Power in Ethnic and Racial Studies in the United States*. Atlantic Highlands, N.J.: Humanities Press.

Saran, Parmatma. 1980. *Asian Indian Experience in the United States*. Cambridge, Mass.: Schenkman.

Schloss, Joseph. 2004. *Making Beats: The Art of Sample-Based Hip-Hop*. Middletown, Conn.: Wesleyan University Press.

Schlund-Vials, Cathy. 2008. "A Transnational Hip Hop Nation: Cambodian American Rap and Memorialisation." *Life Writing* 5 (1): 11–27.

Schmidt, Garbi. 2004. *Islam in Urban America: Sunni Muslims in Chicago*. Philadelphia: Temple University Press.

Scott, David. 2005. "Stuart Hall's Ethics." *Small Axe* 9 (1): 1–16.

Sen, Rinku. 2006. Black Men, Asian Women." In *ColorLines: The National News Magazine on Race and Politics* (spring), http://www.colorlines.com (accessed February 9, 2009).

Shankar, Lavina, and Rajini Srikanth, eds. 1998. *A Part, Yet Apart: South Asians in Asian America*. Philadelphia: Temple University Press.

Shankar, Shalini. 2008. *Desi Land: Teen Culture, Class, and Success in Silicon Valley*. Durham: Duke University Press.

Sharma, Nitasha. 1999. "Down by Law: The Effects and Responses of Copyright Restrictions on Sampling in Rap." *Journal of Political and Legal Anthropology* 21 (1): 1–13.

———. 2001. "Rotten Coconuts and Other Strange Fruit: A Slice of Hip Hop from the West Coast." *Samar: South Asian Magazine for Action and Reflection* 14 (November): 30–32.

———. 2007. "Musical Manifestos: Desi Hip Hop Artists Sound Off on Capitalism and Sexism." *Subcontinental: The Journal of South Asian American Public Affairs* 4 (spring): 25–38.

———. 2008. "Polyvalent Voices: Ethnic and Racialized Desi Hip Hop." In *Desi Rap: South Asian Americans in Hip Hop*, ed. Ajay Nair and Murali Balaji. New York: Lexington.

Sharma, Sanjay, John Hutnyk, and Ashwani Sharma, eds. 1996. *(Dis)-Orienting Rhythms: The Politics of the New Asian Dance Music.* 2nd ed. London: Zed.

Sharpley-Whiting, T. Denean. 2007. *Pimps Up, Ho's Down: Hip Hop's Hold on Young Black Women.* New York: New York University Press.

Shinagawa, Larry, and Gin Yong Pang. 1996. "Asian American Panethnicity and Intermarriage." *Amerasia* 22 (2): 127–52.

Singh, Amritjit. 1996. "African Americans and the New Immigrants." In *Between the Lines: South Asians and Postcoloniality*, ed. Deepika Bahri and Mary Vasudeva. Philadelphia: Temple University Press.

Song, Min. 1998. "Pahkar Singh's Argument with Asian America: Color and the Structure of Race Formation." In *A Part, Yet Apart: South Asians in Asian America*, ed. Lavina Shankar and Rajini Srikanth. Philadelphia: Temple University Press.

Spivak, Gayatri. 1995. *The Spivak Reader: Selected Works of Gayatri Spivak.* New York: Routledge.

Srikanth, Rajini. 2004. *The World Next Door: South Asian American Literature and the Idea of America.* Philadelphia: Temple University Press.

Strauss, Neil. 1999. "The Hip-Hop Nation, Whose Is It? A Land with Rhythm and Beats for All." *New York Times*, April 22.

Swedenburg, Ted. 2002. "The Post-September 11 Arab Wave in World Music." *Middle East Report* 224 (autumn): 44–48.

Takagi, Dana. 2000. "Maiden Voyage: Excursion into Sexuality and Identity Politics in Asian America." In *Asian American Studies: A Reader*, ed. Jean Wu and Min Song. New Brunswick: Rutgers University Press.

Takaki, Ronald. 1979. *Iron Cages: Race and Culture in Nineteenth-Century America.* New York: Alfred A. Knopf.

———. 1989. *Strangers from a Different Shore: A History of Asian Americans.* Boston: Little, Brown.

Tate, Greg. 1992. *Flyboy in the Buttermilk: Essays on Contemporary America.* New York: Simon and Schuster.

———, ed. 2003. *Everything but the Burden: What White People Are Taking from Black Culture.* New York: Broadway.

Tate, Shirley. 2005. *Black Skins, Black Masks: Hybridity, Dialogism, Performativity.* Aldershot, England: Ashgate.

Thayil, Jeet. 2003. "Bappi Lahiri vs Dr. Dre! And the winner is . . ." *India Abroad* (February 14, 2003, Issue 20, page A8; accessed September 27, 2007).

Thompson, Robert. 1983. *Flash of the Spirit: African and Afro-American Art and Philosophy*. New York: Vintage.

Thornton, Michael, and Harold Gates. 2001. "Black, Japanese, and American: An Asian American Identity Yesterday and Today." In *The Sum of Our Parts: Mixed-Heritage Asian Americans*, ed. Teresa Williams-Leon and Cynthia Nakashima. Philadelphia: Temple University Press.

Thuc Phi, Thien-bao. 2008. "Yellow Lines: Asian Americans and Hip Hop." In *Afro Asia: Revolutionary Political and Cultural Connections between African Americans and Asian Americans*, ed. Fred Ho and Bill Mullen. Durham: Duke University Press.

Tiongson, Antonio, Jr. 2006. "Filipino Youth Cultural Politics and DJ Culture." Ph.D. dissertation, University of California, San Diego.

Touré. 1999. "The Hip-Hop Nation: Whose Rap Is It? In the End, Black Men Must Lead." *New York Times*, August 22.

Tseng, Judy. 2007. "Asian American Rap: Expression through Alternative Forms." Model Minority, http://www.modelminority.com (accessed January 20).

Tuan, Mia. 1999. *Forever Foreigners or Honorary Whites? The Asian Ethnic Experience Today*. New Brunswick: Rutgers University Press.

Turner, Victor. 1967. *The Forest of Symbols: Aspects of Ndembu Ritual*. Ithaca: Cornell University Press.

———. 1969. *The Ritual Process: Structure and Anti-Structure*. Chicago: Aldine.

Twine, Frances. 1996. "Heterosexual Alliances: The Romantic Management of Racial Identity." In *The Multiracial Experience: Racial Borders as the New Frontier*, ed. Maria Root. Thousand Oaks, Calif.: Sage.

Valdez, Zulema. 2009. "Agency and Structure in Panethnic Identity Formation: The Case of Latino/a Entrepreneurs." In *How the United States Racializes Latinos: At Home and Abroad*, ed. Jose Cobas, Jorge Duany, and Joe Feagin. Boulder: Paradigm.

van Gennep, Arnold. 1960 [1909]. *Rites of Passage*. London: Routlege and Kegan Paul.

Visweswaran, Kamala. 1993. "Predicaments of the Hyphen." In *Our Feet Walk the Sky: Women of the South Asian Diaspora*, ed. The Women of South Asian Descent Collective. San Francisco: Aunt Lute.

Wald, Gayle. 2000. *Crossing the Line: Racial Passing in Twentieth-Century U.S. Literature and Culture*. Durham: Duke University Press.

Wallace, Michele. 1979. *Black Macho and the Myth of the Superwoman*. New York: Dial.

Wang, Oliver. 2005. "Legions of Boom." Ph.D. dissertation, University of California, Berkeley.

———. 2006. "These Are the Breaks: Hip-Hop and AfroAsian Cultural (Dis)connection." In *AfroAsian Encounters: Culture, History, Politics*, ed.

Heike Raphael-Hernandez and Shannon Steen. New York: New York University Press.

———. 2007. "Rapping and Repping Asian: Race, Authenticity, and the Asian American MC." In *Alien Encounters: Popular Culture in Asian America*, ed. Mimi Nguyen and Thuy Tu. Durham: Duke University Press.

———. Forthcoming 2011. *Legions of Boom: Filipino American Mobile Disc Jockeys of the San Francisco Bay Area*. Durham: Duke University Press.

Waters, Mary. 1990. *Ethnic Options: Choosing Identities in America*. Berkeley: University of California Press.

———. 1995. "Optional Ethnicities: For Whites Only?" In *Origins and Destinies*, ed. Silvia Pedraza and Ruben Rumbaut. Belmont, Calif.: Wadsworth.

Watkins, Craig. 2005. *Hip Hop Matters: Politics, Pop Culture, and the Struggle for the Soul of Movement*. Boston: Beacon.

Weisman, Jan. 1996. "An 'Other' Way of Life: The Empowerment of Alterity in the Interracial Individual." In *The Multiracial Experience: Racial Borders as the New Frontier*, ed. Maria Root. Thousand Oaks, Calif.: Sage.

White, Armond. 1996. "Who Wants to See Ten Niggers Play Basketball?" In *Droppin' Science: Critical Essays on Rap Music and Hip Hop Culture*, ed. William Perkins. Philadelphia: Temple University Press.

Williams, Teresa. 1996. "Race as Process: Reassessing the 'What Are You' Encounters of Biracial Individuals." In *The Multiracial Experience: Racial Borders as the New Frontier*, ed. Maria Root. Thousand Oaks, Calif.: Sage.

Williams-Leon, Teresa, and Cynthia Nakashima, eds. 2001. *The Sum of Our Parts: Mixed-Heritage Asian Americans*. Philadelphia: Temple University Press.

Wolf, Eric. 1982. *Europe and the People without History*. Berkeley: University of California Press.

Wong, Deborah. 2004. *Speak It Louder: Asian Americans Making Music*. New York: Routledge.

Wong, Sau-ling. 1995. "Denationalization Reconsidered: Asian American Cultural Criticism at a Theoretical Crossroads." *Amerasia Journal* 21 (1–2): 1–27.

Wood, Joe. 1998. "The Yellow Negro." *Transition: An International Review* 7: 40–66.

Woods, Clyde. 1998. *Development Arrested: Race, Power, and the Blues in the Mississippi Delta*. New York: Verso.

Wu, Frank. 2002. *Yellow: Race in America beyond Black and White*. New York: Basic.

Yancey, George. 2003. *Who Is White? Latinos, Asians, and the New Black/Nonblack Divide*. Boulder: Lynne Rienner.

Yuh, Ji-Yeon. 2004. *Beyond the Shadow of Camptown: Korean Military Brides in America*. New York: New York University Press.

Yun, Lisa. 2007. *The Coolie Speaks: Chinese Indentured Laborers and African Slaves in Cuba*. Philadelphia: Temple University Press.

Zhou, Min. 2004. "Are Asian Americans Becoming 'White'?" *Context* 3 (1): 29–37.

Zhou, Min, and Carl Bankston III. 1998. *Growing Up American: How Vietnamese Children Adapt to Life in the United States*. New York: Russell Sage Foundation.

Ziff, Bruce, and Pratima Rao. 1997. "Introduction to Cultural Appropriation: A Framework for Analysis." In *Borrowed Power: Essays in Cultural Appropriation*, ed. Bruce Ziff and Pratima Rao. New Brunswick: Rutgers University Press.

Index

Artwallah festival, 79, 82, 149, 307n22
Arun (desi DJ), 117, 221, 231, 234
Asian Americans: appeal of hip hop for, 197; Blackness of hip hop and, 213–16; Black rappers' influence on, 311n5; comparative racial studies through multisited ethnography and, 33–36; ethnic identity and, 39–41, 304n2; gender and sexuality issues for, 142, 169–71; global-historical connections of, 120–29; hip hop and, 10–13, 17–23; identity politics and, 27–29; multiple racial affinities of, 112, 309n13; multiracialism of hip hop and, 218–30; post–September 11 era and identity of, 130–35. See also desis; South Asian Americans
Asian Dub Foundation (British Asian group), 126, 201, 304n25
Asma (desi radio producer), 49, 107–8, 152–53, 209
assimilation: desis' college experiences and, 60–74. See also segmented assimilation
Association of Indians in America, 29–33
authenticity: Afro-Asian identity and, 32–33; anti-essentialism and, 271–82; Blackness of hip hop and, 212–16, 223–30; commodification of hip hop and, 217–30, 249–52; desi college experiences and desire for, 62–73; desi hip hop artists and, 20–23, 191–92, 303n16

Babri Masjid (mosque), 307n20
Bahamadia (Black rapper), 310n11
Baraka, Amiri, 21, 199, 215, 222
Basement Bhangra, 250
battle rapping, 104, 222, 308n7

Bay Area rappers, 18, 43–44, 303n13
Beni B (Black DJ), 248
"Beware of the Boys" (Panjabi MC), 265
bhajan, 270, 280–81
bhangra music, 125–29
bharatanatyam dance movements, 78
Biggie Smalls (Black rapper), 215
Big Pun (Puerto Rican rapper), 215
"Bin Laden" (Immortal Technique), 267
bin Laden, Osama, 267
"Bird in the Hand, A" (Ice Cube), 204
Black British identity: emergence of, 32–33; global-historical connections of South Asians and, 125–29
Black Entertainment Television (BET), 20
"Black Men, Asian Women" (article), 176–77
Black Nationalism, influence on desi hip hop of, xi, 179, 192, 203–12
Black Panthers, 43, 102, 128, 194
Black Power movement: Afro-Asian identity and, 31; Brown Pride and, 203–12; exceptional desis and, 43–44; influence on desi hip hop of, xi, 192, 204
Blacks and Black culture: Afro-Asian precedents for, 29–33; appropriation of, 238–64; Black masculinity and Brown identity in, 180–85; Brown women in, 149–56; community formation in, 209–12; desi hip hop artists and, 2–5, 10–13, 88–91, 160, 191–212, 222–30; desi racialized sexuality and, 161–65; female art-

Chuck D (Black rapper), 201–5, 208

Civil Rights Act of 1964, 115–16

Civil Rights Movement, 116

classism: and appeal of hip hop, 190–91; college experience of desis and, 63–73; desis in racially mixed neighborhoods and, 48–51, 99–104; ethnic identity and, 304n2; ethnic insularity and, 44–47, 305nn5–6; exceptional desis and, 41–44; first-generation desi racial consciousness and, 94–95; middle-class desis and, 105–9; racial consciousness of desis and, 91–99; South Asian American hip hop artists' ambivalence concerning, ix–xi; South Asians as honorary Whites and, 25–29, 303n19

clique formation, desi college experiences and, 57–73

co-ethnicity: appropriation and othering and, 241–64; middle-class desis and, 107–9; second-generation desis and, 99

Coldcut (group), 255

college education: Black-desi stereotypes concerning, 96–99; desis' view of, 57–73; Indian hegemony and non-Indian South Asians and, 65–69; racial differences in experiences of, 102–4

colonialism: Afro-Asian precedents and, 29–33; appeal of hip hop and, 201–2; first-generation desi racial consciousness and, 93–95; global-historical connections of South Asians and Blacks and, 118–29; Hindu religious hegemony and, 53–57

colorism: desi romance and sexuality and, 178–79;

second-generation desi racial consciousness and, 96–99

"Colour Line" (Asian Dub Foundation), 201

Coltrane, John, 309n22

Combs, Sean "Diddy" (Black producer), 259, 313n8

commodification of hip hop: authenticity in face of, 271–79; desi hip hop artists and, 216–32, 312n8

community formation: Black music and, 209–12; desis in racially mixed communities and, 49–51; through hip hop, 286–99; polycultural sampling and, 23–29

comparative racial studies: methodology for, 33–36; political activism and, 296–99

Condry, Ian, 24–25, 265

Connerly, Ward, 17

consumption patterns of hip hop: college experience of desis and, 63–73; and of multiracial hip hop, 216–30, 312n8

Cookie Crew (group), 153

copyright law, 303n17; commercialization of hip hop and, 252

corridos (ballads), 201

crack cocaine, history of hip hop and, 302n12

crosscultural borrowing: appropriation and identification in, 264–71; ethnic hip hop and, 10–13; global-historical connections of hip hop and, 125–29, 222–33; political activism and, 289–99; religious hegemony and, 53–57; in South Asian and Black relations, 235–38

cross-racial studies, comparative racial studies through multisited ethnography and, 34–36

culture: appropriation of, 263–64,

279–82; desi artists' view of, 56–57. *See also* multiculturalism; polyculturalism

Cypress Hill (group), 78, 215

Da Brat (Black rapper), 151, 310n9

dandia raas (Gujarati stick dance), 10, 301n6

Dark Princess: A Romance (Du Bois), 178

Davey D (Black DJ), 192, 200, 213–14

Davis, Angela, 124–25

Dead Prez (group), 201

Deejay Bella (desi DJ), 9–10, 46, 53, 301n5; on appeal of hip hop, 196, 202, 208, 211; Black hip hop and, 150–56; on community formation through hip hop, 211; on family pressures, 166; gender and sexuality issues for, 142–46, 183–85; global-historical connections of hip hop and, 125, 226–30, 277, 280; middle-class background of, 106; political activism of, 286; production by, 106–8, 308n10; Sistrens created by, 186–87

Deep Dickollective (group), 310n11

Def Poetry Jam (TV series), 146

De La Soul (group), 273

Desh Pardesh (Canadian arts festival), 289

Desi Rap: Hip-Hop and South Asian America (Nair and Balaji), 8

desis and desi culture: appeal of hip hop in, 190–212; appropriation of Blackness by, 238–64, 269–71; college experiences of, 57–73; comparative racial studies and, 34–36; conservative backlash against, 197–98; consumption trends among, 238–39; cross-racial identities

of, 88–91; defined, ix; ethnic identity of, 39–41; exceptionalism of, 41–44; female artists and, 171–80; first-generation racial identities among, 93–95; gender and sexuality and, 138–89; geographic concentrations of, 8–10; global-historical connections with Blacks and, 117–29; heterogeneity of, 40–41; Hindu religious hegemony and, 52–57; hip hop production by, x–xi, 6–10, 51–57, 85–87, 106–9, 216–30, 308n10, 308n12; history of hip hop and, 17–23; Indian hegemony and non-Indian South Asians and, 65–69; insularity and classism of, 44–47, 305nn5–6; marriage attitudes of, 159–60, 165–71, 310n14; "model minority" label for, 14–16, 302n10; multiracial affinities of, 48–51, 91–104, 109–17, 220–30, 279–82, 306n10; panethnicity and, 69–73; politicization of, 194–95, 283–99; polycultural sampling and community formation of, 23–29; racial consciousness of, 1–5, 216; racialized masculinity and, 160–65; second-generation desis and hip hop culture, 13–17, 43–44, 218–20; sexuality expressed by, 156–85; stereotypes of hip hop in, 191–92; third-generation, 306n15. *See also* Indian Americans; South Asian Americans

Desis Rising Up and Moving (DRUM), 289

dhol (drum), 78, 307n21

Diasporadics (American arts festival), 288

"Disco" (Slum Village), 266

Disturbing Silence (group), 149

DJ Quik (Black rapper), 249–52, 255

DJ Rekha (desi DJ), 250–52

D'Lo (desi artist), 9, 45–47, 52–53, 64–66, 68, 70–71, 301n4, 305n8, 307n19; on appeal of hip hop, 198, 203, 205, 210; Black hip hop and, 150–56; Black masculinity and Brown identity and, 180–85; on Brown identity, 206–8; global-historical connections of South Asians and Blacks and, 118–19, 127–29, 283; multiracialism of hip hop and, 105–9, 224–26, 270, 278, 280; music production by, 149, 190; political activism of, 209–10, 288–91, 299; post-September 11 era and, 131–35; transgender identity of, 142, 146–49, 156–58, 178, 183–85, 310n5; WADDAG group formed by, 187

Dotbusters violence, 308n4

double consciousness of race: first-generation desis and, 92–93; multiple racial affinities of desis and, 111–17

Doug E. Fresh and the Get Fresh Crew (group), 14, 302n8

Dr. Dre (Black producer), 249–52, 255, 260

Du Bois, W. E. B., 31, 178, 311n19

Dyson, Michael Eric, 242, 311n1

education, desi hip hop culture and influence of, 54–57

Elliott, Missy (Black rapper), 246, 253–54, 260, 266

Eminem (White rapper), 239, 267

Eric B (Black rapper), 255

essentialism: Afro-Asian identity and, 32–33; multiple racial affinities of desis and, 111–17. See also anti-essentialism

ethnic hip hop, 10–13; desi em-brace of, 40–41, 51–57, 190–91, 218–30; South Asian American production of, ix–x

ethnicity: alternative modes of, 37–41; college experiences of desis and, 57–73; desi conceptions of, 88–91; hip hop as expression of, 73–85; hybrid identities and, 303n21; multiple racial affinities of desis and, 119–17; polycultural sampling and, 23–29; South Asian American hip hop artists' ambivalence concerning, ix–xi

"Eyes Closed in America" (D'Lo), 288

family influences: desi marriage pressures and, 165–71; desis' multiracialism and, 49–51, 306n11; Hindu religious hegemony and, 51–57; for second-generation desis, 96–99; South Asian American hip hop artists' ambivalence concerning, ix–xi

family reunification policy (Immigration Act of 1965), Indian immigrants and, 14–15, 302n10

Fanon, Franz, 228

Fat Joe (Puerto Rican rapper), 215

Fear of a Black Planet (Public Enemy), 203

Feenom Circle (group), 12, 94, 164–65, 224

female artists: Black male business environment and, 141–56, 309n1; desi and Black culture and, 139–89; in desi hip hop, 266–67; hip hop misogyny and, x–xi, 151–56, 158; romance and marriage among, 171–80; sexual ambiguity for, 180–85; womanist and queer-friendly spaces for, 185–87

50 Cent (Black rapper), 217, 266
"Fight the Power" (Public Enemy), 196, 203
Filipinos: history of hip hop and, 19–20, 200; in Louisiana, 308n3
first-generation desis, racial consciousness of, 93–95
Fitzpatrick, Chris, 258–59
Flores, Juan, x
Foucault, Michel, 202, 297
Foxy Brown (Black rapper), 153
Fresh, Doug E., 14, 302n8
Fresh Prince of Bel-Air, The (TV series), 306n11
"From Silent Confusion to Blaring Healing" (D'Lo), 45, 156–57
"Fuck tha Police" (N.W.A.), 204
FunDaMental (British Asian group), 33, 126, 304n25

Game, The (Black rapper), 313n7
Gandhi, Mahatma, 12, 123–25, 297; hip hop ethnicity and, 74
gangsta rap, 18, 200–201, 204
garba (Gujarati dance), 144
Garvey, Marcus, 123, 309n19
Gates, Daryl, 204
gender: authenticity in hip hop and, 271–79; college experiences of desis and, 62–73; comparative racial studies through multisited ethnography and, 35–36; consumption patterns of desis and, 64–73; desi culture and negotiations of, 156–85; desis in racially mixed communities and, 49–51; double standard concerning, 159–60, 166–71, 310n12; marriage pressures on desis and, 165–71, 310n14; South Asian hip hop and, 138–89. *See also* sexuality
"Get Ur Freak On" (Elliott), 246, 253–54, 260
"Girls, Girls, Girls" (Jay-Z), 260–61

Giroux, Henry, 118
global capitalism, multicultural music production and, 249–52
global race consciousness: authenticity in hip hop and, 271–79; desi hip hop and, 225–30; polycultural sampling and, 26–29; post–September 11 era and, 130–35; South Asian and Black relations and, 234–38; of South Asian hip hop artists, 1–5
Gopinath, Gayatri, 266
Gramsci, Antonio, 297
Grand Puba (Black rapper), 204
Green Lantern (Italian American DJ), 267, 313n15
Guevara, Che, 267

habitus, desi sexuality and, 187–89
Halberstam, Judith, 161
Hall, Stuart, 28–29, 32, 50, 88–89
hapa (mixed race individuals), 13–14
Hard Kaur (British Asian rapper), 33, 310n4
Haza, Ofra, 255
Hebdige, Dick, 202
hegemonic status of desis, 41–44, 52–57, 65–69
Himalayan Project (album), 119–20
Himalayan Project (group), 9, 75–77, 104, 115, 131, 242–43
Hindu hegemony of Indian Americans, 52–57, 65–69
"Hiphopistan: South Asians in Hip Hop" (event), 6–10, 301n2, 311n4
hip hop music and culture: Bay Area popularity of, 144, 310n3; Blackness of, 212–16, 221–30; in college experience of desis, 63–73; copyright law and, 303n17; cross-racial identifications in, 88–91; cultural criticism of, 16–17, 302n11; demographics of, 8–10; desi

tion of Blackness by, 238–40, 263–64; internment of, 287, 311n3

Jay-Z, 245, 259–63, 265–67, 269

jazz music: hip hop comparisons with, 199, 204, 215–16, 264–65; racial crossings in, 222, 309n22; White fascination with, 264, 313n12

Jin (Chinese American rapper), 19–20, 121, 309n16

Jindal, Bobby, 311n15

Jonny (desi hip hop journalist), 1, 10, 46–47, 59–61, 310n2; on appeal of hip hop, 193–94, 198, 205–6, 210–11; on authenticity in hip hop, 274, 276, 279; middle-class background of, 106; on multiple racial affinities of desis, 111–13; music production by, 107–8

Jungle Fever (Lee), 169, 311n16

Jyoti (Chakravorty), 313n5

"Kaliyon Ka Chaman" (Anand), 251

kanji tattoos, 260

Karmacy (group), 9, 11, 38, 54, 71, 74–75, 77–85, 168, 312n9

KB (desi rapper), 9, 11; on appeal of hip hop, 195–96, 210–12; on appropriation and othering, 242; on authenticity in hip hop, 273; on classism, 48–49; college experiences of, 57–58, 65, 98–99; ethnicity expressed by, 37–38, 72–74, 88; on family influences, 96; global-historical connections of South Asians and, 128–29; on marriage and family pressures, 167–71; on multiracialism of hip hop, 218–21, 312n9; political activism of, 287, 291

Kelley, Robin, 195, 257

Kelly, R. (Black R&B singer), 246–48, 268

Khalnayak (Ghai), 266

Kibria, Nazli, 62, 93–95

Kich, George, 110

Kid Frost (Chicano rapper), 78, 215

King, Martin Luther, Jr., 12, 123–24

King, Rodney, 128

Kitwana, Bakari, 160

Kochiyama, Yuri, 123–24, 285

Kojoe (Japanese rapper), 269

Kool Herc (Black DJ), 19, 100, 215

Korean immigrants, 287, 308n1

KRS-One (Black rapper), 297

Kuttin Kandi (Filipina DJ), 150

Kwanzaa festival, 279–80

La Bella Mafia (Lil' Kim), 312n4

"La Di Da Di (We Like to Party)" (Doug E. Fresh), 14

Lady of Rage (Black rapper), 310n11

Lahiri, Bappi (Indian producer), 249–52

Latino rappers: Blackness of hip hop and, 213–16; ethnic identity politics of, x; multiple affiliations of, 78, 200

Lee, Bruce, 19

"Legitimizing the Spirit Within" (D'Lo), 53

Lil' Kim (Black rapper), 153, 312n4

liminality: of desis in mixed-race neighborhoods, 51; South Asian ethnic identity and, 27–29

Lipsitz, George, x, 22–23, 125–26

Little India (magazine), 286

Lott, Eric, 179, 240

Maira, Sunaina, 21–22, 62–64, 161, 173, 175, 244

Malcolm X, 1, 12, 123–24, 208, 285

Malcolm X Jazz Festival, 177

Mangeshkar, Lata (Indian singer), 249

marginalized groups, Blackness adopted by, 108–9

Marley, Bob (reggae artist), 125–26, 278
marriage and divorce: desi expectations concerning, 159–60, 165–71; desi multiracial affiliations and, 49–51, 306n12; of female artists, 171–80
masculinity: Black hypersexuality stereotype and, 141, 172–80; Black masculinity and Brown identity, 180–85; Blackness of hip hop and, 213–16; female desi artists and tropes of, x–xi, 153–56, 180–85; Indian racialization of, 21–23; racialized sexuality of desi men, 160–65
"Masters Too" (Feenom Circle), 75–76, 94
Mathew, Biju, 42
Mazumdar, Sucheta, 97
MC Lyte (Black rapper), 151, 153
MC PraCh (Cambodian rapper), 19, 209
MC Trouble (Black rapper), 153
McWhorter, John, 196
media images: appropriation of Black culture in, 240–64; foreign stereotypes in, 250–51; gender stereotypes in hip hop and, 152–56; of urban Blacks, 190–91
"Mental Slavery" (Abstract/Humanity), 292
Mexican Americans, history of hip hop and, 19, 208
M.I.A. (British Asian artist), 33, 310n4
middle-class desis: college experiences of, 63–73; contact with Blacks and hip hop of, 105–9
Middle East, hip hop images of, 243–64
Middle Passage, The (Himalayan Project), 115, 119, 131, 242–43
"Middle Passage, The" (Himalayan Project), 76

mind/body dualism, South Asian immigrants and, 308n2
misogyny in hip hop, 151–56, 158
Miss E . . . So Addictive (Elliott), 260
Mississippi Masala (Nair), 29
"Misunderstanding" (Rawj), 102–3
mixed race studies, multiple racial affinities of desis and, 28, 109–17, 136
model minority myth: desi racial consciousness and, 94–95; desis in mixed-race neighborhoods and, 48–51, 101–4; exceptional desis and, 42–44; for Indian immigrants, 14–16; middle-class desis and, 105–9; polycultural sampling and, 25–29, 303n18; racialized sexuality of desi men and, 161–65; Reaganomics and deindustrialization and, 194–95
Mos Def (Black rapper), 267
Mountain Brothers (Chinese American rap group), 19, 127, 309n16
Movement, The (Karmacy), 74, 83–84
Moynihan Report (1965), 194
Mullen, Bill, 118, 177, 270
multiculturalism: Blackness of hip hop and, 214–16; desi ethnic insularity and, 47; desis in mixed-race neighborhoods and, 99–104; exceptional desis and, 42–44; second-generation desis and, 16–17, 19
multilingualism, Karmacy's use of, 77–85
multiracial affinities of hip hop, 109–17, 213–16, 312n7; desi hip hop artists and, 217–33
multisited ethnography, comparative racial studies through, 33–36

"Mundian to Bach Ke" (Panjabi MC), 247

musical production: Blackness of hip hop and, 213–16; Black ownership of, 237–38; gender and sexuality issues in, 142–46; power dynamics in, 246–53, 263–64; racial identity and, 135–37

Musicians United to Win Without War coalition, 266

Muslims: Black/desi connections to, 129–30; class aspirations of, 55–57; ethnic insularity of, 306n9; hip hop images of, 244–64; political activism of, 291–99; post–September 11 era images of, 130–35, 255–57; South Asian attitudes concerning, 287–88

Mystikal (Black rapper), 268

Naipaul, V. S., 119

Nair, Mira (Indian filmmaker), 29

Nas (Black rapper), 200

"Nas's Angels" (Nas), 266, 312n4

Neal, Mark Anthony, 151–52

"Neil" (Karmacy), 168

Nepali immigrants, desiness and panethnic identity of, 69–73

New Asian Cool, 244

"new cosmopolitans," in South Asian community, 55–57

New Right politics, "new cosmopolitans" in South Asian community and, 56

Nihjon, Raeshem (desi filmmaker), 8

Nimo (desi rapper), xiii, 9, 11, 78–80, 82–83, 221

"1964" (Himalayan Project), 115

non-essentialism, global-historical connections of South Asians and, 122–29

non-Indian South Asians, 65–73, 118

"No Shame" (D'Lo), 46–47

Not in Our Name war protest, 149

"Nuttin Nice" (Himalayan Project), 119

Nuyoricans, 215; history of hip hop and, 19, 100, 200, 208

N.W.A. (Niggaz with Attitude) (group), 18, 106, 197, 204, 308n9

Oasis (dance club), 177

Obama, Barack, 313n15

Oblique Brown (Chee Malabar), 9, 132–33, 309n23

"Oblique Brown" (Chee Malabar), 133–34

Omatsu, Glenn, 43–44

Omi, Michael, 27

"One Cry" (Jin), 120–21

"One Struggle" (Vivek), 226–29, 285

Orientalism: American racism and, 95; appropriation of Middle Eastern/South Asian images and, 245–64; Black-desi romance and, 177–80; of desi women, 171–80; global-historical connections to, 122–29; post–September 11 era and, 131–35

otherness: appropriation as, 238–64, 280–82; South Asian and Black relations and, 234–38

"Outcasted" (Karmacy), 82, 128–29

outsider status, multiple racial affinities of desis and, 109–17

ownership of hip hop: debate over, 212–16, 223–30; South Asian and Black relations and, 234–38

Pacifics, The (Filipino American group), 309n16

"Paid in Full" (Rakim), 255–56

Pakistani immigrants: Blacks and, 174; global-historical con-

Pakistani immigrants (*cont.*)
nections of South Asians and
Blacks and, 118–29
Palumbo-Liu, David, 94–95,
304n2
panethnic identity: desi hip hop
and, 222–30; desiness and,
69–73, 307n18; global-
historical connections to, 121–
29; hip hop and, 12–13; Indian
hegemony and non-Indian
South Asians and, 69; political
activism of desis and, 287
Paris (Black rapper), 313n15
"Part 3: Sri Lankan Boi" (D'Lo),
64, 190–91
Party Music (Coup), 312n6
"Passage to India" (Karmacy),
80–81, 83, 291
Patel, Sardar, 81, 307n24
PeaceOUT World Homo Hop Festival, 310n11
peer evaluation in hip hop music,
104, 308n8
Perry, Imani, 213
pimping, desi female artists and,
183–85
police brutality: D'Lo's references
to, 146–49; global-historical
connections and, 127–29; hip
hop references to, 204; interminority relations and, 104–6
"Police Brutality" (D'Lo), 127–28
political activism: authenticity in
hip hop and, 272–79; hip hop
as tool for, 197–212, 257–64,
283–99; minority activism and,
194–95; panethnic identity and,
70–73; racialization of, 108–9
polyculturalism: community formation and, 23–29; desi hip
hop appropriation and, 269–71;
in hip hop music, 192–212,
280–82; political activism and,
287–99
pop locking, 148, 310n7

Pop Master Fabel (Puerto Rican
dancer), 19
PopMatters (magazine), 258
popular culture: appropriation of
Middle East/South Asian images
by, 244–64; commodification of
hip hop and, 279–82; desi hip
hop artists and, 195–212; power
dynamics in, 255
"positive stereotypes" in desi culture, 165–71, 311n15
Posse Foundation, The, 286
"Postcards from Paradise" (Himalayan Project), 121
Pough, Gwendolyn, 183
power dynamics: desi hip hop
and role of, xi, 220–30; desi
sexuality and, 187–89; hip
hop as tool for, 197–212,
283–99; hybrid identities and,
303n21; interminority relations and differences in, 102–4;
multiracialism of hip hop and,
220–30; music production and,
246–53; South Asian and Black
relations and, 234–38
Prashad, Vijay, 23–24, 26, 31,
42, 56, 94, 96, 126, 263, 283,
303n20, 311n1
Presley, Elvis, 239
professional status: desi hip hop
artists and role of, 54–57;
ethnic insularity and, 44–47,
305nn5–6; of exceptional desis,
42–44
Proposition 21 (California), 197
Proposition 187 (California), 197
Public Enemy (group), 10, 196–
97, 200, 202–7, 209, 231, 297,
311n5
Puerto Ricans: history of hip hop
and, 19, 100, 200, 208; women
in hip hop and, 310n8
Punjabi MC (British Asian artist),
201–2, 265, 267, 269
Purkayastha, Bandana, 76

"Put You on the Game" (The Game), 313n7

Queen Latifah (Black rapper), 151, 153, 201–2, 310n9
Queen Pen (Black rapper), 310n9

"racial draft" in military, 259, 313n10

racialized hip hop, 10–13; Blackness and, 212–16; desi production of, x–xi; gender and, 138–89; global-historical connections of Blacks and South Asians in, 117–29; historical context for, 20–23

racism: Afro-Asian identity and, 29–33, 88–91; appeal of hip hop and, 196–212; appropriation and identification and, 264–71; appropriation and othering and, 240–64; authenticity in hip hop and, 271–79; college experiences of desis and, 59–73; comparative racial studies through multisited ethnography and, 33–36; desi ambiguity concerning, 91–99, 217–30; desi ethnic insularity and, 44–47, 240–64; ethnicity and, 37–41; first-generation desis and, 93–95; gender and sexuality and, 140–89; hip hop artists' ambivalence concerning, ix–xi; history of hip hop and, 18–23; middle-class desis' contact with, 105–9; military draft and, 259, 313n10; multiple racial affinities, 109–17; panethnic identity and, 69–73; political activism of desis and, 287–99; polycultural sampling and construction of, 23–29; racialized sexuality of desi men, 160–65; reactive ethnicity and, 305n3; second-generation desis and, 95–99; South Asian and Black

relations and, 1–5, 56–57, 135–37, 171–80, 235–38, 264–71. See also global race consciousness

Radano, Ronald, 234
Radhika (desi fan), 61, 71–72, 153, 175–76
Raimist, Rachel (filmmaker), 150
Rainman (Chinese American rapper), 119
"raja syndrome" in desi culture, 165–66, 310n14
Rakim (Black rapper), 202, 247–49, 255–56
"Ramble-Ations: A One D'Lo Show," 157–58, 184, 310n10
Rao, Sam, 304n26
rap music: by British South Asian musicians, 33, 304n25; on college radio stations, 107–8, 308n11; influence on desi hip hop of, x–xi
"Rapper's Delight" (Sugarhill Gang), 100
Rastafarianism, 53, 123, 125–26
Ravi (desi label founder), 199, 283
Rawj (desi rapper), 8–10, 12, 49, 52, 301n3, 306n11; on ancestry and ethnicity, 75–76; appeal of hip hop for, 211–12; on authenticity in hip hop, 276; on Black culture, 99–100, 127, 222; college experiences of, 60–61, 64; on desi multiracial consciousness, 94–95, 99, 102–3, 222–23; on desi sexuality, 164–65; on family and marriage pressures, 166–67; political activism of, 291
Rawkus Records, 269
"React" (Sermon), 261–62
reactive ethnicity, 40–41, 305n3
Reagan, Ronald, 17, 194, 204, 311n3
"Rebel Music" (Himalayan Project), 131–32

reggae music: Blackness of hip hop and, 215; ethnic groups in, 151

reggaeton, 215

religion, Indian Hindu hegemony and, 52–57

reparations for African Americans, 311n3

research methodology, comparative racial studies through multisited ethnography and, 33–36

resistance ideology, appeal of hip hop and, 199–212

Richmond (California), 37, 304n1

Rock Steady Crew (dance group), 19

Rocky (Canadian desi rapper), 197, 271

Rodney, Walter, 31

Roediger, David, 161

Rose, Tricia, 151

Ruff Ryder Records, 20

Rukus Avenue Records, 78–80, 126, 163, 210–11, 272, 312n9

Rumbaut, Ruben, 307n18

Sammy (desi rapper), 126, 163, 210–11, 218, 220–21

Samoans, history of hip hop and, 19

sampling: as appropriation, 249–55, 262–64, 279–82; authenticity in face of, 271–79; community formation and, 23–29, 303n17; ethnic hip hop ethnography and, 12–13, 51–57; political activism through, 294–95

San Juan, E., Jr., 37

Saregama, 249–50, 313n7

Scott, David, 29

second-generation desis, racial consciousness of, 95–99

segmented assimilation, ethnic hip hop ethnography and, 13, 301n7

self-racialization, by South Asian hip hop artists, 20–23

September 11, 2001, attacks (9/11): desi identity and, 72–73; history of hip hop and, 20–23; Middle East/South Asian images following, 244–45, 257–64; political activism in wake of, 287–99; racial realignments following, 130–35, 226–30; South Asian and Black relations in wake of, 236–38

Sermon, Erick (Black rapper), 261–62

sexism in hip hop culture, 149–56, 257–64

sexuality: Black-desi comparisons of, 96; Blackness of hip hop and, 213–16; desi college experiences and, 62–73; in desi culture, x–xi, 156–85; desi double standard concerning, 159–60, 310n12; in desi hip hop, 266–67; of female artists, 171–80; multiracialization of hip hop and, 246–47, 255–57, 260–64; power and, 187–89; racialized hip hop and, 138–89; racialized sexuality of desi men, 160–65. See also gender

Shakur, Tupac (Black rapper), 204, 261

Shankar, Ravi (Indian musician), 309n22

Shante, Roxanne (Black rapper), 151, 310n11

Shaw Brothers (film producers), 19

"Show, The" (Doug E. Fresh), 14

Shware, Raje (desi artist), 266–67, 269, 313n13

Sikh, Jat, 287

"Silent Scream" (Himalayan Project), 133

Simmons, Russell, 146, 312n3, 313n15

Simpsons, The (TV series), 142
Sistrens gathering, 186
"6 in the Mornin'" (Ice T), 204
slavery: Blackness of hip hop and, 214–16; global-historical connections of South Asians and Blacks and, 118–29; minority status in U.S. and, 32
Slick Rick (Black British rapper), 302n8
sliding signifiers, multiple racial affinities of desis and, 109–17
Slum Village (group), 266
Smith, Will (rapper and actor), 306n11
"Snake (Remix)" (Kelly), 246–47, 257
soca music, 126
social justice: desi hip hop as tool for, xi, 55–57, 283–99; hip hop and, 196
Song, Min, 97–98
Souled Separately (Feenom Circle), 94, 224
Southall Black Sisters, 30
South Asian Americans: Afro-Asian identity and, 29–33; anti-Black attitudes of, 88–91, 171–80; authenticity of hip hop by, 214–16; collaboration with Black hip hoppers of, 265–69; as female hip hop artists, 142–56; first-generation racial identities among, 93–95; gender and hip hop and, 138–89; generation classifications for, 4, 301n1; global-historical connections with Blacks and, 117–29; heterogeneity of, 40–41; hip hop culture within, 41–44, 211–12; hip hop images of, 243–64; as honorary Whites, 25–26, 303nn18–19; immigration patterns of, 14, 302n9; Indian hegemony and non-Indian South Asians,

65–69; insularity and classism of, 44–47; marriage and family pressures for, 165–71; multiracial affinities of, 37–41, 111–17; musical identity of, 270–71; political activism of, 194–95, 283–99; post–September 11 era and, 130–35; second-generation desis and, 13–17, 95–99; sexuality and gender identity issues for, 158–85; socioeconomic conditions for, 25–29, 303n19. See also desis
South Asian Women Creative Circle, 288–89
Spinderella (Black DJ), 150
Sri Lankan immigrants: college experiences in U.S. of, 65–69; D'Lo's tensions with, 181–85; global-historical connections of South Asians and Blacks and, 118–29, 309n17
strategic ambiguity, multiple racial affinities of desis and, 109–17
Strauss, Neil, 231
student organizations, desi bonding through, 59–60
Sugarhill Gang (group), 100
Swap (desi rapper), 9, 11, 78–83, 221
Sweet Tee (Black rapper), 153
syncretism, Hindu religious hegemony for desis and, 53–57

Tamil Eelam, 120
Tamil Tigers, 309n17
the1shanti (desi rapper), 269
The Indus Entrepreneurs (TIE), 305n6
Third World Liberation Front, 43
"Thoda Resham Lagta Hai" (Mangeshkhar), 249
Thompson, Robert, 210
"Thoroughbred" (Chee Malabar), 309n23

Thuc Phi, Thien-bao, 161, 178–79
thug, image of desis and, 190–91,
    311n1
Timbaland (Black producer),
    246, 263, 266–67, 269, 313n7,
    313n13
TLC (group), 153
Trinidad: global-historical con-
    nections of South Asians in,
    126–29; Indian and African
    populations in, 304nn22–23
Truthfully Speaking (Truth Hurts),
    247
Truth Hurts (Black R&B singer),
    246–49, 251–53, 255–59
Tseng, Judy, 127
Tucker, C. Delores, 302n11
Twilight Players (British Asian
    dance group), 310n7
Twine, Frances, 170

Umoja educational organization,
    114–15
United Kingdom: Afro-Asian iden-
    tity in, 31–33, 304n24; Asian
    music in, 201–2; Black music in,
    107–9; global-historical con-
    nections of South Asians and,
    125–29
United States: Afro-Asian migra-
    tion to, 31–33; anti-Asian back-
    lash in, 95, 308n4
Universal Negro Improvement
    Association, 309n19
upward mobility, desi culture and,
    100–104

Vivek (desi rapper), 1–2, 10–11, 29,
    53, 165; on appeal of hip hop,
    197; on appropriation in hip
    hop, 242, 279–80; on authen-
    ticity in hip hop, 274–75, 278;
    on Black consciousness, 217,
    225–30; on desi stereotyping,
    191; on global-historical con-
    nections of South Asians, 123,

125; multiple racial affinities
    of, 114–17; political activism of,
    285–86

WADDAG (group), 187
Wang, Oliver, 19–20, 121, 125, 202,
    309n13, 311n5
War on Terrorism: hip hop refer-
    ences to, 244–64, 267–71;
    political activism of desis and,
    288–99
wealth accumulation: desi hip hop
    culture and influence of, 54–57;
    desi racial consciousness and,
    94–95; second-generation
    desi identity and, 15–17; South
    Asians as honorary Whites and,
    25–29, 303n19
West, Kanye (Black producer), 267
West Indies: cross-culturalism in,
    210; Indians in, 30, 304n22
"When You Have No Choice"
    (D'Lo), 207–8
White, Armond, 312n7
White culture: appropriation of
    Black culture by, 238–39, 263–
    64; appropriation of Middle
    East/South Asian images by,
    244–64; Blackness of hip hop
    and, 213–16, 312n7; commodi-
    fication of hip hop and, 216–30;
    desi ethnic identity and, 39–41,
    44–47, 304n2; desi intermar-
    riage and romance and, 169–
    71; first-generation desis and,
    93–95; history of hip hop and,
    21–23; polycultural sampling
    and, 25–29; second-generation
    desis' view of, 96–99
White supremacy, 2–5
Williams, Teresa, 113, 136
Wilson, Pete, 204
Winant, Howard, 27
Wince at the Sun (Himalayan
    Project), 119–20, 131

Wong, Deborah, 22–23, 197, 264–65
Wood, Joe, 240

Yagnik, Alka (Indian singer), 266
"Yankee Hindutva," 42

Yellow Panthers, 194
Yo! MTV Raps (TV show), 14, 106, 148
Youth Built, 286
Yo Yo (Black rapper), 310n11

Nitasha Tamar Sharma is an assistant professor
of African American studies and Asian American studies
at Northwestern University.

Library of Congress Cataloging-in-Publication Data
Sharma, Nitasha Tamar, 1973–
Hip hop Desis : South Asian Americans, Blackness, and a global race
consciousness / Nitasha Tamar Sharma.
p. cm. — (Refiguring American music)
Includes bibliographical references and index.
ISBN 978-0-8223-4741-5 (cloth : alk. paper)
ISBN 978-0-8223-4760-6 (pbk. : alk. paper)
1. South Asian Americans—Music—Social aspects. 2. Rap (Music)—
Social aspects—United States. 3. Hip-hop—Influence. 4. South
Asian Americans—Race identity. 5. United States—Race relations.
I. Title. II. Series: Refiguring American music.
ML3918.R37S53 2010
782.421649089'914073—dc22   2010006794

THE ART OF
BREATHING

Nancy Zi

Vivi Co.

Vivi Company
Glendale, California

THE ART OF BREATHING

A Vivi Book/February 1994

Designed and produced by The Compage Company, San Francisco, California

Ilustrations by Eric Maché
Book Design by Joy Dickinson
Cover Design by Karyn Young Designs, Santa Barbara, California
Cover painting of clouds by Elaine Tong
Author cover photograph courtesy of Dunlap & Turney, Glendale, CA

All rights reserved
Copyright © 1986, 1994 by Nancy Zi.

This book may not be reproduced in whole or in part by
mimeograph or any other means, without permission.
For information address: Vivi Company

Library of Congress Catalog Card number 94-060023

ISBN 1-884872-62-X (Previously ISBN 0-553-34281-1)

Vivi Books and videos are published by the Vivi Company, P.O. Box 750,
Glendale, California, U.S.A., 91209-0750

NOTE: An earlier version of The Art of Breathing, *without the companion*
video, was published by Bantam Books as part of the Bantam New Age Books
series. This edition has been revised and all exercises have been coordinated
with a self-paced video, The Art of Breathing: A Course of Six Simple
Lessons for Improving Your Performance and Well-Being.

PRINTED IN THE UNITED STATES OF AMERICA

9 8 7 6 5 4 3 2 1

*This book is dedicated
to my mother,
Mrs. Lucy Ma Zi,
and my late father,
Reverend Dr. Benjamin Dung Hwe Zi*

Caution

This or any exercise program may result in injury. Please consult your doctor before beginning this or any exercise program. The exercises, instructions, and advice in this program are in no way intended as a substitute for medical counseling.

Companion Video–Now Available

Because people learn in various ways, and because we have had many requests for a video to accompany the book, a companion video now exists for *The Art of Breathing*.

The video invites you to learn how to convert your breath into inner energy current. It, like the book, is presented in six progressive lessons with imagery drills. These lessons and drills will lead you to acquire a greater sense of vitality and balance, and sharpen your mental and physical coordination. As you develop breath control and awareness through *Chi Yi*, you will find the principles of disciplined breathing moving effortlessly into your daily activities. The results can forever enhance your life by cultivating the power of *Chi*—mental and physical health, energy level, personality, voice, coordination, athletic potential, and more.

Although the book and the video are each independently valuable, taking advantage of both simultaneously can greatly facilitate and enhance the learning process. The book provides more background information, theoretical discussion, and detailed explanation, and places greater emphasis on application. Whereas, the video offers extensive visual aids, thus emphasizing easy execution of the exercises and imagery drills.

The book and the video provide a complete course. Mastering this course will enable you to:

- Apply *Chi Yi* to virtually any endeavor—athletics, theater, singing, yoga, meditation, and more.

- Reduce stress and promote relaxation, as well as combat insomnia and other physical discomforts.

- Find a common center for your mental and physical movements to produce an aura of poise, grace, and ease.

- Look, feel, and be healthier, and bounce back more quickly from illness.

- Gain increased stamina, radiance, and general well-being.

For information regarding this video or additional copies of the book, write to Vivi Company, 222 Monterey Road, Suite 1006, Glendale, California 91206.

Acknowledgments

I wish to express my deepest appreciation to Mr. Wang Chi Chien for writing the calligraphic Chinese characters that so beautifully adorn the part openers of this book.

Mr. Ernie Pereira, retired managing editor of the *Hong Kong Standard* daily newspaper, gave me the first words of encouragement and guided me to write this book. I also wish to extend my thanks to Professor and Mrs. John Hsu of Cornell University, whose wise suggestions and careful scrutiny of the initial manuscript have led this book onto a much wiser course.

The invaluable artistic advice and other counsel of Mrs. Sue Yung Li Ikeda have guided me throughout this project.

I am also very grateful to my son, Vincent Li, and my daughter, Violette Li Huang, for assisting in the preparation of the book.

It is my great fortune to have had the assistance of Charles Hammond and Margaret M. Meier in preparing the manuscript. I am also grateful to Eric Mache for his illustrations.

And finally, I cannot thank Alan Freeland and Kenneth Burke enough. Without them, this book would never have materialized in its present form.

Contents

List of Imagery Drills

THE ART OF
BREATHING

A Singer's Discoveries

Breath is life; and learning to control the breath adds a new dimension of control and ease to every action, no matter how simple or how complex it is. In fact, the effectiveness of every activity we undertake—singing, walking, exercising, working, dancing, public speaking—depends greatly on how we use the air we breathe.

My voice is my career. For more than twenty years, much of my time has been devoted to singing and to voice instruction. My performance schedule is extensive and my teaching schedule full. I have to make certain that my singing voice is always in good condition and that my speaking voice does not strain my vocal cords. To maintain the quality of voice I desire, effective controlled breathing is my most important tool.

During my college days, at Millikin University in Illinois, I sang in student recitals and performed in many opera productions. Deep breathing automatically accompanied me whenever I stepped onstage to sing. Then, during my junior year, I was elected a candidate for Homecoming Queen. I will never forget the parade of candidates, each of us swiveling at center stage in front of a panel of judges. Suddenly I was like a lump of clay! What had happened to my customary poise and stage presence? Years later, the answer became clear to me. My breathing technique had eluded me, and without it I also lost my vibrancy and the ability to project my personality.

In the years that followed, I learned to apply the lesson of that experience: Deep breathing can get me through most situations.

Controlled deep breathing helps the body to transform the air we breathe into energy. The stream of energized air produced by properly executed and controlled deep breathing produces a current of inner energy which radiates throughout the entire body and can be channeled to the body areas that need it the most, on demand. It can be used to fuel a specific physical effort, such as tennis or jogging. Or you can use this current of inner energy to relieve muscular tension throughout the body, revitalize a tired mind, or soothe localized aches and pains.

My years of experience in training and maintaining the human voice have convinced me that the practice of the art of breathing is beneficial to the health of the whole person, regardless of career or activity. In this book I will share with you some of the discoveries I have made as a singer and voice teacher. These experiences have made me aware of the wide applications of disciplined, effective breathing.

As my understanding of the benefits of controlled breathing developed, I began to formulate the principles of what I call *chi yi*. *Chi* means breath, air, atmosphere. Yi means art. Hence *chi yi*—the art of breathing.

Chi yi (pronounced *chee ee)*, the breathing method I have developed, is influenced in part by the basic principles of the ancient Chinese art of breath manipulation known as *chi kung* (pronounced *chee gung)*. For centuries, the Chinese have practiced *chi kung* as a fundamental discipline, and have applied this discipline to many forms of martial arts, meditation, and healing practices. As a Western-trained singer and as a researcher and practitioner of the ancient art of *chi kung* and its related disciplines, I have compared, extracted, and compiled techniques from both East and West to create *chi yi*, a direct and concise way to teach the art of breathing. The current of inner energy that is generated as a result of my method of deep breathing is comparable to the principle of "inner vigor" upon which *chi kung is* based.

The practice of *chi kung is* concerned not only with the process of breathing and self-energizing; it also encompasses the ancient Chinese understanding of disciplined breathing as a means of acquiring total control over body and mind. It gives us physiological and psychological balance and the balance of *yin* and *yang*—a symbolic expression of such universal polarities as masculine and feminine, light and dark, creative and receptive.

In *chi yi,* that energy is manifested through the manipulation of simultaneous inward and-outward muscular pressure, thus creating opposing forces. By properly balancing these forces, we allow energy to emerge.

The ancient practitioners of *chi kung* further associated the inner energy that derives from disciplined breathing with the quality and vigor of the blood. They deduced ways to control and regulate the seemingly automatic breathing function, which they saw as voluntary. By deliberately controlling the breathing process, they found that other functions of the body—heartbeat, blood flow, and many other physical and emotional functions— could be consciously altered. The mind, said *chi kung* practitioners, can control and manipulate the flow of energy that is created through proper breathing. Therefore the mind, coordinated with breathing, can be responsible for the state of one's physical health, one's blood pressure, one's immune system, and one's mental condition. A *chi kung* expert can channel the inner energy to any location in the body at will. In other words, the accomplished practitioner can "think" this inner energy to any destination in the body where it is needed.

As time went on, the philosophical aspect of *chi kung* was explored in many books, but the technical aspect was treated as a closely guarded secret. Without documentation, the words of generations of teachers and pupils varied greatly in interpretation and practice. Therefore, while *chi kung* became the foundation that teaches the manipulation of body, mind, and spirit, different schools evolved that built upon this foundation yet had very different goals. *Tai chi* and other forms of the martial arts and meditation disciplines are all related to *chi kung.*

Centuries passed, and with the advent of machinery and explosive weapons, the martial arts waned in appeal. External sources of strength and power totally overshadowed the internal energy men and women had once learned to create within their own bodies through self-discipline. The specific talent for energizing the body through disciplined breathing was neglected and nearly forgotten. Western modernization seemed to have eclipsed many of the subtle practices of the East. Today, however, a new era of physical awareness has stimulated the reexamination of Eastern culture, with its foundation based on the importance of the inner self.

In effective breathing, of course, there is no East or West. True, different cultures have placed different degrees of emphasis on the importance and development of breathing, and have called their techniques by different names. Their ultimate objective, however, is the same: to derive the maximum efficiency from the inhaled breath.

My intention in *The Art of Breathing* is not to revive or to propagate *chi kung* but to bring attention to and illustrate the existence of the power that is ours if we choose to have it. By cultivating that power through the practice of *chi yi,* we can excel in our endeavors and become more successful and dynamic people. The exercises, applications of *chi yi* principles, and imagery drills described in this book will enable you to build a solid, deep, effective breathing system to support whatever activities you pursue.

PART ONE

The Promise of Chi Yi

Chi Yi: An Art for Today

The newborn infant gasps for its first breath, and life ends with a final exhalation. But breathing is more than just an instinct that is active from birth to death. When properly executed, breathing can help you develop to the utmost, enabling you to acquire a greater sense of power and balance and to sharpen both your mental and physical coordination. This is the promise of *chi yi*.

The demands of today's society, working conditions, and environment are complicated and frequently stressful; and our energy needs, both physical and mental, are forced to change rapidly to cope with all the forms of tension to which we are subjected. Innumerable varieties of relaxation techniques—transcendental meditation, self-hypnosis, physical exercises, biofeedback, and many others—are available today. But no matter what method is practiced, a mode of breathing in one way or another always comes into the picture.

Modern science has done wonders to elevate the standard of human existence, with the expectation that new inventions and medical discoveries will raise our physical and mental well-being to ever-higher states. Advanced education systems sharpen our minds, while vitamins and nutritional supplements ensure that our bodies are well nourished. Great efforts are devoted to developing innumerable variations of exercises that promise to enhance our physical shape and condition. All these avenues for generating and maintaining a high level of energy are pursued with the intention of producing a better, more exciting person.

Ironically, in our search for energy resources to maintain this modern lifestyle, we have overlooked the potential of the greatest energy source available to everyone: the current of vital energy that can be generated within our bodies, using the air we breathe as fuel. The Chinese call that energy *chi*.

Chi yi is a method of deep breathing through which you can stimulate and harness the current of inner energy. By making sure that the air you breathe is effectively inhaled, energized, and exhaled, you can improve your health and bring vitality to all your physical movements and expressions.

We have all experienced the direct link between our breathing and the way we feel physically and emotionally. We speak of a sigh of relief, of gasping in horror, of holding the breath in anticipation, of being breathless with excitement. Laughing, sighing, yawning, yelling, gasping, screaming—nature provides us with all these responses to help us fulfill the emotional demands of the instant. Physically, these acts provide us with the extra oxygen to meet a potential need.

These outbursts stimulate deep breathing—breathing to the "core"—in effect opening up vents to release emotional steam. In the next section, we will look at the core of our bodies—what it is, where it is located, and its role in effective breathing.

The Core

As you learn to apply the principles of *chi yi,* you will develop your core, and you will learn how to lead the breath to the point where the core is located. Your stresses, worries, anger, and other tensions will follow the stream of your breath to this center, where the core will shrink away your negative emotions—pain, fear, anxiety, anger, sadness, and even depression—leaving you ready to meet the challenges that you face.

To understand that a central core exists within all human beings is to open your eyes to a whole new dimension of your being. The core has always been within you. When it is stimulated it becomes increasingly effective. It does not grow in size, but in intensity.

The core is located at the center of the body, measuring from head to toe. That point is located approximately 2 to 5 inches below the navel (see Figure 1). The entire body is coordinated from this center of balance. In fact, this core is the center not only of your physical balance but of your mental and emotional balance as well.

The core thrives on attention and stimulation. The more you practice breathing to the core, the more energy it stores and is prepared to release, thus becoming a stronger pivot point for your physical, mental, and emotional balance and control.

In times of emotional crisis or at other crucial moments of distress or physical pain, we frequently hear the advice, "Take a deep breath and get hold of yourself." A very wise suggestion indeed, if we only knew how to make that "deep breath" effective. Expanding the chest and attempting to fill the lungs with additional air isn't necessarily helpful; the goal is to direct air deep toward the core.

It is impossible to explain in scientific terms the process of breathing to the core. Like energy, the core of a person is an abstract entity. Through exercises and imagery drills we can sense it, develop and cultivate it, manipulate it, and feel the power of its presence, but we cannot see it with our eyes.

Introducing the Imagery Drills

The following exercises are the first of several "imagery drills," which make use of mental pictures to help you experience specific sensations or feelings in the body. These mental pictures are metaphorical descriptions of particular movements that may be otherwise impossible to describe. They communicate a muscular process indirectly, through the use of *images* of movement. Such images are useful in elucidating invisible, internal movements and subtle adjustments of the body. This brief introduction to the awareness of inner energy merely suggests the energy source you will learn to tap in the exercises and applications that follow.

These imagery drills may be difficult for those who are unaccustomed to manipulating their breathing apparatus. Many athletes, singers, and musicians who play wind instruments, for example, are conscientious breathers, and will be able to handle the drills easily. Others will need to wait until they have practiced a good number of the exercises in Part 2 before being able to complete the drills correctly and with little strain.

Practice these drills as they are introduced to become familiar with the internal sensations each one stimulates. Review the drills as necessary to reestablish your awareness of a sensation.

The first of these drills, the Eyedropper Imagery Drill, introduces you to abdominal breathing, an important step in learning to breathe to the core at will.

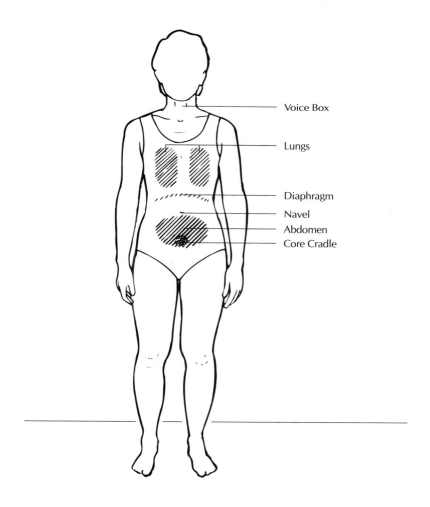

FIGURE 1 Breathing Apparatus

Eyedropper

Stand erect but relaxed, being careful not to tilt or lower your head. Imagine yourself to be an upside-down eyedropper (see Figure 2). Squeeze the bulb, and air is squeezed out. Release the bulb, letting it expand, and air is drawn into the body.

Imagine that the opening tip of the glass tube ends where the back of the nose and the throat meet. Let air flow in and out through this central opening, not simply through the mouth or nose alone.

Practice applying this image as you breathe. You will find that breathing with this image in mind encourages abdominal breathing very naturally.

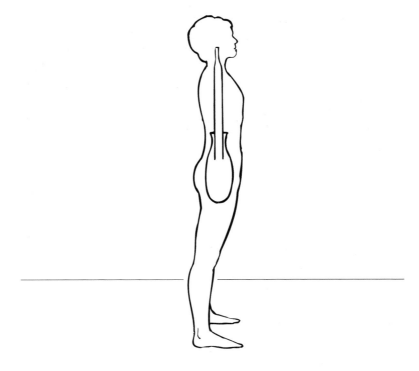

FIGURE 2 Eyedropper

Abdominal breathing does not mean that air enters into the abdomen but rather that the abdominal muscles and the sides and back of the lower torso expand outward to induce the lowering of the diaphragm, thus creating the appearance of an inflated abdomen.

The diaphragm is the main muscle used in breathing (see Figure 1); when it lowers, air is drawn into the lungs. On inhalation, air travels through the nose or mouth to the lungs, passing through the windpipe, which divides into two main bronchial tubes, one going into each lung. Oxygen in the inhaled air is transferred by the lungs to the blood, to be carried to the body tissues. Carbon dioxide, which is formed in this process, is carried by the blood back to the lungs and exhaled.

A simple inhalation of air containing oxygen cannot produce the phenomenal volume, extended range of pitches, and varied sounds and color that are demanded of a singer, nor the force and coordination demanded in the *grand jeté* of a classical dancer. The compounded energy that is developed in the body of the singer or dancer is comparable to the inner energy produced in *chi kung* to attain physical and mental well-being. The former focuses this current of energy outward, whereas the latter circulates it internally.

To further understand abdominal breathing, practice creating the mental image described in the following drill.

IMAGERY DRILL

Accordion

Create the mental image of the diaphragm as a ceiling resting on the abdominal walls (see Figure 3). Imagine that these walls and the ceiling are made of rubber that can be flexed and expanded.

From another perspective, the diaphragm is also a floor on which the lungs rest. Imagine the lungs to be a vertically held accordion. When the diaphragm drops, the accordion elongates, creating a vacuum space that sucks in air.

The whole breathing process can be summarized in this way: Expand your abdomen by curving the downstairs walls outward, causing the downstairs ceiling to lower and the upstairs floor to drop, thereby creating more space on top into which air can flow.

This image will help you to perceive how the abdomen, the lungs, and your exhalations/inhalations interact. In this drill, air is drawn in easily to fill the entire lung, and we have the illusion of air being drawn into the abdomen. In spite of its seeming simplicity, this drill demands the coordination of a juggling act. A central pivot point of control is necessary, and that is the core.

Once you are familiar with the existence and location of the core, you can stimulate it regularly and frequently with proper deep breathing. When the core is energized, all of your mental and physical performances will improve. This improvement comes not merely from being sufficiently energized but also from being able to relax unwanted muscular tension. The core works as a hub with spokes reaching out to the extremities, and the entire body can be saturated with its vibrant energy. Stress and tension can be transferred down those spokes to the core, where they can be converted into useful energy.

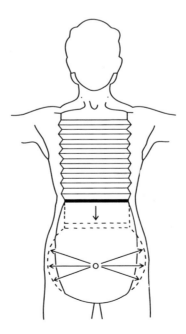

FIGURE 3   Accordian

Now practice the following imagery drills to help you get in touch with the core energy.

Funnel-Balloon

Think of the very back of your nose, where it meets the throat, as the top of a funnel. As you begin an inhalation, imagine the air you breathe as water being poured into this funnel, which leads all the way down to the end of a very long tube.

Imagine a balloon attached to the end of this tube. As you inhale easily and steadily, picture water draining down, and imagine the balloon slowly inflating. Be careful not to overfill and burst the balloon. Stop when it is comfortably full. Hold the inhaled air in the balloon for a second or so, enjoying and dwelling on that pleasant fullness. Now prepare for exhalation.

As you gradually exhale, imagine the full balloon deflating slowly, being careful to let the balloon sit firmly in place until the very end of the exhalation. After several repetitions of this exhalation/ inhalation process, you will feel warmth saturating your lower abdomen. You might even feel a throbbing or tingling sensation in other parts of your body, such as the area between your cheeks and the upper gum in your mouth, at the base of your neck, at your rib cage, and even at your kneecaps or fingertips.

Tumbling Pebble

To stimulate the sensation of activated inner energy in the lower abdomen, imagine a pebble about 1/2 inch in diameter at the center of your lower abdomen. Imagine it tumbling by its own power, over and over, slowly at first, then steadily, about one turn per second.

When you are comfortable with that sensation, you may imagine adding more pebbles to the original one, each turning and tumbling by its own power.

Eventually, with practice of these and later imagery drills, you will be mentally able to stimulate the sensation of activated inner energy. This mental stimulation is vital in order to attain the maximum benefits from your study of *chi yi*.

The Benefits of Chi Yi

Breathing is a natural reflex. So why fuss about it? If we breathe normally, some say, that's good enough. If we follow this line of thinking, we might also ask: If we can stand on our feet, why practice dancing on tiptoe? Why develop any special techniques and abilities if we are meant only to do things easily and naturally? Human beings have developed thousands of exceptional abilities and talents. We develop ourselves in order to be more functional, more wholesome, and more effective.

Among its many benefits, the technique of *chi yi* brings to its practitioners:

☐ The ability to generate inner energy.

☐ The ability to channel this inner energy selectively.

☐ The ability to respond wisely to mental and physical needs.

The core's potential is limitless. The power that comes from core development through *chi yi* will influence every aspect of your daily life—mental and physical health, energy level, personality, voice, coordination, deportment, and many other interrelated activities and characteristics. Through *chi yi*, shyness and timidity can gradually diminish, permitting your full personality to emerge. Your mental and physical movements will find a common center of gravity, and the resulting coordination produces poise, grace, and ease.

In the final section of the book you will learn that *chi yi* has practical applications in relaxation, revitalization, improving your health, reducing or eliminating stress, tension, or pain anywhere in the body, combating insomnia, developing your athletic prowess, and much more. For now, the following section gives a preview of the benefits you may expect.

Building Confidence and Enhancing Personal Presence

In this society of keen competition and the pursuit of excellence, a person must have that extra something in order to succeed. Especially in the fields of artistic and athletic performance, a fully functioning core gives you just that—an extra, indefinable *something*.

You will learn to incorporate an awareness of your core into every sound, motion, and emotion you express: breathing, speaking, smiling, walking, running, waving, and so on. From your inner depth you will exude sincerity, conviction, and strength. From the simplest to the most complex undertaking, you will benefit from this inner support. For example, the simple motion of lifting a teacup, when performed with an awareness of and coordination extending from the core, will be noticeably more steady, graceful, and spontaneous. Similarly, a deep breath flowing from your innermost center to your face will bring a luminous, captivating glow to your complexion.

In any stage performance, alone or in collaboration with others, a successful performer, in addition to possessing talent and mastery of the required skill, must exude a captivating force that propels his or her presence into the audience. This force, often called *stage presence,* is useful to performers and public figures—and to you when you wish to command attention and project an impressive self-image. An effective core can supply this force.

Increasing Stamina, Zest, and Coordination

If you are active in a sport—whether it's tennis, swimming, figure skating, jogging, or aerobic exercise—proper deep breathing can conspicuously improve your performance. With an awareness of the core and the use of its energy, your muscles and nervous system will become more responsive, controlled, and coordinated. This awareness enhances the execution of intricate, exacting movements. You will also be able to channel your energy more effectively, resulting in increased stamina and a higher tolerance for physical exertion.

By visualizing the location of your core, you establish a focal point from which to direct your movements. Imagine that all your limbs are connected to the core, and that all your movements extend from the core. You will quickly recognize the greater sense of coordination this visualization creates, even in a simple movement such as a jumping jack.

Exhalation channels the core's energy into the execution of energetic movements. This is one of the reasons that karate students are taught to emit vocal outbursts when attacking. Some tennis players such as John McEnroe, Chris Evert, and Jimmy Connors frequently grunt with their most powerful hits—a verbal response as they use the inner energy tapped from exhalation.

As you work with the exercises, applications, and drills in this book, you will discover some breathing approaches that are particularly effective for you. Practice a few of these before you engage in your favorite sport. Work on breathing deeply and developing core energy, and see what a difference they make to your performance.

Improving the Complexion

Chi yi stimulates the flow of inner energy, bringing a vibrant glow to the surface of the skin. During the process of stimulating the core with deep breathing, the abdominal muscles flex, knead, and squeeze the organs of the abdomen, producing a massaging effect. This motion, together with activated inner energy, stimulates digestion and helps to relieve uncomfortable internal air bubbles and gas, promoting a clearer, brighter complexion. In addition, the nerve-calming effect of deep breathing will help to control the tension that is so frequently the primary cause of a bad complexion.

Freshening the Breath

Bad breath (halitosis), the kind that persists even though all hygienic precautions and proper eating habits are followed, can be helped through *chi yi* in several ways. Bad breath caused by an acidic stomach resulting from tension can be eased by relaxation through breathing. Bad breath resulting from indigestion may be eliminated through the abdominal stimulation brought on by deep breathing and inner energy. Bad breath caused by shallow breathing that traps stagnant air in the lungs can easily be remedied with a replenishing deep breathing technique.

Preparing for Childbirth

If you are an expectant father who is also a practitioner of *chi* yi, you will be able to calm your own tensions over the next nine months with deep breathing, and you will be well prepared to assist in the delivery of your child by guiding the breathing of the mother.

If you are an expectant mother who has already learned the techniques of *chi yi*, your abdominal muscles are strong and healthy—elastic and responsive. Your breathing is efficient and easy to manipulate. You are sure to benefit from these assets during your pregnancy. These qualities are also a great advantage during the delivery, when your baby—and your doctor—will need all the physical cooperation you can give. Not only will your ability to breathe effectively keep you healthier mentally and emotionally during pregnancy, your baby will benefit from your inner energy too.

If you are planning to use the Psychoprophylactic Method, a psychological and physical preparation for childbirth known also as the Lamaze Method, or any other method of natural childbirth, you will find that your ability in *chi yi is* extremely helpful in learning and carrying out these techniques. All such methods require you to train your breathing to suit the stages of delivery—dilation, transition, and expulsion. With *chi yi*, you are already expert in the control of exhalations and inhalations and in maneuvering their rate, duration, and intensity.

During the prenatal and postpartum periods, numerous physical exercises will probably be prescribed for you to help with your delivery and recovery. Explicit breathing instructions are seldom supplied with these exercises. If you already practice disciplined deep breathing, your ability to incorporate effective breathing into the exercises will greatly increase their beneficial results.

If you have never practiced *chi yi* before, you should consult your doctor before beginning these exercises during pregnancy. Every woman's physical condition varies, and every pregnancy has its own characteristics. For most normal pregnancies, the practice of *chi yi* should be helpful, whether you are a beginner or an experienced practitioner. Moderation must be observed, and your doctor's advice must always take priority. Even through the later part of your pregnancy, your doctor will most likely not object to your continuing with *chi yi*. As with swimming, tennis, and other forms of physical exercise and training, if you have been accustomed to doing it all along, there should be no harm in its continuance during a normal pregnancy.

Madame Ernestine Schumann-Heink, a famed contralto of the late nineteenth and early twentieth centuries, had many children. She was almost constantly pregnant during the prime of her career, and if she had stopped singing during her pregnancies, she would have had no career at all. Her biographers say that she performed almost up to the week of delivery and was back on stage again a few weeks after, breastfeeding her babies backstage between acts. Her breathing practice as a singer must surely have prepared her for such a devoted approach to child rearing.

Relieving Aches, Pains, and Discomforts

Aches and pains and other discomforts can arise for numerous reasons, and you should consult your physician about them if they are serious. However, if the doctor simply prescribes temporary relief such as painkillers, tranquilizers, or decongestants, you can supplement these medications with the inner energy cultivated from the practice of *chi yi*. Pains due to tension, rheumatic and arthritic pains, and lower back pain may be eliminated or greatly eased by channeling core energy to soothe the painful area.

Hastening Convalescence

For those who are convalescing or receiving physical therapy, *chi yi* can offer assistance.

An elderly friend of mine had been hospitalized for several weeks. At home again, she told me that the doctor had ordered her to get out of bed and start moving around, but she could not. She felt too weak even to sit up. I suggested that she should get up while I was visiting, first taking a few deep breaths to muster up some energy. She insisted that she could barely breathe, let alone breathe deeply. I pressed my palm firmly over her lower abdomen. As intended, my palm pressure felt heavy to her, and her abdominal muscle pushed slightly against my hand. If she could resist my palm pressure once, I told her, she could do the same a few more times with more strength.

As she did so, I asked her to synchronize her abdominal movements with her inhalation. "This is abdominal deep breathing," I told her, and she was amazed and encouraged by her accomplishment.

After she had relaxed awhile, I again called her attention to her breathing. This time I pressed against her abdomen with only my middle finger. Then I suggested that she should get up. I asked her to imagine the sensation of my finger pressing continuously against her abdomen: She could focus on that spot and from it draw all the energy she needed to stand up. With a minimum of help from her nurse, she sat up in bed, lifted her feet, and placed them on the floor. Our first goal was accomplished when she stood up by herself and slowly took a few steps to her easy chair. Her rapid recovery from then on amazed not only herself but her doctor as well, as she continued to practice this *chi yi* technique.

Certain *chi yi* exercises can be modified to fit the requirements of convalescence or disability. If you are recovering from a leg injury and are unable to stand, for example, you can execute the standing exercises and applications in this book in a sitting position. If part of your body is in a cast and cannot be moved or bent, you can still practice your breathing by eliminating the impossible motions and striking the postures indicated in the exercise or application as nearly as you can. Sensibly modified exercises and applications are still effective. Most people under physical restraint will pamper the injured area by keeping it immobile. In restricting movement, they also are likely, unconsciously, to restrain their breathing, causing it to be shallow. This limited intake of air reduces stimulation to the core and cuts down the supply of inner energy that is so necessary for recovery and healing.

Minimizing the Effects of Aging

Many people at an advanced age are suddenly confronted with the fact that their health and their very existence could have been greatly enhanced if they had put their lungs to fuller use. Shortness of breath, tight aching chest muscles, an uninspiring voice, tension, the heaving of shoulders in a useless effort to overcome the insufficient inhalation of air—all of these problems are frequently caused by poor breathing habits.

Aging is an unavoidable process characterized by the gradual loss of strength, energy, and coordination. The effects of such physical degeneration can be retarded or minimized through the development and use of core energy. Instead of fumbling aimlessly for the strength to lift yourself up, move, or walk, seek that needed strength at your core. The next time you feel too tired to stand up from sitting or stooping, visualize inward, take a deep breath, and lift up from your core as you stand. You will discover how effortless that movement can be.

Much of the image of aging is reflected in one's movement and carriage. To be able to stand more erect and to move more briskly will help you to look and feel younger.

Inner energy in a person can be likened to the electric current in a battery. When you are young, you are more fully charged, and as you proceed in life, unless you know how to recharge your inner battery, your inner energy circulation decreases steadily. When the inner energy loses some of its power and is no longer functioning at full capacity, the current will gradually withdraw, first from the farthest extremities, such as fingers, hands, and feet, and then from the arms and legs.

The joints, like the elbows in plumbing where clogging tends to occur, will also suffer from this insufficient supply of inner energy. As you grow older, you are likely to be plagued with aches and pains in these extremities—painful knuckles, aching feet, tennis elbow, and charley horses, to name a few. Any part of your body may be deprived of a sufficient supply of this inner current, leaving you unable to ward off or overcome invading illnesses.

If, when you are young and healthy, you have the foresight to develop and practice the skill of regularly generating inner energy, you will avoid the rapid decline of your inner energy stockpile. For the young of today, who frequently burn their candles at both ends, it is especially important to ensure that the supply of inner energy is not depleted but is replaced steadily. For those who are not so young, too, the supply of inner energy can be rapidly replenished and its circulation restored.

Improving Speech and Voice

No other human activity is more influenced by breathing than vocalization. Proper breathing, supported by a healthy core, will ease tension in the vocal apparatus, which is the usual cause of raspiness, hoarseness, squeakiness, breathiness, breathlessness, weakness, nasality, and many other impediments to clear speech. To mend and strengthen a misused, ailing, or underdeveloped voice, you must begin by making sure that the air you take in is correctly inhaled, energized, and exhaled.

Singing, especially classical singing, is a much more intense and demanding form of vocalization than is speech. It is an exaggerated form of elongated speech with built-in self-amplification and with extended range. In addition to musical intelligence and talent, a proficient singer needs extensive and intensive training and practice to master such intricate vocal execution. The singer must above all acquire the important technique of breath support.

When breath support is insufficient for a desired volume, inflection, or tone, whether in singing or in speech, we automatically supplement the missing energy by tensing up the chest, shoulder, or neck muscles, or all of them. But using rigid vocal cords can damage them, leading to functional problems such as soreness, breathiness, raspiness, hoarseness, loss of voice, and even the developing of nodes.

Breath is the foundation on which the voice is built, and it is only sensible to develop a reliable breathing skill, a skill that will provide sufficient energy and control for vocal support.

The image our speaking voice creates is just as important as our physical appearance. Our character, personality, state of mind, and degree of charisma are judged by how we sound. It is also true that how one sounds is related to how one looks.

Energetic, expressive speech generates obvious excitement in the listener, but a raspy, breathless, tired voice can blemish the most attractive appearance. Correct breathing is an essential component of good speech. With the help of deep breathing, a damaged voice can usually be mended. Speech defects can be smoothed out. The tone, the color, the ease, the contour of a voice can be developed. An average voice can be improved. A good voice can become more polished and perfected.

The voice possesses the unique power to express emotions through the laws of exclamatory vowels that are common to all human beings. Although the meanings of "ah," "oh," and "ee" may vary from culture to culture, their use is universal. Pitch denotes degrees of excitement. The depth of the breath relates to the depth of the vocal projection. The deeper the breath, the more thoroughly the feeling is released.

Every deep breath we take should give us a sense of wellbeing and make us feel uplifted. The world grows brighter then, and we want to open up and sing. Singing is healthy. It invites us to control a flowing stream of air and to release any pent-up emotions.

Sing anywhere you can. Sing in the shower, sing in your garden, sing in the car on the way to work. Never mind if you are tone deaf and sing out of tune. Sing for yourself. Don't worry about who may hear you. Memorize the words to a few songs—pop, rock, folk songs, hymns, even your favorite operatic arias. Don't worry if you are no Enrico Caruso or Barbra Streisand; just sing freely, comfortably. If you forget the words, make them up, or sing "la-la-la-la." Don't be shy about hearing your own voice.

Gradually, your true expressive self will emerge. You may even surprise yourself as you hear improvements in your singing. As your breathing method improves through the practice of *chi yi*, your singing voice will improve too. Let it be a barometer of your progress in learning the art of breathing.

Focusing the Breath in Meditation

Through the centuries, Buddhist monks and meditators of many faiths and beliefs have practiced meditation as a means of ascending to higher mental and spiritual plateaus; and they have asserted that the key to successful meditation is proper manipulation of the breath.

The yogis of the Himalayas went further, maintaining that controlled alternate-nostril breathing is essential. They claimed that normal breathing has a natural cycle that alternates between emphasis on the left and right nostrils. The ancient yogis believed that right-nostril breathing induced more active and aggressive instincts, while breathing through the left made one more passive and subdued. This belief brings to mind recent research on the different functions performed by the right and left hemispheres of the brain.

The practice of *chi yi* techniques establishes for you the basic ability to advance into many forms of meditation. In the process of disciplining and controlling breathing, you direct your mental attention inward, thus minimizing or even eliminating external distractions. The ability to centralize and control all mental and physical awareness is the key to total self-control of the body and mind, which is basically what meditation is all about. *Chi yi* trains the mind's eye to look inward and remain in focus, bringing about a state of total relaxation.

The ability to control your own physical and mental state produces immense satisfaction. To lie in sleeplessness or pain without the ability to combat it undermines self-confidence. Being competent in *chi yi* makes the difference between being helpless and being in charge. Begin to learn *chi yi* today!

PART TWO

Exercises for Practicing Chi Yi

Some Suggestions for Practice

What follows is the heart of *chi yi* training. These are thirty exercises, arranged in six progressive lessons, to guide you toward increased awareness of proper breathing habits and greater control of your breath.

Although the theory is easily grasped, diligent practice is required for the muscles and nervous system to handle this new technique reflexively. Learning *chi yi* takes motivation, concentration, and persistence. Eventually, though, taking a shallow breath will require more effort than practicing deep breathing from the abdomen. As your awareness of the breathing process is developed through the exercises, you will soon find the principles of deep breathing moving into your daily activities until you, too, are an artist in the art of breathing.

The deep-breathing skills and the resulting energy to be gained from practicing these exercises can be applied in many ways, to both physical and mental tasks. They can supplement and enhance whatever special physical skill you may be pursuing—making a business presentation, dancing, acting, or general physical activities such as jogging, aerobic exercise, or golf.

Don't be discouraged if you feel lost during your initial attempts to capture certain sensations and physical controls. With careful repetition you will begin to feel and perform as described in this book. As *chi yi* becomes habitual, you will gain in stamina, grace, radiance, and general well-being.

To some readers the exercises in this book, especially those in the first few lessons, may seem overly simple. In fact, they are very demanding because they must be performed precisely. Each detail is directed to an important purpose. The purposes of each exercise may seem abstract at first, but with practice they will soon become evident.

Each of the six lessons takes about 10 to 20 minutes to complete, depending on how much rest you require between exercises. You may decrease the number of repetitions indicated in the exercises according to your endurance. When you first begin to practice controlled breathing, you may feel slightly dizzy. Pause to recover before proceeding. Dizziness may be a signal of overexertion. Take time out for a rest interval whenever you need one, even if no rest break is indicated in the exercise instructions. If you wish to increase the number of repetitions of a particular exercise, do so with caution and with sufficient rest between repetitions.

Dress comfortably to accommodate the various movements and positions called for in the exercises. Loose comfortable clothes are recommended. Avoid constricting collars, waistbands, or belts that might restrict free and easy breathing.

The exercises do not require a lot of space, but it is a good idea to practice in a place where you can concentrate and not be interrupted. You may practice either indoors or outdoors. You will find that a stuffy room is not conducive to the practice of *chi yi*, because after the first couple of minutes of deep breathing you will begin to feel uncomfortably warm. To achieve the maximum benefit from the exercises that follow, open a window or two; it is always revitalizing to inhale fresh air.

For the exercises that are performed lying down, you will need a mat or a carpeted floor. A bare floor is not comfortable, and a soft bed does not give enough support.

You may practice any time during the day or evening, but be sure to rest at least 15 to 20 minutes after practicing before eating a meal. Also wait an hour or two after a meal before practicing, depending on how heavy a meal you have eaten.

Practice each lesson twice daily in two separate sessions. Practice each lesson for at least three days to allow sufficient time to master the skills and for your muscles to develop progressively.

After practicing a lesson twice daily for at least three consecutive days, you are ready to move on to the next lesson. If you cannot always practice twice daily, but feel thoroughly confident in performing all of the exercises in a lesson, you may proceed to the next lesson after three days. If you have skipped practicing for an entire day, it is advisable to go over each exercise once (ignoring repetitions) in the old lesson before going on to the new one. If you have not practiced for more than two days, review the previous lesson or lessons for a day or two before proceeding. In any case, let your own feeling about your mastery of the material be your guide.

Deep breathing means exhalations and inhalations that fill the upper and the lower lungs, involving the muscles of the lower torso, including the front, sides, and lower back. It is necessary to develop and tone the muscles in these areas with exercises that will induce specific results at the appropriate time. Therefore it is important to follow closely all the details specified in the exercises.

We are used to thinking of breathing as a process of inhalation-exhalation, in that order of importance. We seldom give any thought to how we exhale. Most advice on breathing emphasizes inhalation, as in "take a deep breath." The truth is that exhalation is just as important. Exhalations are cultivated and refined inner energy being selectively channeled, the reaping of what we sow when we inhale.

Important: Although the *effects* of these exercises will eventually carry over into normal breathing, the exercises themselves are intended *only* as exercises. They should not be taken as substitute methods for normal, everyday breathing. The exercises are demanding and should not be overpracticed. If signs of dizziness or other discomfort occur, stop! You have done enough for the time being. Divert your attention away from breathing by attending to other activities. Your breathing will automatically return to its normal manner and you will recuperate quickly.

Counting

In exercises where a *slow count is* indicated, each count should be executed at the rate of approximately one per second.

The numbers specified for counting mentally as we breathe are not picked arbitrarily but are chosen to gauge the duration of exhalations and inhalations under specific conditions. However, you will notice a pattern that persists throughout the book: Inhalations end with odd numbers, and exhalations end with even numbers. A psychological reason guides this usage. Most people count in pairs: At an odd number, we are mentally prepared to proceed and are therefore anticipating; at an even number we are more inclined to stop. When we end an inhalation, it is beneficial to feel anticipation and movement, whereas when we end an exhalation, it is preferable to experience a feeling of completion.

Posture

Observe the following points as you practice the exercises:

☐ Proper posture encourages proper breathing.

☐ The shoulders must never be raised or tightened. They should be relaxed and uninvolved during both exhalation and inhalation.

☐ The chest must never feel depressed or sunken.

As you sit, stand, or walk, stay erect, being careful not to stick out behind. Your head should be held straight and upright on an imaginary line drawn from the tailbone to the center top of the head. A tilted or lowered head tightens the muscles under the chin and neck, obstructing the free flow of the stream of breath.

The angle of the pelvis is essential for maintaining good posture. When you tilt your pelvis by lifting the pubic bone up in front, the abdominal and buttocks muscles are best able to support the trunk, and strain on your lower back is minimized. To further minimize straining, practice the following imagery drill.

IMAGERY DRILL

String of Beads

Imagine that your body parts are beads of different shapes. Attach a string to the floor, and string the beads. After the final bead (representing the head) is put on, pull the string taut and straight upward. All the beads should fall perfectly into place in a straight line. The different parts of your body should feel like beads on a string—well aligned, with all parts properly positioned and in place.

After a lifetime of shallow breathing, the top portion of the lungs has had more use and is stretched more than the bottom portion. We need not further emphasize the development of this top portion. On the contrary, this portion of the lungs should be left alone. Any attempt to emphasize its use will distract from and impede the development of the lower portion. Eventually, when the level of functional ability and elasticity of the lower lungs matches that of the top, both will automatically function together as a whole.

If you have ever blown up a long balloon, you will remember that balloons of this shape inflate easily only at the end where air enters. Unless you manipulate the balloon, the far end will scarcely inflate at all. You may have noticed that after several tries the inflated end becomes much looser and more elastic than the other end, creating an even greater tendency toward one-ended inflation. One trick to overcome this situation is to stretch and pull the far end of the balloon manually, loosening up the far end before inflating it.

The lungs are like this long balloon. Due to a variety of physical circumstances the bottom part of the lungs, like the far end of the balloon, is hardly used. Unless we do something about shallow breathing, the lungs will become increasingly top-heavy as we grow older. The progressive exercises in this book will deter this unhealthy condition. You will frequently hear elderly— and sometimes not so elderly—people complaining about the difficulty of breathing. Often this condition arises as the top part of the lungs becomes overburdened and overused and loses its elasticity, while the lower part of the lungs is undeveloped and incapable of undertaking its share of the lungs' function. It is never too late to begin training your lower lungs to be functional through the practice of *chi yi*.

Developing Internal Sensations and Muscular Controls

As you practice each of the exercises in the upcoming six lessons, try to maintain your awareness of the following sensations and means of muscular control. *Refer frequently to these two lists to increase your awareness of these qualities.*

Internal Sensations

☐ Be conscious of the *lower abdominal area,* located below the navel, which is inflatable and deflatable.

☐ Experience the sensation of breath flowing into and inflating the *lower abdomen* during inhalation.

☐ Experience the sensation of the deflation of the *lower abdomen* during exhalation.

☐ Experience a mental image and the sensation of the *tongue* extending from the tip to its root, not ending at the throat or the neck or the chest but extending all the way down to the pit of the stomach.

☐ As the tip of the *tongue* touches the back of the top front teeth during inhalation, imagine the tongue as a conduit. Air travels along this conduit from the nostrils past the tip of the tongue and flows all the way down to the tongue's root. At this point the stream of air loops around and travels back up and out.

☐ Experience the sensation of the *tongue's* relaxed positions. The tongue should feel limp and relaxed, not a tight lump or an inflexible strip. A tense tongue can cause tension in the neck, chest, and shoulder muscles, restricting the free flow of air into the lower abdomen.

☐ Experience the sensation of stimulating the *tongue's root so* that it more fully participates in the visible tongue's control and movement. Elongation, movement, and relaxation of the visible part of the tongue establishes sensation in the root and reinforces your ability to relocate tongue tension to the core as you breathe abdominally.

☐ Whenever "hold breath" is indicated between inhalation and exhalation, create a sensation of that breath continuously sinking and settling down to the bottom of the *abdomen* during the "hold" period.

☐ During exhalation, create a sensation of air being drained through a hole in the bottom of the *abdomen.*

☐ Experience the yawning sensation (at the *back of the throat* and the adjoining *nasal passage)* that creates a central opening for the flow of air.

Muscular Controls

☐ Proper opening of the mouth for exercise will be attained only if the *jaws* are opened in a rounded "reclining U" shape (⊃), not in an angular "reclining V" shape (>). To achieve this, stretch the jaws open not only in front but all the way back to the jaw hinges so that the top and bottom molars form an almost parallel line.

☐ Be sure to breathe freely as you practice the exercises that emphasize your *neck muscles.*

☐ Produce a *steady stream of breath* instead of disjointed short puffs.

☐ Movements of the arms, legs, spine, neck, and so on should be initiated by inner energy from the *lower abdomen.*

☐ Strengthen the *lower abdominal muscles* by expanding outward and pulling inward at will, with or without breathing.

☐ Use your fingertips and palms to assist and monitor the movements of the *abdominal muscles* whenever necessary.

Leading the Breath

Lesson 1 introduces a natural, simple, and effective method of breath discipline. The four exercises in Lesson 1 are designed to stretch your abdominal and lower back torso muscles. These muscles are among the principal elements involved in the kind of deep breathing that comes so naturally to healthy infants and is often lost as we grow older.

Through neglect and lack of exercise, the muscles of the abdominal wall and the lower back torso become rigid and unresponsive. Another factor in the avoidance of diaphragmatic deep breathing is the cultural attitude that regards protrusion of the abdomen as unfashionable. These and other properly designed breathing exercises do not make the stomach muscles protrude. On the contrary, development of these muscles reduces flabbiness, adds strength and elasticity, and increases your ability to hold your stomach in when you desire to do so.

Lesson 1 also helps you to develop your awareness of the yawning sensation at the back of the nose and throat that you achieve when inhaling. This sensation, which is emphasized in the Eyedropper Imagery Drill, induces the nose-throat junction to act as a wide funnel for the deep, free flow of air.

Once you are familiar with the exercises, the first lesson can be completed in 5 to 10 minutes, but be careful not to rush the exercises, or to skip any steps. This first lesson introduces movements and sensations that are essential to the lessons that follow. Practice it carefully twice a day for at least three days, until you feel comfortable with all the exercises.

EXERCISE 1A

Stretching the Abdominal Muscles

In a sitting position, all muscles, especially those of the legs, are more relaxed. In this position you can readily focus your attention on the abdominal muscles.

Sitting straight is important in order to form a right angle at the torso-buttocks junction. This position gives the lower abdominal area a maximum spread upward, which in turn allows greater breath capacity.

1. Sit up straight in a chair with your feet on the floor 6 to 7 inches apart.

2. Place your hands against the lower abdominal wall with your palms inward, fingertips not quite meeting (see Figure 4).

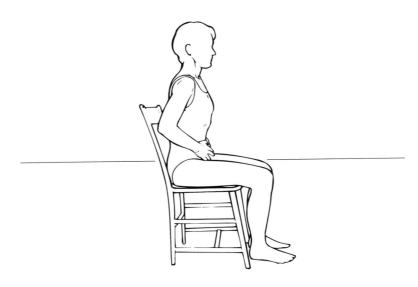

FIGURE 4

3. Place the tip of your tongue behind your bottom front teeth. Exhale through your mouth by blowing gently through slightly pursed lips to a slow count of 1-2-3-4-5. Begin the exhalation from the abdomen, simultaneously deflating the abdominal wall and adding inward pressure from the fingertips. On the sixth count, exert extra pressure to deflate the abdomen completely.

4. Place the tip of your tongue against the back of your top front teeth. Inhale through your nose as you create a yawning sensation in the back of the nose and throat to a slow count of 1-2-3-4-5-6. At the same time, expand the lower abdominal wall outward. On the seventh count, give the lower abdominal wall an extra push outward with an emphatic intake of breath to reach maximum expansion.

5. Without pausing, repeat the exhale-inhale sequence (steps 3 and 4) three times.

6. If you have never attempted to control your breathing before, you may feel slightly dizzy at this time. Don't be alarmed. Just relax for a few minutes before going on to the next exercise.

EXERCISE 1B

Stretching the Lower Back Muscles

When you bend over from a sitting position, the lower back muscles are stretched to their maximum length, and air can easily be inhaled to that area.

Holding your hands on your ankles with your elbows turned outward further encourages the spreading and extending of the lower back torso.

It is important to sit with your feet 10 to 12 inches apart. If the feet are too close together, the lower front abdominal muscle is restricted; if they are too far apart, the tailbone tends to stick out, resulting in a swayback that restricts the lower back muscles.

1. Sit up straight in a chair with your feet on the floor 10 to 12 inches apart. Place your hands in your lap, palms downward. Turn your palms inward with your thumbs toward your body, allowing your elbows to turn outward and forward. Gently grasp your upper thighs with your thumbs on the outside and your fingers on the inside of your thighs (see Figure 5).

2. Bend forward gradually while sliding your hands down your legs toward your ankles (see Figure 6). Firmly grasp the ankles (or the legs as close to the ankles as comfortably possible). Bend your head downward toward the floor, and turn your elbows farther out. In this position, focus your attention on your lower back and tailbone.

3. With your head still down, place the tip of your tongue behind your bottom front teeth. Exhale through your mouth by blowing gently through slightly pursed lips to a slow count of 1-2-3-4. At the same time, gradually deflate the lower abdominal wall.

4. Hold your breath, and remain still for a moment.

5. Place the tip of your tongue against the back of your top front teeth. Inhale through your nose, creating a yawning

sensation at the back of the nose and throat, to a slow count of 1-2-3-4-5. Direct the air you are inhaling toward the base of your torso. Imagine elongating the spine as you inhale while inflating the lower back torso. On the fifth count, give both sides of the lower back torso an extra expansion outward with an emphatic intake of breath.

6. Hold your breath, as you slowly sit up, sliding your hand back onto your lap.

7. Exhale completely.

8. Repeat steps 1 through 7 four times.

9. Relax for a few minutes before going on to Exercise 3.

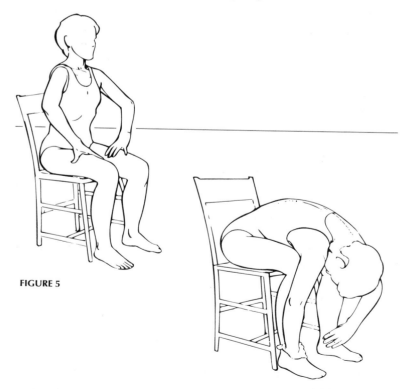

FIGURE 5

FIGURE 6

EXERCISE 1C

Stretching the Muscles at the Base of the Torso

Spreading the knees as far apart as possible in a kneeling position expands the lower torso. This posture draws your attention to the lower abdominal muscles and focuses muscular activity at the point where inflating and deflating most effectively take place.

Sliding your hands downward while inhaling deters your shoulders from heaving and discourages air from flowing uncontrollably and exclusively into the upper torso. The aim of this movement is to fill the lower torso with breath first, and then gradually let the breath pile upward. The feeling of fullness of breath must progress from bottom to top without allowing the lower area to deflate.

1. Kneel with your back and upper legs straight and at a right angle to your lower legs, and with your toes pointing to the back.

2. Spread your knees as far apart as possible without bending your body.

3. Place your hands just above the hips with palms inward, fingers pointing downward, and thumbs forward. Spread your elbows to the sides (see Figure 7).

4. Place the tip of your tongue against your bottom front teeth. Exhale through your mouth by blowing gently through slightly pursed lips to a slow count of 1-2-3-4-5-6 while deflating the lower abdomen.

5. Place the tip of your tongue against your top front teeth. Inhale through your nose, creating a yawning sensation at the back of the nose and throat, to a slow count of 1-2-3-4-5-6-7. Simultaneously inflate the lower abdomen and slide your hands gradually down your thighs until your arms are straight (see Figure 8).

6. Place the tip of your tongue against your bottom front teeth. Exhale through your mouth to a slow count of 1-2-3-4-5-6 while pulling your hands gradually back up to their original upper-hip-level position and deflating the lower abdomen.

7. Repeat steps 5 and 6 three times.

8. Remain in position and breathe freely.

9. Relax for a few minutes before going on to Exercise 4.

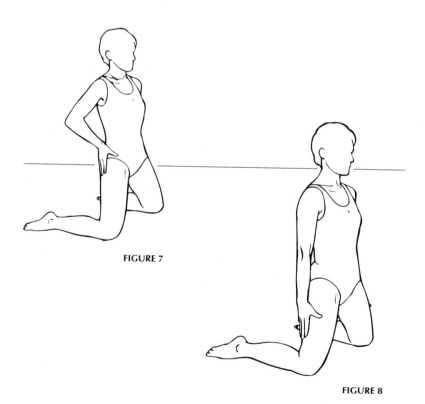

FIGURE 7

FIGURE 8

EXERCISE 1D

Stretching the Lower Front and Back Torso

The standing position does not induce the stretching or flexing of your torso muscles. In this neutral position, a higher degree of mental control of abdominal and lower back muscles is required to achieve the desired physical effect.

Joining hands behind your back and pushing them downward prevents your shoulders from heaving as you extend the front torso. Bending down while exhaling assists the contraction of the lower front abdominal muscles. Then, as you return to the standing position while inhaling, the inhaled air flows easily into the lower front abdominal area.

1. Stand up straight with your feet 18 to 20 inches apart.

2. Hold your head up straight; do not lower your chin (see Figure 9).

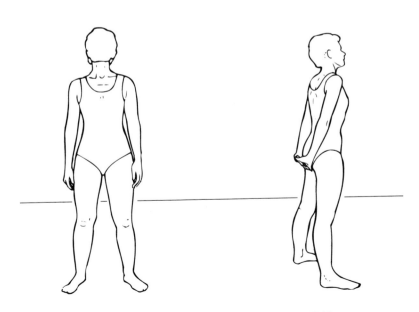

FIGURE 9   **FIGURE 10**

3. Join your hands together behind your back, palms down, locking your fingers.

4. Stretch your locked hands downward as far as possible, being careful not to stick your tailbone out and backward (see Figure 10).

5. Place the tip of your tongue against your bottom front teeth. Exhale through your mouth by blowing gently through slightly pursed lips to a slow count of 1-2-3-4-5-6 while gradually bending forward as far as possible and deflating the lower abdominal wall (see Figure 11).

6. Place the tip of your tongue against your top front teeth. Inhale through your nose, creating a yawning sensation at the back of your nose and throat, to a slow count of 1-2-3-4-5-6-7 while expanding the lower abdominal wall and lower back, returning to the original standing position described in steps 1 through 4.

7. Repeat steps 5 and 6 five times.

8. Exhale, relax, and rest.

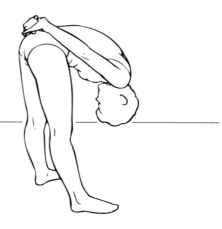

FIGURE 11

Thoughts on Lesson 1

The points made in Lesson 1 are simple, yet frequently the most obvious point may prove to be the one most easily overlooked. The most instinctive act, such as walking, frequently turns out to be difficult or even distorted.

Besides the objectives already discussed in Exercises 1A through 1D of Lesson 1, two very basic mental points must be introduced and established.

First, always think of the breath sequence as exhalation/ inhalation instead of the reverse. At any relaxed instant, some air always remains in the lungs; by expelling this leftover air, you are ready to start your first conscious inhalation afresh.

Second, the outflowing and inflowing of air (exhalation and inhalation) should produce no audible sounds. The sounds of gasping can be very disruptive, and even annoying, especially in speakers, singers, and wind instrumentalists. The split seconds that are allowed for air intake between phrases of speech or music demand that you leave your nose and mouth openings unobstructed. If you think about drawing in air through these openings, the muscles in these areas will be tense and narrow. Instead, apply the mental picture described in the Eyedropper Imagery Drill. Let the air be drawn in by your lower abdomen (the rubber bulb, as you imagine it), simultaneously letting your nose-throat junction act as a passive receptacle, like the top of a funnel. The muscles in these openings will then be relaxed and stretchable, allowing air to flow freely and silently.

Coordinating the Breath

When your tongue is tense and pulled in an inflexible lump toward the back of the throat, it obstructs the free flow of the breath and impairs your speech. Tension in the tongue extends to the throat, shoulder, chest, and abdominal muscles, preventing inhaled air from flowing freely to the bottom of the lungs. The relaxed tongue is crucial to deep breathing.

A continuous muscular connection runs from the tip of the tongue to the pit of the stomach. By learning to relax the tip of the tongue, and to mentally relocate its tension to the core, you will learn to relieve the tension of the tongue and to stimulate the core as well.

Open your mouth wide when doing the tongue exercises in this lesson to give maximum room for free movement of the tongue and the breath. A very small proportion of people may have weak jaw hinge muscles, so be careful not to strain these muscles by performing overexaggerated jaw movements for an extended period of time. If you do strain your jaw hinges, gentle massage with the fingertips will bring instant relief.

RECOMMENDED REVIEW   EXERCISES 1A, 1B, AND 1D

The review exercises can work as an integral part of the lessons. They are designed to fit into a group of exercises that are aimed at a specific purpose. As you do these exercises sequentially, you may become aware of the relationships among them. As you repeat them in the order given in the Review, you will be more aware of the cumulative nature of several exercises. The review of specific exercises, in a specific order, is also designed to strengthen your ability to perform them and to ease you into new exercises.

Review Exercises 1A, 1B, and 1D to recapture the sensations developed in Lesson 1. The specified repetitions in the review exercises can be reduced to leave you enough time and energy to complete Lesson 2.

EXERCISE 2A

Draining Tongue and Tongue Root Tension into the Core

This exercise stretches and extends the neck tendons and muscles and relieves any tension or kinks you may have.

Stretching your locked hands downward behind your back prevents your shoulders from heaving and inhibits inhaled air from flooding the upper torso and blocking the smooth flow of air into the lower abdomen.

If possible, perform Exercise 2A in front of a mirror; it is important to monitor the mouth and tongue positions closely. During this exercise, be sure you don't raise your shoulders while practicing the mouth and tongue movements. Your tongue should remain relaxed at all times.

1. Stand with your feet 10 to 12 inches apart.

2. Tilt your head back as far as possible; then bring it to an upright position in which it is tilted back slightly.

3. Join your hands together behind your back, locking your fingers.

4. Lower your locked hands to your buttocks, being careful not to stick your tailbone out and backward.

5. Open your mouth wide and touch your tongue to your top front teeth at a point about 1/2 to 3/4 inch in from the tip of your tongue (see Figure 12).

6. Inhale through your mouth to a slow count of 1-2-3-4 while inflating the lower abdomen.

7. Place the tip of your relaxed tongue behind your bottom front teeth (see Figure 13). Exhale through your mouth by blowing gently to a slow count of 1-2-3-4-5 while deflating the lower abdomen.

8. Once again, open your mouth wide and touch your tongue to your bottom front teeth at a point 1/2 to 3/4 inch in from the tip (see Figure 14).

9. Inhale through your mouth to a slow count of 1-2-3-4 while inflating the lower abdomen.

10. Place the tip of your tongue behind your bottom front teeth (see Figure 13). Exhale through your mouth to a slow count of 1-2-3-4-5 while deflating the lower abdomen.

11. Repeat steps 5 through 10 two more times.

12. Relax for a few minutes before going on to the next segment.

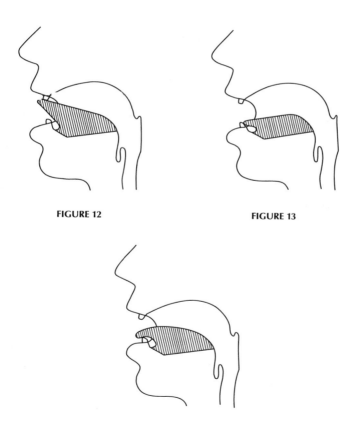

FIGURE 12   FIGURE 13

FIGURE 14

EXERCISE 2A CONTINUED

During this segment, be sure to hold your head erect; in stretching the tongue downward toward the chin, the head tends to dip, causing the under-chin and neck muscles to tighten.

When your tongue is stretched as far as possible toward your chin, as in step 5 below, be sure your mouth remains wide open.

1. Stand up straight with your feet 10 to 12 inches apart.

2. Tilt your head back as far as possible; then return it to an upright position in which it is tilted back slightly. Do not lower your chin.

3. Join your hands together behind your back, locking your fingers.

4. Lower your locked hands to your buttocks, being careful not to stick your tailbone out and backward.

5. Open your mouth wide, stretching the jawbone hinges. Stick your tongue out as far as possible toward your chin (see Figure 15).

6. Keep your mouth wide open and your tongue out. Exhale by blowing gently to a slow count of 1-2-3-4-5 while deflating the lower abdomen.

7. Maintain the mouth and tongue positions as described in steps 5 and 6. Inhale through your mouth to a slow count of 1-2-3-4 while inflating the lower abdomen.

8. Keep your mouth open, and bring your relaxed tongue behind your bottom front teeth (see Figure 16). Exhale through your mouth to a slow count of 1-2-3-4-5 while deflating the lower abdomen.

9. Maintain the mouth and tongue positions described in step 8. Inhale through your mouth to a slow count of 1-2-3-4 while inflating the lower abdomen.

10. Repeat steps 5 through 9 three times.

11. Drop your hands to your sides, loosen your joints, breathe freely, and relax for a few minutes before going on to Exercise 2B.

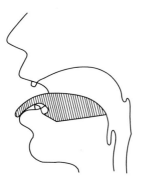

FIGURE 15

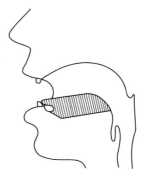

FIGURE 16

EXERCISE 2B

Activating the Tongue Muscles

In this exercise, the syllable *toh is* a nonvocal or aspirated sound, as in whispering, made merely by the quick release of breath. It sounds like *tore* without the r sound, except that it is produced without the involvement of the voice box. Air should explode out between the front teeth and the tip of the tongue to produce a nonvocal outburst.

When making a double *toh-toh* sound, you should produce two explosive snapping sounds, one after the other, using only the lower abdominal muscles and inhaling no additional breath.

IMAGERY DRILL

Cannonball

Imagine an unobstructed channel from the pit of your stomach to the tip of your tongue as you produce nonvocal *tohs. It* may also help to imagine the *tohs* as cannonballs being shot through the channel from the pit of the stomach to the tip of the tongue and beyond.

In the exercise that follows, all snapping inward (rapid deflating) must be done with the lower abdominal and lower back torso muscles only. The only upper torso and chest movements should be slight natural reactions to the abdominal movements. You should experience no upward thrusts or jerks of the shoulders, the top back torso, or the chest.

1. Sit up straight in a chair with your head facing forward. Place both feet on the floor 6 to 8 inches apart, with your toes pointing slightly outward. Place your hands against the lower abdominal wall, palms inward and fingertips almost touching.

2. Place the tip of your tongue against the back of your bottom front teeth. Exhale through your mouth by blowing gently through slightly pursed lips to a slow count of 1-2-3-4-5-6 while deflating the lower abdominal wall, using your fingertips to apply extra pressure.

3. Place the tip of your tongue firmly against your top front teeth. With your mouth closed, inhale through your nose to a slow count of 1-2-3-4-5 while inflating the lower abdominal wall.

4. Bring the tip of your tongue between your top and bottom front teeth. Release the syllable *toh* explosively, dropping your jaw as you do so (see Figure 17). Do not retract your tongue toward your throat but simply release the tip of your tongue from your front teeth while dropping your jaw. Simultaneously snap the lower abdominal wall inward, assisting with pressure from your fingertips.

5. Exhale the remaining air.

6. Repeat steps 3 through 5 four times.

7. Relax, and rest for a moment.

8. Repeat steps 3 through 6 again, substituting a double *toh-toh* sound (staccato) for *toh*.

9. Repeat step 8 six times.

10. Relax, and rest briefly.

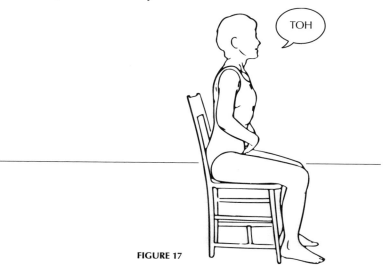

FIGURE 17

EXERCISE 2C

Controlling the Tip and the Root of the Tongue

The purpose of this exercise is to create awareness of core energy. The sound *tse* is a nonvocalized tight hissing sound produced by a continuous stream of breath. To make the *tse* sound, bring your top and bottom teeth together, but do not bite down hard. Place the tip of your tongue gently against the back of your front teeth. It's important for the tongue not to press too strongly against the front teeth, as extreme pressure causes tension in the neck and tongue. Exhale in an even, steady, unrushed stream of breath to produce not a *se* but a *tse* sound.

Although pressure is being produced by a continuous deflation of the lower abdominal wall, this deflation should not be overly exaggerated with too much inward motion of the abdominal wall. You can avoid this tendency by creating an imaginary counterforce from within, such as an expanding sensation within your lower abdomen as you deflate it. In this way, a much more controlled pressure of the abdominal wall can be produced and put to use.

1. Sit up straight in a chair with your head tilted back slightly. Place your feet on the floor 6 to 8 inches apart, with your toes pointing slightly outward. Place your hands against the lower abdominal wall, palms inward, fingertips almost touching.

2. Place the tip of your tongue gently against your bottom front teeth. Exhale through your mouth by blowing through slightly pursed lips to a slow count of 1-2-3-4-5-6, while squeezing in the abdominal wall with added pressure from your fingertips.

3. Place the tip of your tongue firmly against your top front teeth. Inhale through your nose to a slow count of 1-2-3-4-5, while inflating the lower abdomen.

4. Touch your top and bottom teeth together; do not bite hard. Place the tip of your tongue against the inside of your front teeth.

5. Exhale by producing a sustained *tse* sound (see Figure 18) while performing the following steps alternately:

   ☐ Roll your head in a clockwise circle once, then counter-clockwise once.

   ☐ Seesaw your shoulders up and down twice.

6. As you maintain the sustained *tse* sound, you will begin to feel a gradual tightening of a central spot in the depth of the lower abdomen. You are beginning to localize and gain an awareness of your core. Continue making the sustained *tse* sound until your breath is depleted.

7. Hold the deflated position for a few seconds. Then give an extra squeeze of the abdominal muscles, with added pressure from your fingertips, to expel any remaining air with an additional *tse*.

8. Immediately inhale deeply through your nose, with the tip of your tongue firmly against your top front teeth. Settle your breath, and hold it for a few seconds.

9. Exhale and relax for a moment. Repeat steps 2 through 8 once more.

10. Exhale, and rest briefly, and proceed to the following segment.

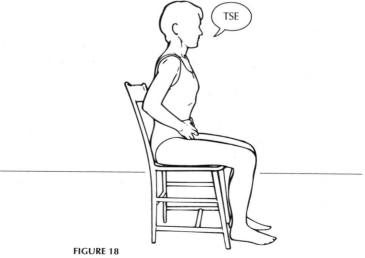

FIGURE 18

EXERCISE 2C CONTINUED

The purpose of this segment is to learn how to maintain constant control of the core while sitting, standing, walking, running, jumping, or performing other movements.

When rising from a sitting to a standing position in step 6, take care not to shift pressure away from the core, the center of the lower abdomen.

In step 7, be especially careful not to let the center point shift to the chest, shoulders, or neck. Steady fingertip pressure on the lower abdomen will help alleviate this tendency to shift.

1. Sit up straight in a chair facing a desk or table. Place your feet on the floor with your weight on your toes, as if you were about to stand up. Place one foot slightly in front of the other.

2. Place your right hand (or your left, if you are left-handed) on the table top, palm down. Place the other hand against the lower abdominal wall, palm inward.

3. Place the tip of your tongue lightly against your bottom front teeth. Exhale through your mouth by blowing through slightly pursed lips to a slow count of 1-2-3-4-5-6, while squeezing the lower abdominal muscle inward and pressing with your fingertips.

4. Place the tip of your tongue firmly against your top front teeth. Inhale deeply through your nose to a slow count of 1-2-3-4-5, while inflating the lower abdomen.

5. Bring your upper and lower teeth together, but do not bite down hard. Place the tip of your tongue gently against the back of your front teeth while maintaining the air pressure in your lower abdomen.

6. Exhale by producing the sustained *tse* sound described in Exercise 2A (see Figure 19). Simultaneously, stand up, using the hand on the table to assist balance. Do not allow your shoulders to rise or your body to bend forward.

7. When you have reached an upright position, continue the *tse* sound evenly and firmly, using your lower abdominal and lower back muscles to maintain breath support (see Figure 20).

8. When your breath is depleted, hold in that state for 2 to 3 seconds. Then blow out forcefully, deflating the abdominal wall to expel any remaining air.

9. Immediately inhale deeply through your nose with the tip of your tongue held firmly against your top front teeth. Hold your breath without straining for a few seconds.

10. Slowly and deeply exhale and inhale three times, with accompanying lower abdomen deflation and inflation.

11. Relax, and rest for a moment.

12. Repeat this exercise two more times with a rest interval between repetitions.

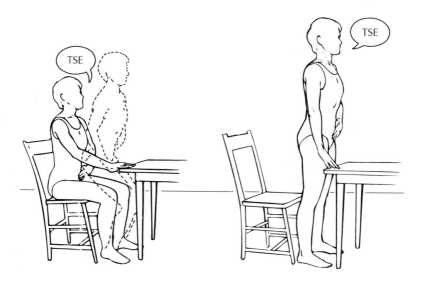

FIGURE 19   **FIGURE 20**

EXERCISE 2D

Stretching the Muscles of the Lower Torso

Raising your hands above your head stretches the torso length-wise. The previous exercises should have stretched your lower torso sideways sufficiently to enable you to maintain a stable, anchored base during this exercise.

In a left-right, backward-forward sequence of movements while inhaling and exhaling, you will learn to squeeze air out of your torso one side at a time, and then draw air back into your torso one side at a time. This action will allow you to make each repeated inhalation and exhalation more emphatic.

1. Stand up straight with your feet spread apart to the width of your shoulders. Point your toes slightly outward.

2. Raise your arms over your head and lock your fingers, palms down, to form an arch (see Figure 21).

FIGURE 21

3. Place the tip of your tongue lightly against your bottom front teeth. Exhale through your mouth by blowing gently through slightly pursed lips to a slow count of 1-2-3-4-5-6-7-8. Simultaneously:

   □ Rock the arch from the waist, left-right-left-right on the counts 1-2-3-4, and slowly deflate the lower abdomen (see Figures 22 and 23).

   □ Return on counts 5 and 6 to the center upright position described in step 2.

4. Place the tip of your tongue firmly against your top front teeth. Inhale deeply through your nose to a slow count of 1-2-3-4-5-6. Simultaneously:

   □ Bend in an arch from the waist, moving forward to a slow count of 1-2 backward to a slow count of 3-4, and inflate the lower back and abdomen (see Figures 24 and 25).

   □ Return to the center upright position on count 5-6 (see Figure 21).

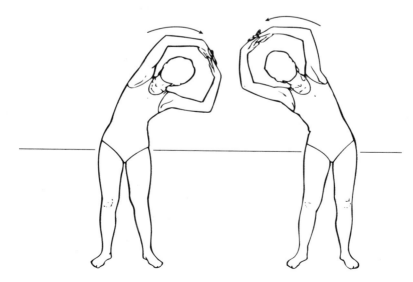

FIGURE 22   **FIGURE 23**

5. Repeat steps 3 and 4 four times.

6. Exhale through your mouth to a slow count of 1-2-3-4-5-6-7-8, while deflating the lower abdomen and lowering your arms to your sides.

7. Inhale, relax, and rest.

FIGURE 24   **FIGURE 25**

Thoughts on Lesson 2

By this time, your muscles should be growing more sensitive and responsive, and your awareness of the core gradually becoming more acute.

Exercises 1A through 2D were geared toward maximum inflation and deflation of the abdomen. Keeping in mind the image of the body as a pyramid, you should begin to cultivate a sensation of physical stability.

You should be able to feel your core glowing with energy, generated from within.

Controlling the Breath

In addition to the tongue, the neck is another part of the body that must be fully relaxed before effective breathing can take place. Without some form of abdominal breathing, however, it is difficult to relax the neck. To break this circle, you must follow a regimen that focuses alternately on developing each of these skills so that they reinforce each other.

It is not easy to get rid of unwanted tension in the neck, tongue, or shoulders. Tension in these areas must be relocated to a place where, properly handled, it can be recycled into useful energy. The core is such a place. Awareness of the core must be established before harmful tensions can be effectively eliminated. This lesson also reestablishes the relationship between the tongue and the core by reviewing Exercise 2B.

From now on, you will no longer be instructed to rest between exercises. Let your physical condition determine when you need to rest, and for how long.

The Elastic Band Imagery Drill will help you to relax your neck as well as your chest and back muscles. You will feel taller, straighter, and free of muscle tension, especially in the neck area.

IMAGERY DRILL

Elastic Band

Visualize your spine, with its ability to bend in any direction. Imagine one elastic band attached from your chin to your lower abdomen, and another attached from the back of your head (at the top) to your lower back. Bend backward, with your chin lifted high, and feel the front elastic band stretching to its utmost. Bend forward with your head dipping low and feel the back elastic band stretching as much as possible.

Imagine that these elastic bands are too stiff and tight. As you bend backward and forward you lengthen the bands and relax the stiffness and tightness.

EXERCISE 3A

Directing the Breath to the Lower Abdomen and Lower Back

Lying down should be a very relaxed position, yet many people find themselves unable to relax sufficiently to fall asleep. To do away with unwanted tension, focus your mind on the core by directing the breath there. This will create a magnetic center where tensions can be gathered and dispelled or recycled. In this exercise, tension is maintained at the core and used to bend the knees and pull the feet toward the body. Drawing the knees to the chest further emphasizes the involvement of the lower back in abdominal breathing.

1. Lie on the floor or bed with your feet together. Place your hands, palms down, on the floor by your sides, 12 to 14 inches away from the body (see Figure 26).

2. Bend your knees and slide your feet flat along the floor until they are as close to your body as possible (see Figure 27).

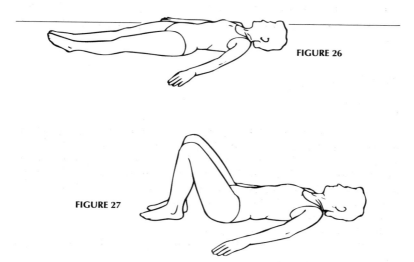

FIGURE 26

FIGURE 27

3. Place the tip of your tongue against your bottom front teeth. Exhale on the counts of 1 and 2 by blowing through your mouth in two strong gusts (one gust to each count), while deflating the lower abdomen and doing the following steps:

   ☐ With the first gust, swing your knees up as close to your chest as possible, lifting your feet off the floor (see Figure 28).

   ☐ With the second gust, return your feet to the floor (see Figure 27).

4. Place the tip of your tongue against your top front teeth. Inhale through your nose in two strong sniffs (one to each count), while inflating the lower abdomen and doing the following steps:

   ☐ With the first sniff, swing your knees up as close to your chest as possible, lifting your feet off the floor (see Figure 28).

   ☐ With the second sniff, return your feet to the floor (see Figure 27).

5. Repeat steps 3 and 4 in a rocking motion ten times.

6. Exhale as you straighten your legs, and return to your original position.

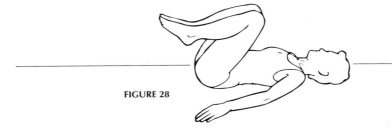

FIGURE 28

EXERCISE 3B

Relieving Neck Tension

This exercise is intended to stretch the spine, back muscles, and tendons at the same time that breathing is being controlled. When you hook your arms under your knees, as in step 3, you stretch the back and side muscles outward and keep your shoulders from heaving. Bending your head and touching your face to your knees extends your back and the back of your neck lengthwise.

In the ball position, with your stomach curled inside, exhaling further shrinks the front abdominal wall. In this position, the back is extended and the front is contracted as much as possible. This position also directs the maximum amount of breath to the lower back while restricting intake to the front. Extreme positions such as this one help you develop agility.

1. Sit up straight on the floor and stretch your legs out in front of you. Place your feet together and point your toes, making sure you are sitting up straight. Hold your head in an upright position, being careful not to drop your chin. Place your hands on your knees, palms down (see Figure 29).

2. Slide your feet toward you, bending your knees (see Figure 30).

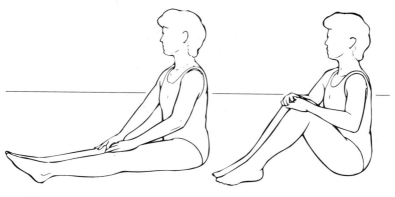

FIGURE 29   **FIGURE 30**

3. Hook your arms under your knees by reaching under the knees with your right hand to hold your left elbow or near to it, and with your left hand to hold your right elbow or near to it (see Figure 31).

4. Bend your head over and touch your face to your knees, or as close as you can comfortably manage (see Figure 32).

5. Place the tip of your tongue against your bottom front teeth. Exhale through your mouth by blowing gently through slightly pursed lips to a slow count of 1-2-3-4-5-6, while completely deflating the lower abdomen.

6. Hold your breath and remain still for a second.

7. Place the tip of your tongue against your top front teeth. Inhale through your nose to a slow count of 1-2-3-4-5-6-7, while inflating the lower abdomen. As you inhale, think of your lower torso as a round balloon that inflates as you inhale steadily to the count of 1-2-3-4-5. On the last two counts, make an extra effort to fully inflate the balloon, using your lower back and side muscles.

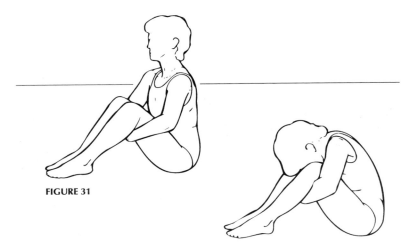

FIGURE 31

FIGURE 32

8. Repeat steps 5 through 7 three times.

9. Slowly let go of all muscle tension, stretching your legs forward and straightening your neck and body.

10. Loosen all your joints. Roll your head clockwise and counter-clockwise several times. Then relax for a moment and proceed with the following segment.

EXERCISE 3B CONTINUED

1. Sit up straight on the floor with your legs spread as far apart as is comfortably possible. Place your hands on your knees, palms down (see Figure 33).

2. Bend your knees to an angle of approximately 120 degrees by sliding your feet along the floor toward you. Keep your feet far apart, and point your toes outward (see Figure 34).

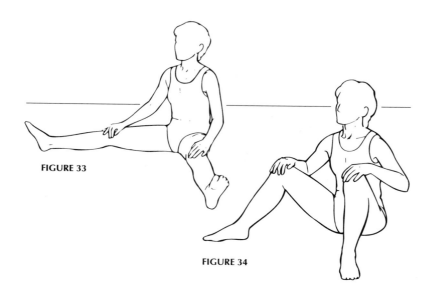

FIGURE 33

FIGURE 34

3. Bend your body forward. Stretch your arms along and over your legs, and gently grasp your ankles (or your legs as near your ankles as possible) with your hands. Spread your elbows out and forward.

4. Let your head dangle toward the floor.

5. Place the tip of your tongue against your bottom front teeth. Exhale through your mouth by blowing gently through slightly pursed lips to a slow count of 1-2-3-4-5-6 in the following manner:

    ☐ Roll your head to the right twice in big circles on counts 1 and 2.

    ☐ Dangle your head forward toward the floor on count 3.

    ☐ Roll your head to the left twice in big circles on counts 4 and 5.

    ☐ Dangle your head forward toward the floor on count 6.

    All these movements are performed as you slowly deflate the lower abdominal and lower back walls (see Figure 35).

6. Place the tip of your tongue against your top front teeth. Inhale through your nose to a slow count of 1-2-3-4, while inflating the lower abdomen and the lower back.

7. Repeat steps 5 and 6 three times.

8. Let go your grip, straighten your legs, lie on the floor facing up, and relax.

FIGURE 35

Sitting up straight with your feet as far apart as possible focuses attention on the lower abdominal area, the core's cradle. Bending your knees with your feet far apart makes you more fully aware of the lower back. Placing your hands on your knees helps you maintain your balance, and lowers and relaxes the shoulders and upper chest muscles as well. Be sure that your shoulders remain relaxed as you bend your knees and shift your hands from knees to ankles.

By rolling your head in a dangling, relaxed position, you ensure that the neck is completely relaxed while the lower torso is energetically controlling the breathing.

RECOMMENDED REVIEW   EXERCISES 1B AND 2B

For the exercises in this lesson, you must be very aware of the relationship between your tongue and the act of breathing to and from the core. Reread the introductory material for Lesson 2 before reviewing Exercise 2B.

A review of Exercise 1B gives you the opportunity to loosen the lower torso and establish a firmer focus on your core. This exercise will also loosen the muscles and tendons at the back of the neck in preparation for Exercise 3C.

EXERCISE 3C

Relieving Neck and Shoulder Tension

Swinging your arms relaxes your shoulders and loosens the base of the neck. Your arms should dangle and swing freely. It is preferable to keep your elbow joints loose by letting your elbows bend slightly, as is their natural tendency.

Your neck muscles should not be tense during the alternating neck stretches. Relax!

1. Stand up straight with your feet 12 to 14 inches apart and your toes pointed slightly outward.

2. Lower your shoulders, and loosen your shoulder joints. Let your arms and hands dangle at your sides (see Figure 36). Stretch and extend your neck upward.

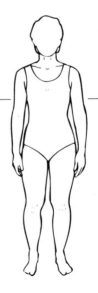

FIGURE 36

3. Place the tip of your tongue against your bottom front teeth. Gently tilt your head back as far as possible to stretch the front of your neck and stretch all the way to the core. Exhale through your mouth by blowing vigorously through slightly pursed lips to a slow count of 1-2, while deflating the lower abdomen and doing the following:

   ☐ On the first count, swing your arms to the left, bringing your hands toward waist level (see Figure 37).

   ☐ On the second count, swing your arms to the right, bringing your hands toward waist level (see Figure 38).

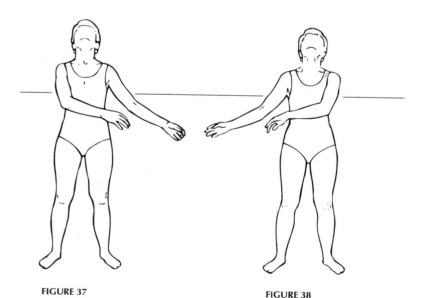

FIGURE 37   **FIGURE 38**

4. Place the tip of your tongue against your top front teeth. Bend your head forward as far as possible to stretch the back of your neck. Inhale vigorously through your nose to a slow count of 1-2, while inflating the lower abdomen and doing the following:

   ☐ On the first count, swing your arms to the left, bringing your hands toward waist level (see Figure 39).

   ☐ On the second count, swing your arms to the right, bringing your hands toward waist level (see Figure 40).

5. Repeat steps 3 and 4 seven times.

6. Return to upright standing position.

7. Relax momentarily and proceed to the following segment.

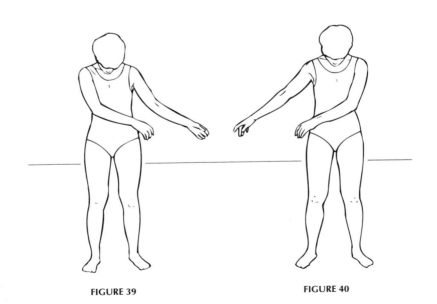

FIGURE 39   FIGURE 40

EXERCISE 3C CONTINUED

Swinging your arms forward and backward as suggested in this segment further relaxes the front and back of the rib cage.

1. Stand up straight with your feet 10 to 12 inches apart and your toes turned slightly outward.

2. Lower your shoulders, and loosen your shoulder joints. Let your arms and hands dangle at your sides. Stretch and extend your neck.

3. Place the tip of your tongue against your bottom front teeth. Tilt your head back as far as possible to stretch the front of your neck from chin to core. Exhale through your mouth by blowing vigorously through slightly pursed lips to a slow count of 1-2, while deflating the lower abdomen and doing the following:

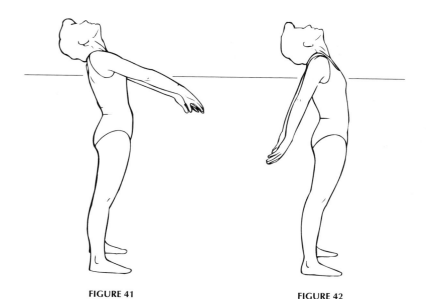

FIGURE 41   FIGURE 42

☐ On the first count, swing your arms forward, bringing your hands toward shoulder height (see Figure 41).

☐ On the second count, keeping your head back, swing your arms back as far as possible (see Figure 42).

4. Place the tip of your tongue against your top front teeth. Bend your head forward as far as possible to stretch the back of your neck. Inhale intensely through your nose to a slow count of 1-2, while inflating the lower abdomen and doing the following:

☐ On the first count, swing your arms forward toward shoulder level (see Figure 43).

☐ On the second count, keeping your head bent, swing your arms back as far as possible (see Figure 44).

5. Repeat steps 3 and 4 seven times.

6. Relax by rotating your shoulder joint and gently shaking your arms and legs.

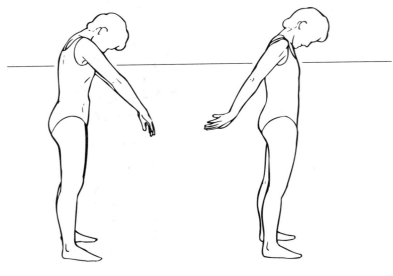

FIGURE 43   **FIGURE 44**

EXERCISE 3D

Leading the Breath to the Core

This long, detailed exercise is divided into two sections. Steps 1 through 7 aim to reveal more completely the location of the core and its cradle through a back-arching movement that induces the lower abdominal wall to stretch as it deflates during exhalation. This movement establishes a strong awareness of the core. After the lower abdomen is completely deflated, you will forcefully expand it, drawing a big gulp of air into the core and its surrounding area. Steps 8 through 10 take advantage of techniques learned in Lesson 1 by repeating deep breathing in a relaxed standing position. Read through the instructions several times so that you understand the steps and will be able to perform the exercise comfortably and easily.

1. Stand up straight with your feet 12 to 14 inches apart and your toes pointed slightly outward. Place your hands on the lower abdominal wall, palms inward, fingers almost touching (see Figure 45).

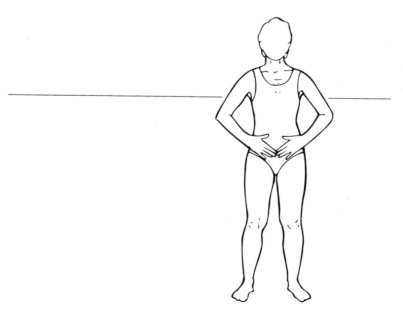

FIGURE 45

2. Place the tip of your tongue against your bottom front teeth. Exhale through your mouth by blowing gently through slightly pursed lips to a slow count of 1-2-3-4-5-6-7-8-9-10-11-12, while gradually deflating the lower abdomen and giving it a big squeeze inward as your breath is depleted

3. As you hold this deflated state, bend your head back with your chin upward (see Figure 46). Steps 3 through 5 should take only a few seconds, so no inhalation is necessary.

4. Bring your arms behind your back, joining your hands by interlocking the fingers. Rest your joined hands on your buttocks (see Figure 47.)

5. Arch back gradually while pushing your locked hands downward and tilting your chin high with your mouth closed. Be sure not to bend your knees (see Figure 48). As you continue to arch back in this manner, you will feel a very strong sensation in the lower abdomen.

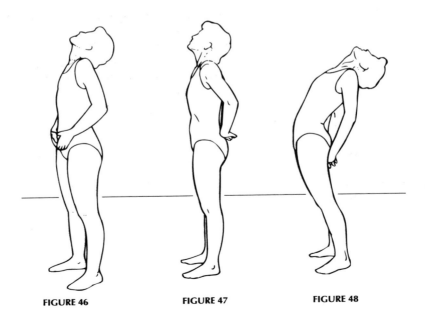

FIGURE 46   **FIGURE 47**   **FIGURE 48**

6. Give a strong squeeze inward with the lower abdominal muscles to expel the last traces of breath.

7. Immediately relax your tongue, resting it against your bottom front teeth, and inhale through your mouth, completely filling the core cradle (lower abdomen). Hold your breath for a few seconds, letting it sink deeply into the core and stabilize and anchor there.

As you continue with the second part of Exercise 3D, do not attempt, in step 8, to squeeze out air excessively. This excessive effort might shift the pivot point upward to the chest, completely undoing your accomplishment of locating the core in order to anchor the breath there.

8. Loosen all muscle tension. Slowly return to a normal standing position, letting your arms and hands dangle at your sides. Place the tip of your tongue against your bottom front teeth. Exhale slowly through your mouth, maintaining the sensation of being anchored. Stop the exhalation when your breath seems completely expelled from the lower abdomen.

9. Place the tip of your relaxed tongue against your slightly parted top and bottom front teeth. Inhale slowly and deeply through your nose, while inflating the lower abdomen. Continue to hold the tip of your tongue at the same position. Exhale slowly and deeply through your nose while deflating the lower abdomen.

10. Repeat step 9 three times.

11. Relax, and rest.

12. Repeat this exercise, steps 1 through 11, two or three times. Rest between each repetition.

Thoughts on Lesson 3

Having completed Lesson 3, you should now be able to apply the abdominal deep-breathing technique to improve your daily breathing. Use the tongue position described in step 9 of Exercise 3D in your everyday breathing. For instance, as you watch TV, walk, exercise, or just relax, inflate and deflate your lower abdomen. Remember, inflate for inhalation and deflate for exhalation. The more you practice this technique, the more habitual it will become.

Since deep breathing stimulates and strengthens the core, it is advisable to do it as frequently as you can. At this stage, you should be able to sense the location of the core without great effort. Think frequently of its location, and familiarize yourself with its presence.

LESSON FOUR

Varying and Extending the Breath

All of the exercises in this book are carefully planned to accomplish specific purposes. It is impossible to design special exercises or to plan special lessons to suit each individual's needs. You have now learned enough about *chi yi* to feel free to repeat those exercises that you find to be especially beneficial, even though they may not be included in a particular lesson. But be careful not to overexert yourself. Allow sufficient rest time between exercises. Always stop to rest if you become dizzy.

In Lesson 4 and later lessons, unless otherwise specified, the term *inhale* will always mean breathing in through the nose with the tip of the tongue against the top front teeth, and *exhale* will always mean blowing out gently through slightly pursed lips with the tip of the tongue placed lightly against the bottom front teeth.

Tongue positions for inhalation and exhalation may now be executed more casually, as long as the tongue remains flexible and unobtrusive and is not tense, retracted, or lumping. As you review Exercise 2C in this lesson, apply the following image.

IMAGERY DRILL

Kite

Imagine controlling your tongue the same way you would fly a kite. You control your kite from the end of the string that you hold in your hand. But to control it well, under conditions of varying wind direction and intensity, you must have great dexterity in your hand.

Likewise, the capability of your tongue relies a great deal on how well you can control it from the core. Imagine your tongue as the kite, and control it from your core, way down in the center of your lower abdomen. You will discover how well your tongue can perform and respond. Apply this image in this lesson as you review Exercise 2C.

RECOMMENDED REVIEW   EXERCISES 3A AND 3B AND EXERCISE 2C

Lesson 4 begins with a review of anchoring the breath in four different positions: lying flat, sitting on the floor, sitting in a chair, and standing up. This review session is fairly strenuous. Be easy on yourself, and take a sufficient break before going on to Exercise 4A. Repeat each of the review exercises as many times as necessary to feel you have mastered them thoroughly.

EXERCISE 4A

Flexing the Lower Abdominal and Lower Back Muscles

In this doubled-up position, the tendons and muscles of the feet and legs are thoroughly stretched. This stretched sensation is passed on up to the base of the torso (the lower abdomen). In bending over, you further extend this sensation up your back to your neck and even to the top of your head. Your entire body is in a state of attention. Centralize all your attention at the core. Focusing in this way will induce your breathing to come and go from the core.

Exhaling while bending over squeezes air out of the abdomen. When you inhale as you sit up, air is drawn easily into the abdomen.

1. Kneel on the floor with your knees together; keep your back straight and sit on your heels. Place your hands in your lap, palms down, fingers pointing forward, and thumbs inward. Keep your elbows by your sides. Lower and relax your shoulders. Hold your head up straight, being careful not to lower your chin (see Figure 49). (If you find it difficult to sit on your heels, place a pillow or cushion on your heels and sit on that.)

FIGURE 49   **FIGURE 50**

2. Exhale to a slow count of 1-2-3-4-5-6-7-8-9-10, while doing the following steps simultaneously (see Figure 50):

   ☐ Bend forward from the hips, and curve your back.

   ☐ Bring your forehead slowly to the floor, or as low as possible.

3. Inhale rapidly to a slow count of 1-2-3, while doing the following steps simultaneously:

   ☐ Straighten up, returning to your original kneeling position (see Figure 51).

   ☐ Expand your lower abdomen and sides. Do not lift your shoulders or raise your chest. Straighten your neck and lift your head slightly.

4. Repeat steps 2 and 3 five times.

5. Sit up, breathe normally, relax for a moment, and proceed to the following segment.

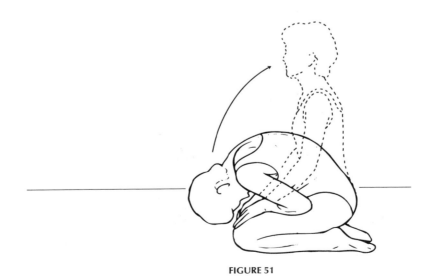

FIGURE 51

EXERCISE 4A CONTINUED

This segment promotes inflation of the lower back torso. Exhaling while deflating all sides of the lower torso in an upright sitting position prepares you for your next inhalation. As you bend over while inhaling, the air you take in will significantly fill up the lower back as the front abdomen is being depressed.

1. Kneel on the floor with your knees together; keep your back straight and sit on your heels. Place your hands in your lap, palms down, fingers pointing forward, and thumbs inward. Keep your elbows at your sides. Lower and relax your shoulders. Hold your head up straight, being careful not to lower your chin (see Figure 52).

2. Exhale to a slow count of 1-2-3-4-5-6-7-8-9-10-11-12, while deflating the lower abdomen.

3. Inhale to a slow count of 1-2-3, while doing the following steps simultaneously (see Figure 53):

   ☐ Bend forward from the hips, bringing your forehead to the floor, or as low as possible.

   ☐ Inflate the lower back and sides.

FIGURE 52   FIGURE 53

4. Exhale to a slow count of 1-2-3-4-5-6-7-8-9-10, while doing the following steps simultaneously:

   □ Straighten up, returning to your original kneeling position (see Figure 54).

   □ Deflate the lower abdomen, back, and sides.

5. Repeat steps 3 and 4 five times.

6. Inhale, and return to the original step 1 position.

7. Exhale and relax.

Note: To help you visualize the deep breathing that involves inflating and deflating of the lower front, the lower back, and the lower sides simultaneously, from now on these areas will be called the *lower circumference* when spoken of as a unit.

RECOMMENDED REVIEW EXERCISES 3B AND 3C

In preparation for Exercises 4C and 4D, this review of Exercises 3B and 3C serves primarily as a reminder of how to relax your neck and shoulders without losing your awareness of the core, the focal point of the flow of breath.

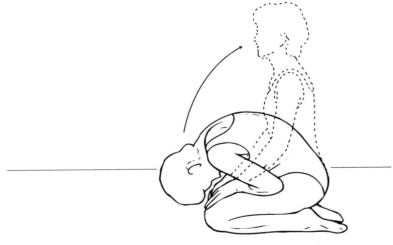

FIGURE 54

EXERCISE 4B

Flexing the Muscles of the Lower Sides and Back

Like Exercise 3A, Exercise 4B helps develop conscious control of a well-anchored breathing technique in a lying position. This exercise also develops the sides of the lower torso.

Practicing *chi yi* while lying in a twisted position will develop your ability to breathe properly in other twisted positions, whether sitting, standing, or moving.

1. Lie flat on your back with your feet 20 to 22 inches apart and your toes pointed. Your head should face the ceiling. Stretch your arms straight out to your sides, palms up (see Figure 55).

2. Exhale completely while deflating the abdomen.

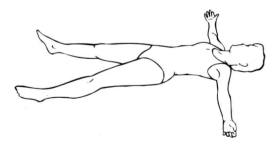

FIGURE 55

3. Inhale deeply while doing the following steps simultaneously (see Figure 56):

   □ Swing your right hand over in a semicircle and clap it to your left hand, turning your head toward the left.

   □ Inflate your abdomen, expanding the lower back and sides.

   □ Keep both heels stationary on the floor.

4. Exhale completely while doing the following steps simultaneously:

   □ Swing your right hand back over to the floor to its original position.

   □ Turn your head back to its original position (see Figure 55)

   □ Deflate your lower abdomen.

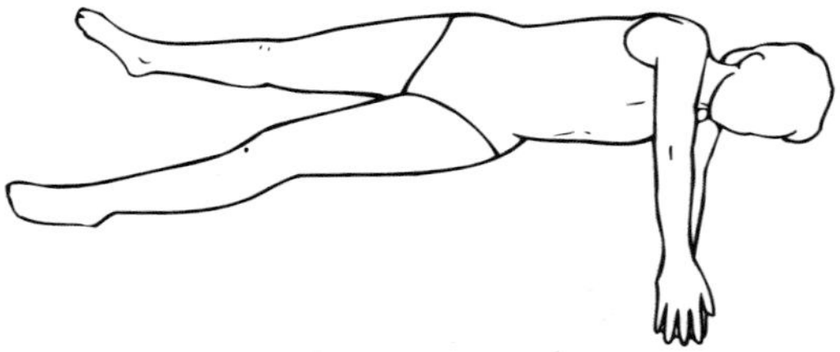

FIGURE 56

5. Inhale deeply while doing the following steps simultaneously (see Figure 57):

- ☐ Swing your left hand over in a semicircle and clap it to your right hand, turning your head toward the right.

- ☐ Inflate your abdomen, expanding the lower back and sides.

6. Exhale completely while doing the following steps simultaneously:

- ☐ Swing your left hand back over to the floor to its original position (see Figure 55).

- ☐ Turn your head back to its original position facing the ceiling.

- ☐ Deflate your lower abdomen.

7. Repeat steps 3 through 6 five times.

8. Lie stretched out on floor, and relax.

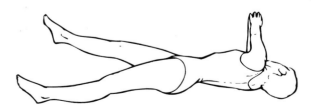

FIGURE 57

EXERCISE 4C

Developing Agility of the Abdominal and Lower Torso Muscles

After completing the neck-shoulder-upper torso relaxation exercises, you should now be ready to add movements that will relax the tongue as well.

Without tension in the neck, shoulders, and upper torso, tongue movement will automatically be controlled by the tongue's roots at the core.

Both the *toh* and *pah* are nonvocal, aspirated, exploding sounds.

1. Stand up straight with your feet 10 to 12 inches apart and your toes pointed slightly out.

2. Place your hands against the lower abdominal wall, palms inward, fingers almost touching, to monitor abdominal wall movements.

3. Place the tip of your tongue firmly against your top front teeth. Inhale deeply and fully. Make an explosive staccato *toh* sound, while snapping the lower abdominal wall inward (see Figure 58).

4. Take a quick, short breath through your nose, while rapidly expanding the lower circumference.

5. Immediately close your mouth, and follow with an exploding staccato *pah* sound while snapping the lower abdominal wall inward.

Note: Do not retract your tongue into the back of the mouth cavity when exploding the *toh* or *pah*. Drop your jaw to assist the rapid opening of the mouth for exploding sounds.

6. Repeat steps 3 through 5 twelve times.

7. Take a slow, deep breath, exhale and relax.

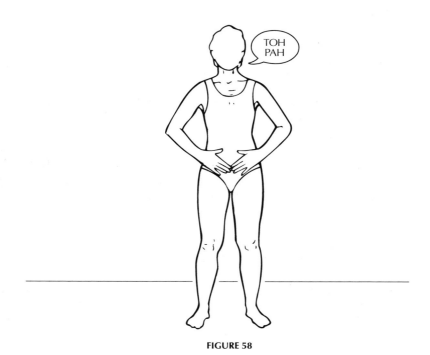

FIGURE 58

EXERCISE 4D

Expanding the Base of the Torso

Now that your lower torso's agility is well developed by the previous exercises, let your upper torso be consciously involved in the breathing process, taking care to maintain your attention and weight consistently in the lower torso. The top and bottom parts of the torso must be very carefully balanced to avoid a tendency toward top-heaviness.

Spreading your arms expands the torso top. Keeping your feet wide apart while bending and unbending the knees prevents loss of awareness of the core.

1. Stand up straight with your feet spread apart a few inches wider than shoulder width. Point your toes slightly outward.

2. Stretch your arms outward to the sides, level with your shoulders. Turn your palms down with your fingers together and extended straight out (see Figure 59).

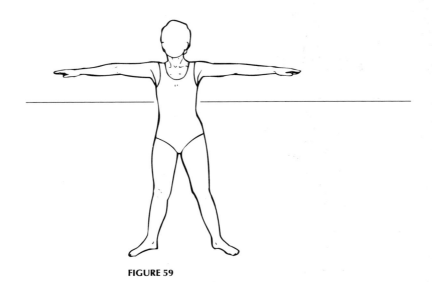

FIGURE 59

3. Inhale rapidly to a slow count of 1-2 and do the following steps simultaneously:

    ☐ Bend your knees outward over your toes (see Figure 60).

    ☐ Keep your elbows stationary and level with your shoulders, and swing your forearms in toward your collarbone. Join your fingertips; your fingers should meet a few inches below your chin.

    ☐ Keep your torso straight; do not allow your buttocks to stick out.

4. Exhale rapidly to a slow count of 1-2, deflating the abdomen and returning to your starting position, standing straight with arms outstretched and pointing out to opposite sides (see Figure 59).

5. Repeat steps 3 and 4 ten times.

6. Repeat step 3, and hold for 5 seconds.

7. Straighten your legs and let your arms dangle at your sides. Exhale slowly, deflate the abdomen, and relax.

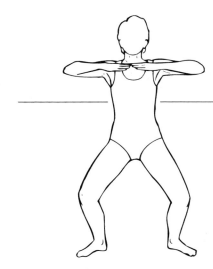

FIGURE 60

Thoughts on Lesson 4

The exercises in this lesson emphasize the lower sides of the torso (the lower waist) by inducing air to these areas with appropriate postures and movements. With your lower abdomen and lower back deflatable and inflatable, your sides should now also be as flexible. Your lower torso is now expandable in four dimensions, forming the lower circumference.

The lower circumference, together with your torso base, envelops the cradle of the core. External stimulation by the lower circumference activates your core to radiate inner energy throughout your entire being.

Throughout this book, we have often used vivid mental pictures to help you visualize how your body functions. If a certain mental image works for you, use it whenever you wish to overcome difficulties. If the following Coil of Rope Imagery Drill, or any other, helps you with your exercises, use it frequently until the effect wears off, and then substitute or invent another one.

IMAGERY DRILL

Coil of Rope

Imagine air entering and leaving your abdomen as a coil of rope with the bottom circle always remaining at the core.

LESSON FIVE

Using the Breath to Develop the Core

This lesson includes more review exercises than any previous lesson. It is important, at this advanced stage, to take the time to reexamine how each of these exercises induces the manner of breathing we seek. A thorough understanding of how certain movements and positions help induce specific breathing mechanisms will build confidence for improvisation in the future.

If you lack time or energy, it is better to cut down the number of repetitions in the review exercises than to skip any exercise entirely, since the order of the exercises—including the reviews—is designed to lead smoothly and effectively from one to the next.

RECOMMENDED REVIEW   EXERCISES 4A AND 4B

Review Exercises 4A and 4B, repeating each one as many times as necessary to accomplish their objectives effectively. You should now be able to perform these exercises more efficiently and meaningfully than you did when they first appeared in the previous lesson.

EXERCISE 5A

Further Expanding the Lower Circumference

The movements in this exercise are very simple. Their purpose is to practice control of the breath flow, extending exhalation time and shortening inhalation time. In speech and singing, we inhale rapidly and exhale slowly to enable the breath to be sustained through a phrase.

A slight dizziness may occur at step 7 if you stand upright too rapidly, or if you are unaccustomed to bending over. Relax, and the feeling will quickly pass.

As you stand and bend over as far as possible, the weight of the torso is borne at and suspended from the torso base. In this position, it is easy to breathe automatically to the core.

During this exercise, be sure to keep track of the pace of your breathing so that you can sustain your exhalation for an extended time.

1. Stand up straight with your feet 18 to 20 inches apart and your toes pointed slightly outward.

2. Place your hands at your waist with palms inward and thumbs pointed toward the back (see Figure 61).

FIGURE 61

3. Bend over gradually from the hips as far as possible (see Figure 62). Simultaneously, exhale by making the sound *"tse"* as in Exercise 2C to a slow count of 1-2-3-4-5-6-7-8-9-10-11-12, while gradually pulling the abdominal wall inward (deflating).

4. Inhale deeply and fully to a slow count of 1-2, while expanding the lower circumference.

5. Gradually stand back up and simultaneously exhale by again making the sound *"tse"* to the slow count of 1-2-3-4-5-6-7-8-9-10-11-12 while deflating your lower abdomen (see Figure 63).

6. Inhale fully, inflating lower abdomen.

7. Repeat steps 3, 4, 5, and 6 five times. Monitor inflation and deflation of your sides with your hands.

8. Exhale slowly, as you lower your hands to your sides.

9. Take a deep breath, and hold it at the core for a few seconds.

10. Relax and return to normal breathing.

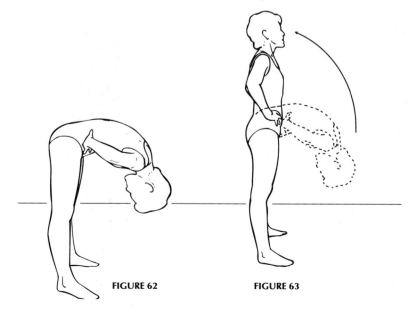

FIGURE 62   FIGURE 63

REVIEW EXERCISES 2D AND 2C AND EXERCISE 3B

After practicing regulating your breath flow in Exercise 5A, you should be able to perform Exercise 2C with much more understanding and skill. This can be made more beneficial by lengthening the *tse* sound by as many counts as possible. It will be interesting for you to test your own endurance.

Make sure that as you use your tongue to produce the *tse* sound you do not tighten your neck and shoulder muscles or unconsciously allow your anchored base (core) to rise. Keep that base low.

EXERCISE 5B

Developing Core Sensation

This exercise focuses on a part of the anatomy that is seldom discussed in Western physical exercise programs. The rectal muscle is a sensitive part of the torso base. When this muscle is tightened at the same time as you swallow, you will feel a direct connection between the base of the core cradle and the opening of the throat. Combining this sensation with regulated exhalation creates an intense awareness of the core.

Pointing your toes downward and pushing your heels upward as indicated in step 5 of the following exercise will intensify the strength that emanates from the lower circumference.

Lowering your feet slowly to the floor as indicated in step 8 results in the greatest awareness of the core.

1. Lie flat on the floor. Place your hands by your sides, palms down, keeping your straightened legs together and pointing your toes (see Figure 64).

2. Inhale deeply and fully to a slow count of 1-2-3 while inflating the lower abdomen.

3. Hold your breath.

FIGURE 64

4. Keeping them together, lift both feet toward the ceiling. (If you have difficulty lifting your feet with your legs straight, bend your knees toward your chest and then straighten your legs upward, allowing your knees to be bent slightly.)

5. Point your toes downward while pushing your heels upward (see Figure 65).

6. Tighten the rectal muscle.

7. Place the tip of your tongue firmly against your front teeth, and swallow.

8. Maintaining the position described in steps 4 through 6, exhale to a slow count of 1-2-3-4-5-6-7-8-9-10, while lowering your legs slowly to their original position on the floor (see Figure 66).

FIGURE 65

9. Inhale rapidly and deeply to a slow count of 1-2-3.

10. Remain lying down, and hold your breath for 3 seconds.

11. Exhale, and relax for a moment as you monitor the pulsing energy throbs in your core and even other areas of your body where *chi* is needed to help your building and healing process.

12. Repeat steps 2 through 11 two more times.

13. Breathe deeply several times, and relax.

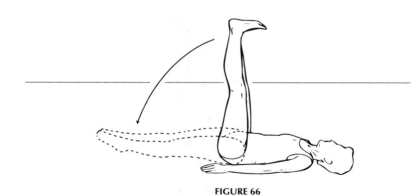

FIGURE 66

EXERCISE 5C

Expanding and Stabilizing the Breath at the Core

Like Exercise 4D, this exercise encourages the top, middle, and lower torso—including the entire length of the lungs—to be well-balanced and to function as a whole.

The arm movements help expand and relax the torso. Standing on tiptoe brings strength to the torso base.

1. Stand up straight with your feet 8 to 10 inches apart. Let your arms and hands dangle at your sides (see Figure 67).

2. Exhale completely to a slow count of 1-2-3-4-5-6-7-8-9-10, deflating the lower abdomen.

3. Inhale fully to a slow count of 1-2-3-4, inflating the lower circumference, while doing the following simultaneously (see Figure 68):

   □ Lift up your heels and stand on tiptoe.

   □ Raise your arms out to your sides at shoulder level.

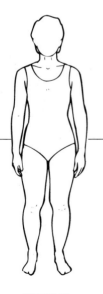

FIGURE 67

4. Exhale completely to a slow count of 1-2-3-4-5, deflating the lower abdomen, while doing the following simultaneously:

☐ Lower your heels to the floor, and stand flat on your feet.

☐ Lower your arms to your sides.

5. Inhale fully to a slow count of 1-2-3-4-5, inflating the lower circumference and doing the following simultaneously (see Figure 69):

☐ Lift up your heels and stand on tiptoe.

☐ Raise your arms forward and upward toward the ceiling.

6. Exhale completely to a slow count of 1-2-3-4-5-6-7, deflating the lower abdomen, and doing the following simultaneously:

☐ Lower your heels to the floor, and stand flat on your feet.

☐ Lower your arms to your sides.

7. Repeat steps 3 through 6 eight times.

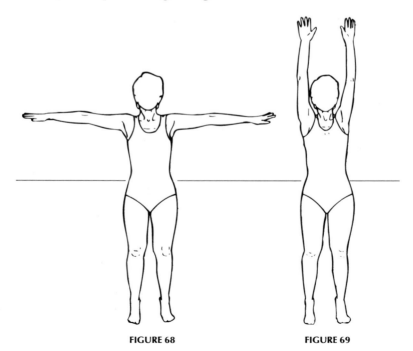

FIGURE 68   **FIGURE 69**

EXERCISE 5D

Intensifying Core Sensation

This exercise puts the rectal muscle into action once more.

Tightening your fists in conjunction with contracting the rectal muscle focuses a pivotal energy at the core, spreading upward to the diaphragm.

When tightening your fists, take care not to tighten your shoulders and neck; in that area tension will obstruct air flow into the bottom of the lungs.

1. Stand up straight with your feet 12 to 14 inches apart. Let your arms dangle.

2. Exhale to a slow count of 1-2-3-4-5-6-7-8, doing the following steps simultaneously:

   □ Slowly bend forward at the hips as far as possible, keeping your knees straight (see Figure 70).

   □ Deflate the lower abdomen.

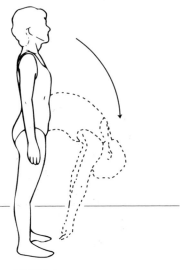

FIGURE 70

3. Holding the bent-over position, place your palms on your knees, fingers pointing inward. Bend your elbows and spread them outward (see Figure 71).

4. Inhale to a slow count of 1-2-3-4-5-6-7, doing the following steps simultaneously:

   ☐ Stand up slowly to an upright position.

   ☐ Raise your hands to head level, palms facing forward in front of your face, with your elbows still bent and spread.

5. Bring your palms to the sides of your head with your arms bent at right angles. Close your palms into tight fists (see Figure 72). Contract the rectal muscle, drawing it slightly upward.

FIGURE 72

FIGURE 71

6. Place the tip of your tongue against your top front teeth. Hold your head erect, tilting it back slightly. Swallow.

7. Immediately exhale as slowly as possible, doing the following steps simultaneously:

   ☐ Blow very slowly

   ☐ Rock your head left, right, left, and right to relax your head and shoulder muscles.

   ☐ Keep your fists tight, and gradually straighten your arms and lower your fists to your sides.

   ☐ Keep the rectal muscle contracted and drawn upward.

8. Continue exhaling slowly. You should be able to feel your core and all the muscles of your lower circumference tightening and exuding energy. Maintain muscle control until your breath is depleted.

9. Loosen your fists. Inhale and exhale deeply several times.

10. Repeat this exercise two more times, with a rest interval between repetitions.

11. Monitor the energy in your core and practice channeling it throughout your body.

Thoughts on the First Five Lessons

Having completed the first five lessons, you should have a clear inner vision of the location of the core, the primary objective of deep breathing. At this advanced stage of exercise, because of your increased awareness of disciplined breathing, you will no longer be given exact breath counts. Inhalation and exhalation can now be more relaxed and spontaneous. These less detailed directions will allow you greater flexibility and an opportunity to experiment sensibly and to adjust these exercises to fit your individual abilities.

You need no longer exaggerate abdominal inflation and deflation. The muscles of the lower circumference should by now be flexible, responsive, and sensitive. Flexing them even slightly should evoke an effective response. However, occasional conscientious repetition of the earlier exercises will prevent these muscles from becoming sloppy and unresponsive.

LESSON SIX

Applying the Breath

In the twenty exercises of the first five lessons, we have covered just about all the important muscular maneuvers that can help induce abdominal deep breathing and lead to an awareness of core energy.

Lesson 6 includes many earlier exercises, reviewing them to reveal further benefits that might not have been obvious during previous executions.

The following imagery drill is designed to deepen your inhalations and extend your exhalations.

IMAGERY DRILL

Book Stacking

Form the mental image of inhaling as a process of stacking books. You start stacking at the bottom, adding books to build a pile. The taller the stack, the more weight the bottom book has to bear. For exhalation, you unload the books from the top, working your way to the bottom book, which remains until the very end. You can stack or unstack rapidly or slowly, so long as you do the job steadily.

From now on, the position of the tip of your tongue as you breathe is less critical, as long as the tip of the tongue touches the front teeth. This position ensures that the tongue is not pulled back to obstruct the flow of air at the back of the throat. A relaxed tongue is always important in deep breathing.

The imagery drill that follows tests your ability to apply the energy that your core can now generate.

Facial Glow

1. Hold a mirror in front of you, and look into it.

2. Take an easy, deep breath, and exhale.

3. Look deeply into your own eyes as you take a long, deep breath and exhale.

4. Put the mirror down, but keep your eyes straight ahead.

5. Think about smiling. Take another easy deep breath, and exhale.

6. Sweep your glance upward, tilting your head back as you inhale deeply through your nose.

7. Hold your breath, and let it surround your core for a moment.

8. Exhale slowly and steadily through your nose as you imagine a warm glow emanating from your core. At the same time, sweep your glance back down, and level your head.

9. Break into a big smile, think a happy thought, and complete your exhalation.

10. Inhale and exhale as you smile. Feel your eyes sparkle, grow warm, and shine.

11. You are looking radiant!

12. Relaxed and content, proceed to Exercise 6A.

EXERCISE 6A

Spreading the Breath to the Base of the Torso

A cross-legged sitting position induces maximum awareness of the lower torso base as a result of the tension that is concentrated there. The tension is produced by assembling the torso weight and the weight of the four limbs at a single pivot platform that supports the entire body. Many people are unaccustomed to the cross-legged position; its awkwardness and discomfort make them more aware of that area.

When you are sitting in the cross-legged position, your shoulders may tense up. By resting your forearms on bent knees, you can thwart that tendency and keep the weight focused downward. In this position, whether you are inhaling or exhaling, imagine yourself as a pyramid that is stable and firmly anchored.

If you find it difficult or uncomfortable to sit cross-legged on the floor, you may sit on one or more firm cushions or on a low stool with your legs crossed in front. Place your hands palm down on your knees or in your lap with your fingers pointing inward.

1. Sit up straight in a cross-legged position. Bend your arms, resting your forearms on your knees. Join your hands by interlocking your fingers (see Figure 73).

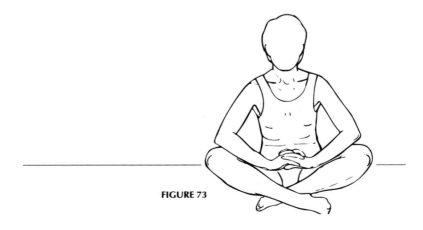

FIGURE 73

2. Place the tip of your tongue against your bottom front teeth. Exhale through your nose to a slow count of 1-2-3-4, while deflating the lower abdominal wall.

3. Place the tip of your tongue against your top front teeth. Inhale through your nose to a slow count of 1-2-3-4-5, while bending forward gradually as far as possible, directing your head toward the floor, and inflating your lower back torso. Let your forearms press on your knees to assist in lowering your knees toward the floor (see Figure 74). (If you are sitting in an elevated position on a cushion or stool, let your elbows and arms spread out and forward.)

4. Place the tip of your tongue against your bottom front teeth. Exhale through your mouth to a slow count of 1-2-3-4, while slowly returning to your original position and relaxing the forearm pressure on your knees. Do not deflate the lower abdominal wall; let the lower back wall react naturally to the sitting up motion.

5. Repeat steps 3 and 4 five times.

6. Remain sitting upright. Breathe freely and relax.

FIGURE 74

EXERCISE 6B

Strengthening the Abdominal Muscles

Raising your arms high and pointing your fingers upward helps you stretch the entire length of your torso as much as possible.

Spreading your feet far apart helps broaden and stabilize the torso base, but in doing so you risk swaying your back and curving out the lower spine. To minimize this risk, stretch your entire top body up as straight as possible. At the same time, pull your abdomen slightly inward even before exhalation begins .

1. Stand up straight with your feet apart a few inches wider than shoulder width. Point your toes slightly outward.

2. Raise your arms high, stretching your fingers toward the ceiling, palms forward (see Figure 75).

3. Exhale completely, doing the following steps simultaneously:

FIGURE 75

☐ Bend over and touch your toes (see Figure 76). If you can't touch your toes, bend as far as you can.

☐ Deflate the lower abdomen.

4. Inhale slowly, filling from the bottom up, doing the following steps simultaneously:

☐ Stand up slowly, stretching your arms and hands above your head (see Figure 77).

☐ Inflate the lower circumference.

5. Repeat steps 3 and 4 three times.

6. Remain standing with your hands reaching high.

7. Hold still for 3 seconds; then lower your hands to your sides.

8. Exhale completely, inhale deeply, and breathe freely as you continue onward with the following segment.

FIGURE 77

FIGURE 76

EXERCISE 6B CONTINUED

Strengthening the Lower Back Muscles

Notice that the emphasis in this segment shifts from the abdomen to the lower back torso by reversing the inhalation-exhalation procedure.

1. Stand up straight with your feet still apart a few inches wider than shoulder width. Point your toes slightly outward.

2. Raise your arms high above your head, stretching your fingers toward the ceiling, palms forward (see Figure 78). Exhale completely through your mouth.

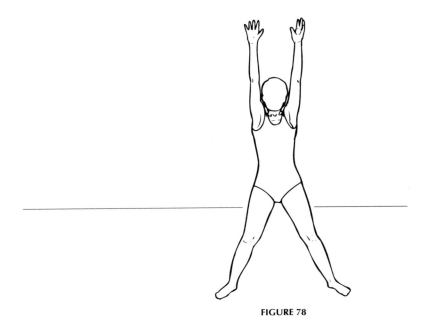

FIGURE 78

3. Inhale slowly from the bottom up, doing the following simultaneously:

   ☐ Bend over and touch your toes (see Figure 79). If you can't touch your toes, bend as far as you can.

   ☐ Inflate the lower circumference.

4. Exhale completely through your mouth, doing the following simultaneously:

   ☐ Stand up slowly, stretching your arms and hands toward the ceiling.

   ☐ Deflate the lower abdomen.

5. Repeat steps 3 and 4 three times.

6. Remain standing with your arms stretched high.

7. Hold your breath for a second.

8. Lower your hands, inhale deeply, exhale steadily, relax and breathe freely.

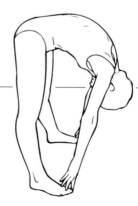

FIGURE 79

REVIEW EXERCISE 3A, EXERCISE 4A, AND EXERCISE 3D

Exercises 3A, 4A, and 3D demonstrate a progression of postures. Apply the following imagery drill during your review.

IMAGERY DRILL

Cream

Create a mental picture of an inhaled breath that is a rich, heavy liquid. On exhaling, leave behind the richness, and let the creaminess stick to the core, where it is converted into energy. You are learning to regulate and absorb that precious energy.

EXERCISE 6C

Strengthening the Diaphragm Muscle and the Core

The breathing action that accompanies this movement thoroughly exercises the diaphragm and stimulates the core.

Steps 3 and 4 may seem difficult. Simply alternate moving your fists up and down as you swing your hips. Bending your knees and tipping your toes helps maintain balance and accommodate easy swaying. In this movement the midtorso, where the diaphragm is located, is being squeezed and stretched on alternate sides to develop flexibility.

1. Stand up straight with your feet spread apart to the width of your shoulders. Raise your arms out to the sides at shoulder height; then bend your elbows upward at right angles. Keep your elbows level with your shoulders. Tighten your hands into fists, palms facing forward (see Figure 80). Exhale completely, deflating the lower abdomen.

2. Inhale slowly, deeply, and fully. Hold your breath. Tighten the rectal muscle, pulling slightly upward. Then swallow, maintaining core tension.

FIGURE 80

3. Keep your rectal muscle tight while blowing forcefully in two consecutive big puffs, deflating the lower abdomen. At the first puff, simultaneously:

   □ Pull your right fist downward, and push your left fist upward.

   □ Swing your right hip to the right.

   □ Bend your left knee slightly forward, raising your left foot on tiptoe (see Figure 81).

   At the second puff, simultaneously:

   □ Push your right fist upward, and pull your left fist downward.

   □ Swing your left hip to the left.

   □ Bend your right knee slightly forward, raising your right foot on tiptoe (see Figure 82).

4. Inhale through your nose forcefully in two consecutive sniffs, inflating the lower abdomen. At the first sniff, simultaneously:

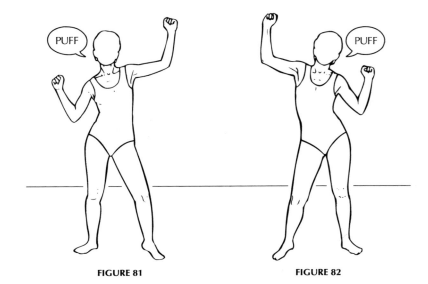

FIGURE 81   **FIGURE 82**

☐ Pull your right fist downward, and push your left fist upward.

☐ Swing your right hip to the right.

☐ Bend your left knee slightly forward, raising your left foot on tiptoe (see Figure 83).

At the second sniff, simultaneously:

☐ Push your right fist upward, and pull your left fist downward.

☐ Swing your left hip to the left.

☐ Bend your right knee slightly forward, raising your right foot on tiptoe (see Figure 84).

5. Repeat steps 3 and 4 ten times, maintaining a tightened rectal muscle. End with an inhalation; level your shoulders and elbows.

6. Exhale slowly, lowering your hands to your sides.

7. Inhale, exhale, relax, and breathe freely.

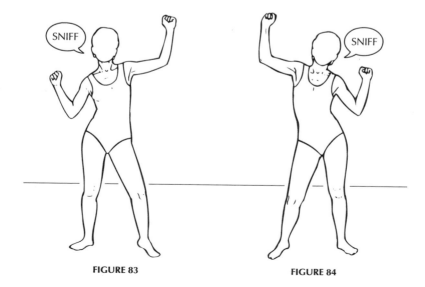

FIGURE 83   FIGURE 84

REVIEW EXERCISES 5D AND 5C

Exercise 6C was a rigorous exercise that placed great emphasis on the midtorso. Forgetting the lower torso and core can make it difficult for the breath to reach its necessary depth. A review of Exercises 5D and 5C will readjust any displacement that may have occurred. Exercise 5C will leave your body ready for Exercise 6D.

EXERCISE 6D

Jogging in Place with Chi Yi

All movement is affected by our manner of breathing. Jogging in place offers *one example* of the application of *chi yi*, showing how, in combination with various stages of physical exercise, you can experiment for improved results through the proper coordination of breathing and exercise.

1. Stand up straight with one foot flat on the floor and the other raised on tiptoe in a stationary jogging position. Keep your arms and hands in a position comfortable for running. Your hands should be loose and relaxed (see Figure 85).

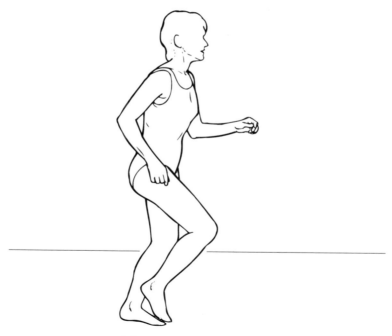

FIGURE 85

2. Throughout this exercise you will breathe in a natural way through the point where the back of the nose and the throat meet. Hold your teeth slightly apart, with your jaws relaxed. Place the tip of your tongue lightly behind your bottom front teeth.

3. Begin stationary jogging, slowly and steadily. Deflate the lower abdomen when exhaling, and inflate the lower circumference when inhaling. Alternately exhale and inhale in the following pattern:

   ☐ Exhale smoothly and steadily for 4 steps.

   ☐ Inhale smoothly and deeply for 4 steps.

   ☐ Exhale smoothly and steadily for 6 steps.

   ☐ Inhale smoothly and deeply for 6 steps.

   ☐ Exhale smoothly and steadily for 8 steps.

   ☐ Inhale smoothly and deeply for 8 steps.

   ☐ Exhale smoothly and steadily for 10 steps.

   ☐ Inhale smoothly and deeply for 10 steps.

   ☐ Exhale smoothly and steadily for 8 steps.

   ☐ Inhale smoothly and deeply for 8 steps.

   ☐ Exhale smoothly and steadily for 6 steps.

   ☐ Inhale smoothly and deeply for 6 steps.

   ☐ Exhale smoothly and steadily for 4 steps.

   ☐ Inhale smoothly and deeply for 4 steps.

   ☐ Exhale smoothly and steadily for 10 steps.

   ☐ Inhale smoothly and deeply for 10 steps.

4. As you continue stationary jogging, slowly and easily adapt to your normal breathing pattern while bringing your steps gradually to a standstill.

Thoughts on Lesson 6

The most important objective of this lesson is to develop a keener awareness of the core and to apply this awareness to *any* activity. By the time you have completed this lesson, the muscles involved in *chi yi* should respond readily to your commands. Feel free to improvise new routines, and to incorporate what you have learned into your daily activities.

Frequently review those exercises that are most effective for you. Do not overlook or underestimate the exercises in the beginning lessons; each one has its particular value.

Be patient and persistent in your practice and application of *chi yi*. Your painstaking effort at the beginning will gradually become spontaneous, and eventually you will find shallow breathing to be uncomfortable, ineffective, and unnatural. It is then that you will recognize that you have mastered the art of breathing.

You may have noticed that your natural breathing patterns sometimes have suspended (rest) intervals between exhalations and inhalations. The length of these suspended intervals depends mainly on the physical and sometimes on the mental and emotional demands at the time. A natural instinct usually takes care of such adjustments. For instance, in running the intervals will be very short. In walking, you may experience an interval to a count of 1 or 2, depending on the amount of energy exerted and the amount of air inhaled and exhaled. In resting, you may experience 3 counts inhale, 3 counts exhale, 3 counts suspended interval. When you are asleep, the suspended period will be extended. Understanding this fact will facilitate the adaptation of *chi yi* into whatever you do.

PART THREE

Applications of Chi Yi

Using the Core Energy

Once you have completed the six lessons outlined in Part 2 of this book, you will have established a strong, sound foundation in *chi yi*. As with all worthwhile skills, the techniques involved must be consistently practiced to maintain the art of breathing. Successful results depend on continued effort and mastery of all the lessons.

Now that your core awareness is well established, you are equipped to function more effectively in every area of your life. The applications that follow will show you how *chi yi* techniques may be applied to the endeavors of daily life, and how they enhance the health and well-being of those who practice them. Once you have worked with these applications, you will be able to adapt them to create your own program of *chi yi* practice.

Disciplined inner energy helps you to realize your full human potential. Uncontrolled inner energy creates tension and stress. It is impossible simply to discard unwanted tension and stress. You must *relocate* them. The practice of *chi yi* enables you to direct unwanted tension and stress to the core, from which it can be circulated throughout the body as beneficial energy.

Now that you have mastered the basic techniques of *chi yi* set forth in the progressive exercises of Part 2, the Steam Funnel Imagery Drill will further assist you in the circulation of inner energy. Keep this image in mind as you practice the applications in Part 3.

In this imagery drill, imagining your inhaled breath as water facilitates the feeling of the breath's flowing downward and hitting bottom. Imagining your exhaled breath as warm water and steam being pumped upward allows you to sense how the breath lingers during the exhalation. As you practice this exercise, you are likely to sense the warm inner energy flowing to your face and head area. Imagining the inner energy as a warm current provides a vivid sensation that can be easily traced and monitored.

IMAGERY DRILL

Steam Funnel

Think of the back of your nose, at the point where it meets the throat, as the top of a funnel emptying into a long tube that leads all the way down to a focal area where a rotating propeller sits ready to spin (see Figure 86). As you begin an inhalation, imagine the air you breathe as water pouring into the funnel and draining down to start the rotor spinning. Let the rotor gain momentum for a few seconds, heating up and setting off an energy that radiates and sparkles and, at the same time, gives off enough power to propel an exhalation in the form of warm water and steam.

It is this return column of energized air that triggers and manipulates the voice. This energized exhalation also gives your face an attractive glow.

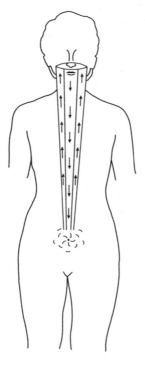

FIGURE 86

During exhalations, you gain the benefit of your inhalations, allowing you to target your inner energy to the body areas that need it most. You can most effectively direct your inner energy with your mind and imagination during the exhalation. You need not have a plan for every exhalation; most of the time it is natural to let your inner energy circulate freely so that your entire being can benefit from it.

Flourishing inner energy naturally attends to the most pressing needs of the various parts of your body. For instance, if you are extremely tired and lie down to rest, you may feel your inner energy throbbing at the parts of your body that are most strained, such as the base of your neck, your head, your legs, and so on. Encourage such sensations with *chi yi* breathing; they will help you to recuperate.

The surges of inner energy may be perceived as throbs, as patches of inner warmth, or as rays or flashes of inner light. These throbs are slower than the pulses of the heart, occurring about one per second or even more slowly. If these sensations come to you in the form of warm patches or light flashes and so have a less vivid rhythm, monitor them by mentally counting at the speed of roughly one count per second.

Whenever and wherever throbbing sensations occur—not painful ones—don't discourage them. They are a sign that your inner energy is surging to where it's needed in your body. For instance, if you have strained muscles at the base of your neck and in your shoulders, lie down and do *chi yi* breathing. Soon you will become aware of a throbbing sensation in that strained area, gradually bringing on relief and comfort.

After you have talked and smiled continuously for a long time, relax and focus your mind on your tired lips, jaws, gums, and on the back of your nose, and you will sense these muscles, bones, and tissues pulsating intensely. They are being helped by your inner energy to relax and recuperate.

When your eyes are tired or strained, close them and bring your attention to that area. Your eyes will be soothed with pulsating inner energy that will relax the eyes themselves and the surrounding muscles.

Painful throbbing is a signal from the body of some injury, tension, or stress. You will learn to blend these throbs with your inner energy surges to dispel pain and tension.

To encourage your awareness of the throbbing sensation created by the concentration of inner energy, practice the following imagery drill.

Sink and Drain

Inhale as if you are filling up a sink from the bottom upward. Exhale as if you are draining a sink through the bottom. Repeat these two steps a few times. Then suspend your breathing for a few seconds, and concentrate on developing a slow throb in your core. Resume breathing as you continue to monitor your throbs. Apply this throbbing sensation to various areas of the body by mentally moving the throbs from the core to other parts of your body.

Suggestions for Practicing the Applications

When you are practicing the applications, remember always to invigorate and back up your inner energy with deep inhalations and lingering exhalations. *Chi yi* breaths may vary in intensity and frequency. As you monitor your throbs, light flashes, or warm patches, your breaths may at times become so faint and infrequent that they seem hardly to be there.

These faint inhalations will be interspersed with some long, intense inhalations whenever your body feels the need. Let your natural instincts be your guide. If the throbs or sensations of light or warmth should hesitate or fade away, regenerate them with a few intense, regulated exhalations and inhalations, almost like deep sighs. Use the Sink and Drain Imagery Drill to encourage these sensations. Whether your breaths are faint or intense, frequent or sparse, the most important point to remember is to inhale to the core and to let your exhalations linger.

You can bring on the sensations of inner energy surges with *chi yi* breathing and exaggerated flexing of the lower abdominal muscles, which stimulates the core. Deep breathing can also be induced with vivid mental pictures, as in the imagery drill below.

Drinking Straw

Imagine an oversized drinking straw with one end at the nose-- throat junction and the other end leading to the center of the core. Both ends are kept open at all times to allow the air to flow freely. As you inhale, imagine air being sucked in through the lower opening, inflating the lower abdomen. Stop, and reverse your mental gears in preparation for exhalation. Now imagine the straw with air flowing out through both ends (without collapsing the straw at any point). Exhale completely. Then proceed again with another inhalation .

The following core awareness imagery drill also cultivates and helps you channel the core's energy. It will be put to use in several of the applications that follow.

IMAGERY DRILL

Red Light Bulb

Do your *chi yi* breathing as you imagine, as vividly as you can, an electric socket at the location of your core. Screw a red light bulb into this socket, and watch it light up. Imagine that the light glows evenly as you exhale and inhale deeply and smoothly. At the pauses between exhalations and inhalations, or when you hold your breath, the light does not flicker or go out, but sustains an even glow.

As soon as *chi yi is* thoroughly integrated into your life, as you work or play or engage in physical activities throughout the day, you may apply an exercise or drill to help you relax or to act more effectively. Throughout the day and night, you will find yourself breathing more deeply, with greater ease. You are enjoying *chi yi*—the art of breathing.

APPLICATION 1

Promoting Relaxation

Whenever you are under pressure, or in a rush, or feeling tense, let *chi yi* help you take stock of the situation. Loosen and lower your shoulders. Breathe to your core, and let your breath linger and filter downward. Do this several times, until you feel your taut nerves and muscles loosen up. You will find that you are better able to control your feelings, and to be more patient, tolerant, and pleasant than before.

Anxiety can be greatly eased or even eliminated by bringing your inner energy throbs to the spot at the center of your chest just below the point where your front ribs meet. Concentrate your inner energy surges there, and let them warm that spot and loosen the knots there. Soon your anxiety will begin to evaporate.

1. Take a few deep breaths to firmly establish an inner vision of the core's location.

2. Analyze and trace your points of tension.

3. Continue breathing deeply and steadily as you direct imaginary lumps of tension, one at a time, to the core and calmly drop them into the core's cradle to dissolve.

4. Tension often gathers at the back of the neck and shoulders, contributing to aches and pains in the arms and from the head down through the spine. To relieve that neck-shoulder tension, check the following vital points, and follow the prescribed remedies.

   □ Tongue. If your tongue is persistently pulled back, away from the front teeth, tension will be created in the jaw and neck. Remedy this condition by pushing the tongue forward gently, filling up the space behind the lower front teeth. Then let the tongue go limp, and breathe.

   □ Shoulders. When your shoulders are heaved (raised), you are fighting against gravity. Seesaw and rotate your shoulders a few times; then smooth your shoulders backward and downward, and breathe comfortably.

APPLICATION 2

Waking Up Alert: The Good Morning Regimen

For many people, just waking up and getting out of bed in the morning requires quite an effort and, in fact, may be very stressful. Many rely on a cup of black coffee or an extra half hour in bed to become their usual social selves. They hope to become alert, bright-eyed, and radiant as the day goes by.

This *chi yi* regimen prepares you for getting out of bed with all your faculties fully functioning. The regimen requires you to stay in bed for 10 minutes or so after you awaken. If you wake up by the alarm clock, set it 10 minutes earlier. You will get out of bed much less blurry-eyed and cranky than you would have after those extra 10 minutes of sleep. This *chi yi* application requires willpower on your part, but you will find the reward more than worth the effort.

At first glance, the regimen may look long and complicated. After you review it a few times, you will find it systematic and easy to remember. Memorize the steps or at least understand and organize them in your mind before you actually do the regimen.

The number of throbs indicated in this application is to be considered a guideline. Use your discretion in this matter according to your physical condition and the time you have allotted for performing the regimen. You can mentally direct inner energy sensations and channel them to whatever location you desire. For instance, if you have a stuffy nose, a sore throat, or an uncomfortable stomach, you will want to let the throbs linger in the sensitive area.

When you wake up in the morning, remain lying in bed with your eyes closed. If you need to make a trip to the bathroom, return immediately to bed. If your room is cool, keep the covers over you so that you are comfortable and warm. You may bend your knees if that position is more comfortable than lying flat. At first you may find lying on your back easier than any other position, but as you become more experienced, you may find it just as easy to perform the regimen lying on either side, as long as you are relaxed and comfortable.

Remember always to invigorate and back up your inner energy with deep inhalations and lingering exhalations.

1. Lie comfortably in bed with your eyes closed.

2. Do the Eyedropper Imagery Drill from Part 1 to refresh the deep breathing sensation.

3. Relax your hands and elbows. Rest your hands one over the other on your lower abdomen. Let your elbows rest on the bed beside your body.

4. Flex your lower abdominal muscles and vigorously deflate the abdomen as you exhale by blowing rapidly through slightly pursed lips. Relax your abdominal muscle; it will pop outward, effecting a rapid, deep inhalation of air. Do this in/out process of flexing the abdominal wall to the count of 1-2. Repeat the process 10 times in succession, ending with a long, slow, deep inhalation followed by a long, slow, thorough exhalation.

5. Relax. Monitor your body for throbs or pulsations. You may sense them at many areas of your body, especially around your eye sockets, between your cheeks and gums, at the back of your nose, and in your neck, your inner shoulders, and your lower abdomen. If you are aware of no such sensations, repeat step 4. If you still have no reaction, do the Simplified Vowel Exercise that appears on page 155. Then proceed to step 6.

6. Concentrate on throbs in one area at a time, starting with the lower abdomen. Mentally direct the throbs to your tailbone. Inch them slowly up the spine to the top of your head (the crown).

7. Mentally direct the throbs toward the eye sockets. Monitor 20 throbs there.

8. Direct 10 to 14 throbs to the center of the bridge of the nose. If you have a stuffy nose, let the throbs dwell longer at that area, and the stuffiness may disappear.

9. Direct 10 to 14 throbs to the tip of your nose.

10. Direct 10 to 14 throbs to your upper gum.

11. Let 10 to 14 throbs spread to your cheeks. You may feel a flush spreading through the center of your face. Direct 10 throbs to that area.

12. Direct 10 to 14 throbs each to your lower gum, tongue, and chin.

13. Direct 10 to 14 throbs to your throat. If you have a sore throat, allow the throbs to dwell at the throat area to soothe away the pain. If a ticklish feeling in the throat is bringing on a cough, hold off the cough as long as you can. Allow the throbs to dwell at that location until the tickling sensation subsides.

14. Direct 10 to 14 throbs to the base of the neck and across the inner shoulders. If you are suffering from a stiff neck or strained shoulders, let the throbs dwell in the neck-shoulder area to relieve tension.

15. Direct throbs in little steps, one throb per step, down the center front of your body. Let the throbs dwell at whatever spot feels tight, uncomfortable, or uneasy. Throbbing in the abdominal area may at times start your stomach rumbling; it may even cause you to pass gas. This response is a good sign; it shows that your stomach is waking up, too! Aim your throbs toward the lower abdomen.

16. Rub your warm hands over your abdomen and the front of your rib cage, gently massaging these areas. Enjoy this stimulation for a few seconds, or longer if you wish.

17. Sit up. Put your feet on the floor.

18. Dangle your head and roll it to the right in big circles slowly 4 times, synchronizing the motion with the breath—inhale-exhale-inhale-exhale. Repeat the process, rolling your head to the left.

19. Bring your right palm to the left side of the base of your neck. Pat gently and firmly, starting at the base of the neck, moving along the left shoulder and down the arm toward

the hand and fingers. Pat more at the spots where you feel tension. Repeat this patting motion 2 times.

Note: During the process of directing the inner energy surges up and down your head and torso in steps 1 through 16, your limbs may have become tense. The patting will relieve any tension. And more importantly, the stimulation of the patting will lead the flow of inner energy you have activated during steps 1 through 16 to the limbs as well.

20. Bring your left palm to the right side of the base of your neck. Pat gently and firmly, starting at the base of the neck, moving along the right shoulder and down the arm toward the hand and fingers. Again, pat more at any tense spots. Repeat this patting motion 2 times.

21. Again bring your right palm to the left side of the base of your neck. Pat along the shoulder to the top of the left arm. At this point, turn your left palm outward, bringing the inside of your left arm outward also. Continue patting downward along the inside of the left arm to the palm, ending at the fingertips. Repeat this patting motion 2 times.

22. Again bring your left palm to the right side of the base of your neck. Pat along the shoulder to the top of the right arm. At this point, turn your right palm outward, bringing the inside of your right arm outward also. Continue patting downward along the inside of the right arm to the palm, ending at the fingertips. Repeat this patting motion 2 times.

23. Stand up. Dangle your hands in front of you and shake them vigorously 20 times.

24. Stand up straight with your feet spread comfortably, 16 to 18 inches apart. Bring your right hand to your left underarm with the palm inward, fingers pointing backward. Gently and firmly pat downward on the left side of your body to the left hip; then proceed toward the center of your lower abdomen. Repeat this patting motion 2 times.

25. In the same standing position, bring your left hand to your right underarm with the palm inward, fingers pointing backward. Gently and firmly pat downward on the right side of your body toward the right hip, and proceed to pat toward the lower center of the abdomen. Repeat this patting motion 2 times.

26. Stand upright with your feet slightly parted, 8 to 10 inches apart. Bring your hands to the sides of your hips, palms inward, fingers pointing toward the center of your back. Gently and firmly pat slowly toward the center lower back, and proceed downward along the backs of your legs to your heels. Bend down gradually as you pat, then straighten up. Repeat this patting motion 2 times.

27. Bend forward with your feet parted at slightly wider than shoulder's width. Bring your hands to your crotch (the very top of the inside of your legs) with the palm inward, fingers pointing backward. Gently and firmly pat downward along the inside of your legs toward the inside ankles, bending down gradually as you pat. Stand up. Repeat this patting motion 2 times.

28. Walk in place or around the room 30 to 40 steps, lifting your feet high. Now you are all set for a good day, with bright eyes and rosy cheeks, full of energy.

Whenever you have the luxury of relaxing in bed for a few extra minutes, take the opportunity to improve your weak areas. For example, if you are susceptible to lower back pain, lie on your side with your knees drawn up in the fetal position. Focus your mind on your lower back. Take a few *chi yi* breaths, then direct your throbs (or patches of warmth, or flashes of light) to your lower back. Let these sensations dwell at the painful area for as long as you like. You may focus your mind on and send your inner energy to soothe and repair any spot in your body—a joint in your finger, a strained calf muscle, or your teeth and gums.

To start the day with a rosy glow, bring the throbs to your face in order to stimulate your skin and facial muscles.

APPLICATION 3

Motivating Movement from the Core

This application of *chi yi* shows you how to make connections between your movements and your core. Breathing affects your core, which in turn affects your movements. If you are lucky, your movements may be instinctively motivated from the core, whether or not you realize how that came about. However, the more fully you understand and exercise your ability to move from the core, the more you can control your movements and improve them at will.

After you have practiced this application, you will find that you are more aware of every movement you make, and you will move with more control. Your penmanship may even improve! At first, practice this application for short periods (5 to 10 minutes). This technique of control will gradually blend into your everyday movements, naturally and easily. Your movements will become more graceful, more steady, and more confident.

1. Stand with your feet 10 to 12 inches apart, toes pointed slightly outward. Hold your hands behind your back, and let them dangle loosely.

2. Inhale deeply, and exhale thoroughly. Inhale again easily, and continue breathing without further attention to your breathing process.

3. Tighten your lower abdominal muscle, and lift the center of the torso floor.

4. Do the Red Light Bulb Imagery Drill. Imagine as vividly as you can an electric socket at the location of your core. Screw a little red light bulb into this socket and watch it light up. Imagine the glowing bulb.

5. Raise on tiptoe and lower yourself several times. As you do this, imagine that the bulb glows with each lift. The more strength your movement requires, the brighter the bulb glows.

6. Place your feet more widely apart. Shift your weight from one foot to the other a few times. As you do this, imagine that the bulb glows more intensely as the movement demands greater energy.

7. Walk around the room. Imagine that the bulb brightens and dims as you pick up and lower your feet and shift your weight.

8. Raise one arm to your head. Notice the reactions of the bulb. Draw big round circles in the air with your hand. Lower your hand gracefully to your side. This movement also takes energy to control. Imagine how the bulb brightens and dims as any part of you moves. Raise your other arm, and put it through various motions. Pick up objects from the table, and put them back down. Mentally watch the reactions of the bulb.

9. Turn your head to one side. Lift it. Turn it to the other side. Keep an image of the bulb in your mind as you move.

10. Make any movement with any part of your body. Lift and wiggle a finger. Roll your eyes. Write with a pencil. Maintain the imagery of the bulb glowing in its various intensities.

APPLICATION 4

Developing Athletic Prowess

The previous application, which develops motivated movements, will adapt easily and beneficially to all your athletic activities. Athletic movements require much more exact execution, strength, and coordination than do the movements of everyday actions. At first you may feel that the application interferes with your spontaneity and natural reflexes; and it may, until you make the technique part of your subconscious mind. If practiced faithfully, however, this technique will soon become spontaneous, and will greatly enhance your athletic movements.

All sports require footwork of some sort. Your steps determine the direction, position, and maneuverability of your entire body. Experiments scrutinizing runners' patterns of running and breathing at various stages of a run, under various conditions, and at different speeds, have concluded that synchronization takes place between pace and breath. The speed of a runner depends on both the rate and the length of his or her stride. Experiments have shown that even when runners aim for a longer stride, their phase-locked pattern of breathing and footsteps need not change. Scientists are continuing to study phase-locked breathing and running patterns.

A 1983 article by Dennis M. Bramble and David R. Carrier (*Science*, Vol. 219, 21 January 1983, p. 251) recorded that four-legged animals normally synchronize their footfalls and their breathing cycles for trots and gallops at a constant 1:1 ratio (one stride per breath). Human runners employ several phaselocked patterns (4:1, 3:1, 2:1, 1:1, 5:2, 3:2), although the 2:1 pattern seems to be the most commonly used. In whatever pattern, the synchronization of breathing and physical movements appears to be necessary during sustained running.

If a phase-locked pattern of movement and breathing is necessary for sustained running, it must also be important for not-so-sustained running, and it may well be helpful in walking in regulated steps. In fact, a phase-locked pattern between breathing and any movement of the body can effect better performance. These patterns, however, vary under different conditions and with different people. No formula has been established for getting the best results. You, or you and your coach, will work out what is best for you.

Where does the runner get the extra energy required for longer strides? I believe that the principles of *chi yi* offer an answer to how the runner gets extra energy: Deeper breathing stimulates the core to produce more inner energy.

Sports vary greatly in their degree of rhythmic involvement. In general, noncompetitive sports—jogging, bicycling, aerobic exercises, rope skipping, skating, and so on—are more highly regulated by rhythm. Competitive sports that engage opponents and require teamwork—tennis, football, baseball, and so on—are usually freer from set rhythms. The more rhythmic the sport, the more your performance can benefit from phase-locked patterns of breathing and movement.

This application will show you how to generate and direct inner energy when participating in athletic activities.

1. Strike the stance that you would normally take as you begin practicing your sport.

2. If an instrument such as a racket is involved, hold it as you normally would at the starting point.

3. Take a *chi yi* breath (exhalation and inhalation).

4. Inhale, and hold your breath without straining. Touch your top and bottom teeth together, but don't bite hard. Place the tip of your tongue against your front teeth.

5. Produce a sustained *tse* sound. To make sure that this sound does not bring on tension of the neck or shoulder muscles, roll your head clockwise and counter-clockwise several times as you proceed with your continuous *tse* sound.

6. As you continue making the *tse* sound, you will feel your core tightening and generating energy. Sustaining the sound, think of the Red Light Bulb Imagery Drill with the bulb plugged into the socket. Imagine the light of the red bulb glowing steadily—as steady as your *tse*—until the end of this exhalation.

7. Inhale.

8. Exhale in the form of disconnected short *tse* syllables. As you exhale, do the following simultaneously:

   □ Do the movements of your sport—swing your racket, take a step, jump, swing, or the like—in a slightly slow motion.

   □ Accompany each movement with a *tse* sound and a profuse glow of the imaginary red bulb. (You can do this step when you are actually playing the game just for practice.)

9. Continue to inhale and exhale freely, at the rate and intensity at which you feel comfortable. As you exhale, the disconnected *tse* sounds should accompany your actions; let the core bulb glow to accompany your *tse* sounds.

10. Continue with steps 7, 8, and 9 as long as you wish and as long as you feel comfortable doing them.

APPLICATION 5

Sustaining Personal Presence

Most virtuoso performers are able to attract the attention of their audience, but the greatest virtuosos are those who can maintain a continuous magnetism so that members of the audience can't take their eyes or ears from them even when they pause. This ability to deliver a skill laced with continuous magnetism adds a charismatic quality to every note, phrase, line, and movement they send forth—a string of perfected pearls strung together not with string but with magnetic inner energy.

Applications 3 and 4 teach you to direct your inner energy to your physical expression and movements. This application shows you how to develop an inner energy capable of sustaining and molding itself so that it corresponds with the demands of artistic performance and stage presence. You may apply this energy to your performance in any situation, in the conference room or on the stage.

First, do the Red Light Bulb Imagery Drill. We will work with the image of the red electric bulb plugged in at your lower abdomen, at the location of your core. Not only must you be able mentally to turn it on and off, but when you are performing, you must know how to keep it on all the time. You don't want it at full power continuously; you want to be able to manipulate its glow as though it had a dimmer switch.

Basically, you must learn to overcome the break between exhalation and inhalation. Your imaginary bulb has a natural tendency to go off at that moment of transition, so that you must mentally make the light come back on after the interruption. This takes additional effort, and you may momentarily lose your audience.

This application helps you overcome the interference of this sporadic "darkness" in the breathing cycle. The steps sound simple, but the application is difficult; it can be mentally exhausting. Be careful not to overpractice, especially at first; 10 or 20 seconds may be enough for beginners. Eventually, however, the application will become a spontaneous part of your skill in appearing before people. Your diligence will be greatly rewarded.

1. Do the Red Light Bulb Imagery Drill.

2. Exhale, as you imagine the light burning brightly.

3. As you approach the end of your exhalation, mentally turn the light bulb to tighten its contact with the socket, and make sure that the light does not flicker, dim, or go off.

4. Inhale without the slightest flickering of the light. Continue inhaling, and keep the light shining.

5. As you approach the end of your inhalation, again mentally turn the light bulb slightly to reassert its contact with the socket. Make sure that the light does not flicker or dim.

6 Repeat steps 2 through 5 as many times as you can manage without overexerting mentally.

APPLICATION 6

Working through Pain

The painful throbs you experience when you are in pain are SOS signals for immediate attention. Do not ignore those throbbing pains. They are calling for the mind to direct inner energy to that area. When your mind focuses on an area of your body, inner energy can be directed to that place to perform its function of soothing, healing, and strengthening. The length of time it takes the pain to ebb away depends on the degree of affliction.

1. Take several deep, full inhalations and lingering, thorough exhalations.

2. Focus your mind on any throbbing pains. Monitor them by mentally counting as you continue with your *chi yi* breathing. Count in a simple sequence such as 1 through 4, or 1 through 10. Repeat the sequence to avoid high numbers with many syllables, which tend to interfere with a free-flowing rhythm.

3. Continue to count. Before long, you will find the pain subsiding and the throbs becoming regular and painless throbs of inner energy.

APPLICATION 7

Relieving Discomfort in the Fingers, Hands, and Arms

You can use *chi yi* to relieve muscle aches in the limbs. For example, if your elbow aches, bring on the inner energy throbbing sensation. Stimulate a few throbs of pain at the elbow by bending or pressing it. Synchronize the energy throbs with the painful throbs in your elbow, while letting your entire arm relax and go limp. Maintain your *chi yi* breathing. The throbs of pain will very quickly become plain throbs. Monitor the throbs at the elbow for at least 50 to 100 counts At the end of this count you will find your pain much relieved, if not completely gone. Your first few tries may not bring on very conspicuous positive results. Give this approach several chances, taking a little rest time between attempts. Repeat this therapy whenever necessary.

This application can be done while you are lying down, sitting, or standing and in any surroundings—in front of a TV set or in a concert hall—as long as your hands are free.

During this application, your inner energy will stimulate the painful areas and cut through any interference that may stagnate the flow of the inner energy current. Let us say, for example, that the joints in your left index finger are painful, due to strain or arthritis.

1. Warm your right hand in any convenient way. Put it in your pocket, or hold it under your coat or your sweater, or even in your armpit.

2. Wrap your warm right hand over your left index finger, gripping it firmly but without squeezing.

3. In seconds you will feel your left index finger throbbing together with your right hand. You are feeling the pulses of your heartbeat. These heart beats, at about 70 to 80 per minute, are faster than the throbs created by your inner energy, at about 45 to 55 per minute.

4. Monitor the heart-related throbs for about 30 seconds.

5. Loosen the grip of your right hand to an easy hold. Continue focusing your mind on your aching index finger.

6. The heart-related throbs will grow faint and, as they seem to be ebbing away, slower-paced throbs will emerge. Your inner energy surges are now taking over.

7. During steps 1 through 6 you have been breathing naturally in a *chi yi* manner and need not have given your breathing any thought. As you monitor the slower throbs, your breathing will adjust itself in rate, intensity, and quantity. At times your breathing may seem to have subsided to almost nothing; at other times you may feel the urge to take very deep, long inhalations. Let your instincts command your course. At this stage, you are equipped with adequate *chi yi* techniques to respond to any demand of breathing. If your inner energy throbs start to fade too soon, intentionally initiate several deep, long inhalations and lingering exhalations, which should strengthen the throbs again.

8. When you feel you can no longer concentrate or that the throbs have done their work, stop and relax.

9. During steps 6, 7, and 8, the pain in your finger should gradually have been eased and perhaps even eliminated. Although your finger may not hurt anymore, it may still feel stiff. Flex your left hand a few times, and massage it with your right.

10. Continue practicing this application frequently, with the intention of improving the condition of the ailing joints and preventing the recurrence of pain.

This approach to easing pain may also be practiced on your knees and upper thighs when you are in a sitting position and your hands can comfortably reach these areas.

APPLICATION 8

Conditioning the Legs and Arms

Our limbs are indispensable for a physically active life. For athletes, dancers, laborers, and many others, limbs are tools of the trade. Even when our limbs are healthy, it's still a good idea to give them some attention. We should develop the ability to lead our inner energy through our legs and arms, first to keep them healthy, and second to become familiar with the technique of directing inner energy through these areas. Then when our limbs need conditioning, soothing, or healing, we will be more adept and efficient at that task.

You can do this application while you watch TV or ride a bus, train, or plane, you can even do it during a dull lecture or conference, if no one is watching—you may look a little absent-minded. You can practice it while lying in bed, although if you are sitting up, it is easier for you to keep your eyes on the areas on which your mind's eye will also concentrate.

When you are thoroughly familiar with this application, you will not need the assistance of your eyesight to guide the movement of inner energy. You can direct and control the flow of inner energy with your mind's eye alone. As long as you are in a place where you are able to concentrate, you can practice this application inconspicuously anywhere and anytime.

It helps if you look at the spot you are concentrating on while you imagine with your mind's eye. Looking will help to induce the throbs or light flashes at that spot.

When your body and mind have become familiar with and adapted to this application, you may combine steps 2 through 6 with steps 7 and 8; that is, you may send inner energy up and down both legs simultaneously. You may also do the same with both arms.

1. Begin with a few *chi yi* breaths and bring on inner energy throbs in your lower abdomen.

2. Look at the top of your right leg.

3. Focus your mind's eye at the same spot at the top of your right leg.

4. Do a few more *chi yi* breaths as you concentrate on feeling a sensation at that spot on your leg. This sensation may be a throb, a warm patch, a flashing spot of light, or some other manifestation.

5. Using both your inner sight and outer sight, slowly guide this small patch of sensation down the length of your right leg to your ankle, foot, and toes. Mentally move this sensation along, down the leg, stopping every inch or so to tap that spot mentally in counts of 1-2 or 1-2-3-4. Dwell longer at the foot and toes by repeating more sequences of taps at each spot.

6. In the same way, return the sensation from your toes up to the top of your right leg (repeating step 5 in the reverse direction).

7. Now shift your inner and outer sight to the top of your left leg.

8. Focus, concentrate, and proceed as described in steps 2 through 6, applying these steps to the left leg.

9. Direct your inner energy sensation to your core. Let it pulse there for a bit. Relax, and rest for a moment.

Note: You may want to end the exercise at this point, or you may continue stimulating your arms by doing the following steps.

10. Direct your inner energy sensation from your core to the base of your neck. (If you had temporarily stopped and are now resuming this exercise, you will need to begin this step with a few *chi yi* breaths to get your inner energy going before you proceed.)

11. Place your right hand palm down in your lap. Look at the top of your right arm (at your right shoulder).

12. Focus your mind's eye at the same spot at the top of your right arm.

13. Concentrate on feeling a sensation at that spot. This sensation may be a throb, a warm patch, a flashing spot of light, or some other manifestation.

14. Using both your inner sight and outer sight, guide this small patch of sensation down the length of your right arm to your wrist, hand, and fingers. Mentally move the sensation along, down the arm, stopping every inch or so to tap that spot mentally in counts of 1-2 or 1-2-3-4. Dwell longer at the hand and fingers by repeating more sequences of taps at each spot.

15. In the same way, return the sensation to the top of your right shoulder (repeating step 14 in the reverse direction).

16. Now shift both your inner and outer sight to the top of your left arm (at your left shoulder). Place your left hand palm down in your lap.

17. Focus, concentrate, and proceed as described in steps 11 through 15, applying these steps to the left arm.

18. Roll your head in big circles, 5 times clockwise and 5 times counter-clockwise. Put both your hands over your lower abdomen.

19. Take several good stabilizing *chi yi* breaths, and relax.

Note: If you are interrupted during the course of this exercise, just take a few deep abdominal breaths to stabilize and anchor your inner energy. You may then proceed to any activity awaiting you.

APPLICATION 9

Creating a Dynamic Image

You had sufficient rest, and you are superbly dressed, yet you feel tired and drab, and you know that you look dull and project little vitality. You are on your way to a very important meeting, a photography session, an audition, an interview, or a party. You want to make an impact upon arrival. You are in your car on the way, or you are waiting for the elevator or in the reception room. You wish you could give yourself a lift. Try this application. You will feel a difference, and that difference will be visible to others.

1. Start your inner energy going by exhaling thoroughly and taking a long, deep inhalation. Imagine that you are deeply drawing in the scent of your favorite flower while also breathing through your mouth. Draw that inhalation into the very depth of you. Savor the fragrance of that inhalation for a few seconds before letting it drain out slowly.

2. Breathe in and out easily 3 times as you purposefully inflate and deflate your lower abdomen.

3. Take another long draw of fragrance, and repeat step 1.

4. Repeat steps 2 and 3 twice.

5. Your face will begin to feel warm, and your inner energy will start throbbing behind your nose and eyes. Let the throbs float through your face, your gums, the tip of your tongue, and your lips. You can almost feel a smile breaking out all over your countenance. Your face is glowing.

6. Take another long drag of air. Exhale by letting the air spill out all over.

7. You are sitting, standing, and walking tall, confident, and radiant. Keep your inner energy throbbing in your face and through your eyes as constantly as you can. You are looking great!

APPLICATION 10

Combating Insomnia

Proper breathing can be applied as if it were a tonic for insomnia First try Application 1, Promoting Relaxation. If that doesn't lull you to sleep, then capture your wandering thoughts by focusing on your abdominal breathing.

Individual sleep requirements vary; *chi yi* will not cause you to sleep naturally for much longer than your normal physical sleep requirement.

1. Breathe deeply to stimulate the core's cradle (the lower abdominal area), and to produce a throbbing sensation at the core. (Try the Tumbling Pebble Imagery Drill, page 15.)

2. Should you need additional stimulation to produce the pulsating sensation, vigorously pump your lower abdomen inward and outward 10 to 15 times, deflating as you exhale and inflating as you inhale.

3. When you have produced the throbbing sensation, focus your full attention on it.

4. As the throbbing gradually strengthens, it dominates your other sensations. Move the throbs to your thighs or toes. Imagine these throbbings as floating bubbles, *never* as bursting bubbles. Images of bursting bubbles will create an agitating effect. Notice that your breathing gradually becomes more subdued and slower, almost as though it were ebbing away. This ebbing, which produces a very calming effect, is to be encouraged.

5. When aches, pains, or discomfort are keeping you awake, extend this throbbing sensation from your core to the affected spot, allowing it to soothe and relieve the affliction.

6. Continue to monitor the throbs by counting them in repeated sequences of four, over and over. Before you realize it, you will fall asleep.

APPLICATION 11

Relieving Gas Pains in the Stomach

Gas pain is often caused by overeating or nervous tension. This application induces surges of core energy to relieve this discomfort.

Important: Be sure your symptoms are not caused by a heart condition, appendicitis, food poisoning, or any other ailment that requires the immediate attention of a physician.

1. Bring on inner energy throbbings with *chi yi* breathing.

2. Move your mind's eye to the uncomfortable spot in your stomach. Focus on that spot for a few seconds, until the throbbing begins there.

3. Monitor this throbbing for at least 50 to 100 counts.

4. You may also put your palms at the spot if your hands are warm; the warmth will encourage and intensify the throbs. You will feel rumbling at the affected area and will begin to burp and pass gas, and you will feel much better.

APPLICATION 12

Relieving Congested Nasal Passages or Sinuses

At the first hint of discomfort, do the following:

1. After you sneeze or blow your nose, concentrate on feeling a throbbing at the facial mask area and the nose.

Note: With no sneeze or nose-blowing to start the throbbing sensation, begin by focusing your mind's eye on the affected spot. Then blow your nose.

2. Pick up on the rhythm of the throbbing, and monitor it.

3. At the same time, encourage inner energy throbbings with *chi yi* breathing.

4. Continue to monitor the throbbings for at least 50 to 100 counts. You should begin to feel relief.

APPLICATION 13

Relieving Motion Sickness

At the first hint of discomfort, do the following:

1. Bring on inner energy throbbings with *chi yi* breathing.

2. Monitor your lower abdominal throbs for at least 10 to 30 seconds.

3. Focus your mind on the most uncomfortable spots in your abdomen, stomach, and throat and activate throbbings in those areas.

4. Continue monitoring these throbbings until you feel relief.

5. Breathe deeply and relax. This application may be repeated as frequently as necessary.

APPLICATION 14

Improving Speech and Singing (Vowel Production)

Each different vowel sound you produce requires a subtle variation in the way you exhale. It is important to realize the connection between such intricate adjustments of exhalation and the flow of inner energy. To some extent those adjustments are made by reflex, without any conscious effort. However, when these sounds are coordinated with selective inner energy support, you can produce each sound with a much higher degree of efficiency, which can help mend a damaged voice or add proficiency to an ordinary voice.

You use one finger to play a note on a piano. It is neither necessary nor effective to use all five fingers at once to play one note. Along this same line of reasoning, you should use your inner energy appropriately and deftly to attain the vocal production of an intended sound and to avoid clumsiness, wasted effort, or even injury.

Figures 87 through 93 show the locations of concentrated inner energy formed for producing various vowels commonly used in English and other European languages. Use these figures as a guide in helping you to direct your inner energy to the appropriate locations.

The following application will help you to achieve increased vocal proficiency. Starting with the vowel "ah" (as in "father"), visualize the image in Figure 87 as you imagine your torso to be a big hollow barrel. (Note that Figures 91 and 93 show the back of the torso.)

1. Inhale deeply to the bottom of the barrel, according to the principles of *chi yi*.

2. Open your mouth wide in preparation for producing a *hah* sound. Be sure your jaws are parted not only in front but all the way back to the jaw hinges so that the top and bottom molars are evenly parted and almost parallel.

3. Exhale with a *hah* sound, as if letting air reverberate in the empty barrel. Simultaneously imagine the shaded area in Figure 87 as air vent(s) cut out at the front of the barrel. Imagine air ventilating through these cutout(s) as you exhale in a long, sustained, aspirated, whispering *hah*. Repeat this step several times.

hah as in father

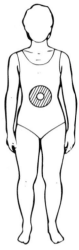

heh as in ever

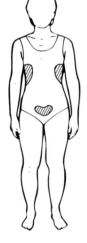

FIGURE 87

FIGURE 88

hee as in ease

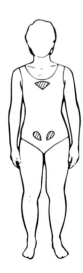

hoh as in of

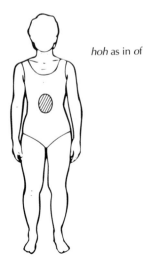

FIGURE 89

FIGURE 90

4. Repeat steps 1 through 3, but in place of the aspirated, sustained, whispering *hah* substitute a vocal *hah*, as in regular speech. (Singers may substitute the singing of a legato *hah* at a comfortable pitch.)

 hu as in w*ou*ld

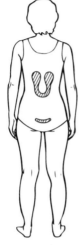

FIGURE 91

he(r) as in h*er*

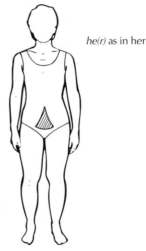

FIGURE 92

hü as in French *u* and German *ü;* combination of *ee* and *ou* sounds, with rounded lips

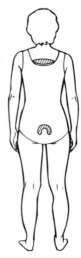

FIGURE 93

Use steps 3 and 4 to practice through all the vowels illustrated in Figures 87 through 93, one vowel at a time, being sure to open your mouth sufficiently. Certain vowels in speech or singing may present you with more difficulty than others, and these problem vowels will cause a scratchy, uncomfortable sensation. If left unattended, the inefficient execution of these vowels in everyday speech will contribute to injury and damage to the vocal cords. Spend more time practicing these problem sounds, being sure to use proper breath support and appropriate mouth and tongue positions. Use the figures as a guide to the distribution of inner energy to improve your placement of vowels and vowel production and to gradually eliminate this vocal difficulty.

As you progress, you will be able to combine various vowels in any sequence to gain further control and versatility in the allocation of inner energy. Try, for instance, to say in one breath *hah—heh—hah—heh—hah—*. As you produce these sounds, train your mind's eye to visualize core energy at the locations shown in Figures 87 and 88, alternating locations as you alternate sounds. In the same manner, you can also try *hah—heh—hee—hoh—hoo—he(r)—hü—*or any other combination that suits your needs. For instance, if you have difficulty in pronouncing or singing the word "into," practice *hee—hoo—hee—hoo—hee—hoo* until this vowel combination is smoothed out.

By selecting a specific vowel to practice, you will isolate a specific area of your torso to develop and strengthen.

Vowels form the backbone of speech and singing; once they have been sturdily constructed, consonants will have a much better chance of falling properly into place.

Simplified-Vowel Exercise

The following simplified version of the previous vowel exercise may be used to help stimulate isolated areas of the torso; to emphatically activate the inner energy flow, a section at a time; and to bring on inner energy surges and throbs.

1. Breath deeply, using the principles learned in this book. Review one or more of the following imagery drills: Eyedropper, Sink and Drain, or Coil of Rope.

2. Open your mouth in preparation for producing a whispering aspirated *hah* sound. Be sure your jaws are parted not only in front but all the way to the jaw hinges, so that the top and bottom molars are almost parallel.

3. Relax your tongue and place the tongue tip behind the bottom front teeth. Exhale air sparingly, producing a sustained *hah* sound. Simultaneously visualize Figure 87, imagining that the shaded area is cut out. Imagine air ventilating through this cutout in your torso in a long, sustained, aspirated, whispering *hah* sound. As you do this several times, you will feel a slight warmth in the part of your body corresponding to the shaded area.

Use the above three steps to produce all the vowels illustrated in Figures 87 through 93 in the same whispering aspirated and sustained manner. As you produce each of these sounds, visualize the figure that corresponds to the sound you are producing. Be sure to imagine the air ventilating through the shaded areas in each figure.

All these vowel sounds may also be aspirated consecutively in one breath. For example, you may aspirate *hah—heh—hee—hoh—hu—he(r)—hü*. Or *hah—hoh—hah—hoh*. Or *hoh—hu—he(r)—hoh—hü—he(r)*.

To get the maximum benefit from this exercise, be sure to accompany each sound with the image of the figure that illustrates it. For example, if you aspirate *hoh* while imagining the air ventilating through the corresponding area at the center of your stomach (see Figure 90), the aspirating of the sound will induce inner energy to that specific area, relieving any discomfort in the stomach. An aspirated *he(r)* will not only benefit the specific area depicted in Figure 92, but will also help anchor the inhalations that follow, drawing the inhaled air to the core.

Afterword

Now that you have completed the exercises, applications of *chi yi* principles, and imagery drills described in this book, you have built a solid, effective deep breathing system to support whatever activities you pursue. You are well on your way to achieving the major objective of *chi yi*—to derive the maximum benefit from every breath you inhale. As you continue to apply the principles of deep breathing to your everyday activities, remember that the more you practice breathing to the core, the more energy is stored and ready for use. By stimulating the core regularly and frequently with proper deep breathing, the compounded energy that you develop will improve both your mental sharpness and your physical performance.

Remember, the more you practice *chi yi*, the more adept you will become, and the easier and more natural the techniques will feel. Motivation, concentration, and persistence will pay off; as *chi yi* becomes habitual, you will gain in stamina, grace, radiance, and well-being.

All of the exercises in this book have been carefully planned to accomplish specific purposes. Now that you have mastered those exercises, you can put together your own program, repeating those exercises that you find especially beneficial and combining them in different sequences. If a particular imagery drill helps you with your *chi yi* breathing, use it frequently until the effect wears off, and then substitute another one—or invent one of your own.

Stay flexible in your approach, experiment sensibly, and adjust these exercises to fit your individual needs. Practice an exercise or two before engaging in your favorite sport, or whenever you feel in need of an energy boost. The investment of a few minutes a day will make an amazing difference in your overall performance.

Above all, it is my sincere hope that you will enjoy not only the actual practice of *chi yi*, but all of the physical and mental benefits it brings as well.

About the Author

Nancy Zi was born in the United States in 1930 to Chinese parents. Raised in China since infancy, she returned to the United States in 1949. She attended Millikin University in Illinois and graduated with a bachelor's degree in music, majoring in vocal performance. She continued her vocal training in Chicago and New York City. She has more than 30 years of experience in teaching singing and has performed extensively as a professional vocal soloist in concerts, operas, operettas, oratorios, and television and radio programs.

Growing up in China, Nancy Zi was greatly influenced by the Eastern belief that our mental and physical well-being is governed by an inner energy called *Chi*. She has been a fervent practitioner of *Chi Kung* for many years. Through this ancient Chinese discipline, which teaches proper handling of breath, body movements, and meditation, she has derived great benefits. With years of experience, Nancy Zi realized that the vital energy used in Western civilization for classical singing and other performances is comparable to *Chi*. She found that in Western culture this inner vitality is directed outward for external accomplishments, whereas in Eastern culture it is directed primarily inward for healing and maintaining good health.

Weaving together the best of these two cultures, Nancy Zi has created *Chi Yi*, which literally means "the art of breathing," a new and simple way to acquire a sound breathing technique. Through the direct approach of teaching *Chi Yi*, the author hopes to dispel the mysticism that surrounds the generating, cultivating, and utilizing of inner energy to improve overall performance and well-being. In her book and video, *The Art of Breathing*, Nancy Zi discusses what she has learned and developed—a program of effective breathing principles accessible to an international audience.

The author and her husband of 38 years, S. Paul Li, spent much of their married life in Hong Kong, but they have now settled in Glendale, California. They have a son and a daughter.